MICROBREWED
ADVENTURES

ALSO BY CHARLIE PAPAZIAN

•••••••••••••

The Complete Joy of Homebrewing, Third Edition

The Homebrewer's Companion

Homebrewer's Gold

Best of Zymurgy

CHARLIE PAPAZIAN

MICROBREWED

ADVENTURES

A Lupulin-Filled Journey to
the Heart and Flavor of the World's
Great Craft Beers

WILLIAM MORROW
An Imprint of HarperCollinsPublishers

Some of these stories have appeared in *Zymurgy* magazine in a slightly different form.

HarperCollins books may be purchased for educational,
business, or sales promotional use. For information please write:
Special Markets Department, HarperCollins Publishers,
10 East 53rd Street, New York, NY 10022.

FIRST EDITION

Designed by Kate Nichols

Library of Congress Cataloging-in-Publication Data has been applied for.

ISBN-10: 0-06-075814-7
ISBN-13: 978-0-06-075814-1

12   WBC/RRD   10   9   8

Microbrewed Adventures is dedicated

to brewers worldwide

who add their passionate spirit for flavor and diversity

to every beer they create

for the pleasures of their friends, family and

beer drinkers everywhere.

Contents

MICROBREWED
ADVENTURES

Introduction

I AM AT HEART a brewer. The romance of beer has been a significant part of my life since the early 1970s. My first homebrew was an amber beer brewed in the basement of a Charlottesville, Virginia, preschool and day care center. I never looked back. Our five senses help me turn the basic ingredients—hops, yeast, malt and water—into beer, but it is my imagination that permits me to experiment and create an endless variety of new and inspired beers.

IMAGINATION IS A powerful factor that influences our view of the world—indeed, it is at the heart of how we interpret our senses of taste, smell, hearing, sight and touch. At recent judgings of beer I have begun cautioning myself about the extent to which we become separated from our imagination as we evaluate beer. As beer drinkers and brewers, we sometimes try to mimic machines too much.

Refreshingly, among the most experienced and passionate of brewers, objective evaluation is mixed with stories of great beers and great brewers. These side trips lend proper perspective to most discussions. A brewer may say, "The character in this beer, though some may consider it a technical flaw, is a real, honest-to-God, traditional character that has beer enjoyment value and is found in some small, genuinely wonderful countryside breweries—and I like it. In fact, I am passionate about the beer's character." You can see the smile on that brewer's face and his daydream expression as he imagines someday recreating the experience. The beer with its eccentric—not technically brewers'-perfect—character has warmth of heart, which is perhaps the real reason we all pay for beer. Simply by inhaling certain aromas, I can recall wonderful memories and moments of pleasure.

I often enjoyed one of my favorite American-made British-style bitters on the rooftop of a popular neighborhood tavern. The view of the Front Range Rocky Mountains, and the warmth of the sun on early spring and late autumn days, brought cheer. The all-malt, full-flavored draft bitter is easily affected by sunlight, yet I loved the beer and being there, at that spot.

Now, whenever I experience the aroma of an all-malt beer that is faintly and freshly sunstruck, I smile. I enjoy these technically destabilized beers, and often prefer them, because of the sunshine and warmth of heart they evoke. And I like the flavor! The memory is all mine, and there is no denying the power of where it can take me.

To "capture the imagination" is to capture our five senses. This is why we buy beer, isn't it? It's not just that India pale ale has pleasurable hop-infested, lupulin-drenched bitterness. Not just that stout is black velvet with a full-bodied, creamy texture. Not only that pale ale is graced with the floral lupulin bouquet of Cascade, Goldings or Fuggles hops. Not just that barley wine ale or Doppelbock has a tantalizing 9.14 percent alcohol, nor that a Hefeweizen is accented with spice and fruity themes. Nor do the finest hops, malt, water and yeast really make a huge difference. No, I don't really believe this is ultimately what we beer drinkers seek. We see a label, we hear the name, we see a designer glass full of beer and tantalizing foam, we smell, we taste, we observe . . . our mind takes us on a journey with first contact.

The moment lasts less than a second, but we connect with our lifelong experiences. Will it be a good experience? Yes? I'll have one. I'll have another. I will remember the moment, perhaps more than the beer, but I *will* remember the beer.

The beer drinker walks out of a store, package of beer playfully swinging at arm's length. The door closes behind and you know for sure that if that beer has been well made, it will transform all those beery characteristics into an experience fully influenced by imagination.

If you still can't quite picture what it is I'm talking about, then sit down quietly with a beer and see where it *really* takes you.

MICROBREWED ADVENTURES is essentially a book about imagination. I have been fortunate in being able to meet many of the world's great brewers and to travel across the United States and the world tasting thousands of amazing beers. My jobs as the founding president of the American Homebrewers Association (1978) and the Brewers Association, founder of the Great American Beer Festival and author of the paradigmatic *Complete Joy of Home Brewing* (1984) have brought me beer opportunities of which I could never have dreamed. Sometimes I realize I am living the ultimate beer fairy tale, with every new beer a happy ending.

I have collected many of these adventures and tastings to share with you. Each story inspired a homebrew recipe that can be found in the back of the book. In many cases it's a recipe from a brewery that I have visited; in others, the recipe captures the flavor of the experience.

My microbrewed adventure begins in 1980 with the pioneers of micro-brewing. These were a small collection of homebrewers who were making beer with the flavor and character of a time past. As their friends cheered them on to their next batch, their beer improved. They were tiring of their jobs and began to dream of life as a brewer. Their enthusiasm and confidence grew. At the time, ours was a world of mass-produced light lager, with virtu-ally no options. Velveeta ruled the world of cheese. Wonder bread sand-wiched our lunch.

The world of beer was about to embark on a new path. New Albion (Sonoma, CA), Sierra Nevada (Chico, CA), Boulder Beer (Boulder, CO), River City (Sacramento, CA), DeBakker (Novato, CA), Cartwright (Portland, OR) and Wm. S. Newman (Albany, NY) were among the handful of small breweries that emerged in the late 1970s and early 1980s. We called them "small breweries" until one day *Zymurgy* magazine small-brewery news editor Stuart Harris suggested that these tiny breweries were like "these new small computers called 'micro-computers'" he used in his day job. The term "micro-brewery" was born.

The half-dozen microbrewers in 1981 were afloat in a sea of light lager when the American Homebrewers Association, founded in 1978, began to gain some momentum. A champion of beer styles, beer flavor and diversity, the AHA was the only beacon microbrewers, homebrewers and beer lovers had to turn to. I don't recall whether we discovered them or they discovered us, but the relationship became one of mutual support.

All-malt beer with distinctive varieties of hops and caramelized and roasted specialty malts provided the distinctive and traditional appeal of those original pale ales, porters and stouts. The microbrewed adventure was en-tirely distinct and different from what the forty-two existing American large and regional breweries were offering.

Now there are more than 1,300 microbreweries in the United States and the numbers are growing worldwide. While many microbreweries have grown in size and are sometimes called craft breweries, they maintain their passion for flavor, diversity and adventure.

The microbreweries of today, such as Sierra Nevada Brewing Company, Dogfish Head Brewing Company, Deschutes Brewery, Left Coast Brewing Company, Stone Brewing Company, Brooklyn Brewery, Boston Beer Company, Rockies Brewing Company and Boulevard Brewing Company, are among the thousand-plus micro and craft brewers producing an amazing array of choice. It's hard to believe that just twenty-five years ago the American beer market was dominated by Big Beer and offered virtually no other options.

Beyond America I have discovered tradition and an equal passion for flavor, diversity and creativity. The second half of *Microbrewed Adventures* reveals many of my most memorable travel adventures outside the United States, tasting exotic, classically traditional and pioneering beers—Andech's German Monastic Bock, Leipziger Gose, Brakspear's Henley-on-Thames Ordinary Bitter, Goose and Firkin Dogbolter, Zimbabwe Zephyr Sorghum Beer, fifty-year-old Cornish mead, spicy Dutch Zeezuiper and legendary Belgian ales and lambics, to name a few. All my microbrewed adventures were invaluable lessons, serving as inspiration for a beer drinker and homebrewer gone "over-the-top." I hope you enjoy . . .

Ya Sure Ya Betcha
The Independent Ale Brewery/
Red Hook Brewery

ALWAYS SHY AWAY from the inevitable question that everyone loves to ask me: "Charlie, what's your favorite beer?" I will always deflect the question with "It's the beer that I'm holding in my hand" or "The locally made beer, and when I'm home that's my homebrew." One of the more memorable beers I've held in my hand—you could have called it my "favorite" at the time—was an American-made British-style bitter I enjoyed frequently on the rooftop of Boulder's West End Tavern. It was called Ballard Bitter. Brewed by the Independent Brewing Company (now called Red Hook Brewing Co.), then located in the Ballard neighborhood of Seattle, Washington, Ballard Bitter was a wonderfully complex hybrid of American and British beers. I perceived a

Gordon Bowker, co-founder of Red Hook Ale, introduces the brewery in 1982.

predominance of American Cascade hop character combined with a mellow background of English Kent countryside hop flavor. You could taste a complexity of hops. Not only that, but perhaps you could see the hops in the ever-so-slight haze that was likely a combination of hops, yeast and full-malt ingredients.

Ballard Bitter was also blessed with one other "flaw" that I loved. It was called diacetyl—one of the textbook brewer's deadly beer sins, producing a flavor and aroma reminiscent of caramel or butterscotch. Textbook brewers despise diacetyl in any amount whatsoever. I am not a textbook brewer, but I *am* a textbook beer drinker. I drink what I like. I like the soft integration of caramel-, toffee-, butterscotch-like flavor that diacetyl harmonically contributes to some styles of English and American ales. A balanced amount of diacetyl contributed to my enjoyment of Ballard Bitter. Yet despite good

ORIGINAL BALLARD BITTER

My attempt to recreate this beer is "Original Ballard Bitter." Ingredient and process information for the original beer was found in various publications and information provided by the brewery. This recipe can be found on page 242.

sales, this wonderfully balanced and distinct ale was eventually purged of its diacetyl by the brewery. Hop intensity was elevated and the brand renamed India Pale Ale–Ballard Bitter. The slogan on the bottle, "Ya Sure Ya Betcha," remains, but it is no longer the Ballard I and thousands in my neighborhood enjoyed.

My intention is not to denounce the brewery. The Red Hook Brewery, founded by passionate beer people and one of the co-founders of Starbucks Coffee as the Independent Brewing Company, began brewing in August of 1982. Paul Shipman, who still leads the brewery, was there at its inception to introduce their original and legendary fruity, yeast-influenced Red Hook Ale. It was a phenomenal success among homebrew enthusiasts and worth a story in and of itself. But I yearn for the original Ballard Bitter.

SECTION ONE

Microbrewed:
American Style

Birth of Style

I WAS TAKING THE F TRAIN from Manhattan to Brooklyn, on my way to the Park Slope Brewery Pub, in the autumn of 1994. Halloween had recently come and gone. Jack-o'-lantern pumpkins still glowered from neighborhood windows. The evening was cold, inspiring me to walk briskly through the Brooklyn neighborhood as I searched for the newly opened brewpub.

My thoughts dwelled on a conference presentation given earlier in the day where the question was asked, "Why are certain areas of the country hotbeds of microbreweries and specialty beers?" An expert presented his reasoning, citing pseudo-facts about culture and demographics. I thought to myself, those reasons are academic bullshit things you say when you really don't know.

It was a longer walk to the Park Slope Brewery than I had imagined. I asked myself the same question. Could it be that specialty beer and microbrewery beer are especially popular in certain areas because of a handful of key individuals and their enthusiasm, dedication and persistence? I believe microbrewed beer's success in certain areas is a result of people such as Ken Grossman (Sierra Nevada), Fritz Maytag (Anchor Steam), Steve Hindy (Brooklyn Brewing Company), Paul Shipman (Red Hook Ale), Fred Bowman (Portland Brewing Company), Kurt Widmer (Widmer Brewing, Portland, OR), John Hickenlooper (Denver's Wynkoop Brewery), Greg Noonan (Vermont Pub and Brewery, Burlington), David Geary (D. L. Geary's Brewing Company, Maine) and others. Demographics and culture contribute nothing compared to the influence of individual acts of heroism, dedication and persistence. But in high-powered industrial economics, never is individual hero-ism an accepted explanation. It does not fit very well into the academic and economic models at board meetings and learned universities. Big-company marketing departments are uncomfortable with this.

I was still walking. In what seemed to be a strictly residential neighbor-hood, I was looking around for a brewpub. There were no signs of beer any-where. A Jack-o-lantern sat in a corner window of a building. I shaded my eyes from the overhead street lamp and peered inside. It was a bar, with glee-ful pumpkins alit with flames. There was beer.

I entered and was greeted by the warmth and glow of friendship and mi-crobrewed beer. There was little doubt—this had to be the place. But where was the brewery? Steve Deptula greeted me with recognition and I was quickly confronted with a decision: California ale, porter, blonde, Kölsch (with 30 percent flaked corn), barley wine or pumpkin ale on tap. A pint of hearty ale soon graced my hand.

Owner and brewer Steve explained the unusual circumstances of his business. Steve was a graduate of the "Complete Joy of Homebrewing" School of Brewing. The brewery pub was a complete do-it-yourself project in-volving a year and a half of renovation. Steve's resources were limited, but his determination obviously was not.

The beautiful mahogany bar, graced by the good cheer of local beer drinkers, was a testimonial to his accomplishment. The small brewery below was retrofitted with equipment. Steve proudly explained how, with limited re-sources, he had had to place the chilled aging tanks in the same room as the fermenters. How did he keep the fermenters warm enough for ale fermenta-tion? An $18 space heater from Wal-Mart.

The brewery has since closed, but not before pleasing thousand of beer drinkers and turning on countless others to the world of flavorful and pas-sionately made microbrewery beer.

THE 1980s were a turning point for American beer. Microbreweries and brewpubs began opening and new American beer styles were born—American pale ale, American wheat beer and American imperial stout.

Raspberry wheat beers, American India pale ale, stouts and porter, rye ale, whiskey-barrel aged stout and several other creations continue to emerge as brewers continue to embark on their own microbrewed adventures. The flavors and diversity of American beer are unparalleled anywhere in the world, bringing a high degree of respect and creating a proud American beer culture for beer drinkers to enjoy.

American Pale Ale
Sierra Nevada Pale Ale

MICROBREWERIES STARTED popping up in the United States around 1981. This was the year I first tried Sierra Nevada Pale Ale. I knew at once that the guys behind this brew were possessed with a passion for beer and excellence. It was the dawn of what was to become the most popular style of microbrewed craft beer, American pale ale, and the Sierra Nevada Brewing Company of Chico, California, pioneered the way. Ken Grossman and Paul Camusi, the founders of the brewery and originally homebrewers, sought to make a commercial beer that emphasized hops.

Indeed not only were there more hops in their now famous pale ale, but they were the unique citruslike Cascade hops. These hops had never been used in large amounts—in any beer, anywhere in the world—except by home-brewers like themselves.

In 1880, there were more than 2,200 registered breweries operating in the United States. In 1980–81, there were only forty-four.

However, this was all soon to change. Homebrewers were indulging in their newfound passion for flavor and diversity in beer. With the fermentations of their efforts as inspiration, they were founding small brewing companies based exclusively on their love of beer. This passionate approach to professional brewing would become known as "microbrewing."

THE MICROBREW ADVENTURE was begun by homebrewers with the opening of breweries such as the New Albion Brewer in Sonoma, California (1976, closed in the early 1980s), the Boulder Brewing Company in Boulder, Colorado (1980, still operating as the Boulder Beer Company), the Cartwright Brewing Company, Portland, Oregon (opened and closed in the early 1980s) and the Debakker Brewing Company, Novato, California (opened and closed in the early 1980s). Others that opened in 1981 included River City Brewing Company (Sacramento, California), William S. Newman Brewing Company (Albany, New York) and Thousand Oaks Brewing Company (Berkeley, California), all closing within a decade.

I FIRST VISITED the Sierra Nevada Brewing Company in 1986, five years after they had opened. At the time there only were a few dozen microbreweries in the United States. Beer choice for most beer drinkers was limited to dozens of brands of same-tasting American light lagers. I came away

Cofounding brewer, Ken Grossman

from my visit knowing that this brewery, with their original Sierra Nevada Pale Ale, Porter and Stout, was getting it right for America.

Sierra Nevada was brewing four to six brews a week in their 17-barrel brewery, cranking out 35 barrels on any given day. Co-founder Ken Grossman, a student of chemistry and a bike mechanic, had run a home beer and

winemaking shop before becoming a
professional brewer. Steve Harrison,
the company's lead salesperson, had
worked as a head clerk in a liquor
store as well as at a retail service center of Sears. His first job at the brewery was part time on the bottling line
and part time selling beer. Ken and
Steve wanted to open a small business that made high-quality beer and
do something they enjoyed.

In 1986 they were planning and
projecting for the future. High profit was not an original goal—survival was.
They didn't realize the size of brewery they would need in order to make money.
In the beginning, the maximum they could brew was 30 barrels a week. At the
time this seemed like a gold mine, but the reality of maintaining beer quality,
the increasing costs of packaging and selling beer and keeping and paying their
employees well and the need to make a profit in order to reinvest in their growing business became evident as the demand for their beer increased.

EVEN THOUGH they are brewing at a much higher level these days, their
goal has stayed the same—to make great beer. Their equipment is larger and
better and their processes have become more efficient, but the beer stays
true. Their production is approaching 600,000 barrels at the time of this
book's publication, and their products have every bit of the "microbrewing" in-
tegrity with which they began in 1981. This is not only a tribute to Sierra
Nevada Brewing Company, but also to what passion for beer and brewing has
done for our American beer culture.

1982 ORIGINAL SIERRA NEVADA PALE ALE

While Sierra Nevada Pale Ale has remained true to its original character,
there have been a few subtle adjustments over the years in order to facili-
tate distribution needs and brewery equipment changes. This original
recipe is based on today's flavor profile and what is known about its formulation and information published in the early 1980s, revealing original
ingredients and processes used at their original small-batch brewery. The
recipe can be found on page 244.

American Wheat Beer
Pyramid Wheaten Ale

THE ADDRESS OF the brewery was 176 First Street, reached by taking Exit 30 off Washington Interstate 5, just above Washington's border with Oregon. It could arguably be called the birthplace of American-style wheat beer. Someone should erect a historic landmark memorial, for there was brewed the original Pyramid Wheaten Ale at the Hart Brewing Company. In 1984, company founder and homebrewer Tom Baune and his wife breathed life back into a building that can only be described at the time of my visit in 1986 as a general store orphaned by the construction of the Interstate.

Tom Baune, founder Hart Brewing Co. and Pyramid brand ale

The brew kettle, keg-washing equipment, fermenters, keg washers and bottling line were all salvaged, reconditioned or self-fabricated. Visiting with a small group of other brewers and aspiring brewers, I was surprised that such a remote brewery in an all-but-abandoned locale could and *did* resurrect the passion of beer and brewing. It was called sweat equity. We were all in awe of owner and jack-of-all-trades Tom Baune, not only for the establishment of such a brewery in such a remote location, but for the quality of his ales brewed in small handcrafted batches.

In the early 1980s, knowledgeable American homebrewers were aware of beers made with a combination of wheat and barley malt, called Weizenbier (wheat beer) in Germany. The recipes were available. The techniques were known. But one important ingredient was essentially inac-

ORIGINAL PYRAMID WHEATEN ALE

Today's Pyramid Wheaten Ale is as vibrant as is it was in 1986, but not without its differences. The brewery's recipe has been adjusted to accommodate large-batch brewing and the evolving preferences of wheat beer enthusiasts. Based on data and descriptions (as well as recollections from my own taste memory bank) published in their early years, this recipe for "Original Pyramid Wheaten Ale" is presented with confidence and for your enjoyment. Smooth, with a mild yet distinctive caramel character, the recipe for this refreshing beer for all sessions can be found on page 247.

cessible to American microbrewers: the wheat beer yeast creating the unique character of German-style wheat beers. Not to be deterred, American homebrewers and microbrewers followed the essential techniques for making German-style wheat beers, but substituted various English-style ale yeasts for the German variety. A new beer style was born: American-style wheat beer.

Brewed with a significant proportion of wheat malt, Pyramid Wheaten Ale was a smooth, subtly caramel-like, light-bodied pale wheat ale balanced with a floral hop character that made it distinct from most other heavily hopped Pacific Northwest homebrewed and microbrewed ales.

Not only a microbrewery pioneer, Tom Baune pioneered diversity with creativity. Pyramid Wheaten Ale remains one of the best-selling beers of the successor to the Hart Brewing Company, Seattle-based Pyramid Brewing Company.

Michael Jackson
His World Is Beer

ONE CANNOT EVEN BEGIN to have a discussion about beer styles without mentioning the world's leading protagonist of flavor and diversity. Michael Jackson serves as an inspiration to all beer drinkers and brewers.

As a thirtieth-birthday gift in 1979, my girlfriend gave me Michael Jackson's *World Guide to Beer*. I had been homebrewing for nine years, and my beer world had yet to become global. This gift became a threshold for me. Michael opened up my world, and my life has never been the same.

Michael Jackson in his London office

In the early 1980s you could hear Michael on radio commercials describing the Cascade hops used in Henry Weinhard's Ale. Perhaps these were the first beer commercials in the twentieth century pontificating on the basis of varietal ingredients. Michael Jackson has always been a beer pioneer.

I tracked Michael down in 1981 and invited him to attend the American Homebrewers Association's third national homebrewers' conference in Boulder, Colorado. I did not have a clue what to expect, never having met him. Because of his radio presence in Henry's beer commercials, I originally thought he might have lived in America. I was surprised when I learned he was from London.

We've shared many pints and liters of beer at locations throughout the world since that time, but none so grounding as those enjoyed on his home turf, where he is most at ease. I don't recall whether our London discussion took place at Michael's flat or at his local pub, The Thatched House, then a classic, well-attended Young's pub in Hammersmith, but it has cemented our friendship that has remained strong for more than two decades.

I had been invited to judge at the Great British Beer Festival in 1981. As part of a panel of three, I helped decide the grand champion beers of England. Awed by my experiences at the festival, I stopped in London on my way home for a final two days and had a second visit with Michael. I asked him, "I was quite impressed with the variety of beers at the festival. Do you think in America we could pull off a 'Great American Beer Festival'?" Michael took a good swallow of his pint of Young's Ordinary and replied, "Yes of course, it would be a great start, but where would you find interesting beer?"

The beer was one of our biggest challenges. In 1982 there were very few breweries making anything other than light American lager. I was helped by Tom Burns, brewmaster at the Boulder Brewing Company, and homebrewers Stuart Harris and Frank Morris. The four of us connected with twenty of America's most flavorful and unique beers. The Great British Beer Festival provided the inspiration, and Michael encouraged and supported us. The rest is history. The Great American Beer Festival now brings together thousands of American's finest beers for the world to taste every autumn in Denver, Colorado.

Michael continues to travel the world in search of good beers. I do the same. Whenever our paths cross I make every effort to buy the beers, unless of course it's at his local in Hammersmith.

American Imperial Stout
Yakima Brewing Company

IN 1984 the Great American Beer Festival moved from Boulder to Denver, Colorado. Begun in 1982 by the American Homebrewers Association, it had attracted hundreds of homebrewers and a passionate group of professional brewers and brewing professors from the United States, Germany and London. There were almost a dozen microbreweries in all of America. There must have been a spark of excitement in 1982 that had ignited a tinder-dry landscape in Boulder, Colorado, and spread. The smoke from the smoldering passions of homebrewers and knights of beer drifted with the winds eastward and westward, eventually reaching both shining seas.

This was to be the year of Yakima Brewing Company, its founder Bert Grant and his aggressively hoppy ales, and the birth of a new style of beer: "American-style" Russian imperial stout. There he was, founder and legendary hop guru Bert Grant turned brewer-owner of a tiny microbrewery in Washington's Yakima valley, where nearly all American hops are grown today. Bert was a self-induced hophead. "Hophead" was a name originally used in the 1950s Beatnik era and associated with the lifestyle of the time. But this was 1984, and Bert Grant turned its meaning an about-face 180 degrees. Never would microbrewed beer be the same.

At the festival, the lines for previously popular microbrews paled in comparison to the excitement generated by Bert Grant's Russian Imperial Stout. Proudly dressed in his Scottish kilt and bonnet, Bert offered thousands of servings of the rich, dark, heavily hopped, robust Grant's Russian Imperial Stout. Conversion was rampant. It seemed almost evangelical. Lupulin and darkness ruled the festival. The world of beer would never be the same. Hop and stout groupies could not fulfill themselves. Bert was smiling. That year Grant's Russian Imperial Stout took top honors in the Consumer Preference Poll. A style was born.

A brief explanation is needed, for Russian imperial stout has had a long and royal history in continental Europe and Great Britain. Brewed for royalty in olden times and still brewed in parts of Europe and the United Kingdom, its original style was not characterized by massive hoppiness. Roasted malts and barley were added with gentle consideration for flavor balance with caramel-flavored malt. Often aged for several months to a year, European versions of Russian imperial stouts were characterized by nuttiness, high alcohol and sherrified flavors. These imperial stouts are an exquisite high point of the brewer's art and offer an experience that is rare but worth seeking. But Bert Grant's Russian Imperial Stout was something other than "Russian."

Bert Grant at the Yakima Brewing and Malting Company, 1986

I would call it "American-style" imperial stout. Massive amounts of hops were added for bitterness, flavor and a

> ## BERT GRANT'S PLANET IMPERIAL STOUT
>
> Robust, black, roasted malt and barley character unveil themselves only to be joined by the massive citruslike hop flavors and aromas of American-grown Galena and Cascade hops and the intense, clean, refreshing bitterness of Northern Brewer hops. Rich and malty, with symphonic ale-fruity notes, this beer is satisfying for all robust stout enthusiasts. The recipe can be found on page 249.

wondrous floral and citruslike aroma. Combined with loads of black malt and roasted barley, this pitch-black ale was supercharged with all-malt ingredients offering an alcohol level of 8.75 percent. At the time, Bert claimed, "This is probably the strongest draft beer in North America and possibly in the world."

There are lots of microbrewed beers that have since surpassed Grant's original Russian imperial stout in alcohol, but no one has so successfully pioneered such a robust style of ale as profoundly as Bert Grant. In 1982 he founded his Yakima Brewing and Malting Company. In 1984 he took the world by storm. When Bert died in 2001, at age 74, beer maven Michael Jackson wrote, "To whom will we turn now when the world needs saving?"

Bert, you did us proud. Your legacy lives on with every imperial strength and imperially hoppy ale. There are many who continue to remember June first and second at the 1984 Great American Beer Festival.

Matters of Beer Style

I T'S FIRST and foremost all about the beer. This is why I first whet your appetite with a few classic brewery adventures and their legendary beers. But once you begin to enjoy the flavor and diversity of beer, there may be nothing more conversational among homebrewers and beer enthusiasts than the questions dealing with what defines beer style.

Some no doubt would prefer to enjoy or make "just beer," and to hell with stylistic endeavors. After all "its the beer, stupid." And then there are the royal guardians of beer styles and notaries of authenticity upholding the grand traditions of beer. I can appreciate both sides of the issue, having developed the beer style guidelines for the Association of Brewers and various competition guidelines since 1979. What strikes me as most important is that beer styles evolve. New ones arrive; old ones fall by the wayside. Old ones help steer a course and uphold the pride and tradition of brewing. New ones give current generations of brewers the opportunity to develop their creative skills and perhaps one day "invent" a beer that 200 hundred years from now will be upheld as a classic.

I AM RELAXING and having a homebrew, taking note of my thoughts and considering that the essence of style has a basis that is other than simply circumstantial. I consider styles based on one of eight principal characters:

1. Malt
2. Hops
3. Yeast
4. Water
5. Alcohol
6. Process
7. Packaging
8. Special ingredients

One may ask, where do color, head retention and mouthfeel fit in? They are considered, to be sure, but in my opinion are not the basis of style. They may help define styles and the variation within a tradition, but if there is an overriding basis, I'll stick to these essential eight.

Let's consider some examples of classic styles that might fit into these eight "boxes."

Malt. The predominant character of a bock beer, such as Heller bock, dark bock, Maibock, Doppelbock and Eisbock, is its maltiness. Malt more than any other character defines this style. The same might be true for English-style brown ale. Yes, hops, yeast, water, alcohol, processing and packaging all have a role in creating this style, but if you don't have a strong malt character you'll never have a bock or brown ale, whereas the other seven characters can vary while still achieving a variation of the true style of these two beers.

Hops. The India pale ale style of beer is based on hops. The style is virtually defined by the audacious employment of this ingredient.

Yeast. Bavarian-style wheat (Weiss or Weizen) beer is singularly defined by the special strains of yeast used in fermentation. No, I am not saying it is the wheat or the lack of hops—these components can be varied. But without the special yeast you cannot authentically achieve this style of beer.

Water. This is a tricky one. I hesitated to include it, but for the sake of discussion I beg the question: Does the peculiarly hard quality of water define the basis of classic Burton-type pale ales? I think it does, more than any other ingredient. The quality of the water affects the final perception of hops and malt, so important in British pale ales. There are dozens of malts, hops, yeasts and processes that can be integrated into the making of pale ale, but perhaps without the uniqueness of the water one cannot brew to tradition. I also contemplated pilseners on this basis. Soft water is essential for pilseners, but is it as essential as the process of lagering to evolve the smoothness of classic pilseners? Then there is the yeast, but with the proper processing ale yeast can achieve closeness to this style. Hops? Yes, the type does help define the classic pilsener. I haven't decided on this one yet. I need another homebrew.

Alcohol. Barley wine and Belgian-style Tripels, for example, have got to have alcohol. Without it these styles do not exist in mind or matter. Hard water, soft water, noble hops, ale hops, American hops, cold or warm fermented, dark or lighter—the essence of this style is alcohol and all the resulting qualities that naturally occur.

Process. German-style Altbiers come immediately to mind. Warm fermentation and cold lagering are the conditions that precede all Altbiers. Without employing this process, which imparts some unique attributes to their overall quality, Altbiers could just as well be another bitter or sweet brown ale or a dark lager. Warm ferment–cold lager is the most important defining basis of this enjoyable brew.

Packaging. This is a tricky one. Can packaging alone define the basis of a style? As beer enthusiasts we'd hate to consider it, but the realities of the beer world may preclude our own preferences. Let's consider many of the sweet fruit lambics that are making their way into the market. They simply could not exist without special considerations during packaging; sweet fruit juice or flavoring is added at packaging time. The beer is then pasteurized to prevent fermentation in the bottle, a process identical to the making of some classic English-style sweet stouts. Millions enjoy these sweet fruit beers and sweet stouts. Packaging more than anything else is the basis of these styles, more so than the specifications of malt, hops and yeast. Would you agree?

Special ingredients. Herein lies the beer that may not be considered classic by most beer enthusiasts—yet. In this day and age, special ingredients have come to overwhelm the character of many beers. Belgian Wit (wheat or white) beers almost qualify for consideration on this basis. Their unique blend of orange peel and coriander and the quality of the yeast seem to be the principal basis of Belgian-style Wit beer. Chili beer, pumpkin beer, spiced holiday-cheer beer, cranberry beer and cherry beer all may represent a style whose basis is a specialty ingredient. Perhaps special ingredients are a catchall second-string basis for all those beers that are in their early stages of evolution. We don't know which of the first seven characteristics to categorize them under—*yet*.

Say you are considering 30 or 40 other classic styles of beer. Under which category would you place them? And why would I want to go through this exercise anyway? It helps me better understand what and why I am brewing. Brewing as a craft involves these kinds of thought processes. It inspires a thirst. If I didn't think about these kinds of things, I'd be pumping out "just" beer. I'm not into that kind of brewing.

The downside of thinking about the essence of brewing is that it can get downright confusing. I especially get confused after relaxing and enjoying one of my own homebrews, homebrews conceived and concocted from creative cauldrons of kettles and mind. On November 26, 1973, I brewed my first honey lager, a beer brewed with 40 percent honey. My friends thought it normal that I waved real monkey hair over the inoculated wort; but the weird thing was using honey in a beer. No doubt honey had been used in beer way before I ever thought of it, but the fact is I had never heard of such a thing. Thus was born Rocky Raccoon's Honey Lager, and as "Rocky met his match and said, 'Doc it's only a scratch,'" we "proceeded to lie on the table."

Yes, it was strange; so were my fruit beers, pale ales and lagers with pounds of fresh fruit added. They were considered "weird" beers, fun, tasty, but not seriously considered by any professionals, unless they were microbrewers.

Michael Jackson, at our 1986 American Homebrewers Conference, thought I'd really gone nuts when I introduced my commemorative conference beer. It was called Blitzweizen Honey Steam Barley Wine Lager. My intention was and still is *not* to make fun of beer traditions, but to peer over the edge and goose the creative possibilities. I have to admit there was no one basis upon which I brewed this beer. It was, rather, a celebration of all styles.

Little does Michael know that he is in part responsible for one of my beer style "gooses," pushing the stylistic envelope. It was at one of the Philadelphia Book and the Cook festivities, where I was handed an absolutely delicious locally brewed imperial stout. With that in hand I was invited to attend Michael's beer tasting being held in the adjoining hall. I quietly entered in the middle of his presentation, happening to sit among a few homebrewers. I still had quite a bit of tasty imperial stout in hand. Michael was halfway through his beer-tasting session and pouring Celis White, a light Belgian-style wheat beer spiced with coriander and Curaçao orange peel.

I looked all about me, pondering the Egyptian mummies and fantastic architecture of the hall. Then, as the ancient spirits swirled around the room, I had an impulse to create and go beyond what everyone in the room was tasting. Before I knew what I had done I was staring at a creation of half Celis White and half imperial stout. I sipped, smiled and shared it with the homebrewers sitting next to me. I think they agreed, but whether or not they did was irrelevant—I thought it had GREAT potential as a new beer. It was a new idea and, as I realize now, its basis was simply special ingredients, with the combination of Belgian traditions. The notion immediately became part of my inventive brewing plans.

Later, in May 1995, I traveled and tasted my way through Belgium. I fortified the knowledge I already had about Belgian ales and specialty beers. I brought the spirit of Belgian beer back to my homebrewery, and in June of 1995, Felicitous Belgian Stout was born. It was a beer I had never tasted before, except in my mind. There was no such style in Belgium.

Why do I call it Belgian stout? I brewed it with my new appreciation and knowledge of Belgian brewing traditions. If there were ever to be Belgian stout, what would it be? I considered the question seriously. It would be strong. Goldings-type hops would be used. A warm ferment would comfort the yeast. And the flavor and aroma of noble Saaz and Hallertauer would subtly finesse an already complex beer.

FELICITOUS STOUT

So what is it like? Felicitous Belgian Stout is a 6½ to 7 percent (I'll be pushing the higher end next time I brew this) alcohol by volume, very dark stout without the sharpness of roasted malt. The roasted malts and barley are mellowed and lightened by the overriding symphonic combination of coriander and orange peel. The floral and earthy character of Saaz and Hersbucker Hallertauer hops lay a foundation of beer quality upon which the sparkle of spice rides. The Vienna and crystal malt help produce an overall malty character without being excessively full bodied. Fully fermentable honey boosts the alcohol while contributing unique fermented character to the beer, much as candi sugar would had it been used. This recipe can be found on page 251.

If I'd had candi sugar on the day I had chosen to impulsively brew Felicitous Belgian Stout, I would have used it, as the Belgians so often do. Instead,
honey would have to do on this inaugural occasion. Many Belgian types of ale
possess the flavor and aromatic character of crushed coriander seed and Cu-
ração orange peel.

Banana aroma and flavor are also part of the character of many Belgian
ales, especially the stronger types. The banana is a byproduct of certain
strains of yeast usually fermented at 70 to 80 degrees F. While I can appreciate these banana esters in certain ales, I chose not to design the stout with
this in mind, but you may do so with your choice of yeast. Wheat could have
been used in the formulation, really authenticating the original half-and-half
mixture of imperial stout and Celis White I had conceived in Philadelphia,
but then again I took homebrewed liberty in deciding not to formulate with
wheat (but then again, you may, if you wish).

2

·············

Brewery in a Goat Shed and
The King Wants a Beer

THE 1980S were a busy time for me and for microbreweries. I put all my energies toward building up the American Homebrewers Association, the Association of Brewers (now called the Brewers Association) and the Great American Beer Festival. At the same time, many landmark breweries were getting their start. These were adventurous times when doctors, airline pilots, computer programmers, lawyers, teachers, social workers, salespeople and many other professionals were giving up their jobs, risking it all to pursue their passion for beer. Theirs was a belief that Americans deserved the opportunity for choice, flavor and diversity. The idea of great full-flavored lager and ale had captured a grassroots following. All of the microbrewed beer brewed in the 1980s didn't amount to even a drop in the bucket—it was more like a wisp of vapor in proportion to the 6.2 billion gallons of light lager beer enjoyed by Americans each year. But everyone involved felt the excitement of being a pioneer on the frontier of a movement that was sure to win over the beer enthusiast who savored the flavor of real beer. Here are a few stories from that time.

Brewery in a Goat Shed
Boulder Brewing Company

FOR THE FEW INDIVIDUALS who were lucky enough to have visited the original Boulder Brewing Company, the brewery will always be remembered as having been started in a farmhouse goat shed in Hygiene, Colorado. Opened in 1980, the Boulder Brewing Company, now called the Boulder Beer Company, is the oldest surviving craft microbrewery in America.

The love of beer and homebrewing provided the inspiration—microbrewing at its essence. Founders Stick Ware, David Hummer and Al Nelson decided that after their 14th single-barrel test batch of bottle-conditioned homebrew they were ready to explore the legal aspects of going professional. It wasn't easy in those days to start a small brewery. Malt was available only in quantities measured by train car loads, hops were sold in bales weighing hundreds of pounds and fresh yeast cultures could be had only at great expense or through long overseas journeys from German and English brewing institutions. Getting a brewery license was an extreme challenge, as the government agencies in charge of regulating brewing laws were more experienced in dealing with million-barrel-size breweries. The hurdles to opening the Boulder Brewing Company in 1980 were unquestionably daunting but were overcome with microbrewing persistence and the assistance of the only other "local" brewery, the Coors Brewing Company (providing them with pale malt).

Otto Zavatone (with hat) at the "Goat Shed"
Brewery with Michael Jackson (right),
Fred Eckhardt (center, right) and Al Andrews (left)

That three guys, homebrewing test batches, managed to acquire the necessary equipment, ingredients and permits to go professional is yet another fantastic tribute to the passion for microbrewing and beer. Their passion is, in my opinion, the only reason they succeeded.

English-accented Boulder Pale Ale, Porter and Stout were their initial styles of ale, introduced by original head brewer Otto Zavatone. Otto once jokingly described how he got the job of head brewer at the "goat-shed" brewery: "They told me I could be the brewmaster, except I had to build the brewery first!"

The beer was truly handcrafted in every way, filled with a gravity-fed bottling system and capped using a manual "homebrew" bottle capper. All the beers were refermented in the bottle, establishing natural carbonation. After moving to their current facility in the late 1980s Boulder's hand-bottling system was abandoned. Today's Boulder beers are of extraordinary quality, and their range of ales and lagers offer a variety of flavors for the beer impassioned. I'm particularly fond of their hoppy Hazed and Infused, a lupulinhead's daydream.

But there was something charmed about their goat-shed ales of the mid-1980s. Otto Zavatone and his successor, Tom Burns, managed to extract unique, full-bodied, full-flavored ales from their small 1,200-square-foot brewery.

I have ever since been drawn to very small breweries, with batch sizes of five barrels or less. There is something unique about beers from breweries of this size. Perhaps it's because of the scientific dynamics involved when brewing in small volumes. I often find myself tasting a new beer not knowing its origins and marveling at characteristics reminiscent of the earliest small microbreweries, only to discover that the beer was brewed in batches of five barrels or less. I'm content to believe that these qualities reflect the original passion of a brewer who started out small, with all the dreams of success dancing in their mind as they tended to every aspect of the beer's production.

1981 BOULDER CHRISTMAS STOUT

In 1981 I shared a unique Christmas stout brewed by Guinness of Ireland with future Boulder head brewer Tom Burns. We both fell in love with the stuff, and Tom was determined to create a similar beer for Boulder. In those years Guinness had a tradition of making a special batch of Christmas ale. Its original gravity would match the year it was made, so that in 1981 the original gravity of their Christmas stout was 1.081—nearly double the strength of traditional draft Guinness stout. Tom Burns's Boulder Brewing Company's Special Christmas stout is rich, malty, smooth, velvety, strong and warming, with a wonderful hop balance that is not overwhelmingly bitter. It was one of the original American-brewed extra-special strong Imperial stouts. This recipe can be found on page 254.

Only a Brick Remained
Jim Koch, St. Louis and
Boston Beer Company

I**T WAS IN 1985** that Samuel Adams Boston Lager washed over the microbrewed beer scene. Like an unsuspected wave, it drenched beer drinkers and was popularly received as an old European-style pilsener lager. That year, the company, only six weeks old, flew in 20 cases of its beer, barely in time for the opening of the Fourth Annual Great American Beer Festival. It took top honors, winning the 1985 festival's consumer preference poll. From that point on, the waves created by Samuel Adams Boston Lager continued to wash over the landscape of American beer drinkers. Within years it could be found wherever beer was sold, paving the way for the thousands of brands of microbrewed beer that were seeking enthusiasts.

The 1980s were difficult years for most microbrewers. Their passion was evidenced by the quality of their beer, but the established ways of America's beer distribution system have always been a major challenge for microbrewers and a frustration for beer lovers seeking a choice. Great beer was being microbrewed, but the system failed to provide beer drinkers the access to beers they were growing to love.

The founder of Boston Beer Company and creator of Samuel Adams was a homebrewer, entrepreneur and, some say, a marketing genius. He recognized that brewing a distinctive and delicious beer was not enough—you had to make it accessible to beer drinkers. In that he succeeded. His name is Jim Koch. His father was in the beer business, and his great-grandfathers were brewers.

There's a little-known fact about Jim Koch's family brewing history that he shares with few people. He shared it with me the year before he introduced his first "Sam Adams."

We met in St. Louis in the fall of 1984. I was attending a Master Brewers Association of the Americas Conference and had taken the afternoon off to rendezvous with Jim and his father, Charles Joseph Koch, Jr. We drove from the conference center to the vicinity of Anheuser-Busch's brewery. "It's near here." Jim said as he sat up with visible excitement in his posture. His father glanced up the side streets, hinting recognition.

We parked the car. After walking several blocks, Jim's father announced, "We've got to be close. I recall that the Anheuser-Busch smokestack was visible from the site." Coming upon a vacant lot overgrown with weeds and strewn with odd refuse, Jim and his father began examining the remnants of a low-lying stone wall paralleling the sidewalk. "I think this is it!" exclaimed Jim, his father agreeing but with a tone of doubt. We walked slowly onto the lot, avoiding rusty cans, the odd discarded tire and gnarly-looking weeds. We came upon a small indentation at the center and kicked away the loose dirt and rubbish. A smile crossed father and son's faces as the evidence revealed we had found what they were seeking: the site of the Louis Koch Lager Brewery, the home of the Koch family—owned business that brewed between the 1860s and the 1880s. All that remained were a few stacked stones along the sidewalk and the wooden brick floor on which we were now standing.

On the southeast corner of Sydney and Buel Streeets, St. Louis

Well preserved and black with the brewer's pitch used to line the inside of wooden barrels, the $4 \times 6 \times 2$-inch wooden bricks was all that remained of the cooperage area of the brewery. It was the area where wooden barrels were built and reconditioned for beer.

Jim Koch and his father, Charles Joseph, in 1984 chipping away masonry souvenirs from the site of the Louis Koch's Brewery in St. Louis. The Anheuser-Busch Brewery is centered in the background.

SAMUEL ADAMS 1880

Neither an American nor a European-style pilsener, Samuel Adams Boston Lager is a re-creation of a historical American-type golden, hinting-at-amber, lager beer. Full-flavored, with a delicate proportion of dark caramel malt complemented by the unique flavor and floral character of German-grown hops, it's every bit as refreshing as classic pilsener. The Louis Koch Lager Brewery created a beer of its time, forgotten until Jim Koch resurrected it. Here is a recipe that may approach today's Samuel Adams Boston Lager, as well as the lager at the family's 1880 brewery. This recipe can be found on page 256.

We each took a brick as a souvenir and as we approached the car, Jim's gait quickened. He opened the trunk and took out a sledgehammer. Returning to the wall, he and his father wailed on the stone in the shadow of the world's largest brewing company. Pieces of the wall crumbled. The two men lifted a few chunks of foundation wall and placed them in the trunk of the car. And left the vacant lot to its destiny.

Since then I have heard Jim remind brewers several times that people DRINK the BEER. It is not a commodity, a label, an added flavor, nor market research. It has soul and heart. I would add, so do the people who make it. Jim has nurtured the new family brewery as one of the world's leading brewers of specialty craft beers in the true spirit of a microbrewery.

> It's true, Samuel Adams Boston Lager started as a homebrew. I brewed the first batch in my kitchen in 1984 using a recipe of my great-great-great-grandfather's from the 1870s . . . I fell in love with the taste of this beer. I thought that if I could taste this beer every day of my life, I'd be a happy man. That was my motivation for starting the Boston Beer Company.
>
> —JIM KOCH, FOUNDING PRESIDENT/CEO, BOSTON BEER COMPANY

Message on a Bottle
Anchor Brewing Company

SOMEWHERE in the United States there is a unique, old and majestic pipe organ. Its spirit comes alive with the touch of human endeavor. It is a very special organ, because it keeps a secret hidden somewhere in its dark recesses—a very special message. Carved in small letters where no one will notice until perhaps another century is the simple message: "Relax. Don't worry. Have a homebrew."

It's the message of a homebrewer who specializes in reconstructing these grand pipe organs.

In 1986 I had the opportunity to tell this story to Fritz Maytag, president of the Anchor Brewing Company in San Francisco. We were both enjoying the beers of our choice. He cracked a small smile, glanced aside quickly and returned with a story of his own.

Fritz knew a very skilled and proud violinmaker who was in love. He'd confided to Fritz that written somewhere inside his most recent violin was a message that, in all probability, no one would notice for another thousand years. The message read: "I love you Susan."

I wonder how many other people take pride in their skills and express their satisfaction in life's endeavors with small, unrewarded messages.

After my conversation with Fritz, I too became a bit inspired. My idea took seed at the Brewers Association of America Conference in 1986, where 14 breweries were represented. Wouldn't it be a great gesture to collect labels from each of the 14 participating breweries and have the CEO/president of each of these breweries sign the back side of everyone's label? In the end, each CEO would receive a collection of each label plus his or her label signed by 13 other CEOs.

I collected the blank labels and organized a sequential mailing. About six months later I received all of the signed labels and redistributed them. Fritz told me that he randomly inserted the signed labels into a bottling run of his Anchor Steam beer. I don't know what became of the others (Jerry Smart, Boulder Brewing Co.; Kendra Elliot, Dixie Brewing Co.; F.X. Matt II, F.X. Matt Brewing Co.; Fred Huber, Joseph Huber Brewing Co.; Paul Mayer, Jacob Leinenkugel Brewing Co.; Bill Smulowitz, The Lion Inc./Gibbons Stegmaier Brewery; Matthew Reich, New Amsterdam Brewing Co.; Bill Smith, Pabst Brewing Co.; Alice Victor, Savannah Beer Co.; George Korkmas, Spoetzel Brewery; Ken Shibilski, Stevens Point Brewing Co.; Dick

Yuengling, D. G. Yuengling and Son). I have my own collection framed on an office wall—a reminder of the passion that brewers share. A little bit of history. Some of those breweries and people are no longer with us.

I often wonder why microbrewing and homebrewing seem to be one of life's frequently celebrated endeavors, an endeavor that often prompts the best from individuals. Every day thousands of brewers leave small, unrewarded messages in each and every drop of beer they make. "Relax. Don't worry. Have my beer." "I love you." "I respect you." "I appreciate that you enjoy my beer." "You are simply the best." "Thank you."

Irish French Ale in the High Country
George Killian's Irish Red

FALLING IN LOVE in France. A desire to marry and relocate to America. The relatives from Ireland who must grant permission. An impassioned relationship; a contract with the parents in Ireland and those that had kept her in France. Moving to America. Arrival. Culture shock. How to introduce her to friends? At first adhering to her origins, she slowly evolves and eventually becomes more American than she is French or Irish. In middle age, she is ignored, shelved for younger passions, but she still survives. Her roots have been misplaced, lost. But her pride persists; she is nominally supported and enjoys an active life as the unknown horizon of twilight approaches.

IT HAS all the intrigue of a movie romance. It began as a passionate love affair in the late 1970s and early 1980s with Irish Red Ale, brewed in France by the Pellforth Brewing Company, which had a license agreement with the Irish company George Killian Lett Brewing Company. Visiting France, Peter Coors of the Coors Brewing Company discovered this wonderfully complex red ale and considered how to brew it in America and successfully introduce it to American beer drinkers. He pursued his company's interest in the ale.

The years of intrigue and initial development were from about 1980 to 1982. During that period I was fortunate enough to be given a 250 ml bottle of George Killian's Irish Red Ale, brewed at the Pellforth brewery. It was a marvelously complex ale with only subtle fruitiness but with big notes of nuttiness and toasted malt, balanced with hop character. Not overly bitter, it was smooth with quite a bit of drinkability. I recall a hint of floral aroma, perhaps from French countryside hops.

Its new home in America necessitated a makeover for the American public. In the early 1980s the pilot brewery at Coors occupied a relatively small space of about 5,000 square feet. Batch sizes were also small, at about 40 barrels. At the time, the brewery was producing over 15 million barrels of Coors, Coors Light and Herman Joseph. The Coors pilot brewery was the largest of the half-dozen microbreweries that existed in 1981.

I had earlier been introduced to the pilot brewery's head pilot brewer, Gil Ortega. One of the charges of the pilot brewery was product development. When homebrewers were invited to stop by and assess their experiments with "Killian's Red Ale," we jumped at the opportunity.

When given creative choices, most brewers who call themselves master-brewers will jump at the opportunity to develop new products. The spirit of beer passion was certainly evident in this tiny section of the Coors brewing factory.

There were many test batches, trying different malt types with varying degrees of toasting. At first different ale yeasts were used, producing full-flavored red ale with hints of fruitiness and, unfortunately, explosively active warm-temperature fermentations frothing out the tops of the fermenters. The brewers and homebrewers seemed to enjoy these earlier prototypes. So did several of the Coors staff, but operationally the brewery had other priorities. The fermentations certainly needed to be tamer, and warm-temperature fermentations would require refitting with accommodating equipment. Ale

Dave Thomas and Chuck Hahn worked on the original versions of Coors' Killian's Irish Red Ale

GEORGE KILLIAN'S IRISH RED ALE
FROM PELLFORTH

Richly flavored with the subtle and romantic floral character of Santiam hops, this ale's long kettle boil accents the toasted and caramel character of malt. The beer's reddish glow is impassioned by the enthusiast who seeks original red ales. This recipe can be found on page 259.

yeast in a lager brewery made Coors nervous. And the looming marketing priority seemed to be "make us something that we can sell to our lager drinkers."

Killian's Irish Red Ale, originally introduced to the public at the first Great American Beer Festival in 1982, was indeed "top fermented" with ale yeast, but likely lagered at cooler temperatures to soften its complexity. I recall it being very well received. Most beer enthusiasts at the time were utterly astonished that Coors would be so bold as to brew distinctive red ale with a notable degree of complexity.

Time passed, and the company probably realized that if Killians were to survive, it had to increase its appeal to the average American beer drinker. In the following years, lager yeast replaced ale yeast and the complexity was reduced to accommodate the more popular tastes of the time.

Killian's has survived. It bears very little resemblance to the original 1982 recipe and it certainly has lost any connection, other than by name, to the red ale Peter Coors romanced in France. Yet it reminds me of the very beginnings of the emergence of microbrewed beer and of Coors's early passion for interesting, flavorful, complex beers.

Coors remains involved with the spirit of microbrewed beers. They produce Blue Moon Pumpkin Ale and Belgian-style Wheat Beer, and at the Sandlot (micro) Brewery at the Coors Stadium in downtown Denver they are brewing a wide variety of ales and lagers. There is also limited production of Barman, an all-malt German-style pilsener, originally brewed for the enjoyment of the Coors family and available at a half-dozen restaurants in the Denver-Boulder area in Colorado.

The King Wants Homebrew

MAY I PLEASE SPEAK with Mr. Charlie Papazian?" asked a deep-voiced gentleman with a European accent.

"Hello, this is Charlie, can I help you?" I replied, with absolutely no idea that this was the beginning of an adventure I would recall for the rest of my life. I vividly remember the moment and recall it over and over. It was in July of 1982.

"Hello Mr. Papazian, my name is George Charalambous and I work for Anheuser-Busch in St. Louis. You have heard of the brewery?"

I liked this guy already. "Yes," I replied with a nervous chuckle.

"May I call you Charlie?"

"Of course."

"Charlie, I am organizing the annual joint meeting of District St. Louis Master Brewers Association of the Americas and the American Society of Brewing Chemists. I would like to invite you to speak at our meeting this coming April 14, 1983. We have heard you are doing some interesting things in Colorado. We cannot pay for your travel or accommodations, but we can offer you a free dinner."

George Charalambous

I hesitated a moment, wondering a big "why?" "What would you want me to discuss?" I replied.

"I understand you have an association and some of your members are making homebrew and have started small microbreweries. I think it would be interesting to hear about them and taste some of their beers."

This was my first contact with the "King," Anheuser-Busch. I accepted knowing I had nine months to think about what to say. The adventure had begun.

One week later, a very enthusiastic George Charalambous called again. "Charlie, I have talked to some of my colleagues and I would like to ask whether you will consider making a batch of homebrew that could be served at the meeting."

I knew I could make good homebrew, but I silently gasped nevertheless. I drew out the first word of my reply, trying to buy time. "Welllllllll," lingering a moment, "yes I can . . ."

Before I could continue, George raised his voice in excitement. "This is wonderful! You will have to tell me what you might brew after you have had time to think about it."

"George, who will be at this meeting?"

"Professional brewers and production engineers and scientists from Anheuser-Busch; Falstaff, which is across the river; other professionals from the Midwest and manufacturers from Europe. We have a lot of fun and there's always plenty of beer."

I did not get a good night's sleep that evening, as I wondered, "Where is all this going? Am I going to be able to make a beer that is up to their standards? Will they like my homebrew? Am I crazy?" Evidently I was.

Two weeks later George called again. There was excitement in his voice exceeding the pitch of the previous conversation by leaps and bounds. "Charlie, I have wonderful news . . ."

"Uh ohhhhh," I thought to myself as I fumbled for the imaginary seat belt on my office chair.

"Charlie I have talked to Ball Metal Container Corporation; you know, they make aluminum cans for us and they have agreed to supply us with cans to put your homebrew in. We will have the two logos of our professional associations as well as the logo of your American Homebrewers Association and your names as president of each organization. This will be great, Charlie."

Now came the hard part. "George, how will you get the beer into cans?" I meekly asked.

"We will send you empty kegs, and after you have filled them we will ship them to St. Louis."

I wondered if George realized that I was a homebrewer, making beer in 6½-gallon carboys fermenting under my kitchen table. "How . . . much . . . will you . . . uhhh . . . ahhh . . . need, George?"

"Charlie, can you make two barrels?"

My brain quickly calculated: Thirty-one gallons in a barrel. Two barrels. Sixty-two gallons. About ten 6½-gallon carboys worth of beer. In other words, over a hundred pounds of malt! I've never had that much malt in my house at one time.

Adrenaline was coursing through my veins. But I remained calm, because brewers who say "yes" simply breathe deeply and repeat three times, "Relax, don't worry, have a homebrew." It works every time.

"Okay George, I'll do it."

"We'll send you eight quarter-barrels in time for you to use."

That was the beginning of that!

YOU'VE GOT to take into perspective that this was 1983. The best commercially available homebrewing yeast was dried yeast and came in small envelopes. Ale yeasts were often not of the best quality, and "dried lager yeast" was not lager yeast at all, but simply ale yeast called lager yeast on the package. Therein lay my dilemma. If I could gain access to a quality culture of ale and lager yeast, I might have a chance at brewing beers that would be acceptable to the people of the "King." The challenge was to avoid compromise. The beers *had* to be good.

I called in a favor to friends at a brewing laboratory. One week later I had two small test tubes, one each of anonymous ale yeast and anonymous lager yeast. I was assured that they were of very good brewing quality and had been removed from a frozen yeast bank and cultured back to activity inside these tubes. I looked disbelievingly at the tiny drops of liquid and the small, almost imperceptible, amount of sediment that dusted the bottom. From these two drops of liquid sprang forth hundreds of beers, the first two emerging as lagers, Masterbrewers Doppelbock and Masterbrewers Celebration Light Lager. Juggling carboys and available space, I brewed several 12-gallon batches to top out at 31 gallons of final beer. Brewed on a stove top in a 5-gallon brewpot, fermented in 6½-gallon glass carboys at room temperature and "lagered" for three weeks at the same room temperature under my kitchen table, the beer was finally ready to keg. I called George, announcing, "You can deliver those kegs."

I'll never, ever forget the look on my neighbor's face when the Anheuser-Busch van stopped in front of my home. He leaned on his yard rake with an expression that spoke for itself. I shrugged my shoulders as the Anheuser-Busch representative wheeled into my front door eight empty quarter-barrels of beer. After the van left, I looked over at my neighbor, who was still frozen leaning on his rake, his mouth wide open. I didn't say a word. He knew I was a homebrewer . . . but the van from Anheuser-Busch?

A short time later, the beer was transferred into each keg with a gravity siphon. A small amount of corn sugar was added for initiating natural carbonation and the hole was ceremoniously bunged with a wooden cork and a hefty whack of a hammer. One week later I summoned Anheuser-Busch to pick up the filled kegs.

My neighbor was doing yard work as the Anheuser-Busch van pulled up to the front of my home for a second time, and he again stopped and with a dropped jaw, stared at the scene in silent disbelief. The two-wheel dolly entered the house empty and emerged with two quarter-barrels of beer—four times. As the King of Beers guy drove away, I turned to my neighbor, feeling that by now I owed him an explanation. I said, with a shrug, "Anheuser-Busch needed some beer, so I'm helping them out." I immediately turned and walked into the house without waiting for a reaction.

THOUGH SATISFIED that the beer entering the keg was excellent, I was nervous. Would it survive the trip to St. Louis? Would it carbonate? How would it survive the journey into the can?

The can. That was the unknown factor beyond my control. I heard months later that a "small" canning line, perhaps used in a pilot brewery, was used to fill and seal the cans. I wondered later why more than half the cans were only half full and there were so many commemorative empties. It was later explained to me that it took more beer to fill the canning line's plumbing than there was beer. The kegs were emptied before the beer began to emerge on the filling end! Empty cans were flying off the conveyor belt and half-fills barely made it to the sealer. Anheuser-Busch was a union brewery·and all the professionals had to keep their hands behind their backs, sweating over the whole procedure as the line workers did the best they could. The way it was described to me, the scene sounded like an episode straight out of "I Love Lucy."

But the beer survived and was enjoyed by the nearly 100 attendees. Both brews were miraculously "clean" and did not suffer from traveling. The Doppelbock was preferred, though both were beers in which I took a great deal of pride. How did I feel? Totally surprised at how well they had turned out. This success inspired me to have no fear and pursue beer as a passion for years to come. The support given by George Charalambous, Anheuser-Busch, the Master Brewers Association of the Americas, the American Society of Brewing Chemists and the Ball Corporation was tremendous. It was the beginning of a long, mutually supportive relationship between homebrewers, microbrewers, craft brewers and the technical people involved with the large brewing companies. For these opportunities I am forever grateful.

There is one more part to this story.

I continued to brew with the lager yeast, using it in virtually all my beer recipes. It behaved extraordinarily well and resulted in great-tasting "ales" and "lagers" even when I knew it was not an ale yeast and I had no facilities to cold lager my lagers. So, my secret was that I was not making true ales nor true lagers for many years. In fact, nearly all of my recipes in the first editions of *The Complete Joy of Homebrewing* (1984 and 1991) and *The Homebrewer's Companion* (1994) were based on having used this unknown strain of lager yeast. Ten years later I asked the source whether they could tell me where this lager yeast had come from. Their answer was a simple "no we can't tell you, sorry." A few years later, I tried one more time. A friend I had taught to homebrew had a job at the company. "Do you think you could tell me where this yeast came from if I told you the catalog name?" I asked. He'd try.

The next day I received a call. "Charlie, I know the source of that yeast you've been using. Are you sitting down?"

"Should I sit down?" I asked, puzzled.

"Well, I would suggest you do." There was a pause, "that yeast was originally cultured from a keg of Budweiser."

I was in shock. And then a huge homebrew inspired grin crossed my face

MASTERBREWERS DOPPELBOCK/MASTERBREWERS CELEBRATION LIGHT LAGER

Chestnut brown, full-flavored, malty and strong, Masterbrewers Doppelbock is an authentic-tasting German-style Doppelbock lager. Masterbrewers Celebration Light Lager, simply made with quality ingredients and a bit of finesse, is every bit as refreshing as a light lager created by a veteran brewer. Cascade hops added at the end contribute a character wonderfully reminiscent of microbrewing and homebrewing roots. These recipes can be found on pages 261 and 263.

and I began chuckling uncontrollably. All those barley wines, doppelbocks, India pale ales, brown ales, porters, pilseners, Oktoberfest beers, English ales and Irish stouts unknowingly made from a culture of Budweiser yeast!

With a deep sense of satisfaction I finally realized what I had done. This colony of yeast and the generations that followed were perhaps the happiest Budweiser yeast in the world! And they made me happy too.

3

. . . .

In Quest of Fresh Beer

F YOU didn't make your own homebrew in the 1980s, the beer landscape was pretty damned bleak. Of course, if you were brewing at home or visiting with homebrewers, craft beers with flavor and soul abounded. But what happened when you went out for dinner? What were the choices? The meager choices almost always included Bud, Miller, Coors, Bud Light, Miller Light and Coors Light. If you wanted something different you might find a Corona, a Heineken or a Beck's. Rarely would you find a microbrewed beer, even at better restaurants. I often made do with what was available. All that has changed, and today I won't patronize a restaurant that doesn't offer a real choice of beer character.

Why? I feel offended. I really do. It shows prejudice or ignorance on the part of a restaurant if customers are not offered a choice of beers. And as much as possible, that choice should include locally brewed options. If the food a restaurant is offering is worth paying good money for, then it is worth being complemented with the flavor of an appropriate beer. A good beer list offers true diversity, not by country of origin, but by flavor. If people will pay $20 to $40 for a good bottle of wine at dinner, why not offer a beer for which one might expect to pay 50 cents to a dollar, even two dollars, more per serving? Our world is a world of different foods and different cultures. Beer is an important contributor to life's pleasures and when all restaurants realize this, not only will their customers be happier, but their profits will grow.

Drinking with Our Eyes

IN 1999, on a tour of breweries of the southwestern United States, I organized a series of beer tastings to make the point that we are all prejudiced. Whether we like to admit it or not, whether we know it or not, we are severely influenced by beer's color, beer labels, beer commercials, the color of beer bottles and beer marketing. There is no way around it—our sense of taste is influenced by our environment and factors besides simply the taste of the beer.

The first stop on my 1999 microbrewery tour of the Southwest was Colorado Spring, where I visited several homebrew shops. Ending up at the Bristol Brewing Company, my wife, Sandra, and I enjoyed their craft microbrewed beers and set up a blind tasting among 50 homebrewers, beer enthusiasts and their guests. The crowd was a mix of avid and casual beer drinkers out for a good time. We presented three pairs of beers. All the tasters were told was to choose the beers they would prefer to continue to drink. There was no indication whether these beers were microbrewed, American, homebrewed, imports—nothing.

After we tallied the votes, the audience was quite amazed. New Belgium Blue Paddle Pilsener easily won over Corona. Sam Adams Boston Lager creamed Heineken, and Boulder Stout was overwhelmingly preferred to Guinness Stout. The point that interested everyone was that American microbrewed craft beers were preferred over brand names. What astounded many in the audience was that several regular Corona, Heineken and Guinness drinkers had made the American choice.

Encountering thunder in Taos, we rolled on through New Mexico, visiting the Second Street Brewery/Pub in Santa Fe, moving on to Albuquerque to

visit the Wolf Canyon Brewpub and Il Vicinos brewpub, and finally rendezvousing with the Santa Fe Homebrewers at the Rio Grand Brewery on the evening of the third day of the tour.

We once again had a blind tasting, among 40 homebrewers and their invited friends. Grolsch Lager tied with Grand Desert Pils, Sam Adams Boston Lager had twice as many votes as Heineken and in-house-brewed

Cabezon Stout garnered more than twice as many votes as Guinness Stout. There was the same astonishment among beer drinkers who had voted against their preferred brands.

We wound our way through the Southwest, on to Tucson, Arizona, visiting Brew Your Own homebrew shop and being welcomed by more than 100 beer enthusiasts and their spouses at the Pusch Ridge Brewing Company and Pub. Another beer tasting was held, and the results were Sam Adams 42 versus Corona 3; bottled Sierra Nevada Pale Ale 27 versus Bass Ale on draft 19; Guinness on Draft 1 (that is correct: 1) versus Pusch Ridge Old Pueblo Stout 47.

The beers were all served in glasses without any indication of origin. Brand-loyal, die-hard Guinness drinkers were stunned. Bass Ale aficionados could not believe their vote. After that evening, a few Corona drinkers were Corona drinkers no more.

The point has been made over and over again in other tastings. Freshly made local craft beers are preferred to imports when taste is the only factor. But the fact is we do enjoy certain beers simply because of the mystique created by their brand and advertising. That is not necessarily a bad thing if you truly enjoy what you are drinking.

If beer is really all about taste, then a real effort must be made to educate that taste—to allow us to recognize what our taste buds really do enjoy. It is my premise that if you can tune in to what you taste and learn to enjoy beer because of taste, the pleasure of beer is magnified.

THERE IS one more point I would like to discuss regarding how we taste beer: the controversy surrounding adjuncts.

The very word *adjunct* will cause many a homebrewer to cringe. In the name of purity, malt, hops, water and the Holy Ghost (yeast was known as godisgood in former times), homebrewers yearning for the full flavor of beer forsake everything else in favor of all-malt beer. But with the skill of an open-minded brewer, it is possible to maintain the full flavor of malted barley while adding the character of grain adjuncts. Grain adjuncts can add desirable character to beers, producing full-flavored beer with warm-weather drinkability. Now don't get me wrong: I do enjoy a cold all-malt porter on the warmest of summer days. My beer-drinking moods are as diverse as there is diversity among homebrewers and microbrewers.

Let's look at this from a fair perspective. If we label any ingredient other than hops and malt as an adjunct, then we've got to include the ripe, flavorful red cherries and raspberries of Belgian lambics and American wheat beers. The roasted barley of stouts. The coriander and orange peel of some Belgian ales. The cinnamon in your holiday brew. The honey in your honey pils and Weizen. The chili pepper and chocolate in your Goat Scrotum Ale. And you know all the other secrets that have been used to create the wonderful experience we have come to know as homebrewed and microbrewed in the U.S.A.

So why is it we have a reaction to rice and corn? I think I know why. We have let the large breweries define for us what we consider "adjunct beer." We've been suckered into a general mind-think about these ingredients. Light-lager brewers throughout the world have manipulated these adjuncts in ways that suit their needs. Let's not forget they have reduced the hop character and increased the carbonation to levels that quite a few of us don't really care for any longer. It's a matter of taste—theirs and ours. Let's not let their taste result in hang-ups we call our own.

How many times does the word *cheap* precede the use of the word *adjuncts*? Wait a minute: my flaked corn isn't any cheaper than the malts I use. In some parts of the world, corn is a lot more expensive than barley malt. So have we been duped? The word *cheap* is really a reaction to a taste many of us simply don't want any part of. But in this day and age as homebrewers are microbrewing craft beer, adjuncts are only figuratively cheap. Let's focus on the qualities we desire and what we can achieve as homebrewers. Our personal indignation shouldn't interfere with the possibilities of using ingredients to our advantage.

KLIBBETY JIBBIT

Klibbety Jibbit Lager is a full-flavored, light-bodied beer brewed with corn and flavored adequately with hops that many a homebrewer would love. It's alive, unfiltered, unpasteurized and refermented in the bottle for conditioning. Hey, all that *does* make a difference. Have you *ever* come across a commercial corn adjunct beer like this? I *know* not, not and double not. It's a European-type lager with the added microbrewed character of flavor hops. Its fresh and unfiltered character is one you've learned to appreciate as beer enthusiasts. You must inhibit your prejudices. Don't let marketing taint your brain. If you let that happen, you don't get to create your own thing anymore.

So that's the premise behind the formulation. This isn't an apology or justification. It's about, hey, brewing it and enjoying it and realizing what naturally made, fresh, unpasteurized homebrew and microbrew is always all about. The recipe can be found on page 264.

Have I heard microbrewers and homebrewers criticize large brewers for the grain adjuncts they use? Have I heard the large brewers poke fun at the weird (say "adjuncts," please) ingredients small brewers and homebrewers use? Yes and yes. It's all relative, and it's really about what you do with the process. It's about what YOU like. It's about your perspective. And it's about not being a victim of someone else's mind-think.

America's First Brewpubs

THE WHOLESOME QUALITIES of malt liquors greatly recommend themselves to general use as an important means of preserving the health of the citizens of this commonwealth," concluded the Massachusetts legislature passing an act in 1789 "to encourage manufacture of strong beer, ale and other malt liquors."

It was only 149 years earlier, in 1640, that the Massachusetts Bay Colony passed a regulation that "no one should be allowed to brew beer unless he is a good brewer." So it was with a great deal of anticipated pleasure that a group of microbrewery enthusiasts headed north into Massachusetts's emerging beer country in 1987.

As we slept off the beers we'd had earlier in the day from the as-true-as-it-gets German-style Vernon Valley Brewery in northern New Jersey, the bus quietly dieseled through Connecticut. It was late in August and we were headed for the small Massachusetts town of Northampton, a town that had recently taken great pride in the opening of their own Northampton Brewery and Brewster Court Pub. The brewpub's having opened only about six weeks before our arrival, we beer travelers were eager to see and experience a brewery restaurant that had been only a kitchen-table conversation 10 months earlier.

Arriving in the early evening, we checked into the venerable Hotel Northampton, and in true colonial fashion we wasted little time in hightailing it to the brewpub. Down a small hill off the main street we could see a brightly lit building as we approached our quarry for the evening. Blue neon cleanly outlined a large second-story circular picture window. The scene was reminiscent of an airbrushed painting one might have called "beer fantasyland."

People had come from miles around for the pleasure of each other's com-

Peter Egelston, 1987

pany and the fine beers brewed right there on the premises. Behind the bar, a glass wall separated the "New England Deco" pub from the small, beautifully lit 800-square-foot brewery.

A table awaited us with glasses of beer (pitchers had recently and ridiculously been outlawed in Massachusetts; certainly the founding fathers were turning over in their graves). Gold, amber and bock beers complemented the warm ambience, quiet conversation and excellent food. We spoke with the four owners; Peter Egelston brewed the beer while the other three managed the restaurant and bar. (Peter later moved on to establish New Hampshire brewpub Portsmouth Brewery and microbrewery Smuttynose Brewing Company.)

The passion for homebrewing and good beer got the better of the four founders of the Northampton Brewery, and now there they were, operating a brewery and restaurant/bar filled with enthusiastic customers in a small town in western Massachusetts. In 1987 they were among only 21 brewpubs in the entire United States. Only a few years earlier, in 1982, brewpubs were illegal in most of the country. There were none. As brewpub laws were enacted, permitting breweries to serve fresh beer at their own pubs, the numbers have grown.

Russ Scherer, co-founding brewmaster at the Wynkoop Brewery, 1988

In my home state of Colorado, brewpub legislation was slow to be en-acted. Pioneer John Hickenlooper was instrumental in helping enact brew-pub laws in late 1987. It was in 1988 that he and partner-brewer Russ Scherer founded Denver's first brewpub, the Wynkoop Brewery. Having been homebrewers inspired both of them. Russ had won the American Home-brewers Association's top honors as Homebrewer of the Year in 1985. He was certainly one of the most creative homebrewers and microbrewers up until his death in the 1990s. Although homebrewers were experimenting years ear-lier, Russ can certainly be credited with having brewed one of the first micro-brewed chili beers in the country at the Wynkoop Brewery. In 2003, John Hickenlooper was elected mayor of Denver.

MILE-HIGH GREEN CHILI ALE

The British would never dream of doing this to their pale ale, but Russ Scherer's pioneering roasted chili pale ale provides both a spicy and an exotic flavor to an otherwise smooth, purely drinkable English-style pale ale. It has to be brewed to believe. If you love the flavor of green chili, you will adore this beer. The recipe can be found on page 267.

There are now more than 1,000 brewpubs throughout the United States. Each has its own fascinating story. The invariable common thread is that they were all born of the passion for homebrewing and microbrewing. You will almost always find a founder, brewer or investor with roots in homebrewing and a passion for beer. Certainly the most successful brewpubs in America embrace the passion that is the very definition of the joy of microbrewing.

Beware the Puritanical State

DID YOU KNOW that you are in a puritanical state?" a member of the audience asked me during a speech I was giving on a 1991 book-signing tour in Philadelphia. Suddenly you could hear a feather float. Silent was the room as I hesitated in panicked thought. I had just taken a sip of water to clear my voice. Had they thought I had forsaken them? Everyone's face seemed to have a shocked expression, staring straight at my hand as if thinking, "Look. He's drinking water."

I scratched my head in confusion and asked, "What'd I do?" I had never been accused of being puritanical, and now my mind began to race, "Oh my God. This is *not* good. I certainly don't want to project that kind of image. Quick. Someone get me a beer."

On the verge of panic, my questioner began to see the beads of sweat on my forehead and came to the rescue. "No, no, no. I mean you are in a puritanical state; this state of Pennsylvania is very puritanical when it comes to beer laws. You can't buy anything less than a case of twenty-four 12-ounce bottles of beer in a liquor store. That makes it really difficult to try something new. What if you don't like it? Well, then, you're stuck with 23 bottles of, well, er . . . 23 bottles . . . and the laws are restrictive in the amount of alcohol allowed in beer and all agricultural products must be approved by the state before they can be sold here."

I was both relieved (I wasn't being accused of being puritanical after all) and sympathetic. Yes, in these 50 United States we now enjoy more than 14,000 American-made beers from more than 1,300 breweries spread across the land. Irish-style stouts, Belgian-style Dubbel and Tripels, fruit beers, German-style ales and lagers, British-style real ales and so much more. There are some laws that apply nationally, but the truly weird laws are enacted at the state level. In some states, if a beer is in excess of a certain level of alcohol you must call it ale, even if it is a lager. Elsewhere, if you brew a traditional stout you can't call it stout, because wise liquor commissioners translate the word *stout* as a reference to strength—and it seems they don't want you to know you are drinking strong beer. How about the state that allows commercial brewing only if you have a farm that grows the ingredients you would use? (Now, of course, you don't have to use your own farm-grown product, but you do have to go through the motions of growing it. Such is wisdom!)

Weird laws? You bet. All 50 states have the option to regulate the sale and production of alcoholic beverages. It's obvious that few of these regulators are homebrewers yet. But perhaps someday things will change.

Meanwhile, there is homebrewing. Ahhhh, home sweet homebrew! The beauty of it all! The regulations are quite simple: brew it for personal consumption and don't sell it. No label laws, no alcohol limits and no ingredient limitations. Homebrewing is a personal thing. It's a statement about you. It is an interpretation of your priorities and an expression of the freedom you've been given. I don't know of any other hobbies that express themselves as wonderfully as homebrewing.

If you wish to make a traditional German Altbier, brew it. A potato beer— brew it. A chocolate, chili pepper beer—brew it. A Down Under light lager—brew it. An Irish stout— brew it. A kiwi-flavored ale—brew it. You need no one's approval but your own.

What a great advantage homebrewers have! Brew it your own way, from a kit, from extracts, from grains. With the quality of ingredients, instructions and the wonderful supply of quality brewing yeasts available, excellent beer can be made using the simplest or most sophisticated of methods. You can immerse yourself in the science and technology of small-scale brewing or masterfully hover while communing with the art. But keep in mind that science and technical knowledge is best used as a tool

PURITANICAL NUT BROWN ALE

This nut brown ale blends aromatic malts with caramel-flavored malts, fermented as a slightly fruity ale with the subtle bite of roasted chocolate malt. It offers a mouthful of soft, smooth nutlike flavor balanced with a blend of flavors and aromatically floral hops. It will sway even the most puritanical to indulge in brown ale. This recipe can be found on page 269.

and not to be embraced as the final word. You can become a master of brewing only through your own experiences and awareness of the qualities of great beer at whatever level of brewing you choose to pursue.

Your homebrewery, your recipes, your process—homebrewing is about you. And there is every reason to take pride in your beer and brewing endeavors, no matter what degree of sophistication you choose to pursue. If you like your beer, that's all that matters, isn't it? If you already brew, you know of what I speak. If you don't already homebrew—please do.

The guiding principle of homebrewing is remembering that you are an individual with individual taste preferences and priorities. And don't ever forget that homebrewing is supposed to be fun. Relax. Don't worry. Have a homebrew.

Sure, there's room for serious discussion and seriously good beer (and even for enjoying beers that are commercially made), but when you lose sight of the enjoyment of homebrewing, you've lost the microbrew touch. You may as well be in that "puritanical state." I thought I was there for a moment. It was a frightening experience.

Drinking Deliberately

WAS IN TELLURIDE, Colorado, faced with the daunting task of picking from seven excellent brews, house-brewed by Archie Byers at the San Juan Brewing Company's brewpub, and I was very, very thirsty.

My new friends Ann, Melanie, Tom, and Sandy and I had just spent the better part of the day attempting to climb Wilson Peak. Telluride, tucked away in a tiny valley in southwestern Colorado, is surrounded by dozens of 14,000-foot peaks. Wilson Peak, at 14,087 feet, loomed above us in the clear morning sunshine. It should have been a three-hour walk and scramble to the top—but wasn't.

By the time we had reached timberline, the billowy clouds we had seen earlier on the western horizon surrounded us. At 12,000 feet we paused on a stretch of pink glacier snow and discussed whether we should proceed. Thunder rolled on the other side of the valley. The storm patterns were four to five miles on either side of us. This valley seemed to be spared from rain and storm. We proceeded.

We reached the 13,000-foot ridge. Preparing for the final ascent we paused again, lingering over lunch. With growing anxiety we seriously considered whether to proceed. The weather cleared and on we went, taking a deliberate breath with each step, hand holding the rocks we scrambled upon.

At 14,000 feet we were within 50 yards of the top. The rarefied air twists your perceptions. Colors were more intense, and a sense of otherworldliness washed over me in gentle waves. Looking down it was easily noted that we were very, very high. On a small outcrop of exposed rock, all five of us regrouped. Ann was putting on warmer clothes and taking pictures. Sandy was catching her breath. Tom was gazing longingly toward the summit. Melanie seemed intent on completing the hair-raising final 50 yards. And I was gazing down, down, down to the pinprick buildings I knew were towns, far below. I was thinking: "Now. Right now there are people down there enjoying a beer." We all had our priorities. Life is about priorities, and given certain circumstances we are intensely reminded of them.

We were all brought back together in discussion as the wind picked up, the sun disappeared and it began to ominously snow in July. There was a clap of thunder somewhere in the distance.

Suddenly we reached consensus. None of us wanted to be there. We were booking ourselves out of there. I mean scooting, vaminosing, fleeing. Tom did so reluctantly, frequently looking back over his shoulder. This was his fourth unsuccessful attempt at conquering Wilson Peak. Rain, snow and wind had defeated him on three previous tries. Under his breath he was cursing repeatedly, "F——— you, Wilson Peak." He was visibly pissed.

All of us wanted to get back down, but Melanie and Tom wanted to get down faster than the rest of us. They began descending an avalanche chute. The rest of us followed, but some yards down as rock scree cascaded down the mountain with every disturbing step I heartily embraced Annie's wisdom: "This was the stupidest thing we've tried all day." Three of us opted to go back and descend the way we'd come and help assure ourselves that we'd live to

have another beer and try another time. Life is full of choices, and this choice
was easy for me.

We all made it down. At the bottom of the valley we learned Tom was
overcome with anger and stubbornness at the high altitude. He couldn't take
defeat a fourth time. Incredibly, he had decided to go back up and made it to
the top. He told us later, his face still a bit ashen from the experience, "The
rocks began humming like a beehive, but there were no bees." Strangely, his
hair had stood on end from the building electrical charge the mountain and
atmosphere could have released at any moment. He'd fallen flatly onto the
ground, crawling and scraping his belly as he slowly slithered from the top of
the mountain. He was quite certain he was about to die. He was very, very
lucky, and it wasn't because he had finally conquered Wilson Peak.

On the mountain we each had our own priorities. Now that we were off
the mountain, those priorities changed. We all headed straight for the San
Juan Brewery. I think Ann chose the golden ale, as did Tom and Melanie.
Sandy may have had the red. I was ready for my first beer of a long day. I was
tired, dehydrated and very thirsty. It was a tall glass of India pale ale, alongside a tall glass of water. I alternated between the two and savored every wonderful nuance of what seemed to be the best beer I'd ever had in my life. A
part of me savored my glass of water. But the rest of me—the conscious, living me—gleefully established my priorities. While most of the beer-drinking
world might have preferred a light beer at this moment, I chose to drink deliberately.

Drink deliberately!

Only the day before had I come across a trendy advertisement for
footwear. It encouraged, "Live Deliberately." Never mind the product they
were selling; I thought, "Yeah, live deliberately. I like that."

TELLURIDE INDIA PALE ALE

Loaded with hops, but not overdone, this ale is characterized by malt balanced with the unique twist of a healthy handful of Belgian Special-B and toasted biscuit malt. Crisp and refreshing, it's highly drinkable at any altitude. The recipe can be found on page 272.

Perhaps it was the bubbles rising in my second India pale ale (alongside another glass of water) as I gazed hypnotically into my glass. "Drink Deliberately" floated to the surface of my mind like the creamy head on my nourishing ale.

We all have our priorities. I had chosen to come down off the mountain, not having reached the top, to try again another time. I don't regret most of the choices I've made in my life. My priorities continue to evolve. I often think about how lucky we are in America to have so many choices, though most of us don't exercise our opportunity to choose. Beer? Beer is one of those wonderful things in life. Does it dismay me that I've observed so many mindless choices across so many bars and dining tables? No, although I wonder why people bother to make a mindless choice of what beer to drink when there are so many wonderful options.

I suppose at any given moment it's all about priorities. There are so many wonderful beers . . . if people would only take a moment to think about their priorities.

For now, I choose to live deliberately, and when it comes to beer I'll take that moment to drink deliberately.

That day in Telluride in the mid-1990s, I was lucky. I could drink Archie's India Pale Ale after a long day's journey. But if I hadn't been so fortunate and had found myself trapped on top of the mountain with my own ingredients and equipment, I'd have brewed a simple but most excellent batch of my own . . .

The Bad Boys of Beer

WHILE THE MICROBREWS of today owe much to the pioneering work of the brewmasters of the early 1980s, they have contributed their own personality and twists to America's growing lexicon of beer. There are now more than 1,300 microbrewies across the country, offering thousands of choices from Dogfish Head's Raison d' Etre to Rogue Ales' Morimoto Imperial Pilsner and Stone Brewing's Arrogant Bastard ale.

No longer simply content to brew world-class German-style kölsch, bock, Altbier, pilsener, Dunkel, and having perfected English- and Belgian-style stout, porter, India pale ale, gueuze-lambic, barley wine, mild, Tripel, Dubbels and Kriekbiers, today's brewers continue the adventure beyond all boundaries. They are always on the frontier, with beers aged in sherry, bourbon, port and wine barrels, infusing hops at the point of serving, using indigenous and exotic sugar, spicing their beers with the perfect balance of cocoa, coffee, coconut, exotic fruits and herbs. Today's brewers maintain their reverence of classic styles while creating new balanced beer flavors that offer even the avowed non–beer drinker new opportunities to indulge in a vibrant and convivial beer culture.

Rogue Ales
Charlie 1981

JOHN MAIER, brewmaster at Rogue Ales, Newport, Oregon, has brewed more than 30 million pints for Rogue. So states John's short bio, but I beg to differ. John has brewed more than 30 million pints of Rogue Ales for *beer drinkers*!

Article 2 of Rogue Ales's "Beer Manifesto" reads, "We hold that beer is worthy of passion." Agreed.

Rogue Ales is a unique and "beer-alive" brewing company, owing much of its growth in popularity to John Maier's creative skills.

I don't quite recall the very first time I met John. It was probably in the mid-1980s. He began his beer journey in 1981 brewing his first batch of homebrew from my book *The Complete Joy of Homebrewing*. Entering numerous beer competitions, he saw his newfound passion rewarded with several top honors at homebrew competitions. In 1987 he took a job as assistant brewer at Juneau's Alaskan Brewing Company.

It was in the year 1988 that I truly recognized the talents of John Maier. The American Homebrewers Association was celebrating its tenth anniversary at their annual conference. I was wearing only a white toga and a wreath of hops. The celebrations were beginning. I was roasted and then twice pied in the face by hooded "pie terrorists." Speeches were made to embarrass me further. It was all in fun, and the buildup to the final ceremonies awarding the winners of the American Homebrewers Association's National Homebrew Competition. I had the honors of presenting the top award, best of show and Homebrewer of the Year. It was to John Maier.

When he came to accept his award John whispered to me, "Charlie, it was your recipe for barleywine ale, right out of your book." In his acceptance

---

JOHN 1981

First and foremost a "wow!" experience, this beer has lots of malt, lots of hops and lots of passion. Fermented with a vigorous yeast strain providing a relatively dry finish to a very complex ale that will continue to age well, it's a homebrewed version of Charlie 1981. The recipe can be found on page 274.

Rogue Brewmaster John Maier in a mountain of hops

speech, he encouraged all by reminding us that quality beer needs passion and anyone can make great beer at home using simple techniques.

In 1989 John became the head brewer at Rogue Ales. I visited the brewery a few short years after it had opened. There was that ever-present sparkle of passion and excitement in John's eyes and a small grin while he juggled brewhouse, fermentation and packaging activities. They had just received new bottling equipment and were in process of fine-tuning its operation. Since then the beers of John Maier have continued to roll off the conveyers at this small coastal-town brewery.

Would a professionally trained brewmaster with neither homebrewing experience nor passion for beer be capable of what John has achieved? I think not. I can't keep up with the proliferation of beers Rogue offers to the beer drinker. Go to their website (www.rogueales.com) and count them yourself. John brews more than 30 actively available beers, among them Chipotle Ale, Chocolate Stout, Dead Guy Ale, Hazelnut Brown Nectar, Imperial India Pale Ale, Mocha Porter, Morimoto Imperial Pilsner, Santa's Private Reserve and Rogue Smoke.

One of John Maier and Rogue Ales's award-winning and briefly popular beers was "Charlie 1981," brewed to commemorate the 2001 Association of

Brewers' Annual Craft Brewers Conference. Confronted with a bottle of Charlie 1981, bearing my likeness on the label, I was taken by surprise. John had commemorated his first batch of homebrew (1981) using the book that had started his career.

Charlie 1981 was a bottle-conditioned strong ale with a unique balance of hops and malt that rewarded John and the Rogue brewery with honors at several international competitions. Intended to be a once-only brew, Rogue rebrewed Charlie 1981 once again in 2002, but there are no long-term plans to brew this widely acclaimed ale.

The *Book with the Little Rose*
New Belgium

WHEN I AM DEVELOPING a new beer and have certain ideas of what it should be, I don't brew test batches by aiming at the 'center of the target.' I like to brew test batches that explore the areas of ingredients and process so I learn what is happening all around the central idea I am ultimately trying to brew."

These are the words of Peter Bouckaert, head brewer and brewmaster of New Belgium Brewery in Fort Collins, Colorado, makers of the very popular Fat Tire amber lager. Peter is Belgian, with experience and friends at several breweries in Belgium. Now he has relocated to Colorado, bringing with him special skills and an attitude that admires both the obvious and the not-so-obvious world of brewing's science and art.

Speaking English with a Flemish accent, Peter confides, "It is so nice, yes, that in America there are so many people experimenting with all aspects of brewing. The large brewers in Europe are not doing this. The homebrewers, microbrewers and craft brewers are all important to helping us all understand and explore all these interrelationships and very new ways of doing things. If you have many brewing projects that you and others may be working on, it is very valuable to be able to take little pieces of knowledge from each project and fit the pieces together to achieve a new beer."

Others have often said that there are so many good beers in the world, but so little time to try them all. Peter is one who realizes that there is so much to learn and do in creating beers, but so little time to brew them all. He possesses a wealth of knowledge and experience, gained from delving into matters of brewing frontiers.

We discuss the addition of herbs and fruits to beer. There are secrets Peter won't tell me, but he makes me realize that not all herbs and fruits can be treated equally, explaining, "It all depends on the chemical nature of the flavor and character you are trying to finally end up with in your beer." You need to understand very specifically the chemical nature of a cherry's or a raspberry's flavor. For example, raspberry flavors have ketones in their makeup. If they are fermented, certain other flavors are derived from the fermentation and aging process of these compounds.

How do you maintain the red color of cherries? "This is something I know about through experimentation and discussion with colleagues," Peter says with a smile. "I can't tell you too much about this because now we consider it is confidential." He leaves me with the thought that the answer is both process and ingredient related.

"You have to treat spices the same way," he says. For example, if you use kaffir lime leaves, the flavor compound that you want to perceive in the final beer is related to citronellal. He explains that this is chemically described as an aldehyde. If this is acted upon during the fermentation process, it can be broken down into alcohol, and this in turn can be broken down into esters. All have the elements of citrus character, but at each stage the flavor and aroma threshold can increase or decrease dramatically. So you have to be careful about how much you add, as well as when you add it. Every spice and herb is different. "If you are seeking a desired final balance of flavors then it is nice to be able to understand these things," Peter adds.

There are many creative beers brewed at the New Belgium Brewery. The tasting room/pub is worth a visit, for some of the most interesting and experimental beers are available only on site and at the brewery. One beer that is available nearly everywhere is their well-known Fat Tire. But New Belgium also has unusual beers such as their 1554, which intrigues me as a beer enthusiast and homebrewer. Its recipe is based on references to a Belgian-style black ale, brewed as far back as 1447 and quite popular in the 18th and 19th centuries.

"Zwart bier," or black beer, is virtually unknown in today's Belgium. Phil Benstein, one of the brewers Peter works with at New Belgium, came across a reference to black beer at the Colorado State University library. Further research led Peter to other references in the 1903 book *One Hundred Years of Brewing*, but he could not find any Belgian brewers who knew of this historic beer. On one of his frequent journeys back to Belgium, Peter enlisted the help of a Belgian friend and historian, who uncovered a book published in 1554 referencing black ale and a 1447 book called *Het Boeck mette Rooskens*, translated "Book with the Little Rose."

The idea to recreate a historic version of this black ale was proceeding at the brewery, using malted barley, hops and selected spices. The beer, label and packaging were ready to be introduced to beer drinkers as "1554."

Book with a Little Rose

Through good fortune and lucky circumstances, Peter found a copy of *Het Boeck mette Rooskens* in the city archives of Brussels. It was handwritten on parchment, dated September 27, 1447. Written in old Flemish, in stylistic cursive, the book deals with legislated city laws, of which about 32 pages concern *"swart ofte zwert bier"* beer-related matters. Peter believes that Brussels at the time was a small town of perhaps 15,000 people and 1,000 breweries.

Peter recalls, "Everyone was making beer at the time and there were rules in each town that governed what could be used and how you could make beer. Some references to black beers used oats while others may have used barley and wheat. Some reference hops and others reference gruits, the mixture of herbs and spices that were used more often than hops to flavor beer."

1447 BELGIUM ZWARTE ROSE ALE

Brewed with ingredients of the 15th and 16th century such as grains of paradise, amber-colored Munich malt, wheat, oats and crystallized caramel malt, "1447" is a dark beer with no roasted malts. My recipe takes liberty with the addition of rose petals. It's unlikely they were used in 15th-century Belgium, but they remind me of the creative Belgian spirit of brewing and this is the year 2005. This recipe can be found on page 277.

Peter admits he is not a historian, but he certainly values the historic as well as modern-day creativity involved in the mystical process of making craft microbrewed beers. When he can find time, or someone to help translate the difficult old Flemish, Peter plans to learn more about his Belgian brewing roots and perhaps some old wisdom that can be applied to his modern brewery, to brew beer for all of us beer drinkers to savor.

Had he found the "Book with the Little Rose" soon enough, we might be enjoying 1447 rather than 1554.

Hop Whompus
Oggi's Pizza & Brewing and
Left Coast Brewing Company

TOM NICKEL is the brewmaster of Oggi's Pizza and Brewing Company's Left Coast Brewery. His birthday is August 13, the same day as my wife's and also of lifelong friend Whitey Jensen, so I have some insight into the Leo the Lion personality behind the passion for taste, adventure and discovery. I've never studied astrology, nor do I know what the books say about Leos, but I do know what an adventure it is to hang out with them.

Tom Nickel

I'm glad I made the effort to spend a day with Tom in July 2004, visiting the brewery where he has created world-class award-winning ales. To say that Tom is passionate about beer is an understatement. Beer springs forth from every pore of his body and soul. When he is around beer, the guy is all about the planet Microbrew!

Tom's beers are notable for their stylistic balance of flavors, while venturing to the edge of creativity, forging new territories. He is an extraordinary brewer and an extraordinary teacher. While discussing beer and brewing with Rick Smets, Tom's assistant

Rick Smets, Andy Schwartz and Tom Nickel

brewer, it became quite obvious why the beer was so excellent. With a glass of vat-fresh pale ale, Rick explains, "I get up every day in the morning and come to work and am so thankful to have this job as a brewer. I love being a brewer. I couldn't ask for better work. Some beers are more work than others, but that's part of the job and I don't mind the extra hassle and work, because I know that the beer is going to be extra good. My grandmother was a Belgian brewer and my uncle turned me on to making beer when I was 16 years old. I love making beer." Rick was smiling during every bit of the conversation.

Both Rick and Tom explained the "secrets" about their pioneering Double India Pale Ale, a style that one might safely say originated in Southern California.

Using three to four pounds of hops per barrel (that's about 10 ounces per 5 gallons, or a 20-liter batch of homebrew!), the hops are dosed throughout the process to emphasize hop flavors and aromas. They are added to the malt mash, to the kettle boiling, during the lautering process, to the fermenters and even into the "bright tanks" just before kegging. What one ends up with is infused pale ale bursting with vibrantly fresh hop character.

JEFF BAGBY'S HOP WHOMPUS 2004

Jeff sent me a three-page e-mail detailing his recipe and procedures for his award-winning beer. This homebrewed version is an adaptation, extravagantly full of hop flavor and aroma. Yet it is unrepentantly balanced with a foundation of malt. Superbly drinkable and not just for sipping, it's a winner for your own brewing pleasure. This recipe can be found on page 279.

There's excitement in Rick's conversation as he adds details. Later he points out how Tom has encouraged him to learn about everything that he has access to, especially by tasting the beer throughout its journey from malt and hops to finished product. He notes that tasting the beer at all points of the process really helps a brewer to become a master. I agree, as I, too, find myself tasting ingredients, tasting unfermented wort, fermentation and finished beer before bottling and noting how beer flavors evolve with time and patience.

Oggi is the Italian word for "today." All three of us are enjoying today's still-fermenting India pale ale fresh out of the vat, while knowledgeably imagining what tomorrow holds for the glass of beer in our hand. We are microbrewers.

THERE ARE SEVERAL "location" brewmasters working at other Oggi's Pizza breweries. We visited brewmaster Jeff Bagby, award-winning brewer at Oggi's in Vista, California. Jeff offered us a quick taste of a smooth, velvety imperial stout and a new fermenting barley wine sort of ale. As bubbles rose in our glasses from ongoing fermentation, Jeff, Tom and I all agreed that the future was huge for this smooth, hard-to-characterize ale with a unique balanced blend of hops. Little did Jeff know that 68 days after my visit he would be awarded a Gold Medal in the Imperial/Double Red Ale category at the 2004 Great American Beer Festival.

New Frontiers on the Edge of a Continent
Stone Brewing Company, San Diego

You are not worthy of drinking this beer. It is quite doubtful that you have the taste or sophistication to appreciate an ale of this quality and depth . . .

The preceding is part of the statement you will behold when reading the label of Arrogant Bastard Ale. It may be quite true: you are not worthy of this beer unless, as they continue to say, you like big, flavorful brews that are not hyped by multimillion-dollar advertising campaigns that convince you that yellow fizzy beer makes you more sexy. This statement at first struck me as quite confrontational, but I wasn't convinced that this was all there was to the attitude of the brewers and makers of a wide variety of beers at the San Diego area's Stone Brewing Company.

Steve Wagner and Greg Koch (not related to Boston Beer's Jim Koch) are the figurative "bastards" who with their attitude co-founded Stone Brewing in 1998. They were homebrewers and beer enthusiasts before starting what is now Southern California's most successful microbrewer turned craft brewer.

Arrogant Bastard is their hugely big-humongous-grand-colossal red ale loaded with malt, hops and flavor. In a way it has been their affrontal mascot, but it represents only one of the most distinctively named of their growing list of explosively complex beers: Stone Pale Ale, Stone Levitation Ale, Stone Smoked Porter, Stone India Pale Ale, Stone Ruination IPA and Arrogant Bastard Ale, along with Stone Limited Special Releases such as Stone Old Guardian Barley Wine, Double Bastard Ale, Stone Imperial Russian Stout and the Stone Vertical Epic series.

Arrogant Bastard courtesy Stone Brewing Co.

I made a pilgrimage to the brewery in July 2004 in an effort to understand where these beers were coming from and discover the people and spirit behind the brew. Some guy with shockingly bright blue hair greeted me at the door. "Hi Charlie, I'm Steve; we've met before. Welcome to our brewery," welcomed the company president. It was "blue do" time at the brewery. All staff members had been encouraged to dye their hair blue for a charity fundraiser and the brewery's upcoming eighth anniversary.

The brewery was a beehive of activity, brewing, bottling, shipping and receiving, and it was obvious why an expansive new brewery on the other side of town was being built.

I've known Greg Koch, chairman and CEO, for several years and have watched and tasted his beers throughout Stone Brewing's six-year history. "What's the 'arrogant' all about, Greg?" I ask. He smiles and says it represents a viewpoint: "It's about what we think a great beer is all about." Greg and I resolve that not all Stone's beers are malty and hugely hoppy. I'm wondering whether perhaps the attitude is about making interesting, flavorful beers that are always complex. I came away from that conversation still wondering, "What is the Stone style?" Giving it my best shot, I might conclude what Greg hinted at when he said, "We don't like to paint ourselves into a box."

Did he mean "We don't like to paint ourselves into a corner?" or "We don't like to put ourselves into a box?" I suppose mixed metaphors are not in anyone's box or corner. As Humpty Dumpty said, "When I use a word, it means just what I choose it to mean—neither more nor less." To which Alice replied, "The question is, whether you can make words mean so many different things." Humpty concluded the discussion from his precarious perch on the wall: "The question is, which is to be the master—that is all."

Greg had just opened a preview bottle of Stone Brewing's Eighth Anniversary Ale, and I felt as though I was playing Humpty Dumpty with him. Or perhaps it was the beer playing games and being the "master."

It was all becoming clear for me when Greg explained the style of Anniversary Ale: "Hmmmm. Maybe it's an imperial mild?" If you looked carefully, you'd notice a grin on his face.

Imperial—implying big, bold, strong beers. Mild—implying low-alcohol, easy-drinking, mild-tasting brown ale. Who was the master, Greg or the beer? It all seemed quite logical at first, but then contrarian.

Don't ever attempt to figure out the beers of Stone Brewing and why they do what they do. They are all complex and a mirrored vision of only themselves. Expect the unexpected. Anticipate excitement and what is next. It's as though every "box" you want to put them in, they'll punch themselves out of, and then you realize that they weren't in a box to begin with!

Greg Koch, Stone Brewing Co., San Diego, Calif.

A visit to Stone Brewing's website will introduce you to the passion behind their beers and their spirited support for those who homebrew. For example, here's Stone Brewing Company on the making of beer:

> To get started, you usually want to have a stock of a couple of beers that
> you are going to taste to keep you inspired (while brewing). Not that it is
> necessary, but it can keep you focused.

STONE 03.03.03 VERTICAL EPIC ALE

Stone Vertical Ales are a series of brews whose essence goes well beyond the bounds of a recipe. They are brewed with an attitude and the poetry of the moment. Follow the journey of a Stone epic and then brew your own. This recipe is excerpted from their web page, with my own adaptation for homebrewers. This complex, full-flavored ale is one of America's great "laying down" ales. (No, not the beer drinker—lay down the beer for aging!) The recipe can be found on page 284.

. . . you are doing the right thing by bringing some flavorful beer to life.

On fizzy yellow beer:

. . . if a can of carbonated emptiness falls in the trash and no one hears it, is it a waste?

Apples in a Big Beer
New Glarus Brewing Company

I N A REMOTE STRETCH of southern Wisconsin, a half hour southwest of Madison, lies the small community of New Glarus. As we left the vibrant, beer-savvy college town and approached our destination, it seemed that we had been transported to the rolling foothills of the Swiss Alps: green pastures, forests, cows, farmland and a brewery.

I've known Dan and Deb Carey for many years. Dan, a German brewing university graduate, first found brewery work in the early 1980s at one of America's first microbreweries, the Montana Beverage Company, a revival of Montana's old Kessler brewery. In a rustic setting and with limited access to modern equipment and technology, Dan was able to brew the most exquisite German-style bock, pale and Oktoberfest lagers. There were no other breweries in America, large or micro, that were making lager beer of this quality. But the reality of the situation emerged by the late 1980s. Most Montanans were disinterested in quality and diversity in their beers. There were no other microbreweries within hundreds of miles. Helena was briefly an oasis in the high plains, eventually going dry for lack of local beer enthusiasm. Sadly, I never had the opportunity to visit Helena in its microbrewery heyday.

Dan worked awhile with Anheuser-Busch and eventually managed to start a family-owned brewery with wife, Deb. I tasted their award-winning beers at the Great American Beer Festival and assured myself I was not going to let my beer life slip by without a visit to Dan and Deb Carey's New Glarus Brewing Company.

It was blustery and snowing lightly when Sandra and I arrived in April 2002. I felt as though I had made a pilgrimage to a brewery destined to become a model of success—a microbrewery whose success was solidly founded on the quality and diversity of its ales and lagers.

Though Dan has a German brewmaster's education, this doesn't limit

Deb and Dan Carey, New Glarus Brewing Company

him to traditional German beer styles. In fact, besides very traditional German beers such as Uff Da Bock and Edel Pils, at New Glarus you'll find beers like Belgian-inspired Raspberry Tart and Wisconsin Belgian Red (cherry).

The small countryside brewery takes care to use local ingredients whenever they can; local cherries, barley malt, wheat, corn and honey are but a few ingredients used to make their expertly brewed ales and lagers. Speaking of ales, cask-conditioned Spotted Cow Ale and playfully inspired Fat Squirrel Nut Brown Ale are but a couple.

"Drink indigenous" is a theme of New Glarus Brewing Company. Fat Squirrel is explained on their website:

One deceptively springlike winter day, Brewmaster Dan walked home from the brewery, sat down to dinner and said, "Boy, there are some fat squirrels out there. They're running all over the place. I think I should brew a Fat Squirrel Nut Brown Ale." Deb agreed and so another beer legend was born.

One hundred percent Wisconsin malt of six different varieties impart the natural toasted color to the bottle-conditioned unfiltered ale. Clean hazelnut notes result from these carefully chosen barley malts. Hops from Slovenia, Bavaria and the Pacific Northwest give Fat Squirrel its backbone.

I could make New Glarus's pils, bock or spotted cow a regular habit, but while I was at the brewery I wanted to ask about the beers that I would make a special habit. In particular I have always flipped out over Wisconsin Belgian Red, Raspberry Tart and an apple beer no longer brewed. They are all refreshingly fruity and tart, and the intensity of the cherries, raspberry or apple is as true as fresh fruit. How did they do it?

I've made lots of fruit lagers and ales in my day. I've tried hundreds of

NEW WISCONSIN APPLE/RASPBERRY/CHERRY BEER

Boisterously fruity and fresh tasting, this fruit beer has the character of real beer. A short acidic bacteria fermentation creates complexity not possible with simple fruit additions. This beer is all about using local and indigenous ingredients and incorporating your skills as a brewmaster. The recipe can be found on page 289.

fruit beers made by homebrewers and microbrewers, but none were as fresh and vibrant as New Glarus.

Their secrets are not shared. (Otherwise they wouldn't be secrets.) However, applying some basic brewing principles, homebrewers can begin to approach what Dan has accomplished. It took Dan several years of experimentation. Each time he tried, he came closer to the perfection that has won him several beer competition medals throughout the world. So get brewing!

Changing How People Think About Beer, One Minute at a Time Dogfish Head Brewery

FOR SAM CALAGIONE, president of one of America's most "explosive" craft breweries, it all began in a small New York City apartment. It was 1992 and Sam, attending Columbia University, dwelled on a future MBA degree. But then he fell in love. Romancing the specialty and microbrewed beers offered at Nacho Mamas, his local Manhattan beer bar, Sam was caught up in the intrigue of such beers as Sierra Nevada Pale Ale, Brooklyn Lager and other cosmically insightful microbrews.

"It took up half the space in my apartment," admits Sam of his pursuit of homebrew. Inspired by the unique character of microbrewed beers, he immediately pursued the fringes of craft brewing. His first beer was cherry pale ale. He never looked back.

Connecting with area beer aficionados such as Richie Link in New Jersey, Sam soon switched his educational track, finding himself shoveling grain at various breweries along America's eastern seaboard and pursuing course work with such teachers as Shipyard Brewing Company (Portland, Maine) brewmaster Alan Pugsley.

Sam and I are enjoying his 90-minute India Pale Ales at Denver's 2004 Great American Beer Festival as he reminisces, "I was 25 years old and nobody was in much of a hurry to invest in my ideas." He made do with whatever resources he had, essentially setting up a glorified 12-gallon homebrew system and opening up his Dogfish Head Brewpub in Rehoboth Beach, Delaware, in 1995. "I brewed 390 batches of beer the first year," he recalls. "Before that I had only brewed 70 batches of homebrew. Brewing so often really sucked, but I learned a lot about brewing and about what my customers really liked. Some beers really took off in popularity. It did really suck to have to brew so often but experimenting with so many small batches really provided the foundation for our beer philosophy at Dogfish Head Brewery.

"We were really small and Rehoboth Beach isn't exactly the brewery capital of the country, but we are located just two hours from Philadelphia, Baltimore and Washington, D.C. Manhattan was only three and a half hours away. People

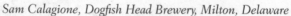

Sam Calagione, Dogfish Head Brewery, Milton, Delaware

who had visited the brewpub were calling and wanting our beers in their area, remembering the flavors of our really eccentric beers. Our Chicory Stout is made with roasted chicory, organic coffee, licorice root and St. John's wort. Our Immort Ale was very popular with our customers, brewed with maple syrup, vanilla beans, peat-smoked malt and juniper berries. People thought we were really crazy when we offered our first pale ale at a price of $12.99 for a six-pack."

Sam's journey toward providing beer drinkers access to his special beers was wrought with challenging times. He does not for a minute think his was an overnight success. The restaurant barely kept the venture afloat in the beginning. First there were six people that were his regular customers and over time there were 12, then 14, and slowly his following grew to a sustainable base. It was five years later that Sam considered his brewing business to be profitable and sustainable.

After having tried Dogfish Head's Raison d' Etre, an extraordinary complex ale made with friendly "help," malt, hops, Belgian yeast, beet sugar and green raisins, I asked Sam what beer he likes to drink and contemplate with. His "default" beer always seems to be his 60-minute India Pale Ale, but he admits, "Whenever everyone is asleep in our household and I can't sleep, I'll turn to one or two servings of our (18-plus percent alcohol) Worldwide Stout. This beer is really a symbolic beer for me because we would often ask ourselves, 'What's stopping us from brewing the biggest beer in the world?' When I'm feeling a warm buzz, I feel a great deal of pride and at the same time remember how scary it was in the late 1990s when we were really on the edge as a company and how difficult it was. I remember well how the passion of the people who really cared came through during difficult times to get us to where we are today. Being able to enjoy Worldwide Stout makes it all worthwhile. For me it is a reflection of celebrating the pride and journey of the Dogfish Head Brewery and all the other small breweries who have also gone through a lot of tough times to get to their own points of success."

Dogfish Head's beers are big and eccentric, but perhaps their very popular 60-, 90- and 120-minute India Pale Ales reflect a lot of the passion and microbrewing craft that is the foundation of this particular brewery. Sam re-

65-65-65-6.5 INDIA PALE ALE

An India pale ale with the Dogfish Head difference, this recipe has been reduced down to homebrew-scale procedures and ingredients. Lots of hops are added at five-minute intervals. The recipe can be found on page 292.

calls, "Our first 60-minute IPA was brewed in 2000. I took one of those vibrating football games, you know the ones you used to play with as a kid
where the players would move as the playing field vibrated. Well, we set a
five-gallon bucket full of hop pellets, made a hole at the bottom and set it on
the vibrating playing field. As the game field vibrated, the hops would slowly
emerge from the bucket and drift down the field and drop into our five-barrel
kettle. So the hops are constantly being added to the kettle during a 60-
minute period. We called the first batch Sir Hops-a-lot."

Their twelve-plus regularly offered beers join special editions of 15 percent barley wine brewed with dates and figs; Liquor de Malt with red, white
and blue corn; Pangea with Australian crystallized ginger, African moscavado
sugar and Asian basmati rice; Festina Lente with peaches, aged with oak; and
other evolving experiments sure to enliven the palate. They've moved from
12-gallon batches to 5-barrel, to 30-barrel, and now to 50-barrel batch sizes
in their packaging brewery, established in 2002.

"We're the antithesis of industrial homogeneity," Sam says. "Microbrew-
ing/craft brewing/homebrewing is all about education, knowledge and creating a community. It begins at the table in everyone's home. Events like
the Great American Beer Festival are a culmination of craft brewing where
we can all 'break bread' together. Brewers, distributors, retailers and
beer drinkers. Knowledge and edu-cation has brought us to this place."

If you have the pleasure of meet-ing Sam, be prepared to meet him
on the run. He doesn't slow down for anyone. *Energetic* is a word that
does not do justice to Sam's spirit. Just when you think you "get it" and
perhaps have had the opportunity to taste his bewildering array of beers,
he's off on new tangents, a dozen ideas at once, concocting the next
generation of ales on the frontier of American brewing on the edge of a
continent.

*Sam Calagione with his Randall—draft beer
dispensed through a bed of fresh hops*

Purposefully Local
Flying Fish Brewing Company

AN EMPHATIC "YOUR book, man!" was the reply I received from Gene Muller, the founder of the Flying Fish Brewing Company, when asked how he ever got hooked up with craft beer. Since 1996 at their micro-brewery in Cherry Hill, New Jersey, Gene and his 12 employees have been dedicated to the crafting of beers with balance and flavor. Gene says, "It's not about the alcohol and not about the most hops. Though we began with Belgian-style beers we've evolved to beers created for their likeability, flavor, balance and complement to food. We always emphasize that we are local. 'Why local?' we're often asked. 'What's so special about local beer?' We like to reply, 'It's like enjoying fresh local New Jersey tomatoes in August.' People can relate to that. Local beer is fresh all year long."

Recognizing and always appreciative of his company's roots, Gene quite

Gene Muller, founder Flying Fish Brewing Co.

often reflects, "Homebrewing is our root. If it weren't for homebrewers I wouldn't have a brewery today." Every year on National Homebrew Day (the first Saturday in May), the Flying Fish Brewing Company invites local home-brewers to the brewery. "Bring your beer so we can taste what you are brew-ing and we'll give you yeast" indicates the passion Flying Fish Brewing Company shares with homebrewers.

"We don't necessarily preach to the converted," Gene notes. "A lot of the time we focus on quality restaurants and develop great relationships with chefs in the New Jersey, Philadelphia, Washington, DC, and Delaware area. We are a hands-on brewery when it comes to service and making and distrib-uting our own beer. What I love about the craft beer business is that everyone has a different approach for success. Right now we are brewing just under 10,000 barrels of beer a year, and we're happy to grow slowly and steadily. I still personally reply to all e-mails and publish a monthly newsletter for our customers and fans."

I recently had the pleasure of sharing a few beers with Gene at a beer gar-den in Italy. We were both participating at Slow Food's Salone del Gusto (Great Hall of Taste) and were blessed with some time to enjoy some won-derful Italian microbrewed beers. Gene passionately conveyed the story of his brewery and his courtship with beer and brewing. After about 30 minutes of effervescent recollection, I interrupted his train of thought with the most important question: "Gene, where does the beer take you? I mean, when you really have the opportunity to relax and appreciate what you are involved in?" There was only a brief pause and he was on a roll once again: "Being a brewer is a wonderful job and passion. But it is a lot of work and having a beer is sometimes like taking a vacation. It takes you to places that are what the beer is all about. A particular beer might take me back to memories of sandstone cliffs in New Mexico, or I always seem to reminisce about the desert when enjoying a Belgian Tripel, because these are my experiences.

"One of my most favorite beers is our Flying Fish Farmhouse Summer Ale. It's a 4.4 percent alcohol-by-volume sour mashed beer that's great with

FLYING FISH BABY SAISON FARMHOUSE ALE

This mildly tart, refreshing summertime ale is brewed in the tradition of the Flemish countryside. Wheat malt adds dry refreshment and the earthy tones of Styrian hops are a favorite of brewer Gene Muller, who shared his recipe with me. This recipe can be found on page 295.

spicy food or sprayed on chicken barbecues. I love the spicy character that Styrian Goldings hops adds to this ale. When the summer comes to an end and the last bottle-conditioned beer leaves the brewery I always feel a sadness and silently reminisce, 'Good-bye, friend, see you next April.'"

Gene assessed the beer culture in New Jersey: "The laws here regulating the sale of beer are very prohibitive for small business owners. New Jersey and much of the mid-Atlantic area of the United States have always trailed behind the craft beer movement in the western part of the United States."

I can assure you that Gene is one of many quality-oriented craft brewers in the mid-Atlantic area that are doing all they can to bring great locally brewed fresh, flavorful ales and lagers to beer lovers in the New Jersey area.

Beer in the Big Apple
Brooklyn Brewery

THERE HAVE BEEN several breweries that have come and gone in New York City. The Manhattan Brewing Company and the New Amsterdam Brewing Company were ambitious brewery projects that succeeded only for a brief time. The oldest of the active breweries and brewpubs in the New York City area is the Brooklyn Brewing Company. Founded in 1988, at first it had its beer made exclusively in Utica, in upstate New York, at the F. X. Matt Brewing Company. Stephen Hindy, co-founder and still active CEO and president, made homebrew before leaving his job as an Associated Press Middle East correspondent, taking the plunge into the world of microbreweries.

Based on a pre-Prohibition Brooklyn brewery's all-malt light lager recipe, Brooklyn Lager has become New York City's best-selling draft beer. That's quite an accomplishment. As Steve emphasizes, "New York City beer drinkers want the best and they don't necessarily care where it comes from. That's a tall order. An important element that differentiates Brooklyn Brewery's beers from all the others available in New York City is that we're a local brewery. People really take quite a bit of pride in having the opportunity and choice to enjoy locally made beer."

Steve, like most every other microbrewer in America, was inspired by his homebrewing hobby and the popularity of his beers. He says, "Good dark beer seemed easier to make at home than lighter beer and in the beginning I really took a liking to roasted barley and chocolate and black malt. My choco-

Steve Hindy, Brooklyn Beer

late stout quickly became my résumé. Once I brought a case of what I thought was our Brooklyn Lager to a beer tasting and by mistake I had 12 bottles of my own homebrewed chocolate stout in the box. The stout was all that anyone wanted to talk about." Steve is quick to give his brewmaster, Garrett Oliver, all the credit for the success enjoyed by the brewery-versioned Brooklyn Black Chocolate Stout.

When Steve has time to relax and enjoy a beer, he reflects "on the days when I would come home from selling beer and crack open my own homebrew. We're extremely proud that the Brooklyn Brewery is a part of New York City's community. It warms my heart whenever I see one of our trucks rumbling down a Manhattan avenue."

The beer's success, along with the establishment of a craft beer distributing company, allows Steve and Garrett to pursue their passion for making several unique styles of beer. Their seemingly slow and deliberate growth has provided a means to offer consumers diversity and flavor, especially with skillfully brewed beers such as Brooklyn Black Chocolate Stout, English-American-style Brooklyn East India Pale Ale, German-style Brooklyner

BROOKLYN'S ORIGINAL CHOCOLATE STOUT

Steve Hindy shares his original recipe. A robust roasted malt and barley character rounds off the combination of English and American hops. The balance is reminiscent of cocoa with a pleasant hop finish. The result is simple, straightforward and deliciously inspiring. This recipe can be found on page 297.

Weisse and Belgian-inspired Saison de Brooklyn and Blanche de Brooklyn, as well as seasonal brown ales, Oktoberfest lagers and Monster Mash Barley wine ales.

In the fall of 1994 on a trip to East Coast, Steve and I sat down to discuss specialty beers and beer distributors. We had concluded with disappointment that most beer distributors have little knowledge about providing beer drinkers access to microbrewery beers. This was a time when several microbrewers in America were beginning to grow quite rapidly. Most mainstream beer businesspeople perceived the growing phenomenon and popularity of microbrewed beers as an overnight success.

As we enjoyed our Brooklyn beers, we both agreed that it takes a lot of time and patience to be perceived as successful. No one is really that interested in all the hard work and failures that come before success. Admired for his product, passion and creativity, Steve was once told by a very successful Coca-Cola ad manager, "If you stick with this for ten years, with a little luck you'll become an overnight success." Big-beer businesspeople are really only interested in trying to establish models based upon apparent success in order to apply those models to their own future growth for growth's sake. They have never figured out that *there is no model to be built*, except for the ones of individual persistence, dedication and enthusiasm for beer quality and diversity. True and successful microbrewers have always put quality, diversity and the people who will enjoy their beer first on their list of priorities. Sales are essential for a brewery, but selling beer for the simple sake of selling beer usually dooms a dispassionate brewer. I've seen this happen over and over again.

Psychographic Resonations
The Magic Hat Brewing Company

WHILE SOME BREWERIES don't like to paint themselves into a corner nor put themselves into a box, there is at least one brewery that you might say presents themselves as *the* box. But they'll let you determine what's inside. As if reaching into a magic hat, you'll take out surprises, delights and joys with every plunge, every adventure, every indulgence and every pleasure. "We believe that the people who enjoy our beer don't really need to be told 'what's in the box,'" explains Alan Newman, the full-bearded, energetic founder of the Magic Hat Brewing Company.

"So who is the poet, the artist, the contrarian, the joker, the gamesman at Magic Hat?" I ask Alan after taking a step inside their virtual address at www.magichat.net. Without any hesitation whatsoever, Alan shoots back, "I am!"

Taking a cruise with the brews of Magic Hat, one is taken on a journey, swirling, turning, breaking out, double-taking and becoming entranced. "You get to choose the level of involvement you have with Magic Hat. It could be the messages under our bottle caps, the beer, the label, a pilgrimage to the magic brewery, the website, our community," explains Alan, the grand wizard.

"The fact that we are in Burlington, Vermont, is really not that relevant to Magic Hat. The community we want to embrace and reach out to is not geographic, it's a psychographic community we are trying to resonate with," Alan continues, knowing exactly what direction he is taking the beers that seem to be mystically brewed at the Magic Hat Brewery. "We are not Burlington. We are not northern Vermont. We are not about New England."

Alan Newman, founder of Magic Hat

He explains that in a sense they and the people who enjoy Magic Hat beer are night people, grown adults; of the stars and the moon. Magic Hat beers are an adult beverage for an adult community. Like the Nike "swoosh," Magic Hat has its little crescent moon embedded in a bursting magical eight-pointed star.

The original Magic Hat head brewer, Bob Johnson, was a talented homebrewer. Alan was looking for something new to develop. Bob was a friend, and it took only a few sips of his homebrew to evoke the excited question, "What the hell is this?" Alan was not a passionate beer enthusiast. "I drank beer," he admits, "but I never really got into the tastes of microbrewery beers . . . until I noticed the beers Bob was brewing at his kitchen sink." One magic taste led to another, and soon thereafter, in 1994, Alan founded the brewery. Beer drinkers recognized the magic, and their appreciation for the "elixirs" has continued to grow.

Now head brewer and brewmaster Todd Haire is brewing up elixirs at Magic Hat. Todd, too, got his start in homebrewing. Originally from Texas, he eventually migrated to Vermont. How did he learn? I asked. "I learned by making mistakes. I love to teach people, because I never had the opportunity to really have a mentor or be taught. Teaching people about brewing is one of the great joys I have with this job."

Todd loves his job. "We have an open palette to experiment," he says. "We're encouraged to be as creative as possible with what resources they have available."

I often ask brewmasters that if they had a moment to relax with a beer and reflect, what beer it would be and where that beer would take them. Todd gushed, "I'd definitely have our 10 percent–plus Thumbsucker Imperial Stout. We started this high-priced product (our "Humdinger" series) as a barrel-aged beer. Thumbsucker goes into Bourbon barrels in which our barley wine had aged for three years. It all began as a homebrewing experiment and my wife and I often reflect on how it all started. People's response to this beer is fantastic. I can't help reflect and appreciate how much depth the Thumbsucker has and how maturing really creates flavor nuances. These beers aren't ready until they are ready; the alcohol complexity changes with time."

Todd goes on to tell me that they also brew a Braggot, a strong, 10 percent–plus ale brewed with one-third honey fermentables, saying, "We keep bees outside the brewery in a small apiary. The 15 hives provided over 300 pounds of honey we used in this year's barrel-aged Braggot." Chamomile flowers were also added, and the ale was eventually aged in French oak.

In the near future they will be blending Cabernet grapes, pomegranates

Number 9, their most popular beer. Label courtesy of Magic Hat Brewing Co.

MAGIC BOLO #9.1

With an apricot aroma and smooth, fruity flavor, this is a year-round drinking beer, low on lupulin but high on smoothness. Recipe details were
shared by the brewer at Magic Hat and adapted to a homebrewed-size
recipe. This recipe can be found on page 300.

and blueberries into a Belgian Flanders–style brown ale infused with a fruity-
producing Brettanomyces yeast culture and aging it in used Cabernet wine
barrels.

Todd recalls one of their most unusual brews: "We made a bottled garlic
beer, also flavored with rosemary and horehound. It was an elixir for our Halloween bash, 'Night of the Living Dead.' We put one clove of garlic in each
bottle. I didn't reminisce too much about that beer."

As we finished our conversation, Todd had one final bit of wisdom:
"Things that ferment have such great taste."

I've had the pleasure of having almost all of the elixirs presented to me
and getting to choose the order in which to try them. It was like beginning a
journey into a secret and mystical universe, where up is down and east is
west. As I gazed into the foamy head of each brew, I could appreciate where
those bubbles come from as they slowly rise to their surface. To say that these
beers have personality would be an understatement. I asked Alan, "So if there
is one beer that epitomizes all that could be in a Magic Hat, what beer would
that be?" He knew the answer: "That would be #9. It's a beer that brings it all
together, a low-hopped 'not quite pale ale' with this wonderfully evocative
apricot character. It comes through much more in the aroma than in the flavor. It's very distinctive and it's our best-selling beer." And I mentally noted he
concluded his description with "yet undefined." It's not your typical fruit
beer.

I am realizing the addiction that can build for Magic Hat beers. It draws
you farther and farther into the matrix of what Magic Hat is all about. Alan reminds me that it's not necessarily all about the beer. Yes, you must have a
world-class beer. That's what Bob Johnson started, and now head brewer
Todd Haire carries the scriptured tradition forward. Great beer is your "entry
card" to play as a brewery. Alan says, "We strive to resonate with our customer. Connecting emotionally drives success."

The Magic Hat Brewery is not just a brewery, it's a community. Visit with
a beer or stroll into the mystical at www.magichat.net.

A Mindset for Sustainability
Otter Creek Brewery & Wolaver's
Organic Beer

COMFORTABLY NESTLED in the northern Vermont community of Middlebury, the popularly acclaimed Otter Creek Brewery has enjoyed a passionate following among beer drinkers since 1991. Every season celebrates the rites of brewing and Otter Creek beers. Now under the leadership of Morgan Wolaver, the brewery continues to brew Otter Creek brands in addition to Wolaver's Organic Beer.

Morgan says, "The first thing Otter Creek beer fans told us was, 'Don't change my beer.' Some even insinuated that we might use tofu in fermentation." Morgan knows not to mess around with a good thing, yet he confided, "Organic products and sustainability is an umbrella for a mindset advocating environmental caretaking, energy efficiency, proper processing of wastewater and supporting organic farmers."

Morgan recalls, "Back in high school my chemistry experiment was brewing beer." Before I could ask the obvious question, he added, "Yes I drank it."

Morgan Wolaver

But his first intention in starting a business was not so much about beer as about advocating and practicing sustainability. He had traveled quite a bit while working in the oil industry as an oceanographer. There were lots of opportunities to taste great beer while working in England. Morgan expresses a passion for sustainability and reveals that it was an odd quirk of serendipity that caused him to embrace beer: "I tasted some organic beer from overseas. It didn't taste good at all! Rather than discourage me, I was inspired. I asked myself, 'Why couldn't one brew great organic beer?'"

With the expert help of brewmaster Steve Parkes, he set out by contracting with six American microbreweries to brew his beer. Steve, a veteran brewer whose focus has always been on quality control, guided the brewing of Wolaver's Organic Beer in California, Colorado and Chicago and at Otter Creek. Before moving to the United States in 1988, Steve brewed in very small-scale breweries in England. He's been brewing in America ever since. In high school, Steve reflects, "I wanted to do biochemistry, but when I began my coursework at Heriot-Watts University in Edinburgh I realized that the blending of science and art manifested itself in brewing and an end product. Now, every day I consider it an honor to get up, go to work and make beer." Steve has had brewing endeavors with such successful brands as Oxford Class in the mid-Atlantic area and Red Nectar in northern California. He says, "What has been great about Wolaver's and Otter Creek is that I never needed to be sold on the idea of 'organic.' The whole concept of sustainability meshes perfectly with craft-brewing ideals. We need to be supporting the people who support us in the long run. And now that we've made a commitment to organic farming we are already seeing an improvement in the quality of ingredients such as organic barley. Currently all New Zealand hops are organic and we've found a few varieties we really like such as New Zealand Hallertauer and Saaz. Cascade hops are the only organic American hop available right now. We use organic oats in our stout and organic raw wheat grown 10 miles from the brewery in our Wit Beer."

Steve Parkes

Succeeding in growing beer drinkers' appreciation of Wolaver's ales from 27,000 cases to nearly 70,000 cases in a short while, Morgan and Steve soon realized there was quality and a lot of opportunity with Otter Creek. Morgan bought the brewery in 2002. They have continued to grow the reputation of the small craft brewery.

"'Organic' is value added," Morgan says adamantly. "Organic grains look like healthier malt. One of the premises we try to instill in all of our organic beers is complexity. The wine industry would go broke if they had to have consistency. It's a plus for the wine industry; why can't it be a plus for brewers and their beer?"

Asked about the difference between the two brands brewed at the Otter Creek Brewery, Morgan emphasizes that Wolaver's beers are bigger beers, being "bigger interpretations" of the classic American microbrewed styles such as IPA, brown ale and Belgian-style wheat (wit) beer. Their beer drinker's table of beers include Wolaver's Brown Ale, India Pale Ale, Pale Ale, Wit Bier and Oatmeal Stout.

Otter Creek brands offer beer drinkers in the Northeast a selection of light and dark ales as well as German-style light, amber and dark bock lagers. Morgan notes, "The pale ale is the closest we come to competing styles between the two brands. Generally the Otter Creek brands are not as 'big' as the Wolaver's brands."

When I asked Steve about his thoughts after having a few relaxing beers, he reflects, "It is so satisfying to get up every morning and go to work and make beer. There's a tremendous amount of satisfaction when for example we received a call on our toll-free number printed on our six-pack cases, from a customer who left a message, 'I love your beer. Thank you.'" Steve most appreciates beer fresh out of the brewer's tank or tap, but realizes that this is not always accessible and notes, "I like hops, but I like balance in beers where I can taste a crisp malt character as well as delicate fermentation characters."

Where do Morgan's favorite beers take him when he finds time to relax? "A good, well-balanced pale ale with a good hop finish really is my usual pref-

WOLAVER'S ORGANIC OATMEAL STOUT

This recipe shared by brewmaster Steve Parkes has been adapted for homebrewers. Caramel, nutlike and cocoa character accents this wonderfully balanced stout. Oatmeal provides body and a velvety texture. Adequate hops accent its thirst-soothing personality, while Cascade aromatics endure throughout the experience of this organic oatmeal stout. The recipe can be found on page 302.

erence. It doesn't seem to matter what mood I'm in. When I'm able to relax and appreciate what the beer is telling me I think about getting away fishing, hiking and generally appreciating the outdoors." He adds that he often thinks about small-time farmers, slowing down, decompressing and appreciating home.

And as a final thought, "Being a good citizen is a big part of where we're going."

THERE ARE many other great microbreweries across America making extraordinary beer. Beer festivals are a good place to find out what is new in beer and to try new flavors and brewers' new adventures. I also recommend going to full-service beer stores that offer a wide variety of local and regional craft and microbrewed beers. In many states that are microbrew friendly you'll be permitted to embark on your own adventure by putting together your own selection of mixed six-packs of beers. Mix a six of stouts or a six of bock beer. Seasonal six-packs from favorite breweries become an anticipated annual adventure for many. See how many different types of beer you can select for a mixed case. Just as you taste wine from a particular region, you can organize your own tasting of great regional beers, and at far less cost than a case of great wine. . . . For starters, check out these two websites for more info on beer festivals and what's new in beer: www.realbeer.com and www.beer town.org.

On the Road with Charlie

AT LEAST ONCE A YEAR I try to take a beer adventure. Sometimes it's to Asia, Europe, Africa or down to South America, but more often than not I'm right in our American backyard encountering local beers with both hands at the ready. I've gone from North Dakota to Tennessee, the deep South, down East, the far West and all the way up to Alaska, tasting for the love of beer.

You might consider it part of a fairy tale or an evang-*ale*-cal passion I have to spread the word about the beer-wonderful world of flavor and diversity. Each trip is organized with the indispensable help of my association assistant Mark Snyder, who plans the details of every moment of the itinerary. But as beer is often a catalyst for digression, so is each trip. Every beer journey becomes a microbrewed adventure of meeting friends old and new; beers wonderful, mystical, complex and creative. Nowhere on the planet can you travel 100 miles and encounter so many different beers of such exquisite quality. It all becomes a blur sometimes. The line between homebrew, microbrew and craft brew evaporates. The journey simply becomes all about the beer. It's a journey I've taken often and look forward to each time. The following stories recount some of those classic moments on the road in pursuit of the ultimate beer.

Noon Moons, Midnight Sun
Bean Mead and Barley Wine Ales
Anchorage and Juneau, Alaska

WITH ONE BREWERY for every 60,000 people, Alaska ranks as the state with the sixth-highest number of breweries per capita (Vermont ranks number one, with one brewery for every 36,000). That's encouraging information for the beer enthusiast living in Alaska. It's also encouraging information for all beer-loving Americans, for at these ratios, one might calculate a potential of 5,000 to 8,000 breweries nationwide.

Because I am a homebrewer and there are thousands of homebrewers in Alaska, I've had the great fortune to visit the state more than just a couple of times. Each time I depart I am in awe of the fanatical passion Alaskans have for both the environment in which they live and for microbrewed beer. People who live in Alaska live there by choice. It is a place they love and cherish. It isn't surprising, given this lifestyle and attitude, that they would demand quality and passion in the beers they enjoy. They are particular about their choices and they seek to explore life's pleasures. Inspired by their environment, I have discovered some uniquely brewed fermentations in Alaska.

On my visit in 1995, two of the first brews I encountered were made by local homebrewer Angie. While most brewers were pushing the limits of barley malt beers and fruit, herb and honey meads, Angie was floating in an entirely different universe. The midnight sun does strange things to the mind. Soy-milk mead and rice-milk mead were her specialties at the moment. At first, I recoiled instinctively as she introduced me to a glass. Recounting the initial fermentation as "milky white and curdy," Angie assured me that with time and the passing of two equinoxes the mead be-

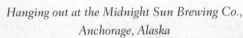

Hanging out at the Midnight Sun Brewing Co., Anchorage, Alaska

Sampling Barleywines at the Glacier Brewhouse, Anchorage, Alaska

comes a crystal clear, deep golden elixir. *Flabbergasted* is the only word I can use to describe my surprise at how mellow and smooth this bean mead had become. It was indeed some of the best mead I had ever had.

Thus encouraged, Angie looked forward to her next experiments, with hazelnut milk. Confident that she could figure out how to make hazelnut milk, she took her inspiration from a reference in Robert Gayre's book *Brewing Mead*, where she found a reference to an ancient mead made with hazelnuts.

I've had the pleasures of visiting and exploring parts of Alaska both in the seasons of the midnight sun and what might be called the high noon moon. Homebrewing in Alaska is prolific, and from this passion has sprung forth a culture of microbrewed beer. In Anchorage, Juneau and most large towns you'll find a good assortment of locally made beers, as well as other passionately made American microbrewed beer.

Summertime is work time, fishing time and being-outdoors time. It all then leads to winter and the Great Alaskan Beer and Barleywine Festival, held each January in Anchorage.

In 2001, Sandra and I arrived a few days ahead of the festival to explore and to visit with local homebrewers and microbrewers. You can safely expect to be up before dawn, which isn't too difficult at that time of year, and to be having your first beer shortly after sunrise. What a wonderful concept! Anchorage is blessed with the likes of the Midnight Sun Brewing Company, Moose's Tooth Brewing Company, Glacier Brewhouse and the Sleeping Lady Brewing Company (the large hanging quilts are spectacular, and to see them is itself worth a visit). Makers of microbrewed and crafted brown ales, pale ales, barleywine aged in oak, stouts, porters and other world-class styles, the brewers of Anchorage are always anticipating the excitement of their annual festival.

Every brewery in Alaska is represented, including small homebrewery brewpubs from the coastal communities of Haines and Homer, the Silver Gulch Brewery from frigid Fairbanks (they brewed a lager) and Alaska's largest craft brewer, Juneau's Alaskan Brewing Company, brewers of a famous alder-smoked porter, a spruce tip–flavored winter ale and a popular top-fermented, cold-lagered Alaskan-style "alt" beer, Alaskan Amber.

The Great Alaskan Beer and Barleywine Festival is a must-do event for anyone who considers him- or herself a serious beer enthusiast. There are other similar events hosted throughout the United States, but none—and I say this from experience, *none*—embraces the passion of barleywine as much as does the Alaskan festival. The nights are very long. You may need crampons to navigate the icy sidewalks. It can be very cold. There will be snow on the ground. Your friends will think you are out of your mind for going to Alaska in January. But nowhere will a beer enthusiast encounter more camaraderie and excitement about beer than in Anchorage in January. Alaska's microbrewers are truly making their world a better place to live. Great barley wine enjoyed and savored in the bosom of winter is one of life's quintessential experiences.

ALASKAN WINTER SPRUCE OLD ALE

"It's the quality of the spruce tips that ultimately determines the character of spruce beer. Don't be afraid to try your local spruce tips in the spring, but do pick them young." These are the suggestions of Alaskan Brewing Company founder and brewer Geoff Larson. This version of spruce-flavored beer is based on strong brown ale. Hop bitterness is mild, allowing the essence and freshness of spruce to shine through. This recipe can be found on page 305.

Winter Warmer Tour
In the Footsteps of the Revolution

O**N FEBRUARY 22,** 1999, my wife Sandra left our home in Colorado to embark on what I now refer to as "The 14-Day Charlie Does Beer–Winter Warmer Tour," just one of countless beer journeys I've experienced.

It was an extraordinary expedition, filled with beer, beer and more beer to warm our souls as we wended our way through upstate New York, dipping down into New Jersey and back up through New York City, and continued to cruise for brews in Connecticut, Massachusetts and New Hampshire. The snow, rain and cold always seemed to follow us, yet the beers and the hospitality of homebrewers and microbrewers everywhere warmed our hearts. Sandra was travel administrator and membership recruiter, while we both accepted and tasted beer all along the way.

Day 1: Getting up at 5 A.M. and continuing until we crashed at our Ramada Inn motel room at 11 P.M. somewhere in Newburgh, New York made for a long day. Getting our flight upgraded to first class with a coupon was no great accomplishment; a fruit plate for breakfast, no lunch and no drinking water (they were out of stock!) developed our thirst for the beers that lay ahead. Perhaps the disregard for in-flight amenities was reverse karma intended to balance the good stuff that lay ahead of us. We hoped to be greeted with the best beers of the Northeast upon our arrival.

Winter is very, very cold in upstate New York. The wind blows. There's ice everywhere. But after checking into our motel and changing clothes, we soon found warmth wherever there was good beer. An enthusiastic reception of 40 or 50 homebrewers at Joe Burke's McGonigles Homebrew Supply Shop at 9 West Main Street in Washingtonville cheered us with an endless variety of homebrew. A quick dinner was followed by a very cold walk to the local homebrew club's meeting place. I was glad to be indoors and greeted with a winter-warming chilled homebrewed stout. The warm reception of my presentation and an endless variety of beer foretold of the days to come.

Day 2: We drove along the eastern bank of the Hudson River on our way to Rhinebeck, New York, a town steeped in American history and contemporary great beer culture. Hosted by the local beer community, Sandra and I stayed at the Beekman Arms Inn, America's oldest continually operating hotel and inn. The second evening we indulged in a magnificent "Dinner with

Charlie" hosted by the St. Andrews Restaurant on the Culinary Institute of America's campus. It was a unique experience in their dining series, as all the beers on the menu were homebrewed by local homebrewers! For each of the six courses there were these beers: a 2 percent ginger lager (brewed by Lyn Howard), an English-style bitter (Anthony Becampis), Pre-Prohibition Pilsener (Jim Taylor), Malt-Tease Maerzen (Bruce Franconi), Robust Porter (Greg Holton) and Bit o' Spice Cider (Cider Maker of the Year, Gloria Franconi). Organized by Bill Woodring (American Homebrewers Association Board of Advisors) and Ken Turow (CIA Dean of Students), the evening was a celebration of pure and indulgent pleasure.

Arriving at our inn after dinner, Sandra and I turned to each other and asked, "How about one more beer?" "You bet!" We snuck off to the inn's bar for a nightcap before retiring. It was biting cold outside; snow covered the ground in moonstruck patches. We entered to the warmth of a fire in the hearth. A sense of something special filled the air. Here the low wood-beamed ceilings and antique floors captured the ambience of 250 years past. George Washington, Alexander Hamilton, John Adams and other revolutionary forefathers of America congregated in this very space and enjoyed locally made porters and other ales—I'm certain of that. The walls told me. The cold winter unchanged from that time to now.

It was quiet—well, almost quiet. Sitting in a wooden booth, we were the last two customers in the bar. The bartender and waitress were finalizing their evening's work. The floors creaked, the air was filled with the faint smell of smoke and the candles' flickering flames engraved their memorable glow upon us. The atmosphere was just as it must have been in 1766. But I couldn't quite connect with the lack of beer choice. I settled on an imported British ale but drank it with disappointment. It had lost its edge, just as the British had in 1776, suffering from the ravages of age and staling. Spice Girls and En Vogue hip-hop music thumped in the background . . . Old George Washington, I wonder how he would've handled it. He probably could have taken the hip hop, but stale English ale? No bloody way! George knew better. He made his own homebrew; this is well known. Beer passion inspires revolution as needed. I am glad to be part of the current American Revolution, a revolution championing beer flavor and diversity.

One small five-gallon batch at a time. Times a million American homebrewers inspiring the spirit of local microbrewed beer.

The next day, we visit the Gilded Otter Brewpub in nearby New Paltz. I am captivated by the spectacular $2 million view of the Hudson Valley countryside. Now this is a place that singularly made the revolution worth fighting for.

Day 3: I have an early-morning telephone interview with Lee Graves, a beer columnist for the *Richmond Times Dispatch* about my Northeast tour. "When are you coming to Virginia, Charlie?" (I would tour New Jersey, Maryland, Virginia and the Carolinas the very next year.)

It's still cold cold cold.

We are picked up by local homebrewer Bill Woodring, Dean of Students at the Culinary Institute; Ken Turow; and John Eccles, brewer at Hyde Park Brewery. We travel through the countryside and visit Gloria and Bruce Franconia's Party Creations Homebrew Supply Shop in Red Hook, New York, a small homebrew shop in a converted barn situated in an all-too-pleasant and relaxing backyard forest. It is a comforting destination as well as a great place to buy supplies from knowledgeable and passionate people. Nat Collins, brewmaster at the Woodstock Brewery in Kingston, drops by as we begin enjoying an imperial stout and a big-brew barley wine to the accompaniment of Gloria's praline-drizzled chocolate cream cake. A killer combination!!! We leave with both the imperial stout and the cake recipe.

As I am leaving, a new customer comes in. At my encouragement he

Nat Collins, Bruce and Gloria Franconia, Woodstock/Redhook, NY

confides, "Well, my mother's brother had a brewery and so I have brewing in my blood." His grandmother's brother was F. X. Matt of the F. X. Matt Brewing Company in Utica, New York. He had discovered homebrewing through my book in a library when he was in high school.

We return in time for dinner at the Hyde Park Brewery, and then quickly stop by our inn for a short hour of downtime. I dare not lie down for fear of falling asleep and never waking up. This is Rip Van Winkle country. So I have a beer, one of many that had already been given me.

In the evening we return to the CIA to meet and talk to 90 members of the student beer society, ALES (Ale and Lager Education Society). We finish a fun evening by 11:30 after watching a few beer videos I'd brought along, tasting and talking beer and food.

Day 4: Departing the Rhinebeck area, we already miss the hundreds of kindred spirits who are in their own special ways all cultivating a passion for beer and brewing. This morning Sandra and I visit friends at the Egg Farm Dairy in Peekskill, a small organic producer of traditional and local cheeses. We share homebrew, and Jonathan White offers us some of the best cheese I have ever tasted.

By evening there are already eight inches of snow on the ground, but that doesn't seem to have stopped 120 beer enthusiasts from coming to the Hud-

Richie Stolarz, Beers International

son Valley Homebrewers/Woodstock Brewing Company "rendezvous" in Kingston. There is nothing maniacal about the people who turned out this evening. Everyone is dead serious about their love of beer and brewing. Dozens of locally made homebrews, as well as fresh specialties and cask-conditioned ales from the Woodstock Brewing Company cellars, flow freely.

Those who attend learn one important lesson: if anyone dares serve me a beer, they had better serve my wife too. More than once she charges to the podium during my presentation to steal my porter, IPA and best bitter, leaving me empty handed, each time to the howling applause of the audience. The last homebrewer who comes up to fill my glass gets it right, one for Sandra and then one for me. I can't really complain about a spouse who in thirst will steal my IPA and enjoy drinking it herself!

Late that night, sleep and bed. How sweet it is, but I'm beginning to wake up wondering where in the world we are.

Day 5: The snow stopped last night and it's starting to get a bit warmer. We drive down to New Jersey and rendezvous with Richie Stolarz of Beers International. Beer enthusiast extraordinaire Richie had arranged for the evening's sold-out 80-person beer event. There'll be a lot of homebrewers in attendance tonight.

True to anticipation, the evening is overflowing with beer. The venue is the Gaslight Brewery in South Orange. More than 15 beers are formally tasted. Several are homebrews, while most are imported strong Belgian ales. And then there are dozens of beers informally tasted ("Charlie, will you taste my homebrew?"). It's still cold outside, and a winter-warming homebrew is a welcome sight.

Day 6: We're not even halfway through our journey. With seven days ahead of us, we're still in the "just warming up" mode.

Dropping off our rental car at Newark airport, we haul our luggage (our extra duffel bag for gift T-shirts gets bigger every day) onto a bus and into New York City. The Big Apple homebrewers and microbrewers are waiting with outstretched arms, beer grins and cheer. We stash our belongings at a friend's apartment on the Bowery, have a quick lunch, change clothes and take the subway to Brooklyn Brewery, arriving in time to judge at the Malted Barley Appreciation Society's second annual homebrew competition. There are 420 entries, up from about 250 the year before. Lots of homebrewers, judges, brewers, fun, winners, food and beer stories.

After judging 420 beers it's time for . . . well, beer and dinner a short walk over to the local beer haven, the Mugz Bar. And that's where and when the evening begins to drift off.

Day 7: A day off. It rains all day, so we sleep in and relax. We have dim sum in Manhattan and home-prepared mussels, asparagus and Jay Sims's pie-to-die for dinner. And some of her own homebrewed beer, of course.

Day 8: Three morning business appointments in Manhattan are followed by an afternoon visit to D.B.A. bar in the East Village. With great selections of cask-conditioned beers on draft, this is the real thing and as good as it gets in New York City.

As I come up from the subway in the evening I notice the first full moon of March high above. Perhaps it's the first time I've glanced up from a beer in eight days.

Later in the evening I host a Café Centro (at Grand Central Station–Met Life Building) gourmet beer dinner organized by Steve Hindy and the good folks at Brooklyn Brewing Company. Great food and great beer are enjoyed by the attending homebrewers and beer enthusiasts.

Day 9: Packed and out of the apartment by 8:30 A.M. Tony Forder, publisher of *Ale Street News* and co–media sponsor of our "beer to heaven" tour, picks us up, and we're suddenly on the road to Connecticut. Our first stop is at Hartford's Troutfish Brewery and Restaurant for a lunch with American Homebrewers Association members and homebrew enthusiasts. There, Bill Metzger, publisher of *Yankee Brew News* and co–media sponsor of the tour, joins us. Lunch is over, but the afternoon beers have just begun. We are soon off to Connecticut's first brewpub, the Hartford Brewery. Afterward we walk over to Ron Page's realm, the relatively new City Steam Brewery and Restaurant.

Paul Zocco, our driving and organizational host of the day, continues to herd us forward as we migrate to a small homebrew shop in East Hartford for a sampling of beers.

We stop briefly to pick up our rental car for the next five days. There's no time to waste, as we're instantly off to the Hop River Homebrew "Clubhouse" for a quick peek at a great little home brewery and meeting site.

It is 5:45 and we are in the small town of Willimantic, checking into our bed-and-breakfast accommodations. After a 15-minute catnap and a change of clothes, we crawl to the Willimantic Brewery and Main Street Café to be greeted by a packed house of 80-plus American Homebrewers Association members and beer enthusiasts. The brewery is in a historic post office building. The grand ceilings, artwork, sight of brewing kettles and excitement of the evening instantly rejuvenate both Sandra and me. The specially prepared beer dinner is superb and is complemented with beers exquisite. If ever there is doubt that small-town America cannot support a small brewery, visit Willi-

Ron Page and Tony Forder "fluting" in the City Steam Brewery, Hartford

mantic. The hospitality, food and beer are worth the journey. The energy is uplifting, and Sandra and I enjoy the company well into the night.

Day 10: A short trip down the road we make a quick morning stop at the under-consideration Old Wyndham Brewery, located at a picturesque mill site along the Shetucket River. Then we drive northeast to Natick, Massachusetts, for a lunch visit at Barley Corn Craft Brew "Brew-on-Premise" and Homebrew Supply. There are lots of customers, and a sunny day greets us in downtown Natick. By 2 P.M. we're leaving, driving off toward Worcester, Massachusetts.

We check in at the no-frills Super 8 somewhere motel along an interstate, then have dinner with Phil Tetarult, president of the WIZARDS homebrew club, Brian Powers (Strangebrew Homebrew Shop) and Bruce Susel (Vinotheque) at the Gentle Lentil, a super restaurant serving natural and locally made cuisine. Greg Hagopian, the owner, is an enthusiastic homebrewer, and it shows in his restaurant.

This evening's gig is at the Plantation Club Draft House for a speaking engagement and more beer tasting with about 100 American Homebrewers Association members, homebrewers, beer enthusiasts and shop owners. Outside it's cold and pouring buckets of rain, but it doesn't matter—we're warming with beer and friends.

Day 11: Yet again we head north, this time to Manchester, New Hampshire. By noon we arrive for a grand reception at Steve and Darlene Friedman's Red White and Brew Brew-on-Premise and Homebrew Shop. Television, newspapers, brewspapers and 40 to 50 local American Homebrewers Association members, beer enthusiasts and homebrewers are on hand for two and a half hours. The hospitality is so good, we have a hard time getting away for our next destination.

We need to be in Portsmouth this evening. Taking a wrong turn, we end up driving the scenic route along the coast. It's nice to see the ocean, even in all of its grayness. It continues to be cold and raining. We check in at the local inn at 5:55 P.M. With no time to change, we walk down the cold and windy streets of Portsmouth to Don Wagoner's Stout Billy homebrew shop. Some good beer, cider and lots of great customers are there to greet us before Don whisks us away to the nearby Redhook Brewery, perhaps America's most state-of-the-art brewhouse and craft brewery. At this point I make the very accurate observation that 99 percent of all of the craft breweries in America are run by former homebrewers, including the good folks at Redhook. Now that's something special. It says a lot about why craft microbrewed beer is so special.

After a few good beers, including Red Hook Ale and Black Hook Ale, in their hospitality and restaurant area, there's no time to waste. It's onward to a 7 P.M. appearance at Peter Egelston's Portsmouth Brewery for food, drink and

Rolling out Samuel Adams Triple Bock Barrel in Boston

SAM ADAMS TRIPLE BOCK HOMEBREW RECIPE

Truly the most complex and alcoholic bock beer in the world, this is the beer that began Boston Beer Company's expedition to strive for extreme achievement. It's the beer that put the brewing world on alert: nothing is impossible. Many brewers have since embarked on their own tangential brewing endeavors, but Sam Adams Triple Bock is the beer that turned the beer world. It is not an easy beer to make. Your success will require all of your brewing skills in order to manage the complex fermentation. Brewing a beer to 18 percent alcohol will be a challenge. Aging and cellaring in wooden casks to impart the unique characters of this beer will push your skills and patience to the limit. They said Triple Bock couldn't be done. Likewise, you may believe you are not worthy to succeed. But that won't stop you, will it? This recipe can be found on page 307.

addressing homebrewers gathered for the evening. It's a fun place with great beer and a homebrew-friendly management.

Sandra and I duck out later in the evening with Peter and his partner JoAnne for a quiet late-night meal of delicious spicy-hot Thai food downed with—of course—local microbrewed ale. The food burns, and it feels good to chase it with a cold one.

Day 12: A snowstorm is impending. We move on to the Boston area, staying with my brother Rich's family in Lexington. That evening they join us and 50 others at the Cambridge Hyatt Hotel for a beer tasting organized by local homebrewers and a gourmet dinner arranged by Jim Koch and his Boston Beer Company. There is always more to say, but let it suffice to tell you: good food, good company and the small oak keg of Sam Adams Triple Bock is something special for all of us. It goes well with the crème brûlée.

Day 13: A day off. We chill out and watch the snowstorm arrive.

Day 14: With eight inches of snow and still falling, we drive the last leg slowly to Boston's Logan airport, return the car and know that we will soon be back home in Colorado. Sandra and I are both a bit worn, but energized. As she put it, "The people we met gave us a lot of energy all along the way."

Beer in America's Heartland
Fargo to Cleveland

AS SANDRA AND I slowly descend the airport escalator I'm staring downward, wondering what the small group of crazy, fanatical people are cheering and waving about. Sandra whispers in a worried tone, "Are these your friends?" I shrug, unknowingly. As we approach, I begin to make out the signs: "Welcome Charlie."

Day 1: This is the beginning of an eight-day journey though America's homebrewing heartland, from Fargo to Cleveland, in 2002. First stop—Fargo.

It doesn't take long to figure it out: this small group of folks is representing the legendary Prairie Homebrewing Companions beer and homebrew club. It's Monday, April 1, 2002, and they are not fooling around! There are already five inches of snow on the ground and it's still snowing as they escort us into an awaiting stretch limousine, complete with a bar stocked with homebrew.

Every homebrewer in Fargo—and there are a lot of homebrewers in Fargo—seems to have taken the day off. As we stop by the Country Cannery Homebrew Shop, we walk through to the rear into a nearby woodworking shop where more than 30 homebrewers are actively brewing and finishing four separate batches of homebrew. The sweet, tantalizing aroma of malt and hops fills the air and fogs the windows as the snow continues to fall outside. There are dozens of different homebrews offered in bottles and on tap.

Next limo stop on the prairie: the Granite City Pub and Restaurant, a unique brewpub importing unfermented brewed wort from their sister brew-

Limos with the Prairie Homebrewing Companions

pub in Sioux Falls, South Dakota, to lovingly ferment in the tanks at Granite City. The cask-conditioned dark and English-style bitter are magnificently welcome. It is still snowing.

Prairie Homebrewing Companions' ringleader and brewster supreme, Susan Rudd, leads us to the club meeting at the Hjemkomst Center, where we are greeted by 65 more club members. Two commemorative beers were brewed, bottled and labeled for the evening's events.

Beer'd, it is 10:30 in the evening and still snowing as we wrap up the first day of our tour. Tomorrow is going to be another workday.

Day 2: We arrive in Minneapolis. It is still snowing. We check into our hotel, visit two homebrew shops and rendezvous at the Minneapolis Rock Bottom Brewery Restaurant with 40 members of the Minneapolis Homebrewers Association, local brewmasters and beer enthusiasts. It's a long day.

Day 3: In the morning we're off early, heading for Madison, Wisconsin. I'm deeply disappointed about not having allowed enough time to visit the Summit Brewing Company and brewmaster Horace Cunningham, whom I had met many years earlier while he was the head brewer at Banks Brewing Company on the Caribbean island of Barbados.

On our way to Madison, we stop for lunch at the legendary all-American Norske's Nook in Osseo, Wisconsin—an absolutely *must* stop for any person who considers himself a pie aficionado.

With no time to check into our hotel, we head directly toward the Wine and Hop Shop, one of the oldest and most supportive homebrew shops in the country. Then on to visits at brewpubs JT Whitneys, Angelic Brewing Company and Great Dane. It's a day and evening filled with meeting new friends and reunions with those who have continued to be involved with homebrewing for more than 20 years. I recognize Dean Coffey, the multi-award-winning brewmaster at Angelic Brewpub, as the guy who years ago had worked at Lolita's delicatessen, across the street from the Association of Brewers' office in Boulder, Colorado, often making my lunch sandwiches to go. Dean had begun homebrewing years ago. Inspired by the experience, he moved to Madison and became a brewmaster, going on to win several medals at the Great American Beer Festival and more awards at the 2002 World Beer Cup than any other brewmaster in the world. The essence of microbrewing has trickled into our souls.

We leave late in the evening to check into the Landhaus Inn by 11 P.M. in New Glarus, 30 minutes to the southwest.

Day 4: After our morning visit and lunch with New Glarus Brewing Company owners Deb and Dan Carey, we head east to Chicago. It was snowing when we left New Glarus, but the warmth of our journeys made us oblivious to the cold April weather.

We spend the rest of the evening visiting at Chicago's Goose Island Brewpub with one of the nation's largest beer clubs, the Chicago Beer Society. More than 80 beer enthusiasts and relations turned out for the event, presentations, food and beer. I'm greeted by two Korean women as I enjoy a glass of Honker Ale. They introduce themselves as the wife and daughter of the Korean brewmaster from the Oriental Brewery in South Korea who had won an award in the 1996 World Beer Cup. He had asked his daughter to get me to autograph a copy of my book *Homebrewer's Gold,* in which he was featured.

Day 5: Leaving Chicago on Friday, we stop at Beer Gear Homebrew Supply Shop on our way out of the suburbs and then visit the Flossmoor Station Brewpub, where several more homebrewers are awaiting a luncheon. Onward we drive to Lafayette, Indiana, where the Tippecanoe Homebrew Club is hosting an evening at the Lafayette Brewing Company. We have dinner, talks, beer and good times with more than 40 area homebrewers, some whom I knew when they joined the American Homebrewers Association in 1980.

Day 6: The Great Fermentations of Indianapolis homebrew shop is our next stop, with lunch across the street at the Broad Ripple Brewpub. In the evening we join area homebrewers at the Ram Brewery in downtown Indianapolis to enjoy award-winning beer and dinner extraordinaire.

Day 7 and 8: On our final days we cruise to Cleveland, where we rendezvous at the Association of Brewers' annual Craft Brewers Conference. There's dinner with local club members at the Great Lakes Brewpub and another evening event at their brewery tasting room to speak to 200 homebrew and microbrew enthusiasts. Beer maven Michael Jackson and I tell stories of beer digressions and the experiences that brought us to Cleveland.

MICKVIRAY PAPAZIAN PILSENER

A cause for celebration Mick, Vi and Ray shared with me their beer and their recipe for their commemorative "Charlie on the Road" pilsener. These folks are award-winning champion homebrewers with a knack for brewing up the perfect beer every time. This is a classic all-malt Czech-style pilsener lager hopped exclusively with Saaz hops—the way it used to be in the Czech Republic. It's clean, crisp, malty and refreshing, with an aftertaste that entices your very soul to have another and another. This recipe can be found on page 310.

Eight days of beer, beer and more beer. Sandra and I are tired, yet strangely energized from our experience and the endless welcomes across the prairies and rolling hills between Fargo and Cleveland. Homebrewing and microbrewing has indeed woven itself into the fabric of a quality lifestyle for the thousands of people we met on our journeys.

Completely Joyous Tour
Tennessee, Alabama and Arkansas

WHILE EACH OF THESE short stories offers you a taste of one of my adventures, words can never express the delights of every beer, every homebrewer and every unexpected brewing encounter. Four and a half days seems like an eternity when you are on the road tasting all those beers, searching for the ones that scream "ultimate." The 14 stops on this trip really don't signify an end or a beginning. The beer just flows into one continuous beer experience when your mission is beer in America.

We visited eight different breweries on this southern sojourn but as I said, we never seemed to really stop as we tasted our way through 32 microbrewed beers. And in between this continuous flow we squeezed in visits to two homebrew shops and five homebrew clubs, tasting more than 130 different homebrewed ales, lagers and meads.

Sleep? What was that, we often wondered? We knew it was precious, for there was very little of it. We were compensated for lack of sleep by the quality of beers all along the way. With 300 people visited and three states, four cities and 525 miles driven, we all felt the experience was priceless.

Day 1: Our trip begins as the "Completely Joyous" Association of Brewers On-the-Road expedition in Nashville, Tennessee, where we visit Boscos Restaurant and Brewery, Blackstone Restaurant and Brewery, Bohannon Brewing Company and All Seasons Gardening & Brewing Supply. Great places, great food, great people, great microbrew and great homebrew in April 2003.

Day 2: From Nashville, we continue on, driving to rendezvous with the Rocket City Homebrewers and Birmingham Masterbrewers in Huntsville, Alabama. Our traveling entourage, my wife Sandra (who brewed her first homebrew, a Belgian Witbier, two weeks earlier), Boscos Nashville brewmaster Fred Scheer and super host, driver and organizer Chuck Skypeck, owner

Rocket City Homebrewers

of Boscos, is welcomed by a massive turnout of homebrewers and homebrew. The beer seems to flow from endless taps and a bottomless well of bottled homebrew.

Day 3: From Huntsville, we drive to Memphis, stopping at Hops Restaurant Bar and Brewery and Boscos Restaurant and Brewery, tasting masterly impressive beers and gathering insights from the brewmasters themselves. The evening eventually ends at a rendezvous with the Bluff City Brewers. Of course, it's homebrew emerging at every opportunity that provides the evening's nightcaps.

Day 4: We cross the Mississippi River as it flows its meandering way toward the delta country of Louisiana. I can't help feel as one with the river, one long ribbon of liquid that has been the lifeblood of the population. Surely beer seems a lifeblood of these impassioned southern brewers who are brewing some of the most excellent and memorable beers I've ever had. Like the river, our adventure seems to meander endlessly. We roll toward Little Rock, Arkansas, to meet its homebrewers and craft brewers. There we experience the taste of mighty fine microbrewed beers at Vinos Pizza Pub and Brewery, homebrews at Fermentables Homebrew and Winemakers Supply and a packed brewhouse finale of pride and passion, beers brewed at the Diamond Bear Brewing Company.

Like a springtime tornado, we have whirled our way through parts of the South, tasting southern microbrewed beers made with soul. Make no mistake about it: here live brewers as passionate and as skilled as in any well-known beer city.

The ultimate beer? As always, there never is one ultimate beer. Just when

Boscos beer lover

you have experienced what you believe is the beer you want to be engaged to for the rest of your life, along comes another quintessential brew. And so it goes.

One thing I always appreciate during these tours is the privilege of tasting new and classically brewed beers. This adventure through the South included a unique personal experience. Beers brewed from recipes in my book *The Complete Joy of Homebrewing* were judged in three separate "Completely Joyous" competitions in Nashville, Memphis and Little Rock. What a taste delight for me, sampling old favorites brewed from recipes out of my books: Get Rio Light Lager, Rocky Raccoon's Honey Lager, Goat Scrotum Ale, Toad Spit Stout, Sparrow Hawk Porter, Armenian Imperial Stout, Who's in the Garden Grand Cru, Buzdigh Moog Double Brown Ale and, most memorably, the wondrous sparkle and refreshing Wailailale Chablis Ginger Mead. Then there was the nefarious Cock (that's Cock as in "rooster") Ale. They were all winners in my opinion, but the ribbons went to the Chablis Ginger Mead and the Cock Ale (made with chicken and spices), which is reminiscent of spiced malty holiday ale. Both of these brews won respective first places.

I'll never forget the taste treat of Memphis-brewed Armenian imperial stout with added oak chips—wow! And I'll always recall the ale brewed in

Tapping into a keg of real ale at Boscos

Huntsville with five different breakfast cereals by the ten-year-old daughter of one of our hosts. At the All Seasons Gardening and Homebrew Supply Company in Nashville, I encountered a mead brewed with sour cherries and the Middle Eastern ingredient *mahleb*, ground cherrystones that offer a wondrous cherry aroma. I was astonished because of my familiarity with this spice: my grandmother used this ingredient when making braided Armenian *choereg* (bread).

As with any microbrewed adventure, it was always comforting to know that while I was away things were getting better at home. My homebrew had a chance to age and improve for one more week. I was inspired by all those five-gallon batches and the skill of all the master homebrewers and master microbrewers I met along the way. I became inspired to brew within days of returning home. You simply can't keep me down.

IRISH COCOA WOOD PORTER

Here's a recipe I'm inspired to brew based on beer tastings offered by homebrewers in Tennessee, Alabama and Arkansas. It's an Irish-style stout, but untraditionally, it has no roasted barley. An extra accent of cocoa flavor and aromatic malts, along with a finishing touch of toasted oak chips, gives this beer the soul of the South and the spirit of your finesse. The recipe can be found on page 312.

Raising the Drinking Age to 40
The Lyons Brewery Depot

SUNOL LIES about an hour southwest of San Francisco's Bay Area. When I managed a pilgrimage there in the late 1980s, Sunol was a small town. No, actually, it was a place, near a railroad crossing, where Judy Ashworth owned and ran her original specialty beer bar. It was called the Lyons Brewery Depot. A pioneer beer establishment, it was a mecca for beer enthusiasts in an age when yellow fizzy beer predominated the American landscapes.

Upon my autumnal arrival, I couldn't help but notice the only two other businesses in town: the feed store to the left and another tavern 50 feet down the road, a classic "biker bar" where shots of tequila and ice-cold Bud, Miller and Coors contrasted with what was happening at the Depot.

I did want to make an appearance at the biker bar. Outside, 50 choppers were parked, gleaming in the late afternoon sun. Intrigued, I took a brief side trip, entered, talked "hog" and had a cold one, but the other adventure—of spending time at Judy Ashworth's historic Lyons Brewery Depot—was more my style.

Entering the Depot I was greeted excitedly: "Charlie, how about a Stanley Steamer?" Was this yet another new beer from another new California microbrewer? No. With pride and enthusiasm, Judy explained, "I invented it myself. It's terrific. You blend half a draft of Anchor Steam beer with half of St. Stan's Dark Alt beer. The richness of the alt beer hits you first, but oh . . . ," she was just beginning to get really excited, "how the Steam beer comes through in the aftertaste! It's all Steam in the aftertaste." Before I could even consider the implications of what she had confided, I was confronted with a short glass of Stanley Steamer.

Judy's 20 beers on draft included an assortment of California microbrews, making the pilgrimage well worth the trip. She took great pride in being the first and now one of the few taverns serving Anchor's Old Foghorn barleywine-style ale on draft. The hop harvest at the back of the tavern had recently been completed. As she preached the virtues of hops to one of her beer patrons, yet another glass of beer appeared: "Foggy Night in the Sierras. You'll love this, Charlie! It's Old Foghorn and Sierra Nevada Pale Ale." I did. The strength and the classic fruitiness of the barley wine served to round out the thirst-quenching hoppy dryness of the pale ale.

Old Foghorn and Guinness Stout were combined next to further cheer

Judy Ashworth at the Lyons Brewery Depot

me up with what Judy called "Irish Mist." The afternoon went on. The sun made motions in the west and as it set, Judy continued to educate me in the fine art of beer blending. There were many more blends, but she saved the best for last.

"Okay, Charlie. . . . This is it. The *ultimate of ultimates*." Her level of excitement was peaking. The new Sierra Nevada Celebration Ale had just come in the day before and already she had a combination for it. A glass appeared before me, seething with a dense creamy head of foam. Judy warned me, "You have to be 40 years old or over to be allowed to drink this one." I lied and told her I was, and then took one sip. My sensory paraphernalia shifted four dimensions, all in opposite ways. "What do you think? I call it 'A Foggy Christmas Eve.'" There was no doubt about it. She had combined Old Foghorn and Sierra Nevada's Celebration Ale in a way that would probably make each brewmaster cringe at the thought, yet for this palate, the experience was absolutely inspiring.

OLD LIGHTHOUSE IN THE FOG BARLEYWINE ALE

Anchor released their first draft barley wine to the Lyons Brewery Depot. It was a momentous event in the history of microbrewed beer—barley wine on draft. The formulation for Foghorn is a guarded secret, but here's a recipe for something that will surely guide you through the fog. This recipe can be found on page 315.

When I returned home I took a walk in 1980s downtown Boulder and visited one of my local beer bars. As I entered I silently chuckled to myself, wondering what kind of mischief I could get myself into. "I'd like a 'Goose the Moose,' please," I announced—an 80–20 blend of Moosehead Lager and Sierra Nevada's Bigfoot Barleywine Ale.

Or how about a "Red Velvet," a combination of Lindeman's (cherry) Kriek and Boulder Stout?

For light beer drinkers who are considering the adventure of microbrewed beer and the sensual pleasure of hops, I'd suggest trying an Anchor Liberty Ale or other microbrewed India pale ale with a light beer and mix to suit a developing taste. Call it "Pursuit of Hoppiness."

The Lyons Brewery Depot in Sunol burnt down soon after my visit. With the support of California microbrewers Judy rebuilt in a nearby town, but the spirit of the place seemed to have faded away after her retirement from the bar business. Judy embodied the passion of microbrewery beer and what it meant to brewers, the beer drinker and those who sell it. In the late 1980s, hers was one of a handful of bars in the entire United States with a passion for microbrewed beer. She helped pioneer the thousands that have followed.

SECTION TWO

Microbrewed:
The World

Introduction

I LOVE MY HOME, my wife, my friends, my garden and homebrew, but to travel and discover new places, new perspectives and new beers is my longest-running and most sustained passion. I recall the first month after I graduated from the University of Virginia with a bachelor's degree in Nuclear Engineering. On a whim, I packed one bag and headed west from New Jersey, where I grew up, and landed in Boulder, Colorado. That was in 1972.

One year later, still restless, I quit my meaningless job, packed my backpack, stuck my thumb out and hitchhiked thousands of miles for 10 weeks, all on $300. Yes, even in those days I had a stash of homebrew awaiting my return.

For the next eight years I lucked into a job teaching children for nine months of the year. The other three months I traveled. The adventure was endless. My first sojourn off the continent of North America took me to Bali and the Fiji Islands for nine weeks, with $500 cash in my pocket. Palm toddy and Fiji homebrew emerged as memorable and unanticipated experiences.

I have not been able to arrest my addiction to adventure, nor do I care to. I have traveled to all 50 United States many times over and have had the privilege of being a guest in more than 60 foreign countries, many a dozen or more times.

Traveling is either in your blood or not. For me it is not only an exercise in patience and observation, but a means of discovering and understanding the true nature of human beings and the dynamics of the world we live in.

Beer seems to always be one important aspect of my travels these days. But I do not travel for the beer. I travel to encounter people and the environment they inhabit, observe their behavior and consider how and why everything fits together in all of its initially apparent inconsistency. Beer becomes a thread, but it is only a part of the bigger picture of why we do the things we do.

Beer has taken mankind to many places. One way I see America is through the world of beer. It is one way in which I see my friends, my home, myself. Certainly there are other ways in which I interpret my world that are as or even more meaningful, but beer is one of them.

Beer is quite meaningless taken out of the context of our lifestyle. It is void of any interest whatsoever without the culture of people and an appreciation of flavor and diversity. Tasteless, pale, fizzy beer presented for mass consumption, brewed with little passion and with no cultural context, becomes a meaningless drag in and of itself.

The adventure is really about life. Beer adds an element of pleasure accessible to virtually every person who inhabits our world. Beer is not a religion. Impassioned beer enthusiasts and brewers neither convert nor preach—a brewer's passion enables our freedom to choose according to flavor, diversity and pleasure. Microbrewers, craft brewers and homebrewers provide the opportunity to enjoy one's own choices.

My microbrewed adventures have taken me to the far corners of the world. Clearly it is the people who are involved with beer that are most important for me—the culture in which they brew, why they brew, how they dance, what they eat, whom they play with. The beer always becomes that much more special. That is really what makes my adventures so interesting to me.

THE FIRST ADVENTURE I want to share with you is about two individuals I met in 1981. David and Louise Bruce weren't *just* starting a brewpub in London; they were living their lives in a creative, passionate manner. Through their trials, tribulations, humor and extraordinary passion, they transformed the world of beer.

The Brewpub that Started
a World Revolution
London—David and Louise Bruce

I BELIEVE that David and Louise Bruce, more than any other individuals, were responsible for igniting the worldwide brewpub revolution. In 1979 they opened the Goose and Firkin in London, the first brewery/pub to be opened in all of twentieth-century England. From the years 1880 through 1970, the number of active brewery pub licenses in England dropped from 12,000 to five. David Bruce, who had been involved in production or as a brewer with Courage, Theakston's and Bass Charington, learned the basis of his serendipitously adopted trade as a brewpub owner and brewer.

By 1982, he had opened several other "Firkin" brewpubs in London. The Fox and Firkin, Goose and Firkin, Frog and Firkin and Fleece and Firkin were the first of dozens of Firkin pubs. They were unique in that they were fun, lively pubs, with a sense of humor unparalleled in the British beer business. Ales were brewed on premise and served directly to the customer.

The Bruces' was not an overnight success. The couple had no personal wealth to invest in a new and promising enterprise, and the investors and brewers they approached thought they were absolutely daft. David had been unemployed for eight months before coming up with the idea of renovating a condemned pub and turning it into a brewery pub. Both he and Louise invested barrels of sweat equity and their own time, while skillfully working the British brewing industry's money-for-beer sales system to help finance their enterprise.

David had a passion for business and entrepreneurial projects. He embraced beer as a lively means to connect with enjoyable work and enjoyable people. His entrepreneurial spirit and brewer's skills qualify him as one of England's original microbrewers. David's sense of humor should not go unmentioned, as evidenced by this anecdote: "One thing we did was a brew called 'Knee Trembler.' The grist for five [British] barrels at 1.075 (18.2 B) original gravity was 330 pounds of pale malt, 110 pounds of crystal malt, 7 pounds of black malt and 11 pounds of hops. Knee Trembler at the time was the strongest draft beer mashed in the country, and someone said after trying it, 'My word, if you ever feel the bottom falling out of your life, drink the stuff and the world will fall out of your bottom.' Apart from that, it did cause quite a bit of problem with the police because people actually couldn't quite get to their cars. After it had been on sale a couple of weeks we had to assure the

David Bruce and the beginning of the Firkin Empire

police that we would only sell it in half pints. Of course, everybody started ordering it in half pints." It surprises me that David has not yet been knighted for his achievements.

It was all well and good in provincial merry old London, but news of their success did not electrify the world until David and Louise attended the 1982 American Homebrewers Association annual conference in Boulder, Colorado, at my invitation. I first met the Bruces in 1981, while attending the

DOGBOLTER

Originally this brew was intended to become Knee Trembler, but David got stuck on a phone call and the mash ran off a bit longer than planned, diluting the beer to 1.060 gravity. He fermented it as is and called it Dogbolter. It was a legendary success. A strong brown ale with rich caramel and a distinctive roasted malt bite provides the foundation. The UK Goldings hops is truly as English as hops can be, perhaps with the exception of Fuggles hops. This is a rich beer, full of flavor and the personality of the world's brewpub pioneers. The recipe can be found on page 317.

Campaign For Real Ale's (CAMRA) Great British Beer Festival. Upon encountering David I was overcome with joy that there was an individual who had such a wacky sense of humor and inspired beer drinkers in a revolutionary manner. We have since been close friends.

At the 1982 conference, David gave a presentation entitled "The English Brewpub and the Resurgence of the Small, Local Brewery in England and America." It was attended by homebrewers and America's founding microbrewers. David electrified the audience with the revolutionary idea of brewing your own beer and then selling it to your customers in your own pub. Within one year's time, America's first brewpubs were operational in Hopland, California; Yakima, Washington; and West Vancouver, British Columbia.

David and Louise had ignited not only America, but the world. Brewpubs were opening and offering diverse styles of ales and lagers. Because the microbrewers that were making the beers had once been beer-passionate homebrewers, they enjoyed a wide variety of beer styles. For starters, brewpubs usually offered no fewer than six regular styles of ales, such as porter, stout, pale ale, India pale ale, brown ale and amber ale. These were the first pubs and bars that regularly extended the choice for American beer drinkers beyond the pale selection of brand-name light lagers. The phenomenon has now reached every corner of the beer-drinking world.

Progress has been slow, but in 2005 America can pride itself in offering beer drinkers a stunning choice of beer styles in more than 1,000 brewpubs. And it all began with David and Louise's London Goose and Firkin.

Extraordinary Times with Ordinary Ale
Brakspear's Brewery, Henley-on-Thames

DAVID AND LOUISE BRUCE inspired the revival of the world's brew-pub tradition. The Campaign for Real Ale (CAMRA) is an organization that has done much to try to save other English brewing traditions, especially that of naturally fermented and traditionally served real ale. There have been a rough few years for the British brewing tradition. Some of the most classic of ales are only shells of their once proud tradition. And worse, pubs that do serve real ale are often not serving it in the best of conditions. I recently encountered two classic examples of a beer served to me in ruins, Fullers ESB and Bass Ale—both were pitifully undrinkable in a downtown London pub, sour and full of diacetyl (an intense butterscotch character). I left full pints on the bar and settled for a Guinness, which I wasn't quite in the mood for at the time but enjoyed nonetheless as my third choice of the moment.

This example of tradition gone awry is common throughout the United Kingdom. Not only should the beer be brewed to standards of excellence, but it also must be kept in proper condition while served and the beer lines cleaned and maintained. My experiences have left me with the impression that Britain is in the midst of major apathy with regards to its real ale traditions, despite the best efforts of CAMRA.

My personal opinion is that CAMRA's zeal for tradition has not taken into enough consideration that real ale consumption continues to decline, and without the ubiquitous consumption from which the tradition was derived, real ale in pubs simply does not get enough attention from consumers and barkeeps. When a cask of real ale does not get consumers' attention, the product eventually goes sour and flat. Beer is money, and rather than appropriately dumping the spoiled beer down the drain, the barkeep often serves the customer rubbish.

Meanwhile, without a compromise of tradition the number of good-quality real ales served will continue to dwindle. Many that are forced through dirty taps will turn off new beer drinkers, just as they have momentarily turned me off.

YET I ALWAYS RETURN to the motherland of traditional ale in search of unforgettable experiences, enjoying relatively low-alcohol yet full-flavored "ordinary bitter" in well-kept pubs. In my recurrent journeys, I am often guided to the best England has to offer. These memorable encounters with

BEYOND-THE-ORDINARY ORDINARY BITTER

I have come within 90 percent of achieving what I consider a Brakspear's Bitter clone. I have refined the technique, ingredients and process to my satisfaction. Inspired by a legendary beer made by a legendary brewery, I regularly brew my own Beyond-the-Ordinary Ordinary.

The Brakspear's brewery would condition their water to assure there was enough calcium and sulfate ions. They used invert sugar #2 (a brown sugar, rich in toffeelike flavor) as an adjunct. Most of their hops were whole East Kent Goldings, aged in a cool room for as long as six to nine months. After pitching the yeast, the beer is observed as it ferments for the first 24 hours. Then it is transferred, with some aeration, into another open fermentation tank. This is called their "double-drop" process.

The resulting ale had a soft degree of fruitiness, full flavor and an aroma of earthy mineral-like hops with a balance of caramel/toffee flavors, all contributing to a complex and harmonious balance that reflects the peak achievements of a brewer's passion for beer.

The invert sugar #2 used by the brewery lends a rich flavor to even their mildest ales. Aging their Kent Goldings hops at cool room temperatures enhances cold hop oxidation and promotes good flavor. American brewers are so obsessed with fresh hops and oxygen barrier packaging that the positive evolution of flavor in an oxygen environment under proper conditions is all but lacking as a choice for beer drinkers in most American "English-style" ales. During the transfer of the just-beginning fermenting wort, much oxygen is picked up. This creates a mixed fermentation-respiration cycle, which seems to positively affect the complexity of character. I am convinced that you can begin to capture the tradition of Brakspear's Henley-on-Thames Ordinary Bitter by brewing your own at home. This recipe can be found on page 319.

place, time, people and pint after pint of delicious ordinary ale are the best examples of how good life can be.

On one such journey, while touring the countryside along the river Thames west of London, I was absolutely thrilled to encounter the ales of the Brakspear's Brewery at Henley-on-Thames. Brakspear's Bitter was considered one of England's greatest beers. It certainly enlivened my heart as I enjoyed the rich taste of East Kent Goldings hops and the full flavor of countryside English malt, skillfully brewed and fermented at the 200-plus-year-old brewery. I found the malt and hop character I seek in English ales both on tap as real ale and in bottles. What was most extraordinary was that I especially enjoyed the Ordinary, likely brewed at 1.038 or thereabouts, low in alcohol (3.4 percent by volume) but bursting with flavor. Keep in mind that this was a full-flavored ale that you won't find in most American brewpubs or in a craft-brewed bottle. How many craft pale ales can you name that start with gravities *below* 1.040 (10 B)? They hardly exist. But to tell you the truth, you can get a full-flavored and satisfying ale at these low gravities by infusing extra malt and hop flavor.

British ale enthusiasts mourned the closing and razing of the brewery in 2002, making way for profit-friendly housing developments in the small town of Henley-on-Thames. The beer became contract brewed elsewhere, but it has been a shadow of its former self. The brewers continue to adjust their brewing process, attempting to bring back the original character of a national treasure. They will come close, but I fear that technology and new techniques will interfere with the traditions that once produced one of the finest ales on earth.

The anomalies of Brakspear's will never be studied in today's brewing research laboratories, simply because their methods do not agree with modern brewing and fermentation theories and philosophies. That's too bad. There is much that could have been learned from breweries like the historical Brakspear's Henley-on-Thames brewery and their superb world-class beers. The beer speaks for itself, though the techniques are contentious to many of the learned and the scholarly trained.

I'VE BEGUN my world beer adventures with recollections of England. These beers and brewers were the beginnings of my own homebrew journey. But I have discovered since, as you will too, that the world is full of great beer endeavors, and one country's border is yet another's frontier. I continue striding out of bounds and normality, into the intimate realm of personal experiences. Each journey provides the foundation of all great beer, great brewers and microbrewed adventures.

CHAPTER 6

....

Unraveling the Mysteries

of Mead

MEAD IS THE HOLY GRAIL of brewing. It has a storied history dating back thousands of years. The earliest written records of mead—the Sanskrit Rig-veda—date back to 3000 B.C. There is no doubt in my mind that the unwritten history reaches back even farther, 10,000 years or more. The Anglo-Saxon epic *Beowulf* from 700 A.D. describes mead halls and mead benches. The Welsh king Howl the Great introduced royal legislation on making meads in 950 A.D. In the 14th century, mead reached its greatest popularity in England and was prominently featured in Chaucer's seminal work, *The Canterbury Tales*. In the 1400s, large-scale importation of cheap foreign wines into England brought a rapid decline in mead production, but it continued to be made commercially for another 300 years. The last written reference to the public sale of meads in England is seen in 1712, in Addison's "Coverly Papers."[1] So what has happened to mead, the original ale, nectar of the gods, an elixir derived from the fermentation of honey, water and yeast? How has it managed to survive the past 300 years? Well, a few great mead makers, microbrewers in their own right, have kept the tradition alive, and I have been lucky enough to meet and linger in the wisdom and company of two of them. . . .

1 Dates and references taken from *A Brief History of Mead*, originally published in *Mead and Other Honey Liquors* by Lieutenant Colonel Robert Gayre.

The Secrets of Buckfast Abbey
Brother Adam

I **ENJOY** tasting all of life's small and big flavors. Some beckon, some flirt, while others attempt to escape. Not all reveal themselves completely, but the ones that do are epic.

In the summer of 1993 I found myself sharing dinner with 40 Benedictine monks in the Devonshire countryside of England. The ceilings arched above while the evening light filtered through the narrow windows to the west, creating a mood of reverence and awe. Prayers had been read, and only the busy clatter of knives and forks broke the silence in this centuries-old dining hall furnished with simple wooden tables and chairs. I tasted, savored and dwelled on the moments. They were everywhere. A background smell of furniture polish and the mustiness of old stones crept into my being. The experience of dining with monks swept my imagination back in time within the walls of this old monastery.

The meal was accompanied by a stoneware jug of amber liquid. I poured myself a glass. It was ale, English ale. Almost flat, served at room temperature, it was a bit ciderlike. Had it been homebrewed at the abbey? Knowing its origins seemed irrelevant. The recipe was nothing I'd ever pursue. Still, its mere presence enhanced its quality. I continued to taste and savor the moments. They were everywhere.

I spent that night in the monastery. Robed, hooded and slippered monks quietly walked the dark halls of the cloister. At the 9:15 curfew, the doors would be bolted shut from the inside. The lure of local ale collided with the fear of being locked out, almost discouraging me from a few evening pints just down the road at one of the quiet town pubs. Temptation won out, and I managed to make the most of the twilight hour, enjoying a few pints and rushing back to the stone abbey, returning in time to hear the bolts slam shut throughout the building five minutes later. The halls were dark. My footsteps echoed on the hard stone floors as I groped my way back to my room. All was still as I retired. The single high, small window in my room promised morning's first light and the sound of bells at 5 A.M.

I had not come to the monastery for spiritual reasons, or so I thought. Why, then, had I found myself at Buckfast Abbey, asleep inside a small, spartan room? I had traveled all this way from America to the Devon countryside in the southwest of England to see a man whom I had admired from afar for many years. I must admit that the admiration was not one that at first seemed to be a profound calling. But for a kind of reason that always seems mysterious to me, I had appointed myself seven years earlier to make the pilgrimage to this place, across the Atlantic, to meet and be in the presence of Brother Adam. Why? Because Brother Adam and I shared a rare interest in making and appreciating honey mead, a fermented "wine" of honey and water. Mead enjoys a tradition preceding beer and wine. There are very few people who know its secrets. For years I have been slowly trying to discover and unravel them.

Born in 1898, Brother Adam had retired from a life of devotion at Buckfast Abbey, a life that began upon entering the monastery at the age of 12 after having emigrated from Germany to England. His interests led him to study and breed honeybees for more than 75 years, traveling hundreds of thousands of miles throughout the world to crossbreed his very personal collection of bees. The hybrid Buckfast bee is known throughout the world for its favorable characteristics and resistance to disease and parasites.

In his own small but magnificently significant way, Brother Adam had helped assure fruit, vegetable and nut harvests throughout the world by developing bees that survive to pollinate flowers and assure crops.

Brother Adam

Brother Adam's mead-making began as a pleasant byproduct of bee breeding in 1940. When I visited in 1993, it was still a tradition at Buckfast Abbey, reserved for moderate enjoyment by monks at the monastery. For over 50 years he had found the challenge of making traditional mead a side interest, much as I have found brewing and drinking beer and mead a side interest of mine and one of the many intriguing and beguiling aspects of life.

Far more than a mead

maker, Brother Adam provided me with an insight into devotion. A man of 95 years, his spirited walk and generous hospitality were mere reflections of a long and meaningful life. His memorable voice, though somewhat unclear with age, was a reflection of unfathomable knowledge, patience and sentience only devoted persons possess.

I spent all of my morning pouring through Brother Adam's file on mead making—short articles on the subject, references, recipes, experiments and formulations recorded over the past 30 or so years. They all fit into a small hatbox. The formulations were rather simple. Experimentation was indeed part of the progression over the years. Yet there were no copious stacks of recipes or piles of research papers. Brother Adam's procedures were as modest as those of any modern-day homebrewer or mead maker. He "brewed" mead in 60-gallon batches and fermented it in large oak barrels. Wine yeasts were used, but were often difficult to get in England during the early days of mead-making at the abbey. Nutrients were essential, and his experimentation with small amounts of cream of tartar, ammonium phosphate and citric acid provided the vitamins needed for complete and dependable fermentation.

Light clover honey was found best for dry and/or sparkling meads, while darker honeys such as the abundant heather honey found throughout Britain was more suitable for sweeter, sherry-type meads. Brother Adam found soft water to be essential, along with a brief two- or three-minute simmering boil and a skimming off of the coagulated protein rising to the surface.

The fermentations were long and complete. And if the strength or gravity of mead was lacking during the initial stages of fermentation, more honey was judiciously added.

After lunch with the brothers of the abbey, I returned to Brother Adam's office, now brightly lit as the afternoon sun accented the blues and greens of the world outside. Inside, the golden walls were trimmed with natural wood. Not far outside his office door, very large vats of honey provided comfort. But not as much comfort as his storied conversation, accompanied with bottles of his 10-year-old heather honey sherry mead and four-year-old sparkling clover mead.

Brother Adam spoke of his life, about which I had known very little. For two hours we talked. There were frequent pauses of silence as he attempted to recall memories of his past 83 years at the abbey. Brother Adam apologized for his frequent yawning. When one reaches the age of 95, he confided, weariness comes more often.

We spoke of mead, but I soon realized that this was only a very small part of his story; a morsel, a little flavor, but one that no doubt inspires someone like myself to explore the meanings of the reasons why.

We both often paused to contemplate and savor the ambrosia in our glasses. Saturated with antiquity, the mead refracted sunlight as deep amber. Its aroma was very big, floral and honeylike. Closing my eyes, I perceived an earthy aroma. An infusion of alcohol titillated my nostrils. The flavor began unusually soft and gently sweet, then flirted with fruitlike acidity, finally retreating to a wonderful sherrylike aftertaste—nutty, but not overbearing nor overly sweet. The green grass outside in the courtyard sparkled in the sunlight. I began to hear bees buzzing. They were on the other side of the window, seeking our glasses of mead. Smart bees.

Brother Adam recounted the making of his first batch of mead. That was in 1940. There was an abundance of heather honey. What to do with it? Heather honey, having somewhat of a gelatinous nature, was not as suitable for sale as other types of honey. The first batch of mead was made with very little knowledge of the process. I couldn't help but reflect that 53 years later, the mysteries of mead-making remained enveloped in antiquity, awaiting discovery by individual mead makers.

I am not the monastic type. I spent only 24 hours in Buckfast Abbey, but I came away wondering how my small, whimsical notion of seven years back could have led to such an inspiring experience.

Brother Adam, Buckfast Abbey 1993

ST. BARTHOLOMEW'S MEAD

Saint Bartholomew is the patron saint of mead. Considered mystical and held in the highest esteem, mead was originally made from the washings of beeswax. Every church used candles. Honey was washed from the beeswax and fermented into the ambrosia whose sale often provided welcome revenue to the church. St. Bartholomew's Mead is my original and simple recipe. This mead is the pure essence of the art and tradition of mead. It's easy to make, while offering all the complexity and pleasure mead has wrought for thousands of years. The recipe can be found on page 322.

Short glimpses, small tastes and brief digressions. With no real agenda I had wandered onto the grounds of Buckfast Abbey, somewhat purposefully but not expectant. An immersion into the sights, sounds, feelings, aromas and flavors of this place slowly impressed upon me the value of seeing with your eyes closed, tasting with your mouth empty, smelling with only your mind, feeling without touching and hearing through sound barriers.

I bade farewell to Brother Adam late in the morning. I happened to find him walking the halls of the cloister carrying an electronic typewriter. I thanked him for offering me some of his time. He hoped that I found his conversation and information of interest. They were.

Was it a mere whim I had had seven years earlier? Perhaps. Or perhaps it was something else, something that mead makers understand. A yearning for a simple small taste had led me to something much more intriguing. The unexpected always surpasses the expectations of original desire.

Little tastes, little flavors, notions, whims, fancies and small gestures. This time they've complemented a journey I will never forget. This seems always to be the story of mead and its mysteries. A friend of mead is a friend indeed.

One year after my visit, Brother Adam died. His passion surely has left an indelible mark on these lives we still live.

Minard Castle,
Argyll, Scotland

FROM THE DEVON COUNTRYSIDE I journeyed north to the brisk and rustic landscape west of Glasgow, Scotland. Mead had been foremost in my mind for a week, and now I had arrived at the beginning of another adventure back in time. I found myself sipping 45-year-old mead in the wine cellar of a centuries-old Victorian castle. In my hands I held experimental meads brewed both before and during World War II. The walls of the castle were several feet thick. The silence of the room was total, though the rain and gales blew outside, scouring the Scottish countryside.

I had to remember to breathe as I excitedly found myself poring over the original notes of perhaps the 20th century's greatest mead historian and professional and amateur mead maker.

What else would I find inside these castle walls? Were there other bottles of old mead hidden? Very few knew for sure, until I discovered a dusty rack and a box full of mead made over 50 years ago.

But I'm getting ahead of myself. For a moment I need to impress upon you the small gestures and the impulses of a moment in 1983 that had led me to the opposite side of the world seeking whatever knowledge of mead might exist.

It was December, and I wanted to be somewhere warm and have the time to appreciate it. I had totally dedicated the previous summer in Colorado to researching and writing the manuscript for my book *The Complete Joy of Homebrewing*. I had rarely seen the light of day. With my manuscript off to the publisher, I fulfilled the promise to myself to go somewhere warm.

Two weeks into my stay in New Zealand I found myself at the top of the South Island, near the town of Nelson. I had been visiting the recently established RocMac Brewery, the nation's one and only microbrewery at the time. For one reason or another, the brewer and I had begun a discussion about mead. On a whim, he suggested I go have a look at the stock of wines carried by the bottle shop across the street from the brewery.

"I'll be a blue-nosed gopher," I thought to myself as I discovered a bottle of something called Havill's Mazer Mead. There was a telephone number on the bottle and I did not hesitate to ask the shopkeeper if I might make a call to this meadery.

Within minutes I was on the phone talking to Leon Havill. "Where is Rangiora?" I asked, as that was listed on the label as the bottle's source. Leon had only to reply "near Christchurch," and I was making air reservations five minutes later. I was suddenly leaving the next day for a part of New Zealand I'd originally had no intention of visiting. Christchurch? Rangiora? Havill's Mazer Mead? Was I nuts? I had second thoughts, but it was too late.

The visit with Leon and Gay Havill was the beginning of a long and warm friendship. Leon's mead was excellent, and his knowledge and experience were inspiring. During the telling of many tales (all true, I'm sure) he showed me a book about mead he'd found, written in 1948 by a Lieutenant Colonel Robert Gayre, called *Wassail! In Mazers of Mead*. I was fascinated by the depth of historical knowledge this book contained.

It was over a year later that I found a copy of Gayre's book through a rare-book search service. The price seemed high, a painful $80, but I wasn't about to lose the opportunity. I read it with great interest. I continued my own mead-making, somewhat more inspired, but it wasn't until 1985 that I had a strange impulse to wonder if this Lieutenant Colonel Robert Gayre was still alive. Perhaps if he was, he might be interested in participating as a speaker at the American Homebrewers Association's National Homebrewers Conference.

Where does one begin?

I called my friend and advisor Michael Jackson, wondering if he might have the resources to track the whereabouts of Colonel Gayre. Michael called one week later to report that the publisher of the book had gone out of business decades ago, but he had some other leads he still needed to pursue. I couldn't imagine success at this point, but then I didn't know Michael, the world's number-one fermentation detective, as well as I do today. He was in hot pursuit of something, and one week later he had a telephone number for me, saying, "I don't know if it will work, but it's supposed to be his home phone number." I couldn't quite believe it. And Michael hadn't finished. "Oh yes, by the way, he lives in a castle in Scotland, so I'm told."

It was too late to call that day, but early the next morning I direct dialed the number. A rather formal-sounding "Hello, Minard Castle" was the response.

"May I speak to Mr. Gayre, please?"

"This is he."

I was a bit dumbfounded. I had anticipated a secretary to answer. It was Lieutenant Colonel Gayre. The guy who'd written the book I was holding in my hand, published nearly 40 years ago. My mind briefly flashed back to New Zealand and that original unassuming conversation with the brewmaster at

RocMac Brewery, the impulsive trip to visit Havill's meadery and a freak finding of an original copy of this book. Now, several years later, I was speaking with the author.

I briefly explained who I was and where I was from, and asked whether he would consider attending our convention to speak on mead. I had no idea how old this man was (he was 76 at the time). He simply replied, "Yes I would."

Seventeen passionate friends of mead privately donated $1,200 in order to cover the expenses of his travel to Colorado, as the American Homebrewers Association was in no position to come up with that kind of money at the time.

Colonel Gayre attended the 1985 AHA convention, and from that visit the Association of Brewers made arrangements to reprint his book, retitled *Brewing Mead*. Before he departed, the colonel gave me two picture postcards of his castle and invited me to visit, should I ever be in Scotland.

That was in 1985. For eight years a visit to the castle had been on my list of things to do.

This is the abbreviated story of my visit to the home of the 20th century's most knowledgeable, passionate and accomplished mead maker.

I arrived at Minard Castle on a cool, rainy and typically Scottish spring

Minard Castle

day. The imposing castle gate heightened the promise of what might lie within the high walls.

With a view of Loch Fyne bordering the "backyard," Colonel Gayre's son, Reinold, and Reinold's wife, Marion, graciously received me. My arrival turned out to be quite auspicious, as no sooner had I been shown to my room (which was nearly the size of my own house) than I hurried down to one of the castle libraries, where a small celebration of the colonel's 86th birthday had commenced.

Unfortunately, the strokes he had suffered several years earlier had left Lieutenant Colonel Robert Gayre in poor health, but he continued his tradition of enjoying a glass of mead with lunch every day. I had brought two bottles of my own mead to share with him. Little had I known they would be birthday gifts.

I spent two full days with the Gayre family. Their hospitality was gratefully received, and Reinold and Marion's help in locating what was left of Colonel Gayre's mead files led me to some important insights about mead.

I had the freedom to roam among the castle's numerous rooms, most filled with antiques, artifacts, paintings, books, cantilevered staircases, majestic fireplaces, long carpets and coats of arms. Every room seemed appointed with history. I learned much about the colonel during my brief stay. Mead was a relatively small part of his long and active life. During World War II he

Lt. Colonel Robert Gayre (left), son Reinold Gayre (right)

worked in military intelligence against the Nazis in Germany. After the war he was assigned as Chief of Education and Religious Affairs for Germany. He had held a similar position in postwar Italy as well. His specialty was ethnology with related study and work in anthropology, archeology, biology and genealogy. In the late 1940s he published his book *Wassail! In Mazers of Mead*, a cultural and ethnological study of mead tracing its origins back to the Middle Ages and beyond. At about that time Colonel Gayre established and assumed the role of managing director of Mead Makers Ltd. of Gulval in Cornwall, England.

Mead Makers became a commercial meadery, flourishing for several years before its demise in the mid-1950s. Housed in a refurbished abandoned flour mill, the company grew herbs, made mead, sold mead-making kits, showcased their products in a visitor's center and operated a grand mead hall, where exotic banquets were offered combining mead cookery with melage (vintage) meads. Melages were always assigned to the company's mead. St. Bartholomew's Day, on August 24, was celebrated annually with great ceremony.

Sack mead, metheglin, sack metheglin, pyment, hippocras, sack brochet, cyser and melomel were regularly made at Gulval. Preaching that mead was the liquor of the upper classes and the gourmet, Gayre promoted the tradition of old English mead cookery and mead at every opportunity. An old copy of his booklet *Mead Hall Cookery* describes in appetizing and fanciful detail several recipes such as Prawn Sack Mead Soup, Pheasant Hippocras Soup, Cyser Cream of Sole Soup, Oyster Pyment Soup, Rabbit cooked in Melomel, Cyser Omelet and Trevylor Mead Sauce.

Gayre noted in one of several articles he authored in the 1940s that "ambrosia" and "nectar of the gods" referred to ancient meads and were the terms used to describe the best of the best. We still use these terms today, but forget they originally referred to mead.

Mead Makers also harvested their own honey and used it until the price of imported Australian honey could be had for one-hundredth the price of the lighter and more delicious English honey.

Success at Mead Makers lasted only a few years. In 1955 the mead hall, herb garden and meadery and the brief popularity of mead were abandoned, it is thought due largely to the reduction of imported wine tariffs. While these events surely had a profound effect on the popularity and sales of Gayre's mead, Brother Adam of Buckfast Abbey told me that during the final years of the meadery, inexpensive and strongly flavored Australian eucalyptus honey was used in Mead Maker's mead. The unusual flavors, he thought, might have contributed to mead's falling out of favor with the English.

Silver Mazer Mead Chalices

Gayre's autobiography mentions only briefly his mead endeavors, attributing their failure to quarreling among the directors of the company.

Regardless of the reasons for its demise, Mead Makers and Gayre brought great attention to mead and mead making. Several stories about it were published in magazines of the time. The spirit of the articles mirrored the current enthusiasm and attention given to today's microbrewery phenomenon in the United States. Except among a few friends of mead, the western world was to forget Gayre's great accomplishments and abandon the culture of mead. Gulval had been the center of a brief revival.

I recall how Colonel Gayre sparkled during his visit to Colorado in 1985 when he appeared at the American Homebrewers Association National Conference. His small audience was avid and appreciative. He discussed his experiences and mead wisdom, much as he must have done 35 years earlier when he addressed a meeting of beekeepers in England. At the American Homebrewers Association conference he emphasized the need for sanitation and strong yeast strains and the destructive nature of oxygen and oxidation. The following excerpt from a presentation Gayre made in 1950 indicates the passion he had always had for mead:

One of the characteristics of mead is that it is drinkable at a much earlier stage than would be wine. One reason for this is that in honey there are practically no toxic properties whatsoever, whereas even in the making of the finest wines there are derived from pips, leaves and stems, all of which in most cases at one time or another come into contact with the juice. The result of this is that mead never appears to affect the head in the sense of giving a headache—what is commonly called a hangover—nor does it affect the liver and make for much the same effect with feeling of nausea or sickness. There is from an excess of mead drinking—and all good things can be abused—a tendency for a certain irrational rationality! That is, a person may do a most irrational thing in the most rational way, and be fully conscious of it both at the time and afterwards. There is not that sort of blackout with failure to remember what has been done. Traditionally, mead is able to affect the legs rather seriously when taken excessively, and there are instances known to the writer where the drinkers have said that, after a prolonged session at mead drinking, they have had some difficulty in rising. The moral of this is not to drink in excess, or, if you are determined to do so—in which case no one will be able to stop you—the thing is to drink where you intend to sleep!" (Excerpted from The British Bee Journal, *July 22, 1950*)

Irrational rationality and difficulty in rising! I've never known anything closer to the truth.

The stone walls of the castle within which I undertook my brief research were imposingly silent in the vastness of Colonel Gayre's home. The wide Victorian main stairs spiraled to the second floor. The halls were decorated with larger-than-life-size paintings of European dignitaries in times past. Thousands of books from all over the world lay on shelves seemingly extending forever. They were all perfectly dusted. In one room, a large kitchen with a long table bore a full complement of pewter plates, drinking vessels and silverware. The kitchen hearth set out as it may have been two hundred years ago. A stacked pyramid of grapefruit-size cannonballs lay in a corner, a small triangular metal corral called a brass monkey keeping them from rolling away. (Now I understood where the phrase "cold as balls on a brass monkey" came from.) Full sheaths of armor, swords, hunting bows, muskets, lanterns and other ancient paraphernalia filled the room.

Gayre was indeed a collector of stuff and I admired that, being a collector of stuff myself. Nothing seemed spectacularly valuable, but there was a lot of it. And all of it was very old, mysterious and intriguing. Somewhere in this vast collection of stuff I was searching for information about mead. But I couldn't help being distracted by the tall and rippled windows peering out over this Scottish estate.

Outside, a walled garden flourished under the caretaking of John the gardener. I learned he was also an avid all-grain homebrewer. Orchids grew in several corners, while fruit trees and exotic grasses grew elsewhere. Beyond the walls the Gayre family had planted spruce trees, planning to sell them as Christmas trees in years to come. The sun shone briefly as I took advantage of the fleeting glimpse of blue sky to don boots and walk about the castle grounds. The grass between the loch and the castle was a rich, soggy deep green as I peered back and contemplated the stone walls and the secrets of mead.

In my room that night, I typed my thoughts and transcribed a few records and recipes onto my notebook computer, which posed a strange contrast of 20th-century technology with medieval surroundings. Outside the rain was driven by gale winds, yet I could not hear any sound through the three-foot-thick walls. Despite the eerie silence and a permeating coolness, I slept well that night.

After a morning walk I returned to my research within the walls of the castle. My wanderings found me in a room I had not visited. Toward the rear of the castle and beneath a set of cantilevered spiral stairs is a small room that served as the wine cellar. I entered through the small door with anticipation that was soon to be rewarded. Scattered on the floor were boxes of marked and unmarked bottles of mead and a dusty wine rack silently upholding several more. As I was very carefully sorting through these relics I discovered what remained of Lieutenant Colonel Robert Gayre's stash of commercial and experimentally homemade mead. Bottled in the years 1944 through 1949, there were perhaps 40 labeled bottles remaining of sack mead, sack metheglin, cyser, melomel, brochet and hippocras.

I also discovered a box on the floor containing 16 bottles of mead, some of which were hand labeled. All seemed to be from about 1944, when Gayre was experimenting with various recipes as well as beginning his career working for military intelligence against Nazi Germany. I held this mead and thought of how only eight years earlier, in 1936, Gayre had met with Hitler in Berlin, Hitler having been interested in his ethnological ideas. Now it was August 1993 and I was sorting through several cysers, metheglins and melomels.

Most of the bottles were still intact, though a few had oozed part of their contents through failing corks and broken wax seals. My intent was to take a few photographs of these rare bottles and bring to the attention of Reinold and Marion the significance of what was in their basement.

Remaining mead from 1940s Mead Makers Meadery, Gulval, Cornwall

Over the years various castle residents may have squandered much of what had been there. Who was to know? Now only a few bottles remained.

As I took stock of the small inventory, Marion brought in a steaming plate of lightly sautéed chanterelle mushrooms, along with a complement of several wineglasses and a corkscrew. I was about to be immersed in mead heaven. Reinold joined us and invited me to open two bottles of melage mead.

The first was a 1948 melomel made by Mead Makers. The bottle had leaked. A quarter of its contents were gone, replaced with air. There was very little hope that the contents would be good. The cork disintegrated as I pried it out. To our astonishment the mead was not only drinkable, but quite good. It tasted very rich and dense, almost salty from the concentration of solids due to evaporation; it was very sweet, sherrylike and somewhat spicy in character. There was very little suggestion of oxidation and no acidification had taken place.

The next bottle we opened was a 1948 bottle of sack metheglin. It was in perfect condition. The aroma was herbal and honeylike. There was not the slightest evidence of oxidation. The label stated that the contents were no less than 14 percent a.b.v. The character of this sack metheglin was deep and complex; it was crystal clear, bearing no sediment. The aroma also expressed a slight lavender/herbal character. The taste mystified me. My mind continued to unravel the flavor. After several sips and savoring the long aftertaste, several characters unfolded themselves. I thought I could identify lavender, thyme, rosemary, cinnamon, allspice and nutmeg, though they were all interwoven into one marvelous and unifying expression. Curiously, it was the aftertaste that really helped unravel the flavor for me. It still lingered 30 minutes later, and it was at that time that a rosemary-and-thyme (almost oregano-like) character became clearly evident.

I later learned from reading Gayre's mead notes that the gruit (herbal mixture) from which metheglins were made consisted of those herbs I had perceived, as well as a long list of others.

A slight burnt and smoky flavor contributed to the overall character. I would guess that this might have been the result of certain root herbs such as orris (powdered Florentine iris, of which Gayre writes in one of his herbal books: "a most valuable ingredient in flavoring fine metheglin") and of being aged in oak for a year or two before bottling. There was also a soft acidity blessing the overall character.

We tried no other meads, though I could hardly contain my desire. I noted that the melomels and hippocras and particularly the cysers all had deposits in the bottle, likely from the tannic additions from grapes, apples or other fruit.

The experience of enjoying Colonel Gayre's mead must have had a mystical effect upon Reinold, for as soon after we had sampled the meads, he mentioned that there was a journal in one of the bookcases of the library in which the colonel had kept notes on his mead experimentation. I searched the rest of the day, but it wasn't until the next morning that I discovered it. I was leaving later that morning and had little time to view it, though. I did quickly note a few handwritten formulations. The first was for an early sack metheglin, surely a less potent predecessor of what I had experienced the night before:

for **SACK METHEGLIN**

> *18 quarts* [Imperial, or approximately 5½ U.S. gallons] *of water, 9 pounds of honey and 2 tight handfuls of gruit.* [the gruit consisting of] *1 handful of fresh fennel and equal parts* [to make up the other handful] *of lemon balm, thyme in flower and sage.*

Another formulation for gruit appeared later in his journal and may be more indicative of the gruit of which the sack metheglin from the previous night had been made. Question marks appear where the handwritten notes were not quite legible.

3 parts	bog myrtle (sweet gale)
3 parts	rosemary
3 parts	yarrow
1 part	ginger
9 parts	fennel
1 part	rue (ceaser?)
1 part	thyme
2 parts	sweet criar(?)
1 part	tansy
2 parts	balm
1 part	peppermint

Here is another recipe for gruit, in which Gayre apparently experiments with clove, cinnamon and nutmeg:

Metheglin *for 5 imperial gallons [6 U.S. gallons]*

2 oz.	fresh fennel
2 oz.	lemon balm, thyme and sage in flower
2 oz.	elder flowers, fresh
1 oz.	bay leaf, tansy (fresh), parsley (fresh) and mint
½ oz.	clove, cinnamon and nutmeg

The first formulation for sack-type mead related to the above gruit formulations indicates the use of 2 pounds of honey per imperial gallon. This must have been an earlier experiment, as further on in his journal Gayre refines his formulations to become more indicative of a truer sack mead with ratios of 5 pounds (2.3 kg) of honey per imperial gallon (1.2 U.S. gallon, or 4.6 l) for sack mead and 6 pounds (2.7 kg) per imperial gallon for melage sack mead.

To assure the cessation of fermentation, Gayre would add spirits (alcohol), fortifying some of his concoctions.

While experimenting with yeast, he noted that he isolated some of his yeast cultures from fresh apple juice: *"add ¼ bottle of whisky to 2 gallons of apple juice and 12 # honey . . ."* I wondered, did the whisky inhibit bacterial organisms, while wild yeast survived? Did the wild yeast encourage a more complete fermentation?

Gayre must have experimented with various gruits until he was satisfied, for a later journal entry describes a grander production of metheglin. A large volume of gruit was formulated thusly:

10 lbs.	heads of elder flowers
1 lb.	heads of hawthorn
3 oz.	rosemary
2½ lbs.	fennel [probably not seeds]
4 oz.	thyme
9 oz.	balm
½ oz.	borage
½ oz.	peppermint
½ oz.	marjoram
1 oz.	southernwood (type of wormwood)
1 oz.	rue
1 oz.	horehound
1 oz.	winter savory
1 oz.	hyssop
1 oz.	mint
1 oz.	wormwood [this herb is toxic and not recommended]
1 oz.	pennyroyal
6 oz.	tansy
?	comfrey
?	agrimony
3	bottles of rose hip syrup

The castle remains a sentry on the shores of Loch Fyne, in county Argyll. Marion and Reinold Gayre keep busy with the upkeep of the castle and attending to the six or seven self-catering cottages on the castle grounds. They rent these cottages by the week to vacationers. Theirs is a long and busy day, spent attending to dry rot, leaking roofs, water-damaged floors, dusting, plumbing and window cleaning. Castle upkeep isn't a normal housekeeping job. But a visitor like myself, in awe of antiquity and in search of lost meads, can't help but admire the Gayre family's dedication to traditions.

I emerged from within the castle walls a bit wiser in the ways of mead. Tucked away in my hand-held luggage was one gift of a 1947 sack metheglin.

··
CASTLE METHEGLIN

This is unlike any other mead you have ever made or tasted. If properly cared for, it will age well for 100 years. The gruit of herbs provides a unique blend, taking on the character of the combined ingredients. Individual herbal flavors will briefly emerge when tasting, yet it is the artful blend of these herbs that creates this most majestic of metheglin meads. Patience is a virtue surely rewarded with the eventual emergence of this golden elixir. The recipe can be found on page 323.
··

It is now over 58 years old. So am I. In the meantime I continue to make my own meads. I believe they will improve because of that intangible knowledge one acquires from such a journey.

I often think of Colonel Gayre as I make my annual melage of meads. I also take heart in knowing that thousands of home mead makers throughout the world are now wiser and more aware of how the traditions of mead have contributed to our culture.

Dear Colonel, wherever you may be, know ye that a friend of mead is a friend indeed.

I REVISITED the castle with Sandra in 2003. Marion had sadly and quite suddenly died earlier that year. Reinold has since remarried and continues with the upkeep of Minard Castle. At the time of our visit, the closet of mead was still in good order. Having tried a bottle of 55-year-old brochet, I continue to admire the quality of what Lieutenant Colonel Gayre created.

Beer Heaven Is
in Germany

IN THE MINDS of the world's beer drinkers, Germany is the center of the beer universe. Its reputation for upholding the 1516 Beer Purity Law, the *Reinheitsgebot*, serves as reassurance to all German beer drinkers that purity and quality will reside in every liter of beer brewed and enjoyed in Deutschland.

While the flavor and diversity of beer styles is limited in Germany, the pilseners, wheat beers, Altbiers, Kölschs, bocks and Bavarian light and dark styles are brewed with artisanal pride. Sadly in the last decade, the globalization of beer brands and economic pressures has stressed the fragile infrastructure of German small brewers. Their numbers have dwindled. The pressure to conform to the low taste profile of mass-marketed beers has resulted in the diminished complexity and flavor of many famous German beers from breweries both large and small.

German beer culture has not escaped the very real economic challenges of the early 21st century. Recently there has a been a small rebound in appreciation for passionately brewed German beer made by small brewers, but the struggle for survival continues and the German beer culture flirts precariously close to collapse. Two things may save what I have come to love about German beer: (1) Brewers will maintain their traditional standards and not compromise nor diminish the flavor and complexity of their beers, and (2) beer drinkers may learn that they must pay a small premium for beers whose character is above the trend toward less taste in beer.

My first tour of duty with the beers and brewers of Germany was in 1989. That year may have been the peak of modern German beer culture. The threats of globalizing beer brands had not yet aggressively appeared in Germany. Everywhere I went there was a sense of continuing celebration and a brewer's pride. The anxieties for the future had not yet made their presence. Small countryside breweries created unique versions of classic styles of German lagers and ales, each having their own "house" aromas and flavors. It was a wonderful time to be traveling in search of the beers and brewers of Germany. Those times provided my valued first impression, which has consequently inspired me to champion the passion of the microbrewer and preserve the flavor and diversity of real German beer.

The Monastery at Andechs

SUMMER IN BAVARIA isn't all sunny skies. In fact, when I was there in July 1989 it was cool, rainy and gray. I was making a pilgrimage to Andechs Monastery, Brewery and Beer House, west of Munich, easily accessible by the S-bahn train.

From the train station it is about a three-mile, thirst-provoking walk through the forest to the top of the hill where the monastery peacefully overlooks the valley. The monks brew a variety of beers for which they are famous and I was seeking the one they were most famous for, Andechs bock beer.

I was quite surprised to see the day's chalkboard drink menu absent of my heart's desire. What perplexed me even more was the listing of two other drinks that were completely foreign to me, "Radler" and "Diesel." I was beginning to feel disillusioned and quite disappointed.

I had seen these drinks listed in other parts of Germany but really didn't pay them attention. Now I was annoyed. I drooled at the thought of downing a liter of their famous fresh, microbrewed dark Andechs bock beer but it was not served on the weekend. In the absence of bock beer my choice was limited to Andechs Helles. But what were these intrusions called Radler and Diesel? I was in the land of beer heaven. I was in Germany! They make beer here with only malt, hops, water and yeast. My thoughts were preoccupied with the question, "What is this other stuff?"

To my astonishment, I learned that Germans often mix lemonade with their beer and call it a Radler. Diesel was a popular half-beer, half-cola beverage also

enjoyed by Germans. For me it seemed a best-kept secret that was best kept a secret! They say it's "not bad." But there is no way in beer heaven nor any other part of Planet Beer I will be mixing lemonade or cola with my beer. If word ever got out that Germans add lemonade and cola to their beer, there would be millions of disillusioned beer drinkers throughout the beer-loving world.

Restricted to their Helles lager, I nevertheless enjoyed the experience immensely. But what had happened to the bock beer? The problem, it turned out, was that recently the monks had decided to limit the weekend tourist crowds to their less potent Helles, as they've had problems with drunks who could not handle their higher-strength beers. So if you visit the monastery, go on a weekday (and note that the beer house is closed on Tuesdays).

ANDECH'S WEEKDAY BOCK

In the pure tradition of an all-malt German lager, this bock beer is an excellent rendition of the style: malty, with a balance of piquant German-grown hop flavor, aroma and pleasantly soft bitterness. American Crystal hops offer equal character, providing artisanal nuances. This beer is fresh-tasting and immensely drinkable. Even at 7 percent alcohol this bock beer would be served on weekdays at Andechs, but anytime is fine with me. This recipe can be found on page 325.

German Rye Beer
Thurn und Taxis

IN 1988, while vacationing and trekking through the jungles of Thailand, I was cooling my thirst one evening in a mountain cave not far from the Burmese border. The beer was Singha, the most popular Thai beer at the time. We were sitting around a fire when a German traveler seated across from me agreed that Singha was "an all right beer." He continued about the many good beers in his country, ". . . but if you are ever interested in an unusual beer you must go to Regensburg. There is a brewery called Thurn und Taxis. It is in nearby Schierling and they make a rye beer."

Six months after sharing a beer in a jungle cave, I found myself leaving the Miesbach train station at 10:25 A.M., headed for Regensburg.

Only about three hours north of Munich, Regensburg is steeped in malt and history. It's the birthplace of Martin Luther. Regensburg's population is about 100,000, and it has more than 100 churches and four breweries. Many years ago there were more than 40 breweries. The 20th century had a detrimental effect on this town's beer culture.

When I visited, three of the breweries were "public"; only Thurn und Taxis was privately owned. The public breweries were incorporated in such a way that their profits went to charitable foundations. The Bischof's Brauerei profits went to priests. The Spital Brauerei profits went to a hospital for the aged, and the Knietinger Brauerei, at the time, was a private, family-owned brewery, willed to benefit orphans and children whose parents were unable to care for them.

Lunchtime in Regensburg was a quest fulfilled. I finally drank a very tall, specially endorsed glass of Thurn und Taxis Roggenbier (rye beer). Dark and yeasty, the beer's character is remarkably similar to that of Bavarian Weizenbiers. It has a clovelike essence and is slightly higher in refreshing sour acidity. I didn't

PUMPERNICKEL RYE STOUT

There are plenty of recipes for German-style Roggenbier, brewed with pale barley and rye malt with the addition of a measured small amount of roasted barley malt. It is fermented with German wheat beer yeast to create the banana–clove character that helps define this style. Pumpernickel Rye Stout is not your typical Roggenbier; rather it is an American invention of mine. Brewed with the ingredients of classic pumpernickel, this brew is smooth, with the added spiciness of rye malt. The recipe can be found on page 327.

care for it given my own taste preference, which doesn't favor clove, or banana flavor in beer. However, I did admire the quality of the beer and the care with which Thurn und Taxis developed it, and I was impressed with the enjoyment so many others found in this beer. I was surely in the minority when it came to this beer preference.

Malted rye presents some unique problems for the brewer. It is very gummy when mashed and is notorious for what is called "set" mashes and runoffs. The grain mash becomes so sticky that liquid flows through with great difficulty. The brewery evidently developed a special process to deal with these problems.

The beer is more than 50 percent rye malt and is darkened with roasted malt. According to the brewery, in olden times rye was valued as a grain with high nutritional value. Five hundred years ago it was forbidden in Germany to brew beer with rye; the grain was reserved strictly for breads. Now, with an abundance of rye, Thurn und Taxis brings back the tradition of brewing with rye.

German Brown Ale
Düsseldorf, the Altstadt. Altbier

MY PILGRIMAGE TO beer heaven—Germany—lasted 18 days. On the Fourth of July, I found myself in Düsseldorf in search of Altbier. Without a map or guide, I easily managed to stumble upon Düsseldorf's Altstadt (old city) and four Altbier microbreweries. There were also countless other brands brewed by larger companies in the region. The old beers of Germany, I discovered that evening, were uniquely top-fermented light brown ales, rather dry, with no hop aroma or flavor and often awash with intense hop bitterness.

I began my tasting in the early evening, and by 1 A.M. I was an expert. After tasting a dozen different Altbiers (more than once) at seven (or was it eight?) beer halls, I determined that the crazy old man was my favorite. I ended my evening pilgrimizing Zum Uerige Alt (*Uerige* means crazy old man). Dark, dry and clean, with very little fruitiness (I detected the tiniest hint of apple flavor), no roasted malt flavor and a dense, creamy head, its bitterness quickly asserted itself and lingered provocatively on my palate. It was delectable but not obtrusive. Skillfully designed by the brewer, the beer's bitterness resided only on the back of my tongue, not throughout my mouth. I learned later that Zum Uerige is one of the most exciting and pleasantly bitter examples of the Altbier style.

I indulged in several other Altbiers with pleasure. Rhenania Alt was very fruity, with the aroma of apples. Zum Schluessel's Gatzweiler Alt had a slight banana character and the flavor of hops. Schumacher Alt was characterized

Zum Uerige Bier Haus, Altstadt, Düsseldorf

CRAZY OLD MAN ALTBIER

Fresh Crazy Old Man Altbier, better known as Zum Uerige Alt, is an experience worth seeking if you are in Düsseldorf. The next best thing to being there is to brew it yourself and enjoy the freshness of a traditional centuries-old style of German brown ale right where you live. Smooth and refreshingly bitter, this beer will zap and excite your palate. The recipe can be found on page 330.

by old hops and applelike fruitiness. Im Fuechsen was by far the most bitter of all the Altbiers I tried; it also had a slight coconut-like flavor and an aroma of hops. The bitterness was a bit intense for my mood at the time.

Altbier was the most popular style of beer in the city of Düsseldorf, where it has maintained a tradition for centuries. That evening I delightfully lived my own 19th century. These Altbiers were certainly the most popular styles of the evening. Altbier is difficult to find in other parts of Germany, though bottled versions are sometimes available. A growing number of American and Japanese microbreweries are making true-to-style German Altbier. The Widmer Brothers Brewing Company in Portland, Oregon, was one of the first microbreweries to popularize this style in the United States. Their version is delicious and true to style, yet not quite as bitter as my favorite, Zum Uerige Alt.

Weissbier in Bavaria
Hopfweissbier Brauerei

A T 10 A.M. in Bavaria you are likely to find yourself in the company of others enjoying the traditional late breakfast of Weissbier (wheat beer) and Weisswurst (white sausage of veal). It's a treat any time of day, but uniquely Bavarian when enjoyed before noon.

Whichever you call it, Weizenbier or Weissbier, wheat beer is spectacularly popular in Bavaria. In 1984 this slightly acidic, yeasty, well-carbonated style of beer with its hint of clove and banana flavor accounted for less than 1 percent of German beer drinking. By 1989 it was the second most popular style of beer in Bavaria (pils is first), with a 28 percent share of the beer market. In 2004 its share was 33 percent, and it continues to grow. Bavarians love their Weizenbier, and they like it *mit Hefe* (with yeast).

I had the privilege and great pleasure of spending several days with Hans Hopf and his family in Miesbach, 30 miles south of Munich in the foothills of the Alps. The relatively small Hopfweissbier Brauerei has been in the Hopf family for three generations and continues to slowly grow to meet the demand for wheat beer. It is unique in that it is one of only a few breweries in Germany that brews exclusively wheat beer.

A morning in the brewery and some enjoyable evenings at local beer gardens gave insight into the German wheat beer phenomenon. Hans explained, "I have problems sometimes with my cask wheat beer because the yeast settles too well and the beer comes out too clear. People prefer yeast in their wheat beer. I tell the managers to roll the kegs a little, but that does not seem to help." I was astonished to learn that some beer gardens and beer houses offered yeast dispensers, designed like mustard dispensers. "People will put the yeast in their other beers as well. It is a healthy thing to do because of all the vitamins in the beer yeast."

Hans Hopf

If you are a brewer and are thinking of culturing yeast sediment from the bottom of a bottle of German wheat beer, though, you'd better think twice. Yes, the yeast sediment is alive and naturally carbonates the beer in the bottle, just as in home-brewed beer. The fact is that most wheat beers are filtered before bottling in order to remove the "powdery" top-fermenting yeast that does not settle to the bottom very well. Wheat beer is then inoculated with a more easily sedimented strain of lager yeast and held at relatively warm temperatures to naturally carbonate in the bottle. While touring the brewery, Hans explained that using a different "bottle yeast" really affects the flavor of the beer significantly—and for his beer it made a positive difference.

Bianca Hopf

In the room beneath the kettle it was very warm. It was there Hans had me sample a small batch of fermenting wort. It was so sour my mouth puckered. "That is 1 percent lactic acidity," he explained. Because of the natural carbonate hardness of the local water, Hans had been experimenting with naturally acidifying his mashing regime and wort production. High carbonate levels in water will produce pH ranges that prevent the desired extraction of sugars from grains during the mashing process. By fermenting a portion of naturally produced wort with a strain of lactobacillus bacteria, Hans is able to add a portion of soured extract and obtain a better yield from his grains. By adding a portion of soured wort to his main wort during wort boiling, he found he could also control the flavor balance of his Weissbiers and get better flavors out of the hops he uses.

Because of tradition and Germany's beer purity law, the *Reinheitsgebot,* German brewers cannot use industrially made acids to adjust the pH of their mash or wort. Much of Germany's water has been contaminated with man-made nitrates from fertilizers used in agriculture. The water is unfit for brewing, so almost every brewery I visited filtered and purified its water or used deep well water (which often had high carbonate levels).

The Hopfweissbier Brauerei brews wheat beers exclusively, including Dunkel (dark) Weizen, Weizenbock and Weizen Doppelbock. The brewery is family-owned. At the time of my first visit, Bianca, Hans's 13-year-old daughter, had already expressed an interest in attending Weihenstephan University and taking over as brewmaster someday. In 1989, when I left Miesbach, she was wearing an American Homebrewers Association T-shirt

HANS WEISSBIER

This beer is formulated and brewed in the true German wheat beer tradition. Your brewmaster skills will guide you to the exact temperature conditions in which to manage fermentation of this most delicately wonderful Bavarian wheat beer. The recipe can be found on page 332.

that read, "I brew therefore I am." I recently checked in with her, and she anticipates taking over general manager responsibilities and running the brewery in 2006.

With His Royal Highness
Printz Luitpold von Bayern

HIS ROYAL HIGHNESS PRINTZ LUITPOLD of Bavaria would have been the successor to the throne of Bavaria if such things happened today. Instead, Printz Luitpold is a brewer and in 1989 operated two breweries west of Munich: one in Fuerstenfeldbruck and the other at his castle at Kaltenberg. He also has installed dozens of microbreweries and brewpub systems throughout the world in such places as China, Canada, Hungary, Russia and the United States, as well as in Germany.

After my stop at Miesbach I found myself cruising the countryside with His Royal Highness. The level of excitement could be heard in his voice as he announced, "We are preparing for our annual medieval jousting tournaments and Renaissance festival at the castle. You must come to see the preparations after our brewery visits and have some beer, of course."

We talked of beer, breweries and Germany. Printz Luitpold's royalty made him no less passionate about beer and brewing than the most enthusiastic of beer brewers. Though his two production breweries were rather large scale, they produced beers fit for a king. His passion was obvious. He has the heart and soul of a microbrewer and the spirit of an adventurer.

During our drive, he told me, "There are about 800 private breweries in Germany. Every year there are fewer." I knew this and felt remorse whenever I hear those dwindling statistics, but the prince explained that it was not all the result of poor business management or lack of marketing. He continued to explain, "On the average every 30 years a brewery goes through a generation change. About 30 breweries each year face a family decision: who will manage the brewery? Sometimes there are family disagreements and often no one in the family is interested in continuing."

This was the first time I had heard this perspective, one often hidden from the beer drinker's realm.

We arrived in Fuerstenfeldbruck for a beer at the town's beer festival. Never mind the brewery—we had both seen enough breweries in our

Printz Luitpold, 1987

Free beer for the elderly

lives. The festival was where
the beer and people were!
It was where I found my-
self with the prince. It was
mid-afternoon, midweek, and
there were thousands of
people drinking liter mugs of
Luitpold's Hellesbier. The
brewery was sponsoring free
beer for senior citizens. I
looked around to see that
virtually everyone there was
between the ages of 60 and
100—and many were at the
top end of the scale! Everywhere there were both quiet
and animated conversations
as the oompah band belted
out the Bavarian classics hit
parade. I looked around at
all those wise faces, faces

Printz Luitpold and Papazian, 2004

that knew of other times and many more breweries. It occurred to me that,
yes, more changes are yet to evolve as Germany joins the European Union.

Printz Luitpold's home and brewery, Kaltenberg Castle, is in the quietly
picturesque countryside. Here he brews his increasingly popular dark
Dunkelbier, some of which is lagered in large, century-old oak barrels. It is
also the site of his jousting tournament, an event attracting 200,000 thirsty
people.

The media were visiting that day, covering a promotional story about the
event. One beer led to another and the prince dressed me in a complete suit of
armor for a photo opportunity with him, a fair maiden and, of course, a beer.

Later that day when we parted company, he told me, "If you are interested I can get you a custom-made suit of armor for about $1,500." So far I
have not taken him up on the offer, as it would seriously handicap my drinking style.

I have had the pleasure of joining the prince on several beer occasions, including stops at many of his brewpubs around the world. Truly wonderful
beer. Truly wonderful company, and truly a gentleman of beer passion and a
smile.

PRINTZ HELLES GERMAN LAGER

This is one of my favorite styles of everyday drinking beer. Immensely quaffable, this German-style light lager is rich in the malty tradition of Bavarian beer. My addition of American Crystal hops at the end comes close to providing the authentic character of hard-to-find fresh German aroma hops. Give me a liter of this beer and my imagination quickly drifts to the pleasures I've experienced in German beer gardens and beer halls. The recipe can be found on page 335.

CHAPTER 8

An Underground Beer Culture: France, Italy and Sweden

I F YOU ARE an adventurer and embrace the unexpected, you will discover beer in the most unlikely of places. But I have found "unlikelihood" to really be a matter of prejudice. Microbrewed adventures are everywhere. They can be discovered on remote islands of the South Pacific, in the mountains of Tibet or Japan, on the seashores of the Middle East, in the fjords of Scandinavia, in the jungles of Africa, in the casinos of Las Vegas and in the old cities of Latin America—and if you are lucky, around the corner at your local pub. Beer is ubiquitous. But the microbrewed adventure often lies just beneath the surface. One must be free of assumptions and virtually tuned in to the invisible wavelengths of nearby fermentation. I have encountered brewpubs and microbreweries on the side streets of Madrid and Athens. I stumbled on a small microbrewery sitting on the green horizon while driving the wine country of South Africa. At a brewers' convention in Hanoi I came across the business cards of several local brewpubs, and in my wife's hometown of Natal, Brazil, there is a brewpub just above the seaside.

While the French, Italians and Swedes may have a culture of high-profile wines and distilled spirits, there are many individuals in these countries who have embarked on their own microbrewing adventures. I have been fortunate to share their passion for beer on their terms.

My Paris—My Beer
Frog & Rosbif

MY PARIS is not the typical Paris most people come to see. I was invited there in 1995 to brew a batch of beer. I was excited. It was to be my first-ever commercially brewed beer.

I arrived in Paris at 8:30 in the morning. Taking a train into the city center, I emerged randomly from the Métro and miraculously found myself within two blocks of my hotel and on time for my 10:30 A.M. rendezvous at the Frog & Rosbif at 116, rue St. Denis, four blocks away.

Owners Thor Gugmundson and Paul Chantler and friend David Bruce (formerly of London's Firkin brewpub empire) had schemed to bring me to Paris. "Well, Charlie, what shall we have you brew?" I didn't have a clue what their customers would enjoy. This was my first trip to Paris, and most people here drank wine rather than enjoying the delights of craft microbrewed beer.

I was about to ask who their customers were when they apologized that the brewpub was closed for the day. Being one of the very few English-style pubs in Paris, they had inadvertently attracted soccer thugs, who the night before were handing out trudgeons and knives in preparations for "cheering" their team's match against Spain. Thor and Paul didn't want any part of that, so they had shut down for the day.

With this one exception, the pub is quite civilized, with a mixed clientele of tourists, British expats and local Parisians who appreciate the ambience and British-style ales. What was I to brew? "Whatever you brew, Charlie, it should be unusual, so that we mustn't forget you were here," was the sentiment. "Does it have to be a traditional style?" I asked. They unanimously agreed that it should have flair, be creative and be remembered in Paris.

I was scheduled to brew the next morning. We tossed about some ideas. Well, actually, I asked a few leading questions. "Can I use spices?" I sensed that Thor and Paul were exchanging nervous glances, but David, always the adventurer and joker, charged forward, not hesitating to encourage my direction. "How about casket-conditioned veal ale?" he shouted, his eyes squinting with laughter.

"Could you find some whole coriander seed?" I asked. There was an Indian specialty store in the neighborhood, so we had that problem resolved. I had decided that this was Paris. I was American. The brewpub was thematically English. The owners were Icelandic. Why not create a hybrid with an artistic flair. Ah, Paris in the springtime!

Brewing in Paris

I had decided to make somewhat of a light brown wheat ale, lightly yet flavorfully hopped, with the addition of freshly crushed coriander seed. The ale was a combination of pale lager malt, crystal malt, wheat malt and chocolate malt. Czech Saaz and German Hersbrucker Hallertauer hops were used rather than British hops in order to create a more continental European character. I used 1.4 kilograms of crushed coriander seed to remind the French of the rich Belgian beer culture to their north.

It took the better part of the next morning, as we hand paddle-stirred the mash to perfection and dosed the boiling kettle with hops and coriander at my prescribed times. Tasting the unfermented wort, I was satisfied that it was what I had imagined it to be. If there were any complaints about the beer, I would take full responsibility. Quite frankly, I was very nervous about how my first professionally brewed beer would be accepted.

FROG & ROSBIF'S BROWN WHEAT CORIANDER ALE

This recipe is similar to the beer I brewed in Paris, a light brown wheat ale, lightly yet flavorfully hopped with the addition of freshly crushed coriander seed. A French revolution in the making and a reminder of the rich Belgian beer culture to their north, the recipe can be found on page 337.

I learned later that even at Parisian beer prices of $8 a pint, it had been popular enough that they brewed a second batch. It made me feel quite accomplished as a novice professional. Since that time, Thor and Paul have successfully opened up six more "Frog & . . ." brewpubs in France and Lisbon (www.frogpubs.com).

Poetic Justice in Italy
The Microbrewers of Italy

AGOSTINO ARIOLI IS a craft brewer who continues to serve time as an accused criminal. At first this may be of passive interest to most of you, but his customers aren't likely to dismiss Agostino's crimes against Italian beer drinkers. His brewery, Birrificio Italiano, in Lurago Marinone (a suburb of Como), produces over 700 hectoliters of craft-brewed lagers a year for his successful brewpub. He is accused by his customers of crimes against beer drinkers: "You are a criminal, Agostino. I cannot drink any other beer but yours now."

Italy, a country that seems forever planted to the horizon with vineyards, enjoys a beverage culture deeply immersed in wine and food. However, Italians are drinking a lot more beer these days than one would imagine. More than 25 percent of the beer consumed in Italy is imported from all over the world. Brewpubs and microbrewery numbers have increased from six to more than 50 in less than two years. Estimates in 2004 reveal the numbers of microbrewers has grown to more than 120. On a trip I made in 2000, I discovered a new world of beer and a small but growing number of Italian craft beers.

I traveled with members of *Unionbirrai Microbirrifici* (Italy's microbrewery association) through north-central Italy to visit five microbreweries and brewpubs. There I learned that the poets of the beer world have coalesced and emerged, expressing the traditions of Italian food and beverage. Through their creative combination of American, German, Belgian and British beer traditions, they poetically express themselves with uniquely Italian beers worthy of all beer enthusiasts' attention. They have truly immersed themselves in their own microbrewed adventures.

La Baladin

THE BEERS I tasted at La Baladin (http://www.birreria.com) in the tiny hilltop medieval village of Piozzo were nothing short of magnificent. Teo Musso, owner, troubadour, world music producer and brewmaster, blends his knowledge of Belgian brewing techniques with Italian creativity to skillfully brew a balanced selection of top-fermented beers. His knowledge of brewing, he says, comes from watching. Having spent more than a year working at the Silly Brewery in Belgium, not as a brewer or even as an assistant brewer, he intently observed and digested all he experienced.

Teo Musso with son Isaac and beer

La Baladin opened in 1985 as a non-brewing café. The brewery, Teo's brainchild, was installed in 1996, and beer sales increased 40 percent once his beer was on tap. In his 5-hectoliter brewhouse, Teo continues to provide draft beer for his pub and bottled specialties for fortunate beer sellers around the world.

The Beers of La Baladin

Isaac—Birra Bianca, a Belgian-style wheat beer made with unmalted wheat grown by Teo's mother and father, with the unique addition of whole sweet oranges and coriander. It's well-balanced, with low hop flavor and a refreshing lemon-orange-citrus theme complemented by a lively yet subtle coriander aroma and flavor. Bottle-conditioned in uniquely styled champagne bottles, *Isaac* is named after Teo's then two-year old. What makes this beer uniquely Teo's is homegrown unmalted wheat, whole sweet oranges, English ale yeast and bottle conditioning.

Super Baladin—The brewpub's strongest seller. Beer sales jumped 300 percent after its introduction. At 8 percent alcohol, this bottle-conditioned ale is reminiscent of a Belgian-style Dubbel, but as all Teo's beers are made with English-style ale yeasts, Belgian fruitiness is minimal, resulting in a smooth, clean taste with accents on malt and hops rather than on fermentation esters and fruity alcohols.

Niña—On draft, this brew has a similar profile to an English-style bitter, with a twist—the hop aroma is floral and German in origin! It is dispensed with nitrogen. The result represents an extraordinary combination of traditions.

La Blonde du Baladin—A well-attenuated golden ale with high drinkability and the inviting floral character of German Hersbrucker Hallertau and Spalt hops. The wort is caramelized by a very long boiling time, resulting in a rich, caramel-like malt character that is suggestive of butterscotch but is rather toffeelike. A beer judge could easily mistake this toffee character for diacetyl, but it isn't so. Travel the world and you'd be hard pressed to find this light ale's equal.

Brune du Baladin—Actually, what I might call "Italian Stout." It has a profile similar to that of Guinness but, as Teo emphasized, with milder intentions. Deep, dark and complex, it's brewed with a combination of five different malts yet with no roasted barley. You think stout, but then who cares—it goes down smoothly.

Noel—Teo's wonderfully complex creation that defies categorizing. Bottle conditioned at 9 percent alcohol, it presents a complex and interwoven balance of cocoa and fruitiness, while maintaining its relative dryness on the palate. This is a very special brew with very special packaging. Remember: this is strong brown ale with English ale yeast.

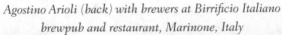

Birrificio Italiano

JUST EAST of Turin (*Torino*), in Marinone outside of Como, Agostino Arioli and his brother Stefano founded the Birrificio Italiano brewpub and restaurant in 1997 with eight other partners. In two years, production grew from 400 hectoliters to 700 hectoliters. All beers are sold only from the pub and restaurant. Most are bottom-fermented. Agostino designed and had his

Agostino Arioli (back) with brewers at Birrificio Italiano
brewpub and restaurant, Marinone, Italy

original 3 hectoliter brewhouse built locally. A new 6 hectoliter system has been installed since then. All his beers are uniquely Italian—they are variations on traditional themes. Most beers at Birrificio Italiano are lagers with nicknames and a story, served on draft or bottled (some bottle-conditioned).

The Beers of Birrificio Italiano

Prima—(L' ingannatrice—the cheater, "who is like a woman who is a liar—beware") This beer has a mild taste, so you may think it is light, but it is 6 percent alcohol. A soft caramel personality dominates this popular brown lager. At first you might think of it as German Dunkel style, but a sweet twist of crème caramel is often used to describe its qualities, so close to butterscotch but most definitely not. The beer does have caramel malts, but Agostino knows that it is the extra boil time that gives this heady lager its special character. Caramunich, carapils, Munich and pils malts are used to brew this complex, well-balanced beer.

Amber Shock—(L' impevedible—"that which is unexpected") At 7 percent alcohol, this beer is lager fermented and lager bottle-conditioned. It's available only in elegant 1-liter bottle-conditioned packages for the customer who comes to the brewery. It is considered the brewery's most special beer and the most "mythical," because it isn't always available. A full-malt and toffeelike flavor creates the overture, followed by a complementary fruity rose, apricot and cherry aroma and flavor. The beer has a slight sulfur note in the aroma, but within a few minutes of breathing after opening, the sulfur notes dissipate. The result is a remarkably playful and complex beer that is light on the palate. It is a lager, yet because of its higher alcohol and bottle conditioning it develops nontypical fruit character.

Tipo Pils—(Autoconscienza—"the self-consciousness; when you finish drinking it you will have reached a state of self-consciousness") With a rich, dense head, this is every bit in the clean, crisp, refreshing and flavorful tradition of a Bavarian-style pilsener—brewed south of the Alps, leaving you wondering if you've gone to another heaven.

Bibock—(La Prepotenza—"strength and power as from a goat; enabling one to do what they want to do"; Agostino encourages you to "get in touch with the Bibock") This is an Italian creation, an amber "Italian bock." It's 6.2 percent alcohol, with more hops than a traditional bock, along with the rich maltiness usually evident in the stronger German version. You wouldn't be able to call it a bock in Germany, but then again, this is Italy. Its aroma is reminiscent of fresh rising bread dough, and its maltiness is complemented with a unique apricot character in both flavor and aroma. German Hallertau and Perle hops are used for aroma.

Weiss Beer—(*L' Mirage*—"a dream of a woman taking a bath in a tub of Weiss beer," explains Agostino.) This seasonal brew was not available when I was there.

Dunkel Weizen—(*Voo Du*—*L' Originia*—"the original because all original styles were dark") This seasonal brew was not available when I was there.

2000—(*La Birra Terzo Millennio*—"the beer of the third millennium") At 6.5 percent alcohol, this is currently Birrificio Italiano's only ale, though, as in Bavarian Weizenbier tradition (but using English ale yeast), it is bottle-conditioned with lager yeast. It's a light brown ale, plumlike and dry, with a soft, well-balanced cocoa and roasted malt character. The beer is served in a special large, robust glass requiring two hands to carry the precious liquid forward to the mouth—most definitely a glass with purpose, to drink deliberately with depth and balance . . . This is Italian beer poetry and "moves towards the new millennium for Italian beer," proclaimed Agostino.

Agostino's departing wisdom: *"Semel in Anno Lecit Insanire"*—Once a year it is okay to be crazy. "At least once a year," he emphasized.

Birrificio Lambrate

EAST OF THE CITY CENTER of Milan (*Milano*) resides a sparkling jewel of a brewpub that features absolutely top-quality beers along with regional specialty foods purchased fresh from the producers. Fresh beer is brewed in the adjacent building. The Skunky Brewpub serves fresh beers brewed by partner-owners Davide Sangiorgi and Rosa Gravina. The Birrificio Lambrate brewing company was founded in 1996 near the heart of Milan.

They brew about 1,500 hectoliters of top-fermented ales annually, served in nearby restaurants and at their own brewpub. Young students, businesspeople, artists and beer enthusiasts flock to this warm, bohemian-style bar to enjoy fresh food and an assortment of ales that reflect the creative and poetic spirit of the Italian brewery renaissance.

The Beers of Birrificio Lambrate

The beers at Birrificio Lambrate are all named after places or cultural elements in the Milan area.

Montestella—An extraordinary hoppy, well-balanced blond ale. At 30 bittering units, the hop flavor of Hallertauer, Hersbrucker and Spalt contribute a wonderful balance to the Pilsener malt base. This is world-class ale, yet lager-like in its smoothness. All the brewery's ales are brewed with dry "English" ale yeast, with world-class results.

Lambrate—Meaning "amber," this ale is strong at 7 percent alcohol. Its overall impression is sweet, with malt flavor being more memorable than hops. It's an excellent, well-balanced ale with suggestions of fruitiness.

Santàmbroeus—A pale 7 percent alcohol ale brewed with 5 percent wheat malt; the balance is brewed with pils malt. A strong malty aroma and flavor dominate. Though it's somewhat "bock"-like, remember, it's an ale.

Porpora—Referred to as a red beer, but more indicative of brown ale at 6.3 percent alcohol. It has evident malty and roast malt characters with no astringency and good balance and is relatively dry. Hop flavors are notable but not assertive.

Ghisa—*Ghisa* is Milanese slang for "street police," in reference to the black uniform they wear. I never had anything quite like this before visiting Birrificio Lambrate. It's a unique, dark, smoke-flavored beer using 30 percent German beechwood-smoked malt, Munich melanoidan malt, caramel and (black huskless) Carafa malts. With 6.2 percent alcohol, this beer is surprisingly smooth in body and flavor. The smoke flavor is well balanced; the dark and toasted malts offer a velvety texture. This smoke-flavored ale is not assertively hopped and is smooth with excellent drinkability. It is both poetry and balance.

POETIC BRIGHELLA ITALIAN-BELGIAN-GERMAN-ENGLISH-AMERICAN ALE

Here's a clear shot at recreating one of the most unusual beers I experienced on my first tour of Italian breweries. As noted above, it is a golden, very fruity ale reminiscent of Belgian Flanders–style old brown ales. This recipe can be found on page 340.

Brighella—Birrificio Lambrate's Christmas beer, at 8 percent alcohol. It's a golden, very fruity ale reminiscent of Belgian Flanders–style old brown ales. Here is expressed the epitome of Italian beer poetry and creativity. The use of 10 percent German-made *sauer* malt is what makes Brighella unique. I have never heard of this being done elsewhere. The *sauer* malt (soured by natural lactic fermentation, often used in very small percentages by German brewers in order to naturally acidify brewing water) contributes remarkably soft acidity without the often overpowering complexity of bacterially fermented Belgian ales, from which this beer's pedigree emerged. Dried English ale yeast is used in this brew, as it is in all of their beers.

INDEED, THE craft brewers of Italy to whom I was introduced in 2000 were unlike any other craft brewers in the world. The combination of their romantic culture, exquisite regional cuisine, respect for their wine heritage and creative brewing techniques gives them the distinction of being the poets of the brewing industry. Currently they are few, but their ranks are growing. The world will be a far better place when the brewing poets of Italy emerge in numbers and offer their quality creations alongside all the other wonderful things Italy has to offer.

The Piozzo Experiment: The Secret Life of Beer La Baladin, Piozzo, Italy

EINSTEIN ONCE SAID, "There are two ways to live your life. One is as though nothing is a miracle. The other is as though everything is a miracle."

There are many facets of beer and brewing that go far beyond art and science. They are the mysteries and miracles. These are the things that intrigue me the most. I enjoy being able to appreciate them even though I don't fully understand them.

Whenever I brew, I still "feel" the beer and am absolutely certain the beer knows that I care. So often I am asked about the difference between home-brewed and microbrewed beer and mass-produced beer. I am dead serious when I say the difference has something to do with the caring spirit that a homebrewer or microbrewer is able to transmit to the very nature of the wort and the care of yeast and fermentation. I'm not talking about scientific care but a frame of mind, which is transmitted. Who can deny that attitude of mind affects humans and their performance?

I've thought to myself, what about other living organisms? It is quite common knowledge that all living organisms respond to a variety of stimuli. Brewing scientists measure the effects of heat, time, pressure, motion and other forms of stress on yeast. The stream of activities is adjusted accordingly to produce beer as efficiently as possible with the desired qualities. This is what most professional brewers do to earn a living.

Homebrewers do not earn a living from making beer. For them, beer is simply a matter of pride and caring. Money and its impact on efficiency are less relevant. Though they consider the science of brewing, homebrewers are closer to and more accepting of the mysteries of brewing.

There is an Italian brewer who brews craft beers in the tiny hilltop village of Piozzo. On a second visit to La Baladin and Teo Musso's brewhouse and fermentation area, a small group of American craft brewers and I marveled at Teo's latest project. He had fitted his fermentation tanks with giant head-phones. Piping in music for several hours a day, Teo had recently embarked on a two-year experiment attempting to discover aspects of "the secret life of beer."

First impressions may elicit the reaction that this is preposterous. Yet Teo is serious, and he is not alone. There are scientists and healers throughout the world who would recognize that Teo might be on to something. Music is not only of a powerful essence in the lives of people, but it has also been a proven factor in the health of plants and other living organisms.

Just before I sat down to write of my experience and thoughts of the little village brewery in Piozzo, I remembered a book about music that author and acquaintance Don Campbell had given me a few years ago called *The Mozart Effect* (Avon Books, 1997). I had never read it, and now I wasn't about to tackle its 350-plus pages. I took it off my shelf for a quick look. I did not thumb through its pages. I magically opened it directly to page 82 and a heading entitled "Sonic Bloom." A brief introduction explored the use of music to enhance plant growth.

Headphones on the tanks; music for yeast

My fingers anticipated that there must be more background and support for the experiment in Piozzo. I then magically turned to page 64, with the heading "How Music Affects Us: A Medley." George Gershwin is quoted: "Music sets up a certain vibration which unquestionably results in a physical reaction. Eventually the proper vibration for every person will be found and utilized."

In the tiny village of Piozzo, Teo Musso embarked on an experiment no brewing scientist would dare risk his reputation on. "Yeast is a living animal. Why shouldn't it be affected by music as other living organisms are?" Teo explains quite emphatically, nurturing the legitimacy of what at first appears to be an exercise in brewing insanity. But then, with contemplation . . .

PIOZZO ITALIAN PALE ALE

While the secret life of beer will forever remain mysterious, there is nothing mysterious about the simplicity and greatness of this India pale ale. Might I suggest exposing this beer to Indian sitar music throughout fermentation and cellaring? At the very least, savor its flavor while listening to music. This recipe can be found on page 342.

There are significant implications to Teo's ideas. Perhaps his experiments and measurements will be inconclusive. Perhaps they will be enlightening. Whatever the results of the Piozzo Experiment, I hope it inspires an ongoing appreciation of yeast. I hope it inspires a variety of perspectives. Yeast is a sensitive living organism that we know very little about. I appreciate the guidance brewing science has given to me as a brewer. It has helped improve my beer. But without appreciation of the mysteries of yeast and the life processes involving beer, all the science in the world is a bunch of hooey.

Islandic Vellosdricke
Gotland Island, Sweden

NEVER EVER EVER EVER trust a homebrewer who says, "This is the last beer we're going to taste." NEVER EVER in a million years EVER!

I LEARNED MANY YEARS AGO that homesick Swedes brought the dandelion to America. Now I could scarcely doubt this as we drove past expansive fields yellow with carpets of dandelions blazing against a startlingly blue springtime sky on the island of Gotland. Surrounded by the Baltic Sea, Gotland is a small island, about 25 miles wide and 50 miles long, situated off the southeast coast of Sweden. There, dense stands of birch and pine trees accent flowering trees and red, white, yellow and blue springtime tulips and daffodils. The sea is dark blue and cold; the winds are brisk.

Sixty-four-year-old Vello Noodapera greeted Swedish Homebrewing Society member Jesper Schmidt and me at the Gotland airport. We were both curious about the legendary beer of Gotland Island. Overwhelmed by the excitement of our arrival, Vello immediately set the record straight: "Do you know what day is today?" Was it something special? I didn't know, and with a thirsty smile I asked him to explain. "It is Folknykterhetens Dag, which roughly translates to 'a day of people's soberness.'" My god, I had arrived on a national day of abstinence! I thought to myself, "Shit! Get a grip, Charlie! You might get off on smelling the dandelions." But Vello quickly confided with a hearty laugh, ". . . but we'll ignore it."

We were on our way to Vello's small farm and later to Sweden's first brewpub (it had officially opened only two weeks before my arrival), the Virungs

Bryggeri. My quest was to discover the mysteries of the island's special beer, Gotlandsdricke. The 45-minute drive along scenic and winding roads was interrupted briefly as we stopped at a roadside parking area. It may have been 10 in the morning, but it was not too early for a homebrew. At this time of year the sun stubbornly sets late anyway. Up popped the trunk of Vello's Saab and within seconds Jesper, Vello and I were toasting the occasion with a mugful of delicious ale, brewed with the local baker's yeast. I knew I was about to have my horizons broadened.

I had no idea how wonderful this day was about to become. As we approached the farm, I noticed in the distance an American flag flying high on a pole. Vello proudly explained, "That is in your honor, Charlie. It flies near my house and home brewery today." Off on the side-wall of a large red barn, a skillfully carved and painted sign proclaimed "The Ardre Brygg" (Ardre Brewery). From the room behind that wall emerged the simple mash, lauter and brewing kettles from which Vello proudly brewed his beer. From home-fashioned tubs and adapted pieces of dairy equipment, Vello Noodapera brewed some of the best damn beer I had in all of Europe. What I was particularly interested in was the specialty of the island, Gotlandsdricke, ale brewed with smoked malt, hops, juniper branches, bread yeast and water.

Vello Noodapera with his brewery kettle and Gotlandsdricke

Now it would be simple to assume that one could learn and brew this unique beer by following a recipe, but I discovered, as with all traditional beers, that if one wishes to come close to authenticity, it is absolutely imperative to experience it firsthand—and in your hand. I did. From this experience I came away with a feeling of admiration for a beer loved by the people who make it.

Gotlandsdricke is brewed everywhere on this tiny island. It is estimated that 5,000 hectoliters of this beer is homebrewed here by its 50,000 residents. That's 10 liters homebrewed for every man, woman and child on the island. The island is self-sufficient, with its own barley, hops, malt houses and yeast strains.

Dan Andersson, one of Vello's brewing neighbors, soon arrived for this occasion with a most recent batch of Gotlandsdricke. I drooled with anticipation, watching amazed as this amber nectar was poured from a wooden vessel into a magnificent mug made from juniper wood. The rich, creamy head and the aromatics from the juniper resulted in love at first sip. Wow, was this stuff ever good! A huge pile of birchwood logs caught my eye and I asked whether the malt was smoked with birch with the bark left on. They confirmed my speculation: "Yes, we leave the bark on the wood when we smoke the malt." No small detail, since birch bark itself has its own unique qualities. "But everyone makes their own style of Gotlandsdricke," Jesper translated to me from a side conversation going on in Swedish. Details, details. How did they do it? Freshly cut juniper (note: juniper is not the same as cedar) branches are boiled in water for about two hours to make an aromatic amber broth. I noted that the juniper was of the variety that is usually low growing and difficult to handle because of the very thorny nature of the needles (I immediately recalled seeing these types of bushes growing in home gardens and on the mountains of my home state, Colorado).

This is the brewing liquor, which is added to crushed malted barley. Thirty percent is malt dried from the heat and smoke of burning birch logs. The remaining malt is the brewer's preference, consisting mostly of pale lager-type malt. Some of the amber water is reserved for sparging. The lauter vessel and bottom screen is lined with more freshly cut boughs of juniper. The mash is then poured into the lauter vessel and sparged (rinsing the grains with hot water), and sweet aromatic malt extract is drawn off the bottom. In the kettle local hops are usually used, though the more experienced homebrewers were now making the effort to import German-grown varieties.

When the mash is cool, what seemed to be an infinitesimal amount of baker's yeast is added. At Vello's brewery, about one square centimeter of cake yeast was used for a 100-liter (about 25 gallons) batch. The beer was snorting, foaming and in full fermentation within six hours. I didn't understand the significance of the careful utilization of yeast until after I visited the brewpub in the nearby village, where Gotlandsdricke also was made. Added to 800 liters (about 200 gallons) of fresh wort was a mere 25 grams (less than one ounce) of cake yeast. This is the equivalent of using a half-ounce of dried yeast for a 200-gallon batch of beer! Infinitesimal by brewing science standards, but it worked well.

Vello Noodapera, Gotland

Someone mentioned, "We tried using cultured brewing yeasts, but the quality was not the same." When asked why so little yeast was used, no one seemed to have a scientific explanation. Though I now postulate that because this yeast is so active, a small amount is desirable to reduce the quantity of heat generated during the initial fermentation. With greater amounts of yeast, the explosive activity would generate heat that might in turn cause the yeast to produce undesirable flavor compounds, typical of high-temperature fermentations. The relatively cool environment and viability of this yeast produced a balance of flavors the people of Gotland Island had learned to love.

At Vello and Dan's homebrewery recordkeeping was not a habit, but from my senses I surmised they brewed a beer at 1.050 (12.5 degrees B) original gravity. Color was about 14 SRM, and the hop character of Hallertauer contributed about 30 units of bitterness. Their Gotlandsdricke had a fruity and pleasant juniper taste and a smooth, distinctive smoky flavor. But friendly rivalries existed among Gotland's homebrewers, and everyone had his own secret recipe and styles: sweet, bitter, strong, weak, dark, pale, sour, with more or less smoke and juniper. We finished Vello and Dan's beer and continued our daylong expedition to Virungs Bryggeri, the island's brewery/brewpub in the small village of Romakloster. In fact, the small cottage and barn compound seemed to be the entire village. There we visited Lillis Svärd and his family, who raise sheep, run a smokehouse and meat house and operate a small malt house, brewery and attached inn. Lillis malts his own barley and was experimenting with growing and malting wheat and spelt.

A lightly smoked (relatively speaking) version of Gotlandsdricke was brewed using 40 percent lightly smoked malt along with some Munich malt bought from a commercial malt house. Lillis's other beer is called Drog öl, brewed with pale and Munich malt and honey. Lillis had been a homebrewer for the past ten years and had recently gone commercial. Though he was working on a system with which to bottle his beers, you would have had to be

VELLO'S GOTLANDSDRICKE

The fruity and refreshing character of juniper boughs and berries combined with the mellow warmth of gently smoked malt emerge as a magical combination. It is not without reason this centuries-old beer tradition remains regionally popular. If you have access to fresh juniper, you can recreate this Scandinavian experience at home. The recipe can be found on page 345.

there to experience the finest essence of his craft. Lillis has since closed his brewery in pursuit of developing concrete tepees, but I can't imagine he has stopped homebrewing.

I believe that as you brew your next batch of beer, whatever your style might be, Lillis and Vello will be tending their most recent batch of Gotlandsdricke. I fell in love with the stuff and was very pleased with how my first homebrewed batch turned out. I did have a little help, since Lillis gave me about 10 pounds of birch-smoked malt he had made, but you can produce your own style of "dricke" using ingredients locally available. Why? Because you're a homebrewer and microbrewer.

And if you can drink it out of a wooden juniper mug, please do. It's simply wonderful.

CHAPTER 9

Flights of the Imagination—
Eccentric, Creative and Wild
The Netherlands and Belgium

"Geezus I'm blasted. No, not wasted. Blasted. Do I get combat pay for this trip? Everyone seems to want to feed me three times more than I could possibly eat and then pour me five times more than I can possibly drink. I am truly saturated. HELP! I mean having a beer at 10 a.m. is one thing but continuing until 1 or 2 A.M. one after another and knowing that the next day begins at 7 A.M. is an awesome thing to consider."

—FROM MY TRAVEL JOURNAL, MAY 1995,
THE YEAR I VISITED THE NETHERLANDS AND BELGIUM.

Long Days' Journeys into Nights

PERHAPS there is no country in the world more under-discovered and under-recognized for its beer culture than the Netherlands. Amsterdam is both a magnificently beautiful and wild city. Explore its streets and alleys with beer in mind and you will discover brewpubs, world-class beer bars/cafés and memorable beers. Go beyond the city limits to the countryside towns and villages and you will begin to realize the beer passion homebrewers and microbrewers have embraced as their own. There is much more to Holland than

Heineken. My introduction began in the small town of Vllesingen, the Netherlands, with beer, homebrew, microbrew, cider, liqueur, distilling, herbal, horticulture and wine master Jan Van Schaik.

Jan has a small goatee and trim mustache, reminding me of photographs I've seen of Louis Pasteur. I learn that Jan frequently gives lectures about Pasteur, one of his favorite scientists and heroes. He has written numerous books on homebrewing, wine, cider and distilling. He not only is an expert at all things alcohol, but has helped lobby the Dutch legislature to legalize home distilling and established the Dutch beer judge program. Born in 1936, Jan continues to love the finer aspects of alcohol, but seems to overflow with a passion for beer more than anything else.

He lives with his wife, Irma, in the small coastal village of Vllesingen, on the most southwesterly tip of the Netherlands. His garage is an experience, magnificent to behold, filled with herbs, spices, brewing ingredients and an unfathomable collection of homemade beer, wine, brandy and liqueur.

Within hours of my arrival from Colorado, Jan whisked me away to a truly micro microbrewery, the Scheldebrouwerj in the village of 'S Gravenpolder/Bergen op Zoon. These guys impressed as the epitome of true homebrewers. Their hand-built microbrewery, with tiled floors and walls, is in immaculate order. They were brewing 10 hectoliters (about 265 gallons) a week—only on the weekends. The owner, Kaees Loenhout, was a social worker involved with the child protection board by week, brewing on the weekends with his assistant, Louis Spoelstra. Louis's day job was as an oil refinery cracker, electrician and mechanic; he had a keen interest in engines, steam engineering and electronic gadgeteering. The brewery has grown a little since my visit in

Jan Van Schaik, the Netherlands

1995, but they continue to brew with skill and passion as only original home-brewers can do. Their beers were unlike anything I had ever had.

The first thought that went through my mind was that American micro-breweries have a lot to discover when it comes to beer character. They made a beer called De Zeezuiper Natuurbier, a 7.5 percent top-fermented bottle-conditioned ale with 5 to 10 percent corn or maize, malt, coriander, curaçao peel and woodruff, all deliciously blanketed with an unbelievable creamy, dense head. They referred to their yeast as Belgian "zampus." Their hopping rates were low at 20 bittering units, but the beers wonderfully impacted my palate as though they had 30 units of hop bitterness. De Zeezuiper is fermented for 10 days, then cold "lagered" or aged for three weeks before bottling. The bottles are conditioned at warmer temperatures for 10 days before being released from their tiny microbrewery. Whew! What a beer!

Brewer and founder Kaees Loenhout of the Scheldebrouwerj

They also brewed a Winter-bier with 8.5 percent alcohol, made with pilsener, amber, crystal and caramel malts. With the skillful addition and balance of cinnamon, coriander, Belgian candi sugar, Czech Saaz and German Hersbrucker hops, this ale becomes indescribably awesome and unlike anything I've ever had by any American home-brewer or microbrewer.

The repertoire of beers went on. They have made a 6.5 percent (low-alcohol beer!) called Lamme Goedzak, as well as a Liberation 1945–1995 Teugs Teugje Meibok Beer. How did they develop all this brewing knowledge? As homebrewers first, but not without some professional training. Kaees went to the University of Ghent for three years of Sundays to study brewing. Every Sunday morning he would commute to Ghent to attend classes. What he has learned he imparts to others as a beer judge and beer judge teacher.

MUG **IS THE DUTCH WORD** for mosquito. It is also the name of one of the most charming pub-restaurants in the Netherlands and Jan's favorite local specialty beer bar. A tiny place and easy to miss, De Mug is wonderfully nestled in the village of Middelburg only a 10-minute drive from Vllesingen. De Mug's regularly published newsletter features news of the beers they offer and events they sponsor. One can't help notice the abundance of candles and large casks of old medium sherry, dry Madeira and rich ruby port behind the "brown" bar, so called because of its ambience. Bottles of Tabasco sauce are tucked away amidst the carved wooden nooks and crannies and an American Express sticker can be seen on the window, but that's as far as 1995 seemed to express itself, except for the selection of 64 classic Dutch and Belgium beers (though they did have Murphy's and Guinness stout and Paulaner Salvator doppelbock as well). Heineken is offered, but it isn't the Heineken light lager the rest of the world knows; rather rare bottles of Heineken "Oud Bruin" and Amstel "Meibok" were offered as world classics.

The pub was established in 1973. Barend Midavaine, the owner, really loves what he is doing—and it shows. At De Mug I met folks who make beer, sell beer, think beer and drink beer. Barend's wife is a homebrewer. Need I say more about the heart and authenticity of this tiny bar near the Zeeland coast?

I enjoyed a few beers, including a Trappist-brewed Westvleteren and a Rochefort. I savored their complexity and freshness, thinking that this was the finale for the day's visits, but I was wrong.

Nearby in the small village of Hilvarenbeek, we approached an old brick building. I was taken behind its unassuming garage door. I glanced to the side and noted that the iron gate had a hop motif designed into one its supporting posts. Inside this unassuming brick building is a brewery that has been turned into a working museum. The two-hectoliter (53 gallons) Stichting Museumbrouwerij De Roos brewhouse, built in 1850, was hidden from the Germans during World War II and thus saved from being scrapped for war materials. The original Stichting De Roos Brewery was a top-fermenting ale brewery, one of but a few breweries that did not change its beer to the more popular lager style. Harrie de Leijer De Roos, son of the founding grandfather, only recently renovated the brewery premises. At the time of our visit he had the support of the local city council for plans on offering to the local homebrew club an opportunity to brew at this historic brewery museum.

Upon returning to Jan and Irma's home we took off our street shoes and slipped into wooden Dutch shoes to roam around the soggy yard and into the crammed floor-to-ceiling garage. We began tasting Jan's various liqueurs, including a homemade Scottish Drambuie indistinguishable from the real thing and a mystery liqueur whose origins Jan asked me to guess. I tasted vanilla, cocoa, coffee and Curaçao. But Jan flabbergasted me when he confided that he had hand roasted his own cocoa beans, saying, "You really can't get the really true taste of cocoa unless you roast your own beans. They were very difficult to find, but I did."

We had dinner, and the beer, brandy and stories continued. I learned that Holland's only Trappist monastery (De Schaapskoot) would be hosting the next year's Dutch National Homebrew Championship and would brew a special beer in honor of homebrewing. Meanwhile I prepared for another day's adventures with a short night's sleep.

DE VAETE BROUWERIJ in Lewedorpwas was a microbrewery I visited, conceived by yet two more homebrewers. Located at the end of a long dirt road running alongside a canal in an extremely small farmer's shed. Inspired by their 10 years of homebrewing, Ton de Bruin and Alexander Roovers had become weekend microbrewers, producing about 25 gallons at a time. Keeping 30 different strains of yeast on culture, they fermented their Plder Blondje, Tripel, Winterbier, pale ale, Dubbel and Pa's Best in five-gallon carboys. By trade, Ton is a laboratory technician and Alexander a microbiology technician. Their annual production at the time of my visit was about 660 gallons a year. All for the love of beer.

Homebrewing activity in the Netherlands is a relatively small part of the beer landscape, but the few dozen homebrew clubs throughout the country have a great impact on beer education and awareness. Each of the clubs inspires homebrewers with beers and the passion of camaraderie. It is clearly evident that their gatherings are about both beer and family. The next evening we joined about 40 people in a small village community center. I talked about homebrewing and beer judging in America. We then all turned our focus on Meibocks (May/Maibocks), a light-colored German-style strong, malty bock beer that the Dutch have embraced as their own. Tasting six commercial Dutch Meibocks and then 12 homebrewed Meibocks, we judged and chose a winner.

IN AMSTERDAM we met 40 beer judges. This was a Dutch Beer Judges Guild special field trip to visit a brewpub, drink beer, go on a walking tour of

Amsterdam brewery sites, drink beer, attend a seminar and, of course, drink beer. These guys are thrifty when it comes to non-alcoholic endeavors. I was tagging along. We stayed at a $10-a-night youth hostel in the center of one of the diciest areas of Amsterdam. There must have been several hundred travelers bunking in the dormitory-style accommodation. I was in Room 7 with at least 60 guys. Despite all the wonderful beer we had indulged in, I had difficulty sleeping. What does a pod of 30 hippos belching and farting on the riverbanks of the Zambezi sound like? This was an experience to be forgotten, but nonethess it was being experienced at least once in my life. Good beer helped. The sound of 50 men snoring started kind of low key with about 10 or 12 snoring randomly. By 2 A.M. there were at least 30 or 40 all snoring their way to wherever their dreams were taking them. But the most interesting thing was that by about 3 A.M. they had all cycled into snoring in unison. I was not hallucinating—the effects of alcohol had worn off by that time. I had difficulty believing what I was hearing: 59 Dutchmen snoring in harmony, lending a spooky ambience to the darkness of the room, lit by one lonely and beckoning exit sign.

I don't know how much any of you know about Amsterdam, but, well, shall we say, it can get pretty damned weird. Strange-looking people, the smell of legalized hashish and marijuana wafting its way out of numerous street cafés. And hookers, their whorehouses lining the alleys and side streets. It was in this atmosphere that we started our two-hour morning brewery tour. While the guide was explaining the sights in Dutch, all these beer guys were focused on was the one building we were told used to be a brewery 100 years ago. It looked like a brick building to me. Meanwhile in my sleep-deprived state, I did not believe what I was seeing in the picture windows on either side of the historic brewery site. As our guide was pointing out architectural features, I was looking across the canal and up the street. It was only about 9 A.M., but there were "ladies" shaking their booties, winking and carrying on in all manners. Farther down the street were dozens of the most bizarre sex shops I'd ever seen. Meanwhile, our guide was rambling on about the brewer in 1789 and the beer and the pubs. Junkies (though friendly ones at that) were staggering around amongst us and the thousands and thousands of other well-to-do tourists, young and old, shopping for chocolates, teacups, T-shirts, postcards and the weirdest-looking dildos I've never even imagined!

My tour of the Netherlands was winding down. I took a pass on a tour of the newly opened microdistillery pub in Amsterdam in the hope of returning to Vllesingen in time for a decent night's sleep. But that was not to be the

---

ZEEZUIPER SPICED NEDERLANDER STRONG ALE

Formulated from my tasting notes and conversations with the brewer, this ale is an effusive expression of creativity on the brewer's part. It's herbal, fruity, mellow yet zesty, with a rich, creamy head. With a potentially head-banging 7.5 percent alcohol, it is to be enjoyed in moderation with friends and on special occasions. A people pleaser and conversation piece. This recipe can be found on page 348.

---

case, as immediately upon our return to Jan and Irma's home we explored the finer points of homemade Calvados and Poire (Pear) Williams brandy.

The next morning we caught the early-morning ferry to Belgium, but not before stopping at one last Dutch microbrewery—De Halve Maan Bier-brouwerij in Hulst, located in a old train station. By 11 A.M. I was sacked out on the ferry and dreaming of the beer and adventures that awaited.

The Mad Brewer of Esen

DE DOULLE BROUWERS (The Mad Brewers) is a small microbrew-ery in the picturesque town of Esen, Belgium. It is legendary among Belgian beer enthusiasts. I was still traveling with the guiding enthusiasm of Jan Van Schaik for one final day. De Doulle Brouwers was our first stop. The extremes, exceptions and the fantastic lengths to which microbrewers will go in order to achieve their dreams and produce the most exceptional beers on Planet Beer never cease to amaze me. De Doulle Brouwers is one of the most admirable brewery operations I have had the pleasure to witness. Not because of the beer or the equipment, but because of the single own-er/employee who operates this "mad" brewery. Chris Herteleer is a man who seems to have kept his priorities in balance. An architect and graphic de-signer, he also paints watercolors and loves brewing beer.

Starting out as a homebrewer, Chris managed to buy a brewery that was founded in 1842. When I visited in 1995 he was still using the original brew-house equipment. He had recently expanded, installing a bottle washer and bottling line. In keeping with his balanced lifestyle, he built a picturesque and artfully designed café, which reminds one of a large, airy, well-lit loft with tables, a bar and a large outdoor deck overlooking green pastures and very contented cows.

Chris brewed once a week (40 times a year, for a total of about 1,200 hectoliters or about 1,000 barrels), working on other operations at the brewery about three days a week. He is the sole employee/owner (except when bottling). His is another story of a passionate homebrewer gone pro. But Chris has also managed to balance the brewery operations with his other life interests.

Obviously, production is limited. Chris sells all he can make at a good price, despite a zero-dollar marketing budget. His most popular beers, some of which are exported to the United States, are:

Oerbier (**Crazy Beer**)—A Belgian Flanders–style strong brown ale at original gravity of 1.100 at 7½ percent alcohol. It uses six malts, three hops and candi sugar and is bottle-conditioned.

Bos Keun (**Easter Bunny**)—A seasonal blanche (pale) beer with a starting gravity of about 1.090 and alcohol of 8 percent. There is some honey used.

Ara Bier—A beer for summer. Starting gravity is at 1.080, with an alcohol content of 8 percent.

Stille Nacht (**Silent Night**)—A very strong Christmas beer, with an incredibly high original gravity at 1.120 and 9 percent alcohol. It is considered one of his classic beers.

Dulle Teve—I can't recall an explanation for the label Chris gave me, but judging from that label and what memory I had left after departing, I think *dulle teve* means mother-in-law. Alcohol is at 10 percent!

After the tour we were joined by Leuven microbrewer Steven Pauwels (now the head brewer at Boulevard Brewing Company, Kansas City) and former American Homebrewers Association vice president Grosvenor Merle-Smith. We entered a dark and damp cellar. It is where Chris Herteleer keeps his special "vintage" beers. We loaded up with a few cobweb-laced bottles that had barely legible labels and rusted bottle caps and headed up to the loft café. It was beer-tasting time.

We began by tasting a 12-year-old bottle prototype and aged Oerbier. It was at this point I discovered that Chris enjoyed an occasional cigar. I gave him a Cuban cigar I had reserved for a special occasion. This was a special

Chris Herteleer and his cellared "vintage" beers

occasion. It wasn't long before Chris disappeared and reemerged with a few more bottles of a beer brewed years earlier and subsequently aged in oak for two years. It was reminiscent of another world-classic Flanders-style sour brown ale, Rodenbach Gran Cru, but not quite as acetic. The beer kept coming!

There appeared in a fresh glass an 11.5 percent alcohol beer brewed 15 years earlier, in 1980. Chris confided that this was a beer he shares only with his best friends. It was a miraculously complex strong Belgian-style ale. We continued tasting other prototypes of his current beers. Finally, just when we thought we were finished (a big mistake—thinking one is ever finished tasting beer), a special corked dark beer brewed in 1980 appeared to climax the late afternoon. It was 12 percent alcohol, chocolaty, with a bit of fruity acidity, winey and very smooth indeed.

It was at that point I noticed two elderly women sitting on a sofa, their feet resting on a giant bellows. They were all smiles and at the end of their glass of a De Doulle Brouwers strong ale. They left quite peacefully, seeming to drift gracefully down the bright red, narrow spiral staircase.

There were once 3,223 breweries in the era of 1900s Belgium. Now there were fewer than 120. Mad brewers such as Chris may resurrect the strong and crazy brewing traditions of Belgium, if we let them. I was doing my part

Intoxication by Ara and "Bunny Rabbit"

and will continue to do so. We soon left—why, I don't quite remember, except it had something to do with dinner in Brugge. Oh, yes. Dinner, and of course more beer.

Brugge is quite a marvelous city, they tell me. We whisked through at such a fast pace and in such a delirious state of mind I don't recall seeing it. We tasted beers at nook-and-cranny pubs and cafés along the way to wherever we were being led. At one of Jan's favorite pubs, the de Garre, we enjoyed a beer (don't ask me to remember it at this point). Listening to classical music, I was just beginning to get comfortable when I was alerted that it was time to go. Was I going crazy, or was it the maniac fermented in all of us?

Down this street, around that corner and soon we were at Raspoetin, a friendly antique restaurant offering food and more beer. Halfway through our meal it was time to go again—to another café. How could we possibly have another beer? No, I wasn't really inebriated and was far from feeling drunk, but I had an intense feeling of saturation. My eyes were looking but not seeing. My ears were hearing but not listening. My mouth was drinking but not tasting. My hands were touching but not feeling. I had become a walking zombie in Brugge. As I walked, I could feel my eyes closing and my arms rising in front of me. I emitted low, rumbling belches. I imagined little children and mothers with babes in arms fleeing as I approached.

The pleasure of Belgian ale

I came to some senses just as we approached 't Brugs Beertje (the Special Beerhouse), serving more than 300 kinds of traditional and not-so-traditional Belgian beers. We had time to order a couple of more beers. This was Brugge; it all seemed to be foam at the top.

Jan, needing to catch the last ferryboat back to the Netherlands, drove us the last hour to Leuven before departing. Thanking him for his superhuman hospitality, Grosvenor and I checked into our hotel. We looked at each other, then at our watches, and together we glanced out the window to the well-lit town square. We weren't done yet. Not by a long shot. Walking down to the square, we sat down at an outdoor café. What did we do? It isn't hard to imagine. Without thinking, we automatically ordered another beer. Strangely, I couldn't even drink half of it.

Grosvenor left the next day, back to Ireland where he had been working. He admitted a certain degree of saturation.

But beer is my business, and I was working late. The next morning Steven Pauwels had planned another full day's itinerary for me. Our first visit was to the Westmalle Trappist Brewery in Malle. It is one of five authentic Trappist breweries in Belgium. Brewing 125,000 hectoliters of beer per year, the monks have decided that they do not wish to expand production any further. Situated in a pastoral setting, surrounded by fields of green and very contented cows (I began to note the common theme here with cows and brewers, or so it seems). Jan Adriaensens, the head brewer, explained the brewing system and confided that they will use the same yeast through 25 generations before starting a new culture. Their beers are primary fermented at 19 to 20 degrees C (66–68 F), then cooled to 8 degrees C (46.5 F), then aged for three to eight weeks depending on whether they are Dubbel or Tripel. They were using German Spalt,

Tettnanger and Hallertauer hops as well as Czech Saaz, Styrian Goldings and hop extract for bittering. Fresh doses of healthy yeast are added at bottling and refermented and conditioned in the bottle at 20 degrees C (68 F) for about three weeks, creating natural carbonation.

The popularity of Westmalle Trappist beers is encouraging to the brewers, but it is also the reason the beer does not get exported out of the region in great quantities. A fresh Westmalle Tripel or Dubbel is a treat to enjoy close to the source, where the passion is not diluted by age or distance.

At the end of our tour we enjoyed an Extra, a light, 5.5 percent alcohol beer brewed three or four times a year for the exclusive consumption of the 30 monks in the monastery.

Kettle and Crucifix, Westmalle Trappist Brewery

We ate lunch across the street at the Trappiste Café. From there, where did we go? Oh, of course, to visit another brewery. North, not too far from Westmalle and almost to the Netherlands to visit the Sterkens Brewery in Hoogstraten. Built in 1880, it is only about a 15,000-hectoliter (about 13,000 barrels) per year operation, a truly original microbrewery. Stan Sterken offered me beer after the tour. I accepted and immensely enjoyed their Poorter. Not to be confused with American- or British-style porter, this beer is velvety smooth, offering dark ale qualities not commonly brewed by other breweries large or small. Sterken's Poorter has a "round" nutty malt character without any of the caramel or crystal malt flavor you'd normally anticipate in an amber or brown ale. Furthermore, despite its coppery color there is virtually no roast malt astringency. There is a slight touch of banana character in the flavor, but not pronounced or anywhere near the level of many of the dark abbey-style ales of Belgium. Alcohol character was not evident in flavor, aroma or mouthfeel.

> ### SWITCH AND TOGGLES PREPOSTEROUS POORTER
>
> This is a prized recipe that achieves the smooth, "round" nutty malt charac-
> ter and complexity of Belgian malts, with a slight touch of banana charac-
> ter in the flavor. The recipe can be found on page 350.

The word *sublime* comes to mind. Honestly, I drank this beer scratching
my head and truly wondered how it possibly could have been made. My 25
years of brewing experience didn't help solve the mystery. What impressed
me the most was the notion that as a brewer I still could find the excitement
of learning about and brewing something new.

After a brief consultation with the importer, I was given direction: "It's the
malt." I learned on my adventures in Belgium how special Belgian malts can
be. I also learned to discern the character of Goldings hops and the important
role they play in many Belgian specialties.

World-Class Belgian Breweries
Belle Vue, Palm, Moortgat and Lindeman

IN OLDEN TIMES spontaneously fermenting lambic breweries prolifer-
ated throughout the area of Brussels. Now only a few remain, and even
fewer offer the traditional unsweetened styles so revered by beer enthusiasts,
who appreciate and savor the tart, acidic, fruity characters of this true "champagne" of beers.

The Belle Vue Brewery is the largest of the Belgian lambic breweries and
is now owned by the Belgian brewery giant Interbev. This was already the
case when I visited in 1995. Their lambics are often criticized for being
sweetened beyond traditional recognition, and some will not even consider
them true lambics.

It is true that the final product is so sweet that it bears very little resemblance to a true lambic. Its base is a true brewed lambic blended with juice
and sweeteners to suit what they perceive as consumer preference. But a tour
of the brewery reveals secrets that very few care to explore because of its
mega-brewery and sugared reputation.

Inside there are over 11,000 large wooden oak barrels fermenting and aging the real thing! I learned that Belle Vue's lambics are aged for years in these barrels. The small bungholes in the barrel remain open for years, during which fermentation foams out and over the barrel.

For the making of Kriek (Belgian cherry) lambic, ripe, whole cherries are harvested in July and added to six-month-fermented lambic. Fermentation resumes with the addition of natural sugar from the cherries and continues for an additional two to two and a half years. It is easy to tell which barrels have fermenting Kriek inside. There are a handful of birchwood twigs stuffed in and partially emerging from each oak barrel. Why? So that the pits don't emerge and clog the hole during the second fermentation, thus avoiding the danger of building pressure and exploding barrels. Eighty kilograms (about 175 pounds) of cherries are added to each 520-liter (about 550 gallons) oak barrel. That is a lot of cherries, and most of the production staff is busy stuffing cherries into bungholes during the two short weeks when the fruit is received at the brewery.

During the maturation process a moldlike skin from wild yeast forms a layer on the surface of the beer, inhibiting oxidation and evaporation. The entire process is natural, from the spontaneous fermentation begun by airborne yeast and bacteria. Spiders abound in the brewery. These are the sacred creatures of every lambic brewery; their webs capture bacteria-laden flies.

After a tour of the main cellars housing the oak barrels, we were led to a smaller cellar tucked away in a quiet corner of the brewery. There, I couldn't believe my eyes. Hundreds of champagne-type bottles were resting on their side, aging and refermenting lambic. What a comforting sight! I was treated to a bottle. This select aged lambic was exquisite and a real treat, but is rarely available. Most fascinating was an explanation of how to translate the sediment inside the bottle. Brewer Jacque De Keersmaecker explained how to "read" the sediment as he lifted a bottle lying on its side, carefully so as not to disturb the sediment. As the light silhouetted the sediment we could see that it had spread itself into a pattern, clinging to the side of the bottle. Jacque explained that there are two types of sediment along the side of the bottle. The dark, dense and somewhat oval-patterned sediment is bacterial; the featherlike sediment that extends up and down from the bacterial center is *Brettanomyces* yeast. The yeast sediment is actually formed in very thin, featherlike strands. You can tell how acidic the beer will be by how large the bacterial sediment is, and how influenced by *Brettanomyces* yeast the lambic will be by the extending patterns of featherlike fronds of sediment.

You can go to the brewery for a tour any time. In 1995 you could also bring your own container and fill it up directly from their unblended barrels— a little-known treat.

Three Breweries in a Day

THE 500,000-HECTOLITER PALM BREWERY is a small brewery
by some standards, but to taste their beers is to taste the soul of Belgian
beer passion. On a tour, the owner took a few of us to the side and showed us
the dried whole hops used in one of their special dry-hopped beers. We were
told that there is a crew of people who individually tear apart each hop cone
by hand before adding it to the aging tanks. I had my doubts until he confided
to us how wonderful American homebrewers are: "I have to thank the homebrew club in Los Angeles. I believe they are called the Maltose Falcons. They
advised me to use Styrian hops when dry hopping. I learned quite a bit from
my visit there."

On the second brewery tour of the day, the brewery Moortgat (brewer of
Duvel and other beers) was explained. Interestingly, this tour was indicative

*Roger Musche tapping gueuze lambic at
Lindeman Brewery*

of many of the other brewery
tours I and several other brewers
experienced while in Belgium.
There were few, if any, secrets
kept from us. The breweries
even handed out flow charts explaining every detail of ingredients, processes and equipment
for each of their brews. American brewers, small or otherwise,
rarely go into as much detail as
the Belgians. I supposed they really didn't feel they had anything
to hide. It would be virtually impossible to duplicate their beer
with another system and even if
you could, you would still be
missing the 100-plus years of
beer tradition and experience.

In the evening I was part of a
private tour of the Lindeman
Brewery, brewers of spontaneously fermented lambic beers

that are widely exported to America. My first impression: What a funked-out, totally bizarre brewery! Words cannot describe the funkiness of this farmhouse brewery just outside of Brussels. Roger Musche, whom I had met in Zimbabwe while enjoying my sorghum beer indulgence, was the head brewer. He greeted us with the compassion of a brewery father and excitedly led us through the inner depths of the brewery. The fermenting rooms smelled like an old urinal and had the ambience of an ancient water closet. As we sampled various batches of lambic from tanks and barrels, Roger tossed leftover beer onto the walls and floor to add to and feed the existing micro flora of bacteria and wild yeasts, so important to the brewery's success.

Tours uncompromisingly lead to the tasting room. We sat comfortably at wooden tables, the walls decorated with labels and posters outlining the history of the brewery. We tried their *kriek* (cherry), *peche* (peach), *framboise* (raspberry) and sweetened faro lambics. But it was unanimous among the invited that the best beers were the refermented gueuze lambic, no longer sold, and their cassis lambic, which was a failure in the marketplace. The most interesting "beer" was called "Tea Beer," actually a blend of sour fermented lambic and green tea.

When you have the opportunity to reciprocate beer for beer, it is a common courtesy to do so. Rarely have I had the opportunity to share my beers with brewers in other parts of the world. But having anticipated this tour for nearly a year, I had brought along my own homebrewed "lambic-style" cherry and raspberry lambics. Unfortunately, they did not hold up to the two weeks of traveling I had just undergone. Through agitation and less-than-ideal conditions they had lost their edge, crispness and complexity. I was not offended

---

BELGIAN-STYLE CHERRY-BLACK CURRANT (KRIEK-CASSIS) LAMBIC

This is one of the most phenomenal lambic-style beers I've tasted—and I made it! I used a combination of sour cherries and chokecherries, but you have the option to use currants if you wish. This beer is a two-year process, but well worth the effort. You'll need a quiet corner to age the slowly fermenting and evolving beer. Avoid extreme temperatures. Use the best-quality fully ripened fruit you can buy or pick yourself. Cherries and currants should have a balance between sweet and sour. Fresh or fresh-frozen are best. Here is the recipe for my finest lambic. It can be found on page 353.

by their less-than-accepting reception. But my 10-year-old Gnarly Roots Lambic-style barley wine was greeted with enthusiasm. I noted with interest that usually this 10 percent alcohol barley wine tasted very strong, but on this occasion, and after tasting 8 and 9 percent Belgian-style ales with regularity for the past two weeks, it did not. I suppose that proves the theory of relativity, doesn't it?

Cerveza Real in Latin America

A LAND OF THIRST, Latin America has some of the lightest-tasting beers on the planet. The beer landscape from Mexico to Tierra del Fuego can be quite monotonous unless you tune in to creative fermentations.

Greatly influenced by German brewers who had immigrated to Latin America, there was at one time a diversity of ales and lagers available regionally in cities and the countryside. However, nationalization of brands and beer monopolies have greatly diminished the choices available to the beer drinker. Even if you wanted to pay more money for a full-flavored beer, it is difficult to find one. Fortunately, there are signs that all this may be changing. Brewpubs and microbreweries are emerging in Mexico, Cuba, Argentina, Chile, Brazil, Colombia, Peru and several other nations. There are home-brewing co-ops and clubs celebrating their discovery of beer flavor and diversity. Even some of the large brewing companies are beginning to offer amber ales, bocks and wheat beers.

Slowly and patiently, the dormant Latin American passion for beer flavor is reemerging. The hot climate does not mean the beer needs to be tasteless. Pioneers are beginning to succeed by providing choice. People are discovering and drinking their beer with a great deal of appreciation. A microbrewed adventurer will find them.

Czech-Mex in Tijuana

JOSÉ WATCHES HIS CUSTOMERS enjoying beer at his taverna in Tijuana, Mexico. Most are guys, local residents, some with their wives or girlfriends. José notes that one guy is enjoying a chilled half-liter of a pilsener-style lager while his female companion seems disinterested, bored and sipping on a glass of water. José walks over to the table and presents a glass of pilsener to the woman, explaining that he is only giving her the beer so she can feel part of the scene. She doesn't need to pay for it nor even drink it. She thanks him, admitting that she really doesn't like beer. "But this beer is different," he insists, then goes on to briefly explain the merits of all-malt beer with flavor and character. He leaves. Five minutes later he observes from afar that there is one inch of beer missing from the complimentary glass. Ten minutes more go by and the glass is half full. Twenty-five minutes later he returns to the table with another glass of beer, offering the same deal—"you only need to keep the beer company and no need to pay."

The woman becomes a convert and wonders why a beer could be so dif-

José Gonzales, Tijuana Beer

ferent from the typical Mexican light lagers she is accustomed to disliking. The year is 2004, and José has begun his own small revolution.

José Antonio González comes from a beer family. All his life he has been surrounded by beer. His father moved from state to state, distributing and selling beer for the large Mexican breweries. José dreamed of one day having his own brewery and developing the Mexican beer drinker's appreciation for microbrewed beer.

The beginning of his microbrew adventure took him to Germany and the Czech Republic, where he discovered the pleasure and drinkability of Czech pilseners. Experiencing the house-brewed dark lager at the Prague Brewery U Flecku, José asserts, "I would drink all day this wonderful beer. My face would feel warm. I would sleep well at night and wake up the next morning with my head feeling wonderful—and by 12 o'clock noon I wanted to drink more beer. I never had these kinds of experiences with the beer I knew in Mexico."

On a visit to Prague, José asked a brewmaster how much corn, rice and sugar was formulated into these beers. The brewmaster explained, "Rice is for making sake. Corn is for making whiskey. Sugar is for making rum. Malt is for making beer." José's world was turning on edge. He had been touched by the passion for good beer. He did not know it at the time, but he was in the company of family brewers from Pilsner Urquell and Královský pivovar Krušovice (Brewery Krušovice).

Soon thereafter a Czech brewhouse, a Czech brewmaster and Czech malt, hops and yeast were on a voyage to Mexico's northwestern coastal city of 3 million, Tijuana. In the year 2000, Cerveza Tijuana was brewing, bottling and distributing all-malt Czech-inspired pilsener (Güera) and dark lager (Morena) along with other specialties available only on the brewery site at its Czech-styled pub-taverna. If you visit and José is there, you will recognize him by the twinkle in his eye and his excitement about Czech-style lager.

José and his son Ozbaldo have become impassioned and recognize that one of their major challenges is the education of the Mexican beer drinker about beer variety and things

CZECH-MEX TIJUANA URQUELL

Czech-style pilseners are something special. They are the original pilsen-ers. They are traditionally unique with their soft, almost honeylike malt aro-matics and flavor. Czech hops are flavorful and deliciously herbal, with a thirst-quenching character. This is a modern-day formulation of traditional Czech pilseners with a touch of Mexican lightness that deserves your at-tention. The recipe can be found on page 355.

like foam, drinking out of a glass, hops, malt, flavor and the fact that lime is not needed for his beer. These are the same challenges microbrewers have faced throughout the world as they return the flavor, culture and tradition to beer.

In the land of Modelo, Corona and Tecate, there are now a few more lagers from which to choose.

The Oldest Brewery in America

ETERNALLY SPRING, at an elevation of nearly 10,000 feet, sur-rounded by volcanoes towering over 20,000 feet and only 50 miles from the hot, humid tangle of the world's largest jungle, stands America's oldest ex-isting brewery. As though its surroundings were not spectacular enough, the brewery's history inspires the mind while contemplating the origins, wisdom and tenacity of its founders over 470 years ago.

The high Andean air in the city of Quito, Ecuador, is bright, clean and easily calmed by the country's readily available pilsener and Club Premium lager beers. Ecuador, a country situated on the equator and the size of Col-orado, has a lot to offer: the towering mountains of the Andes; tropical beaches; the Amazon basin jungle; brilliant deserts; Indian, African and Spanish culture; and America's oldest brewery.

As part of the Spanish conquest, the city of Quito was founded in 1534. It was only a matter of days before work on a church and monastery was ini-tiated. Seven monks who had traveled to the South American continent from Flanders (now part of Belgium) brought their yearning for beer as it had been brewed in the old country. Wheat was imported and cultivated, and soon America's first brewery was malting, brewing and fermenting America's first wheat beer.

In the garden of the monastery one of the padres gave me a short history of the brewery, which has now been restored as a museum. Through an interpreter, he explained that cultivation of wheat was followed in later years with the introduction of barley. The small, simple brewery was popular with the growing population at the monastery and expanded into a more "serious" brewery in 1595.

Up until 1957, the five-to-six-barrel (U.S. size) brewhouse malted its own barley and sun dried it. The brewery continued operation until 1967, when according to the padre, the Pope issued an order halting brewing operations. The tradition of the Franciscan Order of Monks embraced a vow of poverty and humility, and the new Vatican's interpretation did not perceive beer brewing as part of those values.

However, up until the brewery ceased operation the monks were brewing 12 batches of beer per week, half of which the monastery church kept for itself and the other half of which was distributed to other churches and monasteries in the area. Wheat beers and pale beers as well as very dark beers were regularly brewed, according to the padre's story.

These beers are now only a memory in the minds of a select few people residing in Quito. The manager at the small hostel where I stayed in told me that his father used to work in the brewery. He couldn't recall very much except a locally produced proteinous substance that was used in the brewing process. I figured it must have been some sort of clarifying agent similar to isinglass, which is derived from the swim bladders of certain fish. It is often used in traditional English ale brewing.

The brewery was preserved as a museum with the help of two Ecuadorian breweries, Cervezas Nacionales of Guayaquil and Cerveceria Andina of Quito. Adjacent to and part of the museum is a preserved beautifully small, beer hall. The flavor of it all seems to linger as a cross between Flemish and Germanic brewing traditions. A visit to the monastery brewery is well worth the effort if you ever find yourself in the city of Quito. And I know the padre appreciated the bottle of my own homebrew that I gave him after our tour of the brewery at the monastery of San Francisco.

The following is partially excerpted from an article by Paul V. Grano about the brewery and the brewing of one type of beer by the monastery. The article appeared in the January 1966 issue of *The Brewers Digest*.

Established in 1534 the brewery at the San Francisco Monastery, Quito, Ecuador

The brewhouse consists of a copper-lined concrete mash kettle, a wooden lauter tub with a bronze false bottom and a hot water tank made of an old German hop cylinder. All heating is by direct wood fire. Thirty-three pounds of pilsener malt plus 50 pounds of caramel malt and 20 pounds of black malt (milled in a coffee grinder in the monastery) are mashed in and the usual infusion method is followed. Since the agitator, which was installed for the Fathers, is inadequate they have to take turns in stirring the mash in order to avoid burning on the bottom. This is quite a hot and heavy job.

The mash then runs to the lauter tub by gravity, and the wort is pumped back to the mash kettle by hand. Here 100 pounds of brown sugar dissolved in hot water is added. The hop rate for the batch is two pounds. When the boiling of the wort is finished the wort once again runs by gravity to the surface cooler and is left there over night. The next morning, the yeast that we [La Victoria Malting/Brewing Company] provide them is added and fermentation goes on at about 60 degrees F (15.5 C). The original extract is about 10.5 degrees balling and when the beer has fermented down to one degree balling above the end fermentation the beer is bottled immediately. The bottles are filled through four siphons and crowned by hand. The empty bottles as well as the crown corks were [recently] given to the monastery by our brewery when

QUITO ABBEY ALE—1534

Taking the proportions of malt, sugar and hops as revealed in the 1966 recipe, I've formulated a small-batch recipe that closely matches the character of beer brewed in the final and 432nd year at the monastery. This recipe can be found on page 358.

this type of bottle was discontinued for commercial purposes some years ago.

The fermentable extract still in the beer produces about .5 percent CO_2 by weight or 2.7 percent by volume after 10 to 12 days of storage when the beer is ready for consumption. The alcohol is about 3.4 percent by weight and the taste is very pleasant. The Fathers are served one glass for lunch and one for supper. About one hour before serving, the crown corks are lifted slightly; otherwise the beer would pour like champagne.

To conclude, I would mention a small episode, which took place a few weeks after we had first agreed to assist the Fathers. I went over to the monastery to ask the "Brewmaster" how the beer had turned out, to which he answered me with a smile that where he had previously used one padlock to close his storeroom, he now had to use two!

The Brewing Soul of Cuba

THE ELECTRICITY and lights are out in my neighborhood, Charlie, but not to worry. There is no problem." No problem—yes, the universal phrase spoken in every language, taking on infinite degrees of unreality. We found ourselves winding our way through the streets of Havana, ending in a western suburb. One street block was electrified; another was night dark. We stopped, and the noise of his Russian-built automobile slowly gave way to the vibrancy of the tree-lined neighborhood. The engine pinged as it cooled. I slowly rolled up my window and sat bewildered in the front seat, noting the sounds of the neighborhood, breathing the tropical night air. A hum of conversation filled the air, yet no one could be seen. It was dark—very dark.

Then I noticed the open-air porches above me on the second story of each home. The orange glow of a lit cigar slowly swayed in a silent and languid arc.

In his rocking chair an old man bided time, as most Cubans are apt to do in these difficult times of "austerity." Then I realized the night air was filled with dozens of these tiny orange, swaying, arcing embers. The embracing aroma of Cuban tobacco deliciously filled the evening. Laughing, crying, teasing, joking and serious conversation seemed to gently abide in every household visible and invisible.

We walked through a gate and into a secretly lit, small but comfortable home to have one of my first beer tastings in Cuba. But as I left those moments behind, I knew I would never forget them. They so typified my impressions of today's Cuba: mysterious, intriguing, friendly, incredibly complex and a country constantly on the verge of anxiety.

I was 13 years old in 1962 during the Cuban missile crisis. I can recall listening to my younger brother's six-transistor Sony pocket radio (a new invention at the time) in the darkness of our bedroom, wondering if the world were about to end. That was my first and lasting memory of Cuba. Now, with this educational and journalistic trip hosted by the Cuban government I was on my way, in search of the lost beers of Cuba. I knew that beer was being brewed in Cuba, but little else. In my pre-trip research through commercial literature and in conversations with international brewing colleagues, I was surprised to discover that there was virtually no outside knowledge of the Cuban beer market and brewing industry. Curious, I wanted to find out what very few knew. Months of preparation and attempts at organizing this trip proved mostly futile, but as I was determined I went unconfirmed, assuming the most but expecting the least. Through a series of personal and diplomatic contacts I was unofficially told that the Cuban government and the Minister of Food would officially host me as a journalist. Embarkation day arrived with nothing certain, except my determination.

I boarded an airliner in the tropical heat. I certainly could have used a beer, but only rum was offered. Cool air cascaded from overhead vents into the cabin. As it collided with the humid air, a cold, moist cloud mystically layered the aisle a foot deep. I was in the clouds before we took off. I must admit to a few fleeting moments of panic—"Where am I going? Where am I? Am I crazy?" These were real-time thoughts. My heart pounded with the anxiety of the unknown as we headed toward Havana. The clouds swirled both inside and outside the cabin at takeoff. I was on my uncertain way. But as I always realize, anxiety is a very highly overrated experience. Forgive me; I did not have a homebrew with me.

Approaching legendary Havana, I looked down with some trepidation. From high above and among the billowy clouds we glided past dozens of baseball diamonds and deep blue swimming pools languishing in the stillness be-low. "There has to be beer down there somewhere . . . there just has to," I thought to myself. And with beer there are always fine people.

As I disembarked the plane I was met on the tarmac by a translator and the Ministerio de la Industria Alimenticia (Minister of Food). My bags, pass-port, visa and transport were being cared for through the diplomatic lounge as I was offered a rum mojita and introduced to the possibilities for the next few days: the breweries of Havana and the surrounding area, a flight to the east-ern post-revolutionary city and brewery of Holguin, a road trip to Cerveceria Camagüey and a return by air to Havana for an opportunity to give a presen-tation to the marketing, operations and brewery managers of Havana.

Given several options, I chose to make the most of my visit and accepted an offer by my Cuban government hosts of a full itinerary. From this point on, for five days and six nights I immersed myself in the culture and leisure of Cuba. But beer is my business, and I was working overtime.

What little I had read and heard about Cuba before the trip proved to be quite inaccurate. I must admit that I developed a great admiration for the people of Cuba after seeing and touring the existing facilities, listening to the government's assessment of existing conditions and future efforts, freely roaming the streets and seeing and talking with the local people. Yet both during and after my visit, Cuba remained an enigma. What was really going on there? The issues were complex. The opinions were passionate. I left no

more certain about Cuba's beer culture and brewing industry, though I know that it truly exists and remains to be explored. Discovering the soul takes time.

Soon I began to shatter the myths of my imagination, but not without a flood of long-forgotten memories of people, places, cars, food and feelings of what it was like for me, growing up in the 1950s and early 1960s. In a time warp, the cars, the music, the spectacularly beautiful art deco Spanish-American architecture of the 1950s are still much intact. But sadly, there is more crumbling and disrepair. Old Havana is the historic port of the early 1500s as well as a favorite haunt of Ernest Hemingway. I enjoyed a daiquiri where it was invented and a mojito (rum, lime, sugar, ice and mint) at the bar where it was first concocted. Although I was not visiting Cuba as a tourist, my hosts easily found cold beer for my enjoyment. The quality was variable but mostly acceptable.

Cuba's potential for economic development is quite staggering. In 1959 more than 2 million American tourists came to Cuba, many for gambling and an experience of decadence. After the revolution, the government national-ized all industry and property. Gambling fled and later emerged in Las Vegas. Many Cuban businesses and individuals lost fortunes; many who left still hate the existing regime, vowing someday to return and recover their lost property. But this will be difficult for the brewing companies, for at this point

Havana brewers

there is little left to recover but the earth on which these fading breweries barely exist.

On the road, one of every 10 or 15 cars is a 1951–1954 Chevy, Oldsmobile, Plymouth, Packard, Cadillac, Ford or Pontiac. They are truly a breathtaking sight to behold and one of the real and unique tourist "resources" in Cuba. Cubans have kept them running for 40 years with haywire and bubblegum. Carburetors are reconstructed from tin cans if necessary. It would be a crime to see them sold and leave the island to languish in the garage of a car collector. In Cuba these are real cars used by real people. They certainly are proud. Though they have little, it doesn't show in their physical appearance. They are a determined and hard-working people. And they make things work, inside or outside the system. The same is true of the brewing industry. They have developed some incredibly creative ways to remain operational.

During my visit the streets were spotlessly clean—there was no trash to discard.

Stagnation has characterized the brewing industry for the past 35 years. The state "owns" and manages all seven brewing factories. Similar products are produced by more than one brewery and often under different formulations. The lack of capital and materials has drastically affected the manufacture and quality of the products. Almost all of the beer is brewed with 50 percent sugar, few bottles are labeled (labels are in scarce supply) and work-

Early 20th-century Havana brewery

ing equipment is continually being cannibalized to provide spare parts for downsized operations.

Miraculously, the brewers of Cuba continue to brew beer with equipment that by industry standards would be virtually unacceptable elsewhere. But I noted one exception at the post-revolution brewery in Holguin, which was fitted with East German brewery equipment and a canning line. The spirit of the brewers and operations people was inquisitive and searching for many answers during my visits, tours and seminars. Their persistence produced the best product possible under difficult circumstances and was a testament to the league of brewers everywhere and the tenacity of the Cuban people.

Cuba's brewing heritage is proudly evident in the spectacularly grandiose outdoor tropical beer garden at Havana's Tropical Brewery and on display at the brewery museum. There, in a corner of the museum, remain likely the only artifacts of Cuba's best-kept beer secrets: bottles and labels of past Vienna lagers, bock beer, Munich dark and crystal (malt) lagers. They are there as a quiet testament, day and night, year after year, hardly noted by the inside world and noted not at all by the outside world. Seeing is feeling, and one knows immediately that Cuba had a rich brewing heritage in years past. What were these beers? I can only imagine. My hosts knew little about these lagers, yet hinted that there may still be some old-timers on the island with long memories.

Yes, there is beer in Cuba. Tropical, Polar, Tinima, Mayabe, Modelo and Hatuey light lagers can be found easily with American dollars and with difficulty otherwise. They are brewed with pride by brewers who know very little about the international brewing community. Their desire for quality and improvement qualifies them for acceptance into this community.

VIENNA-STYLE OURO DE HABANERA
(HAVANA GOLD)

I imagine a great beer and have thirsted for something other than a characterless light lager. I dreamed: What if I were asked to brew a beer for a Cuban microbrewery? What might it be? This is my answer: a German-influenced full-malt-flavored golden lager with added corn to freshen up the body and increase drinkability. Hop flavor and character are essential. This recipe can be found on page 359.

The brewery personnel were eager to learn of the beer industry beyond their borders. They noted that my visit to Cuba was the very first contact Cubans had had with the American brewing industry in 35 years.

I am fascinated by the possibility that someday once again bock, Vienna- and Munich-style lagers could be reintroduced to a land where beer is no stranger. But for now, if you yearn for a Cuban lager you would be more satis- fied wistfully enjoying rum poured over ice, crushed mint leaves, lime juice and sugar.

African Safaris

A CASTLE GOLDEN PILSENER, please."
I am on my first of several African journeys. It is 1995. I am on a train, comfortable, relaxed and with a cold beer in hand. The landscape slithers by, highlighted by the glow of the setting sun. The steam engine chugs ahead, leading us around another horseshoe bend. Two minutes earlier I had watched the sun balance itself on the horizon. Now, I am viewing the rising full moon. I open the window wider, taking a deep breath and another long draw of beer. A baboon glances at me from the dry grasses along the railroad sidings. Sucking the foam off my mustache, I begin to recount the experiences of the past few days, and in particular . . .

The Zimbabwe Zephyr and the Beer Gardens of Bulawayo
Hari Yemadzisahwira

DURING THE NIGHT the train's frequent stops distracted me. During the overnight journey northward, people were continuously getting off and on in the middle of nowhere. Vehicles were not waiting at any of these stations; only people, donkeys, two-wheeled carts and the glowing embers of

Riding the "Zimbabwe Zephyr"

small fires comforting the stillness along the tracks. The full moon contributed to the mysteries beyond, throwing shadows that silhouetted trees dotting the landscape. I knew there were small villages out there beyond. In these villages I was sure people brewed beer. I was certain of that.

As the train silently pulled away I could hear people chatter in Shonna and Ndeble among bits of English. Yes, there was beer out there, because there were people. I felt a very strong urge to get off at one of the next stops with my one small bag of belongings and encounter the unknown of the African night. I took another sip of Castle and promised myself that I'd be back someday and succumb to temptation.

I was on the Zimbabwe National Railways, journeying from Bulawayo to Victoria Falls to catch my long flight back to Colorado. And at the same time I was enjoying the local beer, thinking about the one in my hand and those of the past few days. I had learned to appreciate the commercially produced beers because I had had the privilege of attending an international convention of southern and central African brewers. The variety of cultures, variety of beer styles and quality of life were far better than what my prejudices had anticipated. The all-malt Reinheitsgebot Windhoek lagers of Namibia, the aromatic and hoppy Zambezi Lager of Zimbabwe, the stouts and fruit beers of South Africa all provided quenching relief from the late summer sun of southern Africa. Castle Lager and Castle Pilsener provided welcome rehydration, as I had earlier in the week paddled a canoe along a three-day stretch of the Zambezi River. The elephants 20 feet away, grazing along the riverbanks; hippos sloshing their way only yards from our evening campsites; the distant roar of lions; the ominous crocs lining the riverbanks and the nighttime hyenas skulking through the campgrounds were not beer hallucinations. They were real, though the beer helped. Believe me. Though I learned that one was wise not to drink too much on evening campouts. Late-night urinations were an invitation to dangerous encounters. The morning sun was always welcoming light to my bladder.

As a brewer and an enthusiast of indigenous beers the real treat on this, my first African journey, was the discovery of native and commercially brewed opaque sorghum beer. I feel quite certain that these beers were among the first beers ever brewed, perhaps paralleling the beers of ancient Mesopotamia and Egypt. Unfortunately for historians, we haven't yet discovered the beer records (if they exist at all) of the peoples of southern and central Africa. Unlike the Mesopotamian and ancient Egyptian brews, these sorghum beers remain a living tradition, though no less historical.

Sorghum is a grain that grows well in the semi-arid regions of Africa. It can easily be made into malt, having adequate enzymes to convert itself into the essential sugars and fermentables needed to brew beer. To produce a variety of flavors and color in their beer, local village and homebrewers may roast all or a portion of their grains and malts.

Did I say beer? Well, yes, I did, though to most of the Western world opaque sorghum beer would hardly be recognized or considered as such. But in reality it has more tradition than any pils, bock, pale ale or stout.

My first encounter with this living history was at a conference of southern and central African brewers. The last night of the event featured traditional African cuisine such as ostrich, impala stew, ox veal tongue in peanut butter sauce and milo/sadza (corn mush), along with sorghum beer brewed by the local Chibuku Brewery. I must have got a little carried away with the Chibuku that night. During the "circumcision dance" and the "tower of power ceremony," one of the African dancers dragged me into the dirt dancing circle. Several hotel employees told me the next morning that they saw me drinking a lot of Chibuku just before I began kicking up the dust, dancing in front of the entire delegation.

I visited the small Chibuku Brewery in the municipality of Dete. The brewery was one of dozens of Chibuku Breweries in southern Africa commercially producing opaque sorghum beer.

More than half of all the beer consumed in South Africa, Botswana, Zimbabwe and neighboring nations is not light lager, but rather Chibuku-type sorghum beer. Here at the tiny brewery in Dete they were churning out 10,000 to 12,000 hectoliters per month (that's about 8,500 to 10,000 U.S. barrels; one barrel equals 31 gallons).

How is it made? Malted sorghum is ground to a medium-fine flour (along with maize, or corn, in some formulations). The flour is "mashed" into hot water and converted into soluble starches and fermentable sugars. From the mashing vessel, the sweet liquid is passed over a simple screen, removing only the coarsest pieces of crushed grain. The sweet liquid with the fine flour enters a stainless steel tank, where it is cooled. Yeast is added and so are a couple of shovelfuls of freshly milled sorghum malt. On the same day, the mixture is packaged and shipped to retail outlets and beer halls. What a concept—brewed and packaged in one day! And get this: the beer is not alcoholic when it leaves the brewery. I wondered what the tax man was going to do now!

The beverage is designed to ferment in the package or in serving tanks holding the draft versions of this brew. After one day, the beer has developed 1 percent alcohol. It has a creamy texture, much like a thick milkshake or smoothie. The yeast has begun to ferment the sugars into alcohol. The shovelful of malt at the end of the brewing process introduces loads of lactobacillus bacteria to the sweet liquid. At the warm African temperatures, a lactic souring slowly evolves during fermentation. After 24 hours the beer has a slight acidic taste and a slight aromatic character reminiscent of yogurt (but remember, there is no milk in this beverage). The tannins from the sorghum husk contribute a drying astringency to the mouthfeel. The overall flavor is a pleasant blend of sweet and sour. Carbonation is beginning to naturally develop, and the bready aroma of yeast soon begins to emerge. I liked the beer quite a bit, though I imagine that something like this would be even more delicious with a fruit or chocolate flavor served at cold temperatures.

Sorghum beer is healthy. As a matter of fact, it is an important part of the nutritional intake of many Africans; fermented grain is nutritionally superior to nonfermented grain.

The alcohol rises to 2 percent on day two and 3 percent on day three, and then on the fourth day the worm will emerge from the package. This is when you know the beer is at its prime, at about 4 to 4½ percent. Alcohol, acidity and flavor balance to the preference of most Chibuku enthusiasts. The worm? No, it is not the wiggly kind, but rather the foaming fermentation that emerges from the pinhole atop the milk-carton-like container.

Enthusiasts may be found wearing a Chibuku Brewery T-shirt with the

slogan "Hari Yemadzisahwira." I believe it is the Chibuku version of "Relax. Don't worry. Have a homebrew." More accurately, it relates that with good beer, there are friends to be made.

Commercially made Chibuku is quite popular, but the home-brewed stuff is even more so. Instant 24-hour homebrew kits are available throughout South Africa, as well as "all-grain" traditional homebrew kits. But most sorghum beer is made to village standards or family recipes handed down through generations, using 100 percent home-malted sorghum.

The soothing clickety-clack of the railroad tracks and my third Castle Pilsener helped me recall my visit to the beer gardens of Bulawayo the day before. As an editor, I had read and published an article in the 1984 issue of *Zymurgy* magazine about the beer gardens of Bulawayo. Now, 13 years later, the intrigue materialized as I traveled through Zimbabwe seeking these fabled beer gardens.

When I arrived in Bulawayo, I learned there were no longer any beer gardens in town. I ended up consulting a cab driver parked outside my hotel. "You wanna do what?" he asked incredulously.

"Yeah man, I wanna go to one of those sorghum beer gardens. Can you take me there, and will I be able to find a cab ride back?"

Richard, the cab driver, looked at me a bit perplexed, but then shrugged his shoulders and abandoned himself to my crazy fantasy. "Sure man, but you aren't gonna find a cab out there to get you back. I'll tell you what; I'll stick with you for as long as you want to stay. Buy me beer and let me know when you want to come back." This was not America!

Off we went to the western suburbs of Bulawayo seeking the Mashumba Beer Garden in Makakoba Township. The streets were dimly lit, but there was no shortage of people walking to everyday destinations. We pulled over and stopped in a well-lit area. Sitting on the graveled surface, women sold vegetables and snack food. There was a bustle of activity. The place was alive.

We enter the walled garden through a high, grand-looking gate. My first impression was one of lots of people, all in quiet, happy conversation. Benches haphazardly lined the grounds extending beyond the maze of tall walls. Curiously, I did not notice anyone drinking any beer. In fact I didn't notice any beer. I followed Richard. To get a "draw" of brew we stood in line and Richard handed me a rather intimidatingly large, five-liter, white plastic bucket. "Where are the glasses?" I recall wondering. I didn't wonder long. As I stepped up to a small window, the draftsman asked, "Two liters or four?" "Two," I quickly blurted, silently thinking, "One can't be too cautious with these kinds of experiences, you know." *Swooooosh*, the brew gushed out of its dispenser and within 0.84 seconds my bucket proudly contained two liters of fermenting, sour-smelling, yeasty, thick, beery, alcoholic and nutritiously wonderful Chibuku. We exited the dispensary and I realized the virtues of all those white plastic buckets being shared at tables throughout the garden.

Richard and I found a bench occupied by several other men and women. We passed around our communal bucket of brew and shared its glories. Every time it was my turn, I grasped the sides of the bucket with my thumbs and fingers to swirl the contents (to get the good stuff into suspension), inhale the pungent lactic aroma (in my mind repeating a mantra, "Charles, there are no known pathogens that can survive in beer. Charles, there are no known pathogens that can survive in beer. Charles, there are . . ."), take a good, healthy swig and begin to feel the camaraderie, the glow, the warm evening air, the conversation, the culture and the urge for another. The conversation became more animated and Isaac, a stringer of tennis racquets seated next to me, found questioning me easier: "Is America very far from here?" "Where is your family?" "Why are you here?" "Who are you?"

I was smiling. After my sixth swirl, swig and swallow I noticed Regina, a rather large, robust woman who had been nervously watching me for the last 20 minutes. She was uncomfortable about something and not smiling. Something bad was in the air and I was beginning to feel nervous. I swirled, swigged and swallowed one more time. Then, while seated, with hands on her wide hips and a slight friendly yet frustrated tilt of her head, she pleaded in a plaintiff command, "Sir," pausing apologetically, "Will you puleeeeeeeeaase keep your *thumbs* out of the bucket." Red faced, shrinking aback and totally embarrassed, I thought to myself, "And I was concerned about pathogens!" This issue of "thumbs out of the bucket" is clearly an important consideration when drinking in the beer gardens of Bulawayo. I learned a very important cultural lesson, one I'm sure is not in any beer etiquette book.

I can still recall the clean aftertaste and the desire to always have just one more swig. The stuff grew on me. I must admit, it grew rather slowly, but one does develop a taste for the unique. It doesn't come easy. But when you've acquired it . . . well, perhaps you will find out for yourself someday.

Richard and I polished off our two liters and some of the others' liters as well. We left, and as I climbed into the cab I couldn't help but notice a sign high on the building next door to the beer garden: "Mushumbo Surgery, M-W-F, 1–4 P.M." Hmmmmmmmm, I wondered if the beer garden was open before noon?

"Let's go Richard," I said. "I need a Castle now."

THE TRAIN PULLED INTO VICTORIA FALLS STATION at 7 A.M. I'd had a reasonable night's rest and was pleasantly recollecting my two and a half weeks' experiences. My plane would leave the next day. I know I'll be back someday. *Gemütlichkeit. Hari Yemadzisahwira.* Or, like I said, "Relax. Don't worry. Have a homebrew."

POSTNOTE: REENTERING THE UNITED STATES, I walked up to immigrations at New York City's JFK Airport wearily holding my passport after 30 hours of traveling. The official looked up at me in surprise, startling me.

"Hey aren't you Charlie Papazian?"

"Well, how the haeeellll did you know who I am? I haven't even given you my passport yet," I drawled sleepily.

"I'm an American Homebrewers Association member," he proudly proclaimed. "I read all your articles in *Zymurgy* magazine. Where have you been lately—on this trip?"

Half astonished as well as half asleep, I replied, "I'm returning from the beer gardens of Bulawayo." And left it at that. It didn't seem to surprise the homebrewing immigration officer—I've come to learn homebrewers' passions can never be too outrageous.

Two year later I continued my African beer adventures to have . . .

ZIMBABWE ZEPHYR SORGHUM BEER

To truly develop an appreciation for African sorghum beer, you must experience it firsthand in the beer gardens where it is served. For those who wish an introduction to the lively, interesting and complex flavor of this ancient tradition, here is a simple recipe and procedure. This recipe can be found on page 362.

The Last Beer in Swakapmund

THERE IS NO AROMA as tantalizing and sensual as that of the Atlantic Ocean at Swakapmund, Namibia. The cold, Antarctic Benguela current graces the coast of this southwestern African country, creating a unique microclimate so very different from that of the interior. Nearby, the largest sand dunes in the world rise 1,000 feet. There, on the average day, temperatures soar above 100 degrees F and drop to near freezing in the evening. Only one slim mile to the west of these magnificent dunes, the Atlantic brings cold water along the coast creating, they say, the oldest desert in the world. Ask around and it hasn't rained here in recent memory. In Swakapmund, an outpost oasis on the coast, the climate is in the 60s and 70s during the day and damn chilly during the evening. A fog rolls in every morning and what vegetation has evolved drinks the morning dew. But I am not a vegetarian, nor was I about to drink mountain dew.

The ocean aroma—to me it is as intoxicating as the perfectly brewed Namibian-brewed German-style lager I tremendously enjoy. This one special evening, I slowly walked the beach. The sun was setting over the south Atlantic. The sky was nothing memorable—no clouds, no glory. But the smell, the wonderful sweet and tantalizing aroma of the cold sea—that is what was

Thirsty landscape, Swakapmund

wonderful. It reminded me of my months exploring the northwest coast of North America in the 1970s, along the cold seas and among the remote wilderness islands of British Columbia. Here in Swakapmund the aroma is similar, but its presence of here and now is ever so much more sweet.

Did you know that the sound of the sea is a function of its temperature? I've never read anything about this, but I know it for sure! The sound of tropical ocean waters crashing on a beach is so distinctly different from that of cold water crashing on this southwest African sand. I know that this sound is indicative of so much more living in these cold waters. My mind drifted earlier over a quenching draft of the local Reinheitsgebot-style Windhoek Lager (am I in Germany or Africa?). I contemplated the sound of the drip and the spray of hot sparge water versus cold water and the sound that is every poured beer. If you listen to your beer, it speaks to you about its personality—if you take the time to listen.

I was in search of Namibian oysters! I found them, but not before a slow walk down the beach, wrapped warmly in my Bar Harbor Brewing Company sweatshirt. A few Windhoek Lagers, a dozen oysters and assorted other sea creatures were my dinner at the Tugboat, recommended for its seafood.

But I digress. Before this small feast I encountered a busload of Africans on the beach. They were a spectacle, a sight to remember for the rest of my life. The sea was ice cold, beautiful and crashing. These men and women were in business suits and dresses. They were rolling their leggings as fast and as far up as they could, but it was never enough as they laughed and played in the foaming surf. All adults, they smiled the grins of the planet's children. They were making Alice in Wonderland's Cheshire cat envious.

These were their first glorious minutes of ocean "baptism." I recalled my first glimpse of the Pacific Ocean, my first mountain climbed and several other special firsts of my life. I continued to watch as they scooped water into their mouths, tasting the salt of the sea for the first time in their lives. Others were busy gathering gallons of ocean and sand into containers. I grinned to myself and was warmed inside as I imagined this little bit of sea taken back to relatives perhaps 500 miles inland, to marvel at the taste of the Atlantic ocean. I've seen oceans a thousand mornings of my life, but this is a sight that is still a marvel even to me, the Atlantic stretching out to the western horizon. The people danced in the glimmer of the setting sun, unable to judge how far the crashing waves thrust their tongues onto the sand. Soaked in their business suits, they laughed, and to be sure loved every minute of the experience.

I asked, "Where are you from?"

"From Botswana. This is the first time we've ever seen the ocean."

You know there are special moments in everyone's lives. This was one for me. I don't quite know why, but I was overcome with a deep emotion, simply watching these children of our planet taking in the great gray-blue sea crashing wildly on this distant coast. I was there. For the moment it seemed I knew that I would be there forever in my mind, watching these 30 people, silhouetted by the setting sun in their suits and dresses as the children we will always be.

After dinner, I walked halfway down the beach, then broke into a light jog as I headed back into town. It was very cool; the ocean dampness was still invigorating and fresh. I glanced up in awe, knowing that just beyond my sight were sand dunes and one of the driest deserts in the world.

But deserts are for exploring, and that would be tomorrow. That night I was in search of one last beer before retiring. The town looked dreadfully quiet. One last beer? In the desert? That evening I had little faith in fate as I dwelled on sarcastic thoughts.

The streets were empty, deserted, dead. I methodically crisscrossed the small grid of city center streets. I was about to give up when, at the last moment, I found the warm glow of incandescent lights. As I approached the artificial twilight, my heart jumped. I had arrived at the doorsteps of "the Last Western Pub." I walked in. There were a few people still there.

My thirst overcame any small talk I may have had in reserve. "Is the draft Tafel or Windhoek Lager?" I asked. "It's all the same and brewed right here in Swakapmund," answered the owner in a German-accented English. I knew the brewery was three blocks down the street and that it brewed all the country's draft beer, but didn't quite believe it was all the same. So I argued. "Are you sure about that?" "Come around the bar and see for yourself," he said. So I strolled past a young lady and mentioned in an overconfident four-Windhoek state, "He doesn't know that beer is my business and I'm working late."

But I was wrong. He proved his point. And one thing led to another, and I'll be damned!! He nonchalantly added to the conversation, "Well, we have a microbrewery just around the corner. We're Namibia's first and Swakapmund's first. Maybe you can help us . . ."

How do I find these places? This country is small but not that small. There are great distances between places and people. The previous day I was encountering black rhinos, giraffes, zebras, oryx, kudus, gemsboks, springboks (great name for a beer, eh?), dikdiks, lions, ostriches and trees stranger than your weirdest dreams—just 500 kilometers to the north. There was a lot of strange desert and sand between there and here. I needed another Wind-hoek Lager. I was in a small state of serendipitous shock. I kept asking myself over and over, "How do I find these places?" I had just been wandering aimlessly, and what the . . . I walked down an alley and eventually wound up at the Swakapmund Brauhaus by way of the Last Western Pub.

To make a long, sad story short, Swakapmund is a desert oasis for Germans and Namibians. The owners of the Last Western Pub had the beer lover's dream—"let's brew our own beer." Their aspirations were noble, but like so many others in undeveloped microbrewery countries, they have been royally ripped off. They spent $40,000 on one of the worst pieces of equipment I've ever seen in all my born-again days as a brewer. I could have done better with $1,000. Needless to say, they were searching for solutions, having shut down the brewery for lack of anything that tasted like beer. "We just want to make three or four barrels of beer a week—quality beer—and we're prepared to find a solution." I told them part of the solution was to scrap most of the system they had. It was worthless as an asset.

And to their credit, not only were they selling the super-quality local beer made by Windhoek, but as well a selection of more than 50 great beers from Europe, and I was drinking it—free. I thought to myself, two hours ago I was heading back to my hotel depressed, discouraged and thirsty. Now I was being asked if I knew of any homebrewers who might wish to spend six months, all expenses paid, to fix their brewery to make three hectoliters a week. Their biggest asset was Swakapmund's one and only license (other than that owned by the Windhoek Brewing Company) to brew and sell beer. And if that was not enough, they were on good terms with the Windhoek Brewing Company and allowed to buy ingredients from the brewery. I told them their goal was not unreasonable and soon departed, binged and light headed.

Before I left, my eyes glanced up at a sign in back of the bar. It said, "Remember when they said sex was safe and flying was dangerous." This was the motto and business card of Rui, the person I had jumped off a mountain

SWAKAPMUND COWBOY LAGER

This German-style pilsener has the spiciness and floral character of Haller-tauer and Santiam hops and helps me recall the fresh, invigorating aroma of the cold Antarctic Benguela sea current. It's a crisp, full-flavored, refreshing pils. The recipe can be found on page 362.

paragliding with in Rio de Janeiro only four weeks earlier. It is truly an amazing, serendipitous world.

What goes around keeps going around and comes around again and again. Remember this. Always. Sometimes I don't remember, but it comes around anyway. They say the fog rolls in here in the morning. In the morning I would be heading east across the desert.

Expecting the Unexpected:
Russia, Asia, Fiji and Grenada

MANY OF MY adventures are an ongoing regionalized collection of experiences with a common theme. Then there are other adventures that just happen. Time and place, reason and cadence are neither logical nor consistent. That is often the nature of having microbrewed adventures: you simply happen to encounter them with no reason for a beginning nor hint at finality. Russia, Asia and Fiji happened to happen . . .

AS DID Grenada in April 1994. I was among twelve intrepid beer enthusiasts who'd checked their day's luggage at the airport on the small Caribbean island of Grenada. Amongst our belongings was a five-gallon keg of homemade American pale ale. Our enthusiasm and the morning were leading us to a day of sailing and camaraderie in the Grenadine Islands. But there was one problem.

We had forgotten to consider that Grenada was one country and we were entering another. Unfortunately, St. Vincent customs would not allow our keg into their country. We even promised to buy at least six cases of their beer! They smiled and assured us that they'd take good care of our beer so that we could return with it to Grenada. But then there was another problem we discovered later.

Having legitimately cleared Grenada customs with our beers earlier in the week, we were to find another shift on duty upon our return from St. Vincent.

Sadly, the opportunity to enjoy our last remaining keg of beer was lost. Our beer became a beer without a country.

FORTUNATELY, all the other beers I've ever encountered have been proudly hosted by the pride of a brewer and their country. Here are a few more adventures to thirst over. Pour yourself another and read on.

The Hope of Global Warming
Lessons from the Baltic Sea

Little beer, oh brother you are stronger than me
You could make strong men fall down
You could blow the taps free of big barrels
Beer, old brother you are older than me
You were there when I was born
And you will be there when I'm gone

Where will you bury me after I die?
Bury me under the table in the pub
So I can hear what the men say
So I should know whether they love girls or remember me
Yes they love girls, but they don't remember me

—LATVIAN BEER SONG

IN LATE OCTOBER 1995 I took a two-week journey, leading a People-to-People Program delegation of brewers to St. Petersburg and overland through Estonia to Latvia. This ongoing program is sponsored by a 50-plus-year-old organization established by President Eisenhower to promote good-will between nations through the interactions of ordinary citizens. We were a group of ten adventurers from the United States, Canada and Belgium observing the beer culture and brewing community. Ours was a mission of informational exchange. For me, it was a visitation to the roots of beer culture and the challenges every brewer confronts.

"Why Russia and the Baltic countries?" was an often asked question. The very question begs the quest, at least for nine others and me.

Latvian farmhouse brewer

We landed in St. Petersburg, a city of 6 million harbored at the same latitude as Anchorage, Alaska, greeted by October's gray skies. As we boarded our tour bus we noted a ragged group of six or seven men bundled against the cold, their tattered luggage by their side. As if by magic, horns and drums emerged, and then there was music. Jet-lagged and awed, we all stared through the bus windows. Somehow they knew. The first notes of their refrain were unmistakable as they completed a rousing version of *The Star Spangled Banner*. We were in Russia for 20 minutes, and something told me that this trip was going to be different. Or was it?

By order of the Russian Empress, Catherine II, the Stephan Razin Brewery was founded in St. Petersburg in 1795. Many breweries throughout Eastern Europe and Russia similarly enjoyed several eras of a proud and productive history. But now this brewery, on their 200th anniversary, was struggling to continue in a country where economic reform was burdened with unbearable taxation and other difficulties. The Soviet system had not been kind to breweries interested in quality.

Perhaps the most devastating blow to the brewing industry in the 20th century was what many refer to as Gorbachev's "June Revolution." To all beer drinkers in the former Soviet Union, Gorbachev will not be remembered for glasnost or perestroika, but rather for the low-alcohol decree he instituted on June 1, 1980. Overnight, the brewing industry was in ruins. A form of prohibition had been installed. Gorbachev destroyed so many economic infrastructures and so many lives without coming close to solving the real problems of alcoholism. This was the beginning of the end for any respect he had developed among many Russians.

But times have changed. The Baltic Republics are now sovereign nations, and Russia is struggling with its transition. We observed varying degrees of progress across the former Soviet Union. We also learned of more than 150 microbreweries built in the last three years—built for reasons other than what Americans might assume.

It was interesting for me to observe here what I had seen in other developing lands: the health of the brewing industry and the quality of their products seem to have a direct correlation with the economic health of a country. Severe excise taxes are often an indication of naive government repression of business and/or foolishness within a government. Surely they are a measure of government awareness and intelligence. There are lessons here that don't need to be repeated.

For me, it soon became obvious that ours was a unique opportunity to observe an emerging economy and examine the principles upon which beer culture evolves: the brewing community, consumer patterns and the politics of alcohol. Sometimes we become so mired in the complexity of our own developed nations that we lose sight of the real reason why the brewing community and beer culture exist. The opportunities to observe the remnants of the past, the struggles of the present and the hopes of the future are rare in this rapidly changing world. Those that exist are fleeting. We were travelers in fortunate times.

Everywhere we visited, we observed an active revival of beer cultures. There was a time when beer was a proud part of these lives. Now the struggle to catch up with the rest of the beer world was in full swing. Today's standards of international beer quality are at various stages of being realized. They are what one strives for as a brewer. First you discover what the standards are and then you attempt to achieve them with whatever resources are available. All brewers know these dynamics between the abundance and scarcity of resources.

Though the ideals were admirable, it was sometimes discomforting for me to see where the road to "progress" could lead. Modern equipment, efficiency of labor force, technically "cleaner" beer, longer shelf life, wider distribution and markets and profitability—yes, certainly these are some of the elements of growth, progress and quality.

But I grew very fond of many of the beers naturally brewed from what today's "experts" could refer to as "low-quality" ingredients. A tankard of microbrewed country beer served from brewer-crafted wooden barrels, naturally carbonated and gravity dispensed, became an adventure we looked forward to each day. This fresh beer was an important and essential tradition that millions had enjoyed. Yes, of course, the beer lasted only one week before spoiling, but that is the character and nature of heritage any beer culture has as its foundation. The best-tasting fruit is picked ripe and directly from the tree. This is a truth that is rarely experienced in the days of modernization and marketplace dynamics. Will these perfectly made country-fresh beers be forgotten at the expense of clean, pasteurized and stable beer brewed with high-yield hop harvests, disease-resistant malted barley, purified yeast and treated water?

Our trip was about cultural and professional exchange. There was one message I hoped they heard from me: Don't forget your traditions and the products that make your beer culture unique from the rest of the world of beer. With these traditions there is little competition. Yes, I understand in order to be profitable in the current international beer market there is a minimum investment required to develop and maintain quality in the brewery. But with profitability and success, please don't forget your beer culture. Without it, you have nothing that can't be done anywhere else in the world.

Aspiring to be big was the common theme among the developing breweries that had resources. We visited several other breweries that were left behind in the backwaters. They produced the most interesting and complex beers. It was fresh and reminisced of tradition and a passion that they struggled to maintain in the face of market economics and distribution dynamics. Theirs was the dream and the soul to which beer drinkers will someday return.

The brewery chief at the Bauska Brewery in Latvia, Karlis Zaltitis, told us of his 43-year career as a brewer. Deported to Siberia and the stalag prison

ZALTITIS BALTIC PORTER

A unique tradition of strong lagered porters is slowly finding its way into the American brewing culture. Smooth, lagered, caramel-like with cocoa notes, this porter is rich and creamy in texture. It is a hybrid of Baltic tradition and the provocatively floral character of certain varieties of American hops. The recipe can be found on page 365.

camps during the Stalin era, he managed to persevere and return to his beloved brewing, becoming a very talented brewer. Each of us was seated in the brewery's comforting wood-walled tasting room, our hands wrapped around mugs of frothy, fresh microbrewed beer. During a small hesitation between stories we finally asked, "What kind of changes occurred after Stalin died and Khrushchev came into power?" Karlis paused and smiled thoughtfully, and through our translator he slowly said in Latvian one distinct word at a time, "The snow began to melt." We were all momentarily silent as he grinned and his eyes clearly sparkled.

Now there is a second thaw brought to the Baltic nations by a very special kind of global warming. It promises much hope for the reemergence of a very proud beer culture.

Wagging the Tail in China

IN 1999 there were more than 600 breweries in China. That number has more than likely shrunk dramatically, while at the same time Chinese beer production has grown from 30 million barrels in 1996 to over 200 million barrels by the year 2000. Small, dysfunctional breweries are disappearing as the transportation infrastructure improves and companies consolidate their resources to increase efficiency and profits. But at what expense?

Despite the decline of small breweries, we enjoyed beers at several brewpubs encountered on our 1999 trip through China.

Eight of us, with beer on our minds, had just finished an intensive 12-day tour of China. Our adventure had begun with a visit to the Zhongce Bejiing Beer Company, a joint venture between Japanese giant Asahi Brewing Company and the Chinese government. Vice General Manager Shuji Fukushima (speaking Japanese), Chief Engineer Youan Yan Fang (speaking Chinese) and our group (speaking English) endeavored an early-morning three-way translated discussion less than 24 hours after we had arrived from America. The experience seemed to typify the extreme and sometimes bewildering nature of our tour.

In 1999, China was on the verge of becoming the world's largest producer of beer in the world (which it has since done), yet the complexity of our experience could be likened to an intricate quest, trying to unravel and make sense of dozens of conflicting logics and traditions of language, politics, economics and the culture of food and beverage. We had all been enjoying Chinese beer in our hotel lobby upon our arrival the day before. Jamie Johnson, our delegate from Denver, observed, "All of us had sampled the brewery's products the previous evening and we agreed it was an excellent beer (considering we're discussing Chinese lagers)." We enjoyed many beers! We learned two truths: (1) A multinational love of beer was quickly developing in China, and (2) the more we spent time with the Chinese and enjoyed their beer, the easier it was to unravel the emerging Chinese passion for beer. But we had to enjoy a lot of beer just to begin unraveling.

During the trip, our group met with brewers from all over China. We learned about their world and told them about ours.

There is currently a mad dash in China—a gold rush, if you will, though the gold is beer rather than metal. Most of the huge European, North American, Asian and African multinational brewing companies are there trying to carve out their own piece of the market and profits. The statistics are all there, ranking who is the largest and who has captured market share: Anheuser-Busch, Heineken, Carlsberg, Fosters, Pabst, Interbrew, Asahi, Bass, South African Breweries, San Miguel, etc.

But, alas, all these numbers take on another meaning when you discover that the average price of beer in China is 16 cents per 650-millileter (20 oz.) bottle. That doesn't leave much room for profit and success—in the short term. The complexity of the marketplace is mind-boggling. China is not one country with a single regulating government. It is a country of regions and a great variety of people, languages and cultures.

To overcome these vast differences, the large multinational beer companies have poured vast amounts of money into China. It's a natural business-as-usual thing big brewing companies do. But a lot of their efforts are wasted. The Chinese-owned brewing companies are number one in their own country. Foreign interests are last.

I asked myself, where is anyone doing anything to develop a culture of beer enjoyment and diversity?

What frightened me were not the huge investments multinational companies have made, but the logic and research behind their decisions. In our 12 days of visiting brewing companies we talked with experts representing the Chinese, Danes, Americans, Japanese, Germans, British, Irish and others in Beijing, Shanghai, Qingdao and Hong Kong. Our experiences and the information we received created an overload and posed more questions than they answered, until those last few pints of Ruddles, Speckled Hen and Guinness during our final day's conversations in Hong Kong. There, it all seemed to come together. It began to make some sense. We knew we were not experts, but the diversity of experiences, conversations, beers, breweries, cultures and perspectives we observed made us all wonder how anyone could endeavor to start a company or enter a new market without inviting diversity and pondering the questions asked in their research. The key to success seemed to hinge on truly becoming involved, immersing yourself in the research and the culture you were trying to win over to your beer. What we observed, with a few small exceptions, seemed to display a disregard for the true nature of the potential beer drinkers themselves.

It seemed clear that on a larger scale, companies didn't understand the situation, they simply threw money around. People always smile when there's money to pick up, but then they go home and couldn't care less about why it was there to find. On the large-company scale you are bound by the reality that you will make big mistakes and encounter unforeseen gnarly situations. We heard plenty about the ridiculous mistakes companies had made, simply because they hadn't really made the effort to "be there" and understand what was actually going on.

Still, there were several encouraging beer experiences that seemed to highlight our group's hopes for the future.

We visited China's largest brewery, the Yanjing Brewery. Its expansive halls and buildings are built of marble. It reminded us of India's Taj Majal.

Enjoying ten-dollar liters of craft beer in Beijing

Yanjing has an annual production capacity of 9 million hectoliters and has 7,800 employees. Their beer is one of the least expensive in the marketplace, and they dominate the Beijing area market. They claim to be profitable. During our visit in mid-November, the place looked empty and was not in production. We learned that most Chinese do not drink beer in the wintertime. In their tasting room we were offered tea, not beer.

On our return to Beijing, our bus passed by a small building where we all noticed gleaming copper and stainless steel tanks in a restaurant window. That evening several of us embarked on an unscheduled adventure, returning to the Duck and Dark to enjoy a brewpub-brewed pils and dark beer, served fresh from tank "pigtails." A completely local establishment, there was no English spoken there. The dark was excellent. The place was empty.

Earlier we had enjoyed the Paulaner Brauhaus, a small brewpub in the Kempinski Hotel in Beijing where in 1997, 70 percent of their customers were foreigners. By 1999, 70 percent of their customers were local Chinese, paying $8 to $10 a liter for their unfiltered German-style Helles, Oktoberfest, pils and Weizen. Compare that with about 20 cents a liter for local beer in the supermarkets and you begin to understand how bewildering things can be. Days later, at a Guinness pub in Shanghai, we heard the same statistics—a 70 percent turnaround from foreigners to locals. These establishments serving specialty or import-style beers are few, but they succeed in their own super-micro way. We were told that there are eight brewpubs in Beijing, but we suspect there are more.

The Chinese enjoy an astounding diversity of foods, yet the only beer they know is very low-hopped light lager. Is there potential for diversity? We asked the question: Isn't there any dark beer in China, made by Chinese breweries? Hardly, though Tsingtao makes an excellent very dark lager (brewed at 14 degrees Plato; 1.056) for some of their Southeast Asian export markets. We found that Tsingtao Dark went extremely well with Chinese food. Furthermore, the locally available Tsingtao light lager was more complex in malt and hop flavor than the same beer they export to America and Europe.

The Chinese government actively encouraged consumption of beer and wine over distilled spirits. Developing the market for female beer drinkers was of much interest. Why? Asian women's capacity to drink alcohol is greater than that of Chinese men, because Asian men have less liver enzyme activity than Asian women to detoxify alcohol. Price rules. Market share rules. Volume rules. There is little brand loyalty. Welcome to the Wild East.

We enjoyed Oktoberfest-style lagers at a brewpub in Shanghai called the Bund Brauhaus Festhaus and visited and sampled at a microbrewery in

QINGDAO DARK LAGER

Tsingtao light lager is brewed in China by the well-known Tsingtao brewery, whose beers are served at most American Chinese restaurants. Their dark lager is a beer type you don't see exported to the United States. Worthy of your brewing efforts, this complex and flavorful dark lager is light and crisp, yet maintains a certain roasted malt complexity and full flavor beer enthusiasts will enjoy. The recipe can be found on page 367.

Hong Kong. Perhaps if you are a contrarian, offering quality microbrewed beers that express beer culture and passion, you may succeed where others are bound to fail.

The city of Qingdao, home of Tsingtao Brewery #1, was of interest to all of us when we heard that the city hosts the largest beer festival in China every year in late August and early September.

American beer? We encountered several Budweiser and Corona billboards in Shanghai, but rarely encountered the beer. In Hong Kong, Samuel Adams Boston Lager was the American beer featured at our hotel. And mind you—it tasted fresh.

Bula! Vale Vakaviti
Fiji Homebrew

AS ALL of those places I have been become special to me because I've been there; so it has been with Lakeba, a tiny island of the Lau group, one of the 300 islands of Fiji. On a globe it is a tiny speck in the South Pacific surrounded by blue, just west of the International Date Line.

From the main Fijian island of Viti Levu, my decision to embark on an adventure to the outer island Lakeba was unplanned, made on a whim. The most important thing I had going for me was what I had already found to be the overwhelming friendliness and generosity of the Fijian people.

Lakeba was to be full of surprises. On first impression, it seemed just one of those South Sea copra islands surrounded by the quiet, clear, blue-green ocean, gentle hills and sandy and sometimes rocky coast. Five small villages were scattered along the encircling coastline. In 1978, there were no hotels nor any other type of "tourist accommodations."

So where did I make my stay? I didn't. I admit that having gone to Lakeba so blindly, I had psychologically prepared myself for the worst. I could very well not have been graciously accepted into the community of these islands. In such faraway places, I could expect this to be the case for any number of reasons or circumstances.

As it turned out, I fortuitously found myself given the most gracious Fijian hospitality by the Vabula family in the tiny village of Tubou. Suffice it to say that a simple series of chance acquaintances the morning of my arrival led me to Johnny Vabula. For 10 magnificent days I lived an intimate Fijian lifestyle. In Fiji, you don't hurry.

Within hours of settling in the household, my thirst for beer overwhelmed me. I asked, "Johnny, would there be a place nearby where I might buy some beer?" I never really expected an encouraging answer. Johnny replied, "You want to drink beer on Lakeba? Yes, you can buy Fiji Bitter, but the price is so dear to us that we do not drink it too much." I became discouraged, but he quickly added with a mischievous smile, "But if you like to drink beer, tomorrow we will drink Fiji Homebrew. And when we drink, we will drink to hell—cowboy style!"

I somehow had stumbled onto a Fijian homebrewer. I was amazed at my luck to find such hospitality. But wait a minute, I thought, why couldn't we have some now? I ventured to ask, somewhat hesitantly, "Johnny, where is your homebrew now?"

"Oh, tomorrow we will have Fiji Homebrew. This afternoon I will make it and tomorrow it will be ready and we will drink to bloody hell." And he unwound a hearty laugh that slowly trailed off to my own anxiety about bloody hell.

I had let the afternoon's conversation trail with the words "bloody hell" and soon resolved, "what the hell." Fate had brought me successfully this far and if it were to make a stop in bloody hell, well, I hadn't been there yet and might as well see about it.

That night, lying in bed, my mosquito coil lit, I reconsidered my initial anxiety about what the "Fiji Homebrew" could possibly be. I managed to forget my anxiety by remembering my American Homebrewers pledge: "Relax. Don't worry. Have a homebrew." I repeated this to myself three times and immediately fell asleep.

My morning came and went, and an afternoon was passed sharing a meal and drinks of kava kava (the national drink of Fiji, derived from the roots of a certain pepper plant) with Fijian prime minister Sir Kamisese Mara, whose home happened to be the village where I was staying. I waited quietly with

Johnny Vabula, Lakemba, Fiji

anticipation, encouraged by Johnny's winks throughout the day as the brew fermented in a corner of his tiny general store. "It is almost ready, Charlie. Almost ready."

Johnny's store closed in the late afternoon. It was time!

Johnny sauntered into a side room and drew a pitcher of his Fiji Homebrew. He proudly poured a tall glassful. I stared at it, looked at his devilish smile, and then together we bottoms-upped on our way to bloody hell, wherever that was going to be.

The beer had a rich yeast appearance and flavor that wasn't at all unpleasant. For sure it was alcoholic. A very mean concoction to be sure. What was it made from, and how? Well, that was easy: water, sugar, a quarter-pound of yeast and the juice of boiled cassava (tapioca). Cassava is a staple food of many South Pacific islands. Incredibly easy to grow, the potato-like root is cooked much the way a potato would be. It is very starchy. As I later learned, Fiji Homebrew can also be made with green coconut water or boiled green papaya juice rather than cassava. And as for the yeast content of Johnny's five-gallon batch of brew, he says, "The more yeast you use, the stronger and quicker it is."

"When I drink—I drink to hell," Johnny said. And so we went into the latter part of the evening, talking about things that two happily tipsy friends talk about. Above all, he impressed upon me his own personal lifestyle—"cowboy style":

VALE VAKAVITI

While not your typical homebrewed beverage, this beer should give you an indication of what beer you might be enjoying if you were stranded on a desert island. The recipe can be found on page 370.

"You know how they do in cowboy movies. If a cowboy wants to put his feet on the table, he puts his feet on the table. If a cowboy wants to smash a glass, he smashes a glass. When a cowboy wants to drink, he drinks. Never mind anything else. That is what we do here in my house—COWBOY STYLE." Rolling into a hearty laugh, he continued, "So, carry on, Charlie. Carry on."

Matters of Homebrew

TO MAKE SURE I have the beer I like to drink whenever I travel, especially to foreign lands, I simply pack a bottle or two. Sometimes, with the help of friends, I'll pack 100 gallons. As any homebrewer already realizes, homebrew is great, especially if you've made it yourself. And it's even greater when you've taken a bottle with you to some remote corner of the world to enjoy with friends or new acquaintances.

Perhaps the most memorable of all my homebrewing travels was in 1984, when 54 other homebrewers and myself journeyed together to the South Pacific islands of Fiji. Twenty five-gallon canisters of homebrewed beer and mead accompanied us. We anticipated that Fiji would be an island paradise with or without our homebrew, but having 100 gallons of our own stuff turned out to be a beer maker's and drinker's heaven.

With the permission of our resort, restaurant and ship's management, we were allowed the freedom to enjoy our own beer in between thirst-quenching quantities of the country's own Fiji Bitter. We used a magnum champagne bottle as a "pitcher" when serving our hand-pumped brews for dinner. What the waitresses didn't realize was that we had our keg stashed in a cool room outside the dining room. Mysteriously and magically, to their astonishment, that one bottle seemed an endless pour of beer and mead for all 55 of us. The entire trip was pure paradise, with good friends, good feelings, great scenery, special experiences and the best beer in the world.

SPARKLING MEAD—TROPICAL CHAMPAGNE

This is the simplest and fastest-maturing type of mead. Perhaps because of its relatively low alcohol and delicate nature, it is not very popular and is certainly not commercially available. Yet this is often the most enjoyable type of mead because of its resemblance to champagne, and you can enjoy more of it. I guarantee that if the idea of a light, effervescent honey champagne sounds good to you, then you will rave about this recipe. The recipe can be found on page 370.

But when you've had one great experience, why not plan for another? Three years later I led an excursion into the jungles of northern Thailand with 18 other homebrewers. In addition to bringing our own homebrew, we proudly hauled a round of Thai One On Pale Ale into remote hill-tribe country on the backs of several elephants (no, we weren't drinking and driving on elephants).

The first day's journey was delayed by several hours by the lack of elephants for our group. I ended up riding bareback and behind the ears of one of the elephants for five hours. We arrived at our first hill-tribe village after dark. It was a cool night. The fire felt good, and I recall the meal of chicken, chopped banana flowers, rice and homebrew as one of the best meals I've ever had. I think that the homebrew saved my butt, literally, after riding five hours on the ears of an elephant, whispering sweet nothings, through darkening jungle. You'd feel the same way about that homebrew as I did, I'm sure.

CHAPTER

13

. . . .

Seeing Beyond the Beer

BY NOW I hope you've engaged yourself with a few beers. Where does the beer take you? You've read the reflections of several brewers in response to this question. You've imagined their songs, dance and poetry and what really makes them tick. You have been awakened to the spirit of the brewer and the personality behind every beer you enjoy.

I, too, get "taken by the beer." Perhaps the opportunity to melt into a comfortable chair and gaze through the bubbles does not present itself as often as I would like, but perhaps that is the nature of being involved with special experiences. They happen, but they do not happen every moment—that is why they are so special.

What is an ultimate beer experience? For me, there are so many. Though, curiously, I recall this experience in the Caribbean as one I would wish to reincarnate in a thousand different ways. Whenever I do have an ultimate beer experience, the beer is always something I see beyond, in the world of my imagination.

An Ultimate Beer Experience
Kriek, Cassis and the French Caribbean

ABOVE ME loomed Mt. Pelée, a volcano that 85 years ago exploded and instantly killed the 30,000 people who had resided in St.-Pierre, a picturesque town on the French West Indies island of Martinique. Below me beckoned a perfectly chilled glass of Belgian-made ale, Leffe Brun. Beyond the glass and the pleasantly warm outdoor café, the seaside view found me hardly believing I was in the Caribbean, able to enjoy a variety of interesting beers.

There are many wonderful islands in the Caribbean, though beer is usually not the primary reason for heading there. But beer is my business, and I was here to work.

I've been pleased to discover dozens of wonderfully small breweries scattered throughout the Caribbean. All of them make thirst-quenching light American/Caribbean-style lagers. Many are contract brewing (or owned by) Heineken or a powerfully tasty and strong (7.5 percent alcohol) special export Guinness. Some also make their own island brands of stout. In April 1994, I flew to Martinique, an island "state" of France, to attend the 33rd annual convention of the Master Brewers of Americas, district Caribbean.

I took the opportunity of having come all this way from snowy Colorado to explore a bit of the island culture before the convention began. While almost all other Caribbean islands are tiny nations, I was often reminded, "Right now you are in France." This was just the beginning of what made this island unique.

While Martinique's own Brasserie Lorraine produces a hard-to-find porter and a light lager with pleasantly discernible malt and hop character, there were other beers I soon discovered. Lorraine was a welcoming, island-brewed fresh lager sufficient for the first few beers of my cultural explorations, but I was soon very intrigued by the tap handles at local bars and restaurants.

Lorraine was not to be found on draft, anywhere. I discovered the available draft was imported Belgian-brewed Stella Artois, Leffe Blonde and Leffe Brun. They were ubiquitously available throughout Martinique. Ahh, the Blonde was refreshingly good, but I really enjoyed the zestiness of the Brun. In all my travels to tropical islands and climates, this was my first encounter with specialty beers (other than stouts and the brewpub beer of Santiago's on Cayman Island)—and this was from Belgium no less! Things were looking up; the volcano was not blowing smoke and there was a warm sea just outside my window.

But never, and I mean never-ever, have I been so pleasantly beer surprised than when I encountered Le Terminal Bar at 104, rue Ernest Deproge, in the capital town of Fort-de-France—a quiet, comfortable, unpretentious second-floor bar with a view of the harbor. As I entered and crossed the stairwell, I noticed many familiar beer labels and signs from around the world, but not knowing French I dismissed them as wishful decorations. But when the beer menu arrived, language posed no barrier. Before me, I suddenly had a choice of 80 different beers from around the world, of which more than 25 came from Belgium and 15 from France. *Whoohoo!* I was in the Caribbean without any homebrew, but I seemed to have found the next best thing.

I recalled that I was "actually in France." With that in mind, I delved into the choices to be made among Jenlain, Adelscott, Bière du Démon, Gueuze de la Bécasse, Lucifer, Abbaye de Leffe Radieuse, Mort Subite Cassis Lambic, Chimay Rouge and Chimay Bleue, Sixtus, Kwak, Duvel and Orval, to name just a few. While sipping on Jenlain, a French country ale, I learned from some of the folks who owned and tended the bar that all their beer, regardless of its origins, had been imported from France. The beers of the United States, Australia, Canada and even Mexico—in some cases just a few hundred miles away—were all, incredibly, first shipped to France and then to this tiny island, where Le Terminal did the best they could in presenting some classic brews. I asked why, but the Frenchman seated beside me shook his head in confusion and only explained in a heavily accented deep, gravelly voice, "Ahhh, but thees ees *France!*"

With this in mind, I chose beers that could hope to do well with age and journeying. But not before my curiosity got the better of me and I asked what a "Picon" was, listed on the menu under the "country" of "Terminal." Someone explained, "It is something we drink in France when the weather is warm. It is quite popular." Half expecting some type of wheat beer with lemon, I pressed for details and found myself with an almost green-colored beer with a strangely citruslike aroma and flavor. "It is artichoke liqueur with light lager," someone offered in explanation with a "wait-and-see-whether-he'll-drink-it" smile. With one half-squinted eye, I paused a moment, then replied cautiously, "You mean like artichoke heart liqueur and beer?" Yes, and so I sniffed, swirled and sipped. Now both my eyes squinted at the sweet, citrus character and warmth of alcohol. I managed to artfully choke down the rest of the graciously complimentary French beverage, but I must admit it's not something you'll find me paying dollars, francs or euros for in the future.

> ## MONASTIC BLEUE STRONG BELGIAN-STYLE ALE
>
> In the spirit of Chimay Blue, one of the world's most famous Trappist ales, I recreated a homebrewed recipe that approaches the richness of the experience. This recipe can be found on page 371.

After this unholy baptism I was not to be disappointed. That evening I had one of my very few "ultimate beer experiences."

I enjoy an occasional good cigar. I had brought one of my favorites with me just in case I found myself with some time to relax. I'm very pleased to report that a Davidoff Corona begun at sunset with a Chimay Bleue (9 percent alcohol), followed with a Cassis Lambic Mort Subite, can only be described as out of this world. The mild nutty-coffee-cocoa aroma and flavor of my cigar. The charm of Cassis Lambic with its rich berry-balsam fir and fruitlike aromatics and the calming sensation of deep red bubbles accompanied with a superbly quenching balance of sweetness and acidity was dreamlike. The warm night air and breeze carried the smell of sea foam. The lingering effects of Chimay Bleue, with its malt and hops, had exquisitely concealed its alcohol—at first.

There are certain combinations of flavors and aromas that can evoke one's spirit with regard to the best things in life. Unknowingly and quite naturally I drifted toward the beers whose essences are microbrewed. A spirit of beer filled the bar, my glass and the evening—all accomplished because of microbrewers somewhere else in the world. They were communicating with me.

That moonlit night in Martinique at Le Terminal began and ended with some memorable bests. My one and only regret was that I couldn't speak French. A place like this certainly may have inspired me to learn to do so. There was much to talk about, but no one seemed to understand—but me.

The American Ark

WHILE WALKING down the grand and long corridors of the train station in Munich in 1997, I had a chance encounter with a member of the American Homebrewers Association. He recognized me, between his train connections. He was Belgian. We talked, and he was very supportive of the direction that American microbrewing has taken. He made a point of telling me, "You can find a greater and truer-to-tradition variety of Belgian beers in the United States than you can in Belgium. Belgians think they have all the tradition. But we are losing it. It is the Americans that are helping save what we Belgians are losing . . . but no one will listen to me. They won't believe me when I tell them what is happening in the United States."

A British real ale personality, judging at the Great American Beer Festival, similarly confided in me, "Good English mild ales are becoming less common in the U.K. I can find better English mild ales in the United States now than I can in the U.K." I, myself, reflect on how the new American breweries have indeed revived the traditions of English porter and oatmeal stout. Some beer journalists of fame often note how some styles of beer were close to extinction before the new brewing revival in America saved them from the archival tombs.

Oktoberfest in Munich often heralds the lamentations from Americans and Germans alike: "They're modeling their Oktoberfestbier after Coors Extra Gold" (adding that Extra Gold was a great beer, but certainly not an Oktoberfest style). "The tradition of Oktoberfest beer is being diluted . . . I can find better Oktoberfest-style beers in America."

I can't help adding my own opinion. The character of the Munich Helles style of lager continues to migrate in flavor toward a low-hopped, mild pils.

The Hellesbiers I remember from my 1989 German beer journey are slowly and quite sadly losing the richness of malt and special flavor of hops. I know that I can make or find a better Helles in the United States than I can generally find in Munich today. Though I do faithfully seek the small countryside breweries where the spirit of microbrewing and beer passion continues, and tradition and flavor are still being preserved, I am concerned for their future.

I often recall my world travels and the country beers, enjoyed from small casks, made by great men and great women. Are they destined to be inundated by the need to modernize and become competitive in the international marketplace? In the face of the floodwaters, their response is often one of panic and almost always a concession to the rising water to abandon their hopes and swim among the light lager waters rather than create a safe harbor. Might I dare say that they must recognize and take heart in their uniqueness?

I believe, as do many of my colleagues, that here the United States of America we have created an American Beer Ark that is not filled with things American. How odd is this? Wouldn't the rest of the world assume that if Americans were to create an ark to protect treasures from impending doom, we would of course protect our own American treasures? For with our newfound sense of tradition, we have created something unique in the world of things important, lasting and of immeasurable value for generations to come.

We have created the American Beer Ark to float above the light-lagered oceans of the world, harboring with care and passionate enthusiasm the great beer traditions of the world. Little does the world recognize the care and effort of American beer enthusiasts and microbrewers in taking aboard the ark the world's well- and lesser-known beer types. With heart and care and without pretension, they seem to be scouring the earth for threatened and lost beers, to revive and explore them here in the United States.

At the risk of seeming a bit too pretentious, I write these thoughts as an American writer, observer and beer enthusiast myself. I share them with you not because they are my own, but because they are those of knowledgeable people who respect the traditions of beer and are not necessarily American.

The American Beer Ark is my own concept, though not without precedent in the world of Slow Food, traditions and cultural treasures. As the waters continue to rise, the question becomes, what will we take on board? Fortunately, arks are only needed until the waters recede. It is my hope that brewers and consumers will take heart in the culture of beer and traditions and that the day will soon arrive where we don't need an ark.

19TH-CENTURY LEIPZIGER GOSE

This wild fermented wheat beer spiced with coriander seed represents a German ale tradition that has nearly disappeared. It seems to be a distant cousin to the Belgian lambic tradition. Three options are given to brew and mingle with this unique traditional beer. The recipe can be found on page 374.

The Pride of a Brewer

SINCE 1978 I have journeyed, meeting and talking with homebrewers, brewmasters and beer enthusiasts throughout the world in quest of understanding not only the brewing world we live in but why it is we pride ourselves as brewers. I recall my origins as a brewer, and to this day there dwells in me a certain undefined pride that I am knowledgeable in the brewers' craft. I'm sure that it dwells in the soul of every brewer, yet its presence is not easy to define.

The mysterious pride we have as brewers always remains. Beyond the simplicity of beginning to brew is a knowledge that emerges within every brewer. Everywhere in the world, whether we are amateur or professional brewers, we build upon our experiences and develop a skill that no one can ever take away. Those evolving skills and worldly knowledge have been shared for more than 5,000 years. Whether one has been brewing for one year or more than twenty, the life skills learned by brewing are not a simple anyone-can-do-it proposition. By becoming and continuing as a brewer one crosses a mystic threshold, not only gaining experience but also using skills to craft works of art and science for the noble reason of promoting pleasure and enjoyment. This is a rarity in today's world. Despite the trends toward speed and convenience, brewers are steadfast in their pursuits. They are able to experience the pride of accomplishment and mastery of skills that no one can ever deny or take away.

Yes, anyone can do it. But to brew and develop knowledge of the brewers' craft is something very special. It is not easy to do. Those of us who endeavor to brew belong to a worldwide community. We take the time to brew and we take the time to cherish the hard-earned insights we have gained as brewers. Those who do not brew can never know what we know about the blending of life sciences, arts and experiences. Take pride in your endeavor as a brewer. You've earned it.

The Gaze from Above, upon the Beer Below
Joining the BierConvent

IN AMSTERDAM, I found myself crossing a castle moat, entering what appeared to be a crumbling ruin, a lone tower protruding into the sky. Inside, there were thick walls that surrounded the spiraling staircase, three-foot-deep window wells allowing light into each balcony. The narrow staircase wound and wound and wound through three, four, then five enormous levels. Large rooms set aside at each floor's pause were decorated in the style of the 15th century. The floorboards creaked. The ceilings were tall and airy. There were gypsies in the attic. Jesters and musicians wandered in the spirit of the time. The tall grand mirror in the second-floor banquet room was grayed with a smoky film.

She was dressed in flowing scarves, muted and well matched to the worn brick walls. "What do you have in your basket?" I asked. "What do you have in your bag?" she replied. I'll show you mine if you show me yours . . . Anna the gypsy with a Dutch smile cocked her head to the side and managed a subtle twist in her lip.

"Will you read my cards?" I asked.

"No, not really thoroughly, but let's see a few."

I chose a card, then changed my mind, choosing a second before the first was revealed. The second card, she told me, is "the past." From the second deck I chose and it revealed "a leader." "But that is not really you. . . . You have struggled with being a leader in the past . . . your real role is of being a spiritual leader. People will turn to you for vision," Anna continued.

I chose another card as she spread the original deck on the castle table. It was my original card: "emotions."

"See, this is really your card . . . it is about your emotions and you should have stuck with this card when you first chose it. You need to feel your emotions and go with them more freely."

From there I chose the card that would suit my emotions. The card I chose revealed "the fool."

"But you really aren't a fool; you see, the dog is the heart and he grounds you. Dare to be the fool. Follow your heart. It will be okay."

I reached into my bag and found a small clay bird whistle, leaving Anna, the gypsy, with the small bird that has breathed the wishes of six continents and traveled with me around the world several times and was meant to be her keepsake that evening. I recall taking the tiny bird whistle out of my pack only one week before, just before departing home, and then replacing it for an impulsive unknown reason. Perhaps I was thinking it was meant to travel with me once again to its final destiny. A small child, a girl dressed in native clothes high in the Andes mountains of Ecuador, had given it to me as I was walking a countryside dirt road. When I left Anna, she was still staring at and holding the little bird whistle in her hand and began crying, "It's about the same wish I've always had in my life." And at that I departed, never having asked what her wish had always been.

"Dare to be the fool . . . your heart will ground you, so follow it and follow the path of your emotions . . ."

THE NEXT DAY, still in Amsterdam, I was celebrating my enthronement into the BierConvent International. Dinner was served over a period of three hours. Dutch jenever and beer flowed abundantly.

BierConvent International is an international organization, based in Munich. Invited to join by Printz Luitpold von Bayern, I am only the second American to join (the first was August Busch III). BCI's members are not only brewers, but people of many backgrounds embracing quality, beer appreciation and sensitivity to the humanity and international pride portraying what beer was always meant to be.

At my enthronement, I reverently sat and watched the enthronement of others from the front row. The presidents of Heineken and Grolsch were among us. Our ceremonies took place inside a massive building, once a cathedral in Amsterdam. I sat among the hundreds gathered as though attending a wedding. A pianist played classical music. A string quartet played Schubert and Mozart. I stared in disbelief at the colored patterns of the immense and extraordinary flower arrangements in the balconies high above; a bright spotlight intensified the colors. There was a ridiculous and imposing red throne in front of me at center stage. Pretentious? Yes, but I can't help but break into a little smile.

At my enthronement they spoke of my background and commented that if the BCI had not been founded in the 1960s, there was no doubt that Charlie Papazian would have founded it in 1996. I walked up to the "altar" and turned to receive my medallion and accompanying ribbon. I was ceremonially invited to drink from a very large pewter mug. I took long swallows, slowly savoring, drafting this brew into my being. The grand pianist banged away in dramatic and fanatical fashion. The room was beginning to spin. I continued swallowing and swallowing, gulping, the beer dribbling down the right side of my beard onto my tuxedo—loving every minute, every swallow.

The beer tasted great, my head tilted skyward, the bottom of the deep pewter mug began to hint of trailing off into an empty darkness. As I neared my finish, the mug tilted skyward and my eyes became distracted. I looked beyond the beer. My eyes changed from near focus to far. There, high, very, very high above, was a huge gilded domed ceiling, every arch coinciding at the center, in all its majestic grandeur. There in the middle at the highest point, beyond the chandeliers, the gold-leaf buttresses, the stained glass windows, the enormous flower arrangements and an impending belch, were two recently released, distantly tiny helium-filled balloons. No one noticed but me. Mickey Mouse and Donald Duck were watching over us, from up on high with their almighty helium-inflated gaze. There was a twinkle in my eye. Nothing seemed to me to be more genuine. I finished this beer nectar that had helped bring me here and everywhere.

The twinkle continues as I realize with the pride every brewer knows that it is all the same—same but joyously different.

Charlie Papazian
Planet Beer

It is not through knowledge but experiences of the world that we are brought into relation with it.

—ALBERT SCHWEITZER

SECTION THREE

Recipes

About the Recipes

Thank you, brewers and suppliers!

Whether you consider yourself a microbrewer or a homebrewer, these recipes will provide you with a jumping-off point for brewing classic, traditional, unique, eccentric, creative and cutting-edge styles of beer. These are recipes gathered from brewers and adapted, or were formulated from my 34 years of brewing experience and a bit of consultation with the wonderful people who supply brewers with malt, yeast, hops and other ingredients and supplies. I extend a very grateful thank-you to all the brewers who have shared with me their insights and knowledge.

Homebrewing

If you are new to homebrewing, my *Complete Joy of Homebrewing, 3rd Edition* (2003), will get you started and hooked with your first batch. Then you'll move on to more recipes, such as those presented in this book.

A few notes about these recipes

- I've adapted nearly all of the recipes to fit a 5-gallon (19 l) batch format.

- Almost all recipes are presented in two versions: one using all-grain techniques and the second using malt-extract brewing techniques.
- All hops are whole hops unless otherwise noted.
- You may substitute hop pellets for whole hops, but the amounts are not equal when used for bittering long boils. Hops boiled for less than 10 minutes may be either whole or pellets in equal amounts. When converting bittering/long boiling hops, substitute 15 percent less Homebrew Bittering Units (see below) if using hop pellets rather than whole hops. For example, if the recipe calls for 10 HBU (280 MBU) using whole hops, you should use 15 percent less, or 8.5 HBU oz. (238 MBU), in pellet form. Read the recipes carefully; be careful not to assume measurements in ounces or grams. A whole-hop version of a particular variety may not be rated at the same alpha acid rated in pellet form.
- In all-grain recipes I assume an 85 percent grain conversion efficiency, because this is what I usually obtain with the crush of my malt and the two-step infusion method used in most of these recipes. If your brewing system achieves less efficiency, you will need to increase the amount of grains proportionally.
- HBU/MBU or Homebrew Bitterness Units
  - HBU = % alpha acid rating of hops multiplied by ounces = Homebrew Bittering Units
  - MBU = % alpha acid rating of hops multiplied by grams = Metric Bittering Units

Homebrew Bitterness Units: A method with which homebrewers can determine how much hops to use involves the concept of Homebrew Bitterness Units (HBU). In metric units it is expressed as Metric Bitterness Units (MBU).

Homebrew Bitterness Units = % alpha acid of hops multiplied by ounces of hops. This is a very useful concept when a recipe for a given volume of beer calls for, say, 2 ounces of 5 percent alpha acid Hallertauer hops, which is equal to 10 HBU. It is important to note the volume of beer being brewed when using Homebrew Bitterness Units as a measurement of hops.

1) If your Hallertauer hops are only 4 percent alpha acid, you will know to use:

$$10 \text{ HBU} \div 4\% = 2.5 \text{ oz. of hops}$$

2) If you wish to use another variety of hops, say Chinook hops at 10 percent alpha acid, you know to use:

$$10 \text{ HBU} \div 10\% = 1 \text{ oz. of Chinook hops}$$

Similarly, for metric units, MBU = % alpha acid of hops multiplied by grams of hops. If 280 MBU are called for in a recipe, then:

1) If your Hallertauer hops are only 4 percent alpha acid, you will know to use:

$$280 \text{ MBU} \div 4\% = 70 \text{ g of hops}$$

OR

2) If you wish to use another variety of hops, say Chinook hops at 10 percent alpha acid, you know to use:

$$280 \text{ MBU} \div 10\% = 28 \text{ g of Chinook hops}$$

"ORIGINAL" BALLARD BITTER

- TARGET ORIGINAL GRAVITY: 1.045 (11 B)
- APPROXIMATE FINAL GRAVITY: 1.014 (3.5 B)
- IBU: ABOUT 32
- APPROXIMATE COLOR: 5 SRM (10 EBC)
- ALCOHOL: 4% BY VOLUME

All-Grain Recipe *for 5 gallons (19 l)*

Ballard Bitter—Ya Sure Ya Betcha

7.5 lbs.	(3.4 kg) American 2-row pale malt
¼ oz.	(7 g) Cluster hops 7.5% alpha (1.9 HBU/53 MBU)—90 minutes boiling
¼ oz.	(7 g) Oregon Fuggles hops 4% alpha (1 HBU/28 MBU)—90 minutes boiling
¼ oz.	(7 g) Galena (originally Eroica hops were used) hops 12% alpha (3 HBU/84 MBU)—60 minutes boiling
½ oz.	(14 g) Cascade hops 5% alpha (2.5 HBU/70 MBU)—30 minutes boiling
½ oz.	(14 g) Cascade hops—1 minute boiling
½ oz.	(14 g) Oregon Fuggles—1 minute boiling
¼ tsp.	(1 g) powdered Irish moss

Wyeast Ringwood Ale yeast #1187 or White Labs Irish Ale yeast WLP004

¾ cup	(175 ml measure) corn sugar (priming bottles) or 0.33 cups (80 ml) corn sugar for kegging

A step infusion mash is employed to mash the grains. Add 7.5 quarts (7.1 l) of 140-degree F (60 C) water to the crushed grain, stir, stabilize and hold the temperature at 132 degrees F (53 C) for 30 minutes. Add 3.75 quarts (3.6 l) of boiling water and add heat to bring temperature up to 155 degrees F (68 C) and hold for about 30 minutes. Then raise temperature to 167 degrees F (75 C), lauter and sparge with 3.5 gallons (13.5 l) of 170-degree F (77 C) water. Collect about 5.5 gallons (21 l) of runoff. Add 90-minute hops and bring to a full and vigorous boil.

The total boil time will be 90 minutes. When 60 minutes remain, add the 60-minute hops. When 30 minutes remain, add the 30-minute hops. When 10 minutes remain, add the Irish moss. When 1 minute remains, add the 1-minute hops. After a total wort boil of 90 minutes, turn off the heat and place the pot (with cover on) in a running cold-water bath for 30 minutes. Continue to chill in the immersion, or use other methods to chill your wort. Then strain and sparge the wort into a sanitized fermenter. Bring the total volume to 5 gallons (19 l) with additional cold water if necessary. Aerate the wort very well.

Pitch the yeast when temperature of wort is about 70 degrees F (21 C). Ferment at about 70 degrees F (21 C) for about 1 week, or until fermentation shows signs of calm and stopping. Rack from your primary to a secondary fermenter and if you have the capability, "cellar" the beer at about 55 degrees F (12.5 C) for about 1 week.

Prime with sugar and bottle or keg when complete.

Malt Extract Recipe *for 5 gallons (19 l)*

6.25 lbs.	(2.8 kg) light malt extract syrup or 5 lbs. (2.3 kg) dry light malt extract
¼ oz.	(7 g) Cluster hops 7.5% alpha (1.9 HBU/53 MBU)—90 minutes boiling
¼ oz.	(7 g) Galena (originally Eroica hops were used) hops 12% alpha (3 HBU/84 MBU)—60 minutes boiling
¾ oz.	(21 g) Oregon Fuggles hops 4% alpha (3 HBU/84 MBU)—60 minutes boiling
½ oz.	(14 g) Cascade hops 5% alpha (2.5 HBU/70 MBU)—30 minutes boiling
½ oz.	(14 g) Cascade hops—1 minute boiling
½ oz.	(14 g) Oregon Fuggles—1 minute boiling
¼ tsp.	(1 g) powdered Irish moss
Wyeast Ringwood Ale yeast #1187 or White Labs Irish Ale yeast WLP004	
¾ cup	(175 ml measure) corn sugar (priming bottles) or 0.33 cups (80 ml) corn sugar for kegging

Dissolve malt extract in 2 gallons (7.6 l) of water, add 90-minute hops and bring to a boil.

The total boil time will be 90 minutes. When 60 minutes remain, add the 60-minute hops. When 30 minutes remain, add the 30-minute hops. When 10 minutes remain, add the Irish moss. When 1 minute remains, add the 1-minute hops. After a total wort boil of 90 minutes, turn off the heat.

Immerse the covered pot of wort in a cold-water bath and let sit for 30 minutes, or the time it takes to have a couple of homebrews.

Then strain out and sparge hops and direct the hot wort into a sanitized fermenter to which 2.5 gallons (9.5 l) of cold water has been added. Bring the total volume to 5 gallons (19 l) with additional cold water if necessary. Aerate the wort very well.

Pitch the yeast when temperature of wort is about 70 degrees F (21 C). Ferment at about 70 degrees F (21 C) for about 1 week, or until fermentation shows signs of calm and stopping. Rack from your primary to a secondary fermenter and if you have the capability, "cellar" the beer at about 55 degrees F (12.5 C) for about 1 week.

Prime with sugar and bottle or keg when complete.

1982 ORIGINAL SIERRA NEVADA PALE ALE

- TARGET ORIGINAL GRAVITY: 1.051 (12.5 B)
- APPROXIMATE FINAL GRAVITY: 1.016 (4 B)
- IBU: 38–40
- APPROXIMATE COLOR: 7 SRM (14 EBC)
- ALCOHOL: 4.5% BY VOLUME

All-Grain Recipe *for 5 gallons (19 l)*

8 lbs.	(3.6 kg) 2-row American pale malt
8 oz.	(225 g) American crystal malt (10-L)
¾ oz.	(21 g) Cluster hops 7.5% alpha (5.6 HBU/156 MBU)— 60 minutes boiling
¾ oz.	(21 g) Cascade hops 5% alpha (3.8 HBU/105 MBU)—30 minutes boiling
½ oz.	(14 g) Tettnanger hops (Santiam may be substituted) 4.5% alpha (2.3 HBU/64 MBU)—30 minutes boiling

½ oz.	(14 g) Cascade hops—1 minute
½ oz.	(14 g) Tettnanger hops (Santiam may be substituted)—1 minute boiling
¼ tsp.	(1 g) powdered Irish moss

Wyeast American Ale yeast #1056

¾ cup	(175 ml measure) corn sugar (priming bottles) or 0.33 cups (80 ml) corn sugar for kegging

A one-step infusion mash is employed to mash the grains. Add 8.5 quarts (8.1 l) of 168-degree F (76 C) water to the crushed grain, stir, stabilize and hold the temperature at 152 degrees F (66.5 C) for 60 minutes. Then raise temperature to 167 degrees F (75 C), lauter and sparge with 4 gallons (15.2 l) of 170-degree F (77 C) water. Collect about 5.5 gallons (21 l) of runoff. Add cluster hops and bring to a full and vigorous boil.

The total boil time will be 60 minutes. When 30 minutes remain, add the 30-minute hops. When 10 minutes remain, add the Irish moss. When 1 minute remains, add the 1-minute hops. After a total wort boil of 60 minutes, turn off the heat and place the pot (with cover on) in a running cold-water bath for 30 minutes. Continue to chill in the immersion or use other methods to chill your wort. Then strain and sparge the wort into a sanitized fermenter. Bring the total volume to 5 gallons (19 l) with additional cold water if necessary. Aerate the wort very well.

Pitch the yeast when temperature of wort is about 70 degrees F (21 C). Ferment at about 70 degrees F (21 C) for about 1 week, or until fermentation shows signs of calm and stopping. Rack from your primary to a secondary fermenter and if you have the capability, "cellar" the beer at about 55 degrees F (12.5 C) for about 1 week.

Prime with sugar and bottle or keg when complete. The original Sierra Nevada Pale Ale was fully bottle conditioned, just like your homebrew.

Malt Extract Recipe *for 5 gallons (19 l)*

6.5 lbs.	(3 kg) American light malt extract syrup
8 oz.	(225 g) American crystal malt (10-L)
1 oz.	(28 g) Cluster hops 7.5% alpha (7.5 HBU/210 MBU)—60 minutes boiling
1 oz.	(28 g) Cascade hops 5% alpha (5 HBU/140 MBU)—30 minutes boiling

¾ oz.	(21 g) Tettnanger hops (Santiam may be substituted) 4.5% alpha (3.4 HBU/95 MBU)—30 minutes boiling
½ oz.	(14 g) Cascade hops—1 minute boiling
½ oz.	(14 g) Tettnanger hops (Santiam may be substituted)—1 minute boiling
¼ tsp.	(1 g) powdered Irish moss
Wyeast American Ale yeast #1056	
¾ cup	(175 ml measure) corn sugar (priming bottles) or 0.33 cups (80 ml) corn sugar for kegging

Place crushed grains in 2 gallons (7.6 l) of 150-degree F (68 C) water and let steep for 30 minutes. Then strain out (and rinse with 3 quarts [3 l] hot water) and discard the crushed grains, reserving the approximately 2.5 gallons (9.5 l) of liquid, to which you will now add malt extract and cluster hops. Heat to boiling.

The total boil time will be 60 minutes. When 30 minutes remain, add the 30-minute hops. When 10 minutes remain, add the Irish moss. When 1 minute remains, add the 1-minute hops. After a total wort boil of 60 minutes, turn off the heat and place the pot (with cover on) in a running cold-water bath for 30 minutes.

Then strain out and sparge hops and direct the hot wort into a sanitized fermenter to which 2.5 gallons (9.5 l) of cold water has been added. Bring the total volume to 5 gallons (19 l) with additional cold water if necessary.

Pitch the yeast when temperature of wort is about 70 degrees F (21 C). Ferment at about 70 degrees F (21 C) for about 1 week, or until fermentation shows signs of calm and stopping. Rack from your primary to a secondary fermenter and if you have the capability, "cellar" the beer at about 55 degrees F (12.5 C) for about 1 week.

Prime with sugar and bottle or keg when complete. The original Sierra Nevada Pale Ale was fully bottle conditioned, just like your homebrew.

ORIGINAL PYRAMID WHEATEN ALE

* TARGET ORIGINAL GRAVITY: 1.045 (11 B)
* APPROXIMATE FINAL GRAVITY: 1.008 (2 B)
* IBU: ABOUT 25
* APPROXIMATE COLOR: 7 SRM (14 EBC)
* ALCOHOL: 4.5% BY VOLUME

All-Grain Recipe *for 5 gallons (19 l)*

3.25 lbs.	(1.5 kg) American 2-row pale malt
3 lbs.	(1.36 kg) American wheat malt
1 lb.	(454 g) crystal malt (10-L)
1 oz.	(28 g) Cascade hops 5% alpha (5 HBU/140 MBU)—120 minutes boiling
¼ oz.	(7 g) Perle hops 8% alpha (2 HBU/56 MBU)—15 minutes boiling
½ oz.	(14 g) Perle hops—1 minute boiling
¼ tsp.	(1 g) powdered Irish moss
English ale yeast	
¾ cup	(175 ml measure) corn sugar (priming bottles) or 0.33 cups (80 ml) corn sugar for kegging

A step infusion mash is employed to mash the grains. Add 7 quarts (6.7 l) of 140-degree F (60 C) water to the crushed grain, stir, stabilize and hold the temperature at 132 degrees F (53 C) for 30 minutes. Add 3.5 quarts (3.3 l) of boiling water, add heat to bring temperature up to 155 degrees F (68 C) and hold for about 30 minutes. Then raise temperature to 167 degrees F (75 C), lauter and sparge with 3.5 gallons (13.5 l) of 170-degree F (77 C) water. Collect about 5.5 gallons (21 l) of runoff. Add 120-minute hops and bring to a full and vigorous boil.

The total boil time will be 120 minutes. When 15 minutes remain, add the 15-minute hops. When 10 minutes remain, add the Irish moss. When 1 minute remains, add the 1-minute hops. After a total wort boil of 120 minutes, turn off the heat and place the pot (with cover on) in a running cold-water bath for 30 minutes. Continue to chill in the immersion or use other methods to chill your wort. Then strain and sparge the wort into a sanitized fermenter. Bring the total volume to 5 gallons (19 l) with additional cold water if necessary. Aerate the wort very well.

Pitch the yeast when temperature of wort is about 70 degrees F (21 C). Ferment at about 70 degrees F (21 C) for about 1 week, or until fermentation shows signs of calm and stopping. Rack from your primary to a secondary fermenter and if you have the capability, "cellar" the beer at about 55 degrees F (12.5 C) for about 1 week.

Prime with sugar and bottle or keg when complete.

Malt Extract Recipe *for 5 gallons (19 l)*

5.5 lbs.	(2.5 kg) wheat malt extract syrup (50/50 wheat/barley)
1 lb.	(454 g) crystal malt (10-L)
1.25 oz.	(35 g) Cascade hops 5% alpha (6.3 HBU/175 MBU)—60 minutes boiling
¼ oz.	(7 g) Perle hops 8% alpha (2 HBU/56 MBU)—15 minutes boiling
½ oz.	(14 g) Perle hops—1 minute boiling
¼ tsp.	(1 g) powdered Irish moss
English ale yeast	
¾ cup	(175 ml measure) corn sugar (priming bottles) or 0.33 cups (80 ml) corn sugar for kegging

Place crushed grains in 2 gallons (7.6 l) of 150-degree F (68 C) water and let steep for 30 minutes. Then strain out (and rinse with 3 quarts [3 l] hot water) and discard the crushed grains, reserving the approximately 2.5 gallons (9.5 l) of liquid, to which you will now add malt extract and 60-minute hops. Bring to a boil.

The total boil time will be 60 minutes. When 15 minutes remain, add the 15-minute hops. When 10 minutes remain, add the Irish moss. When 1 minute remains, add the 1-minute hops. After a total wort boil of 120 minutes, turn off the heat.

Immerse the covered pot of wort in a cold-water bath and let sit for 30 minutes, or the time it takes to have a couple of homebrews.

Then strain out and sparge hops and direct the hot wort into a sanitized fermenter to which 2.5 gallons (9.5 l) of cold water has been added. Bring the total volume to 5 gallons (19 l) with additional cold water if necessary. Aerate the wort very well.

Pitch the yeast when temperature of wort is about 70 degrees F (21 C). Ferment at about 70 degrees F (21 C) for about 1 week, or until fermentation shows signs of calm and stopping. Rack from your primary to a secondary fermenter and if you have the capability, "cellar" the beer at about 55 degrees F (12.5 C) for about 1 week.

Prime with sugar and bottle or keg when complete.

BERT GRANT'S PLANET IMPERIAL STOUT

- TARGET ORIGINAL GRAVITY: 1.076 (18.4 B)
- APPROXIMATE FINAL GRAVITY: 1.016 (4 B)
- IBU: ABOUT 59
- APPROXIMATE COLOR: 67 SRM (134 EBC)
- ALCOHOL: 8% BY VOLUME

All-Grain Recipe *for 5 gallons (19 l)*

10.5 lbs.	(4.8 kg) American 2-row pale malt
1 lb.	(454 g) crystal malt (80-L)
12 oz.	(340 g) roasted barley
8 oz.	(225 g) black malt
8 oz.	(225 g) German black Caraffe malt
½ oz.	(14 g) Galena hops 12% alpha (6 HBU/168 MBU)—60 minutes boiling
½ oz.	(14 g) Northern Brewers hops 8% alpha (4 HBU/112 MBU)—60 minutes boiling
1 oz.	(28 g) Cascade hops 5% alpha (5 HBU/140 MBU)—60 minutes boiling
1 oz.	(28 g) Cascade hops 5% alpha (5 HBU/140 MBU)—30 minutes boiling
1 oz.	(28 g) Cascade hops—1 minute boiling
¼ tsp.	(1 g) powdered Irish moss
Irish-type ale or stout yeast	
¾ cup	(175 ml measure) corn sugar (priming bottles) or 0.33 cups (80 ml) corn sugar for kegging

A step infusion mash is employed to mash the grains. Add 13 quarts (12.4 l) of 140-degree F (60 C) water to the crushed grain, stir, stabilize and hold the temperature at 132 degrees F (53 C) for 30 minutes. Add 6.5 quarts (6.2 l) of boiling water, add heat to bring temperature up to 155 degrees F (68 C) and hold for about 30 minutes. Then raise temperature to 167 degrees F (75 C), lauter and sparge with 3.5 gallons (13.5 l) of 170-degree F (77 C) water. Collect about 5.5 gallons (21 l) of runoff. Add 60-minute hops and bring to a full and vigorous boil.

The total boil time will be 60 minutes. When 30 minutes remain, add the 30-minute hops. When 10 minutes remain, add the Irish moss. When 1 minute remains, add the 1-minute hops. After a total wort boil of 60 minutes, turn off the heat and place the pot (with cover on) in a running cold-water bath for 30 minutes. Continue to chill in the immersion or use other methods to chill your wort. Then strain and sparge the wort into a sanitized fermenter. Bring the total volume to 5 gallons (19 l) with additional cold water if necessary. Aerate the wort very well.

Pitch the yeast when temperature of wort is about 70 degrees F (21 C). Ferment at about 70 degrees F (21 C) for about 1 week, or until fermentation shows signs of calm and stopping. Rack from your primary to a secondary fermenter and if you have the capability, "cellar" the beer at about 55 degrees F (12.5 C) for about 1 week.

Prime with sugar and bottle or keg when complete.

Malt Extract Recipe *for 5 gallons (19 l)*

9 lbs.	(4 kg) very dark extract syrup or 7.25 lbs. (3.3 kg) dark dried malt extract
1 lb.	(454 g) crystal malt (80-L)
12 oz.	(340 g) roasted barley
8 oz.	(225 g) black malt
½ oz.	(14 g) Galena hops 12% alpha (6 HBU/168 MBU)—60 minutes boiling
¾ oz.	(21 g) Northern Brewers hops 8% alpha (6 HBU/168 MBU)—60 minutes boiling
1 oz.	(28 g) Cascade hops 5% alpha (5 HBU/140 MBU)—60 minutes boiling
1 oz.	(28 g) Cascade hops 5% alpha (5 HBU/140 MBU)—30 minutes boiling

1 oz.	(28 g) Cascade hops—1 minute boiling
¼ tsp.	(1 g) powdered Irish moss

Irish-type ale or stout yeast

| ¾ cup | (175 ml measure) corn sugar (priming bottles) or 0.33 cups (80 ml) corn sugar for kegging |

Place crushed grains in 2 gallons (7.6 l) of 150-degree F (68 C) water and let steep for 30 minutes. Then strain out (and rinse with 3 quarts [3 l] hot water) and discard the crushed grains, reserving the approximately 2.5 gallons (9.5 l) of liquid, to which you will now add malt extract and 60-minute hops. Bring to a boil.

The total boil time will be 60 minutes. When 30 minutes remain, add the 30-minute hops. When 10 minutes remain, add the Irish moss. When 1 minute remains, add the 1-minute hops. After a total wort boil of 60 minutes, turn off the heat.

Immerse the covered pot of wort in a cold-water bath and let sit for 30 minutes, or the time it takes to have a couple of homebrews.

Then strain out and sparge hops and direct the hot wort into a sanitized fermenter to which 2 gallons (7.6 l) of cold water has been added. Bring the total volume to 5 gallons (19 l) with additional cold water if necessary. Aerate the wort very well.

Pitch the yeast when temperature of wort is about 70 degrees F (21 C). Ferment at about 70 degrees F (21 C) for about 1 week, or until fermentation shows signs of calm and stopping. Rack from your primary to a secondary fermenter and if you have the capability, "cellar" the beer at about 55 degrees F (12.5 C) for about 1 week.

Prime with sugar and bottle or keg when complete.

FELICITOUS STOUT

- TARGET ORIGINAL GRAVITY: 1.058 (14.5 B)
- APPROXIMATE FINAL GRAVITY: 1.014 (3.5 B)
- IBU: ABOUT 27
- APPROXIMATE COLOR: 36 SRM (72 EBC)
- ALCOHOL: 5.6% BY VOLUME

All-Grain Recipe *for 5 gallons (19 l)*

4.5 lbs.	(2 kg) pale malt
2.5 lbs.	(1.15 kg) Vienna malt
1 lb.	(454 g) crystal malt (40-L)
6 oz.	(168 g) roasted barley
4 oz.	(113 g) black malt
1 oz.	(28 g) chocolate malt
1 lb.	(454 g) honey
1.25 oz.	(35 g) Styrian Goldings hops 5% alpha (6.25 HBU/175 MBU)—60 minutes boiling
½ oz.	(14 g) Czech Saaz hops 3% alpha (1.5 HBU/42 MBU)—15 minutes boiling
¾ oz.	(21 g) German Hersbrucker hops—1 minute boiling
1.5 oz.	(42 g) freshly crushed coriander
½ oz.	(14 g) dried Curaçao orange peel
¼ tsp.	(1 g) powdered Irish moss
English or American-type ale yeast	
¾ cup	(175 ml measure) corn sugar (priming bottles) or 0.33 cups (80 ml) corn sugar for kegging

A step infusion mash is employed to mash the grains. Add 9 quarts (8.6 l) of 140-degree F (60 C) water to the crushed grain, stir, stabilize and hold the temperature at 132 degrees F (53 C) for 30 minutes. Add 4.5 quarts (4.3 l) of boiling water, add heat to bring temperature up to 155 degrees F (68 C) and hold for about 30 minutes. Then raise temperature to 167 degrees F (75 C), lauter and sparge with 3.5 gallons (13.5 l) of 170-degree F (77 C) water. Collect about 5.5 gallons (21 l) of runoff. Add 60-minute hops and honey and bring to a full and vigorous boil.

The total boil time will be 60 minutes. When 15 minutes remain, add the 15-minute hops, ¾ oz. (21 g) coriander and dried orange peel. When 10 minutes remain, add the Irish moss. When 1 minute remains, add the 1-minute hops. After a total wort boil of 60 minutes, turn off the heat and place the pot (with cover on) in a running cold-water bath for 30 minutes. Continue to chill in the immersion or use other methods to chill your wort. Then strain and sparge the wort into a sanitized fermenter. Bring the total volume to 5 gallons (19 l) with additional cold water if necessary. Aerate the wort very well.

Pitch the yeast when temperature of wort is about 70 degrees F (21 C). Ferment at about 70 degrees F (21 C) for about 1 week, or until fermentation

shows signs of calm and stopping. Rack from your primary to a secondary fermenter, add the remaining ¾ oz. (21 g) coriander and if you have the capability, "cellar" the beer at about 55 degrees F (12.5 C) for about 1 week.

Prime with sugar and bottle or keg when complete.

Malt Extract Recipe *for 5 gallons (19 l)*

6 lbs.	(2.7 kg) malt extract
1 lb.	(454 g) crystal malt (40-L)
6 oz.	(168 g) roasted barley
4 oz.	(113 g) black malt
1 oz.	(28 g) chocolate malt
1 lb.	(454 g) honey
1.75 oz.	(49 g) Styrian Goldings hops 5% alpha (8.8 HBU/245 MBU)—60 minutes boiling
¾ oz.	(21 g) Czech Saaz hops 3% alpha (2.3 HBU/63 MBU)—15 minutes boiling
¾ oz.	(21 g) German Hersbrucker hops—1 minute boiling
1.5 oz.	(42 g) freshly crushed coriander
½ oz.	(14 g) dried Curaçāo orange peel
¼ tsp.	(1 g) powdered Irish moss
English or American-type ale yeast	
¾ cup	(175 ml measure) corn sugar (priming bottles) or 0.33 cups (80 ml) corn sugar for kegging

Place crushed grains in 2 gallons (7.6 l) of 150-degree F (68 C) water and let steep for 30 minutes. Then strain out (and rinse with 3 quarts [3 1] hot water) and discard the crushed grains, reserving the approximately 2.5 gallons (9.5 l) of liquid to which you will now add malt extract, honey and 60-minute hops. Bring to a boil.

The total boil time will be 60 minutes. When 15 minutes remain, add the 15-minute hops, ¾ oz. (21 g) coriander and dried orange peel. When 10 minutes remain, add the Irish moss. When 1 minute remains, add the 1-minute hops. After a total wort boil of 60 minutes, turn off the heat.

Immerse the covered pot of wort in a cold-water bath and let sit for 30 minutes, or the time it takes to have a couple of homebrews.

Then strain out and sparge hops and direct the hot wort into a sanitized fermenter to which 2.5 gallons (9.5 l) of cold water has been added. Bring the total volume to 5 gallons (19 l) with additional cold water if necessary. Aerate the wort very well.

Pitch the yeast when temperature of wort is about 70 degrees F (21 C). Ferment at about 70 degrees F (21 C) for about 1 week, or until fermentation shows signs of calm and stopping. Rack from your primary to a secondary fermenter, add the remaining ¾ oz. (21 g) coriander and if you have the capability, "cellar" the beer at about 55 degrees F (12.5 C) for about 1 week.

Prime with sugar and bottle or keg when complete.

1981 BOULDER CHRISTMAS STOUT

- TARGET ORIGINAL GRAVITY: 1.073 (17.5 B)
- APPROXIMATE FINAL GRAVITY: 1.016–1.020 (4–5 B)
- IBU: ABOUT 41
- APPROXIMATE COLOR: 45 SRM (90 EBC)
- ALCOHOL: 7–7.5% BY VOLUME

All-Grain Recipe *for 5 gallons (19 l)*

10.5 lbs.	(4.8 kg) American 6-row pale malt
1 lb.	(454 g) crystal malt (40-L)
12 oz.	(340 g) roasted barley
4 oz.	(113 g) black patent malt
1.5 oz.	(42 g) German Hallertauer hops 5% alpha (7.5 HBU/210 MBU)—60 minutes boiling
½ oz.	(14 g) Cascade hops 5% alpha (2.5 HBU/70 MBU)—60 minutes boiling
¾ oz.	(21 g) Cascade hops 5% alpha (3.8 HBU/106 MBU)—5 minutes boiling
½ oz.	(14 g) German Hallertauer hops—5 minutes boiling
¼ tsp.	(1 g) powdered Irish moss
English ale yeast	
¾ cup	(175 ml measure) corn sugar (priming bottles) or 0.33 cups (80 ml) corn sugar for kegging

A one-step infusion mash is employed to mash the grains. Add 12.5 quarts (12 l) of 168-degree F (76 C) water to the crushed grain, stir, stabilize and hold the temperature at 152 degrees F (66.5 C) for 60 minutes. Then raise temperature to 167 degrees F (75 C), lauter and sparge with 4 gallons (15.2 l) of 170-degree F (77 C) water. Collect about 5.5 gallons (21 l) of runoff. Add 60-minute hops and bring to a full and vigorous boil.

The total boil time will be 60 minutes. When 10 minutes remain, add the Irish moss. When 5 minutes remain, add the 5-minute hops. After a total wort boil of 60 minutes, turn off the heat and place the pot (with cover on) in a running cold-water bath for 30 minutes. Continue to chill in the immersion or use other methods to chill your wort. Then strain and sparge the wort into a sanitized fermenter. Bring the total volume to 5 gallons (19 l) with additional cold water if necessary. Aerate the wort very well.

Pitch the yeast when temperature of wort is about 70 degrees F (21 C). Ferment at about 70 degrees F (21 C) for about 1 week, or until fermentation shows signs of calm and stopping. Rack from your primary to a secondary fermenter and if you have the capability, "cellar" the beer at about 55 degrees F (12.5 C) for about 1 week.

Prime with sugar and bottle or keg when complete. The original Boulder Christmas Stout was fully bottle conditioned, just like your homebrew.

Malt Extract Recipe *for 5 gallons (19 l)*

9 lbs.	(4.1 kg) American dark malt extract syrup
1 lb.	(454 g) crystal malt (40-L)
8 oz.	(225 g) roasted barley
2 oz.	(56 g) German Hallertauer hops 5% alpha (10 HBU/280 MBU)—60 minutes boiling
¾ oz.	(21 g) Cascade hops 5% alpha (3.8 HBU/106 MBU)—60 minutes boiling
¾ oz.	(21 g) Cascade hops 5% alpha (3.8 HBU/106 MBU)—5 minutes boiling
½ oz.	(14 g) German Hallertauer hops—5 minutes boiling
¼ tsp.	(1 g) powdered Irish moss
English ale yeast	
¾ cup	(175 ml measure) corn sugar (priming bottles) or 0.33 cups (80 ml) corn sugar for kegging

Place crushed grains in 2 gallons (7.6 l) of 150-degree F (68 C) water and let steep for 30 minutes. Then strain out (and rinse with 3 quarts [3 l] hot water) and discard the crushed grains, reserving the approximately 2.5 gallons (9.5 l) of liquid to which you will now add malt extract and 60-minute hops. Heat to boiling.

The total boil time will be 60 minutes. When 10 minutes remain, add the Irish moss. When 5 minutes remain, add the 5-minute hops. After a total wort boil of 60 minutes, turn off the heat and place the pot (with cover on) in a running cold-water bath for 30 minutes.

Then strain out and sparge hops and direct the hot wort into a sanitized fermenter to which 2.5 gallons (9.5 l) of cold water has been added. Bring the total volume to 5 gallons (19 l) with additional cold water if necessary. Aerate the wort very well.

Pitch the yeast when temperature of wort is about 70 degrees F (21 C). Ferment at about 70 degrees F (21 C) for about 1 week, or until fermentation shows signs of calm and stopping. Rack from your primary to a secondary fermenter and if you have the capability, "cellar" the beer at about 55 degrees F (12.5 C) for about 1 week.

Prime with sugar and bottle or keg when complete. The original Boulder Christmas Stout was fully bottle conditioned, just like your homebrew.

SAMUEL ADAMS 1880

- TARGET ORIGINAL GRAVITY: 1.052 (13 B)
- APPROXIMATE FINAL GRAVITY: 1.016 (4 B)
- IBU: ABOUT 32
- APPROXIMATE COLOR: 6–7 SRM (12–14 EBC)
- ALCOHOL: 4.9% BY VOLUME

All-Grain Recipe *for 5 gallons (19 l)*

8.5 lbs.	(3.9 kg) German 2-row pilsener malt
4 oz.	(113 g) crystal malt (60-L)
1.1 oz.	(30 g) German Hallertau-Mittelfrueh hop pellets if available, or substitute German Hersbrucker Hallertau hop pellets 3.5% alpha (4.3 HBU/120 MBU)—120 minutes boiling

⅔ oz.	(18 g) German Tettnanger hop pellets if available, or substitute Santiam hop pellets 4% alpha (2.4 HBU/67 MBU)—120 minutes boiling
½ oz.	(14 g) German Hallertau-Mittelfrueh hop pellets if available, or substitute German Hersbrucker Hallertau hop pellets—5 minutes boiling
½ oz.	(14 g) German Tettnanger hop pellets if available, or substitute Santiam hops—5 minutes boiling
½ oz.	(14 g) crystal hop pellets 5.5% alpha—dry hopping
½ oz.	(14 g) German Hallertau-Mittelfrueh hop pellets if available, or substitute German Hersbrucker Hallertau hops pellets 5.5% alpha—dry hopping
¼ tsp.	(1 g) powdered Irish moss
	Pilsener-type lager yeast
¾ cup	(175 ml measure) corn sugar (priming bottles) or 0.33 cups (80 ml) corn sugar for kegging

A step infusion mash is employed to mash the grains. Add 9 quarts (8.6 l) of 140-degree F (60 C) water to the crushed grain, stir, stabilize and hold the temperature at 132 degrees F (53 C) for 30 minutes. Add 4 quarts (4 l) of boiling water, add heat to bring temperature up to 155 degrees F (68 C) and hold for about 30 minutes. Then raise temperature to 167 degrees F (75 C), lauter and sparge with 3.5 gallons (13.5 l) of 170-degree F (77 C) water. Collect about 5.5 gallons (21 l) of runoff. Add 120-minute hops and bring to a full and vigorous boil.

The total boil time will be 120 minutes. When 10 minutes remain, add the Irish moss. When 5 minutes remain, add the 5-minute hops. After a total wort boil of 120 minutes, turn off the heat and place the pot (with cover on) in a running cold-water bath for 30 minutes. Continue to chill in the immersion or use other methods to chill your wort. Then strain and sparge the wort into a sanitized fermenter. Bring the total volume to 5 gallons (19 l) with additional cold water if necessary. Aerate the wort very well.

Pitch the yeast when temperature of wort is about 70 degrees F (21 C). Once visible signs of fermentation are evident, ferment at about 55 degrees F (12.5 C) for about 1 week, or until fermentation shows signs of calm and stopping. Rack from your primary to a secondary fermenter and add the hop pellets for dry hopping. If you have the capability, "lager" the beer at temperatures between 35 and 45 degrees F (1.5–7 C) for 5 weeks.

Prime with sugar and bottle or keg when complete.

Malt Extract Recipe *for 5 gallons (19 l)*

7 lbs.	(3.2 kg) very light malt extract syrup
4 oz.	(113 g) crystal malt (60-L)
1.5 oz.	(42 g) German Hallertau-Mittelfrueh hop pellets if available, or substitute German Hersbrucker Hallertau hop pellets 3.5% alpha (5.3 HBU/147 MBU)—120 minutes boiling
¾ oz.	(21 g) German Tettnanger hop pellets if available, or substitute Santiam hop pellets 4% alpha (3 HBU/84 MBU)—120 minutes boiling
½ oz.	(14 g) German Hallertau-Mittelfrueh hop pellets if available, or substitute German Hersbrucker Hallertau hop pellets—5 minutes boiling
½ oz.	(14 g) German Tettnanger hop pellets if available, or substitute Santiam hops—5 minutes boiling
½ oz.	(14 g) crystal hop pellets 5.5% alpha—dry hopping
½ oz.	(14 g) German Hallertau-Mittelfrueh hop pellets if available, or substitute German Hersbrucker Hallertau hop pellets 5.5% alpha—dry hopping
¼ tsp.	(1 g) powdered Irish moss
Pilsener-type lager yeast	
¾ cup	(175 ml measure) corn sugar (priming bottles) or 0.33 cups (80 ml) corn sugar for kegging

Place crushed grains in 2 gallons (7.6 l) of 150-degree F (68 C) water and let steep for 30 minutes. Then strain out (and rinse with 3 quarts [3 l] hot water) and discard the crushed grains, reserving the approximately 2.5 gallons (9.5 l) of liquid to which you will now add malt extract and 120-minute hops. Bring to a boil.

The total boil time will be 120 minutes. When 10 minutes remain, add the Irish moss. When 5 minutes remain, add the 5-minute hops. After a total wort boil of 120 minutes, turn off the heat.

Immerse the covered pot of wort in a cold-water bath and let sit for 30 minutes, or the time it takes to have a couple of homebrews.

Then strain out and sparge hops and direct the hot wort into a sanitized fermenter to which 2.5 gallons (9.5 l) of cold water has been added. Bring the total volume to 5 gallons (19 l) with additional water if necessary. Aerate the wort very well.

Pitch the yeast when temperature of wort is about 70 degrees F (21 C). Once visible signs of fermentation are evident, ferment at temperatures of about 55 degrees F (12.5 C) for about 1 week, or until fermentation shows signs of calm and stopping. Rack from your primary to a secondary fermenter and add the hop pellets for dry hopping. If you have the capability, "lager" the beer at temperatures between 35 and 45 degrees F (1.5–7 C) for 5 weeks.

Prime with sugar and bottle or keg when complete.

GEORGE KILLIAN'S IRISH RED ALE FROM PELLFORTH

- TARGET ORIGINAL GRAVITY: 1.067 (16.4 B)
- APPROXIMATE FINAL GRAVITY: 1.018 (4.5 B)
- IBU: ABOUT 25
- APPROXIMATE COLOR: 14 SRM (28 EBC)
- ALCOHOL: 6.6% BY VOLUME

All-Grain Recipe *for 5 gallons (19 l)*

5 lbs.	(2.3 kg) pale malt
4.5 lbs.	(2 kg) Munich malt
1 lb.	(454 g) crystal malt (10-L)
8 oz.	(225 g) home-toasted pale malt
1 oz.	(28 g) French Strisselspalt hops 3% alpha (3 HBU/84 MBU)—120 minutes boiling
½ oz.	(14 g) Mt. Hood hops 6% alpha (3 HBU/84 MBU)—120 minutes boiling
½ oz.	(14 g) Santiam hops—5 minutes boiling
⅓ oz.	(10 g) Santiam hop pellets—dry hopping
¼ tsp.	(1 g) powdered Irish moss
German Altbier or German ale yeast	
¾ cup	(175 ml measure) corn sugar (priming bottles) or 0.33 cups (80 ml) corn sugar for kegging

Spread 8 oz. of whole pale malt on a cookie sheet and toast in a moderate oven until you hear popping noises and smell the aroma of toasted malt. Do not toast to a dark brown. Cool this malt before crushing.

A step infusion mash is employed to mash the grains. Add 11 quarts (10.5 l) of 140-degree F (60 C) water to the crushed grain, stir, stabilize and hold the temperature at 132 degrees F (53 C) for 30 minutes. Add 5.5 quarts (5.2 l) of boiling water, add heat to bring temperature up to 155 degrees F (68 C) and hold for about 30 minutes. Then raise temperature to 167 degrees F (75 C), lauter and sparge with 3.5 gallons (13.5 l) of 170-degree F (77 C) water. Collect about 5.5 gallons (21 l) of runoff. Add 120-minute hops and bring to a full and vigorous boil.

The total boil time will be 120 minutes. When 10 minutes remain, add the Irish moss. When 5 minutes remains, add the 5-minute hops. After a total wort boil of 120 minutes, turn off the heat and place the pot (with cover on) in a running cold-water bath for 30 minutes. Continue to chill in the immersion or use other methods to chill your wort. Then strain and sparge the wort into a sanitized fermenter. Bring the total volume to 5 gallons (19 l) with additional cold water if necessary. Aerate the wort very well.

Pitch the yeast when temperature of wort is about 70 degrees F (21 C). Ferment at about 70 degrees F (21 C) for about 1 week, or until fermentation shows signs of calm and stopping. Rack from your primary to a secondary fermenter and add the hop pellets for dry hopping. If you have the capability, "cellar" the beer at about 55 degrees F (12.5 C) for about 2 weeks.

Prime with sugar and bottle or keg when complete.

Malt Extract Recipe *for 5 gallons (19 l)*

8 lbs.	(3.6 kg) amber malt extract or 6.4 lbs. (2.9 kg) amber dried malt extract
1 lb.	(454 g) crystal malt (10-L)
8 oz.	(225 g) home-toasted pale malt
1.5 oz.	(42 g) French Strisselspalt hops 3% alpha (4.5 HBU/126 MBU)—90 minutes boiling
¾ oz.	(21 g) Mt. Hood hops 6% alpha (4.5 HBU/126 MBU)—90 minutes boiling
½ oz.	(14 g) Santiam hops—5 minutes boiling
⅓ oz.	(10 g) Santiam hop pellets—dry hopping

¼ tsp.   (1 g) powdered Irish moss

German Altbier or German ale yeast

¾ cup   (175 ml measure) corn sugar (priming bottles) or 0.33
             cups (80 ml) corn sugar for kegging

Spread 8 oz. of whole pale malt on a cookie sheet and toast in a moderate oven until you hear popping noises and smell the aroma of toasted malt. Do not toast to a dark brown. Cool this malt before crushing.

Place crushed grains in 2 gallons (7.6 l) of 150-degree F (68 C) water and let steep for 30 minutes. Then strain out (and rinse with 3 quarts [3 l] hot water) and discard the crushed grains, reserving the approximately 2.5 gallons (9.5 l) of liquid to which you will now add malt extract and 90-minute hops. Bring to a boil.

The total boil time will be 90 minutes. When 10 minutes remain, add the Irish moss. When 5 minutes remain, add the 5-minute hops. After a total wort boil of 90 minutes, turn off the heat.

Immerse the covered pot of wort in a cold-water bath and let sit for 30 minutes, or the time it takes to have a couple of homebrews.

Then strain out and sparge hops and direct the hot wort into a sanitized fermenter to which 2.5 gallons (9.5 l) of cold water has been added. Bring the total volume to 5 gallons (19 l) with additional cold water if necessary. Aerate the wort very well.

Pitch the yeast when temperature of wort is about 70 degrees F (21 C). Ferment at about 70 degrees F (21 C) for about 1 week, or until fermentation shows signs of calm and stopping. Rack from your primary to a secondary fermenter and add the hop pellets for dry hopping. If you have the capability, "cellar" the beer at about 55 degrees F (12.5 C) for about 2 weeks.

Prime with sugar and bottle or keg when complete.

MASTERBREWERS DOPPELBOCK

- TARGET ORIGINAL GRAVITY: 1.074 (18 B)
- APPROXIMATE FINAL GRAVITY: 1.016 (4 B)
- IBU: ABOUT 25
- APPROXIMATE COLOR: 36 SRM (72 EBC)
- ALCOHOL: 7.7% BY VOLUME

Mash/Extract Recipe *for 5 gallons (19 l)*

2 lbs.	(908 g) 6-row pale malt
6 oz.	(168 g) home-toasted 6-row pale malt
6 oz.	(168 g) Munich malt
6 oz.	(168 g) Cara Pils malt
4 oz.	(113 g) crystal malt (20-L)
4 oz.	(113 g) chocolate malt
3 oz.	(84 g) black malt
6 lbs.	(2.7 kg) dark dried malt extract
1.25 oz.	(35 g) Brewers Gold hops 6% alpha (7.5 HBU/210 MBU)—60 minutes boiling
½ oz.	(14 g) Willamette hops 5% alpha (2.5 HBU/70 MBU)—20 minutes boiling
½ oz.	(14 g) Santiam hops—2 minutes boiling
¼ tsp.	(1 g) powdered Irish moss
German or Bavarian-type lager yeast	
¾ cup	(175 ml measure) corn sugar (priming bottles) or 0.33 cups (80 ml) corn sugar for kegging

Spread 6 oz. of whole pale malt on a cookie sheet and toast in a moderate oven until you hear popping noises and smell the aroma of toasted malt. Do not toast to a dark brown. Cool this malt before crushing.

Heat 1 gallon (3.8 l) water to 172 degrees F (77.5 C) and then add crushed grains to the water. Stir well to distribute heat. Temperature should stabilize at about 155 degrees F (68 C). Wrap a towel around the pot and set aside for about 45 minutes. Have a homebrew.

After 30 minutes, add heat to the mini-mash and raise the temperature to 167 degrees F (75 C). Then pass the liquid and grains into a strainer and rinse with 170-degree F (77 C) water. Discard the grains.

Add more water to the sweet extract you have just produced, bringing the volume up to about 2.5 gallons (9.5 l). Add malt extract and 60-minute hops and bring to a boil.

The total boil time will be 60 minutes. When 20 minutes remain, add the 20-minute hops. When 10 minutes remain, add the Irish moss. When 2 minutes remain, add the 2-minute hops. After a total wort boil of 60 minutes, turn off the heat and place the pot (with cover on) in a running cold-water bath for 30 minutes. Continue to chill in the immersion or use other methods to chill your wort. Then strain and sparge the wort into a sanitized fermenter.

Bring the total volume to 5 gallons (19 l) with additional cold water if necessary. Aerate the wort very well.

Pitch the yeast when temperature of wort is about 70 degrees F (21 C). Once visible signs of fermentation are evident, ferment at about 55 degrees F (12.5 C) for about 1 week, or until fermentation shows signs of calm and stopping. Rack from your primary to a secondary fermenter and if you have the capability, "lager" the beer at temperatures between 35 and 45 degrees F (1.5–7 C) for 3 to 6 weeks.

Prime with sugar and bottle or keg when complete.

MASTERBREWERS CELEBRATION LIGHT LAGER

- TARGET ORIGINAL GRAVITY: 1.046 (11.5 B)
- APPROXIMATE FINAL GRAVITY: 1.008 (2 B)
- IBU: ABOUT 27
- APPROXIMATE COLOR: 7 SRM (14 EBC)
- ALCOHOL: 5% BY VOLUME

Mash/Extract Recipe *for 5 gallons (19 l)*

2 lbs.	(908 g) 6-row pale malt
8 oz.	(225 g) home-toasted 6-row pale malt
8 oz.	(225 g) Cara Pils malt
4 lbs.	(1.82 kg) extra-light malt extract syrup
1.5 oz.	(42 g) Willamette hops 5% alpha (7.5 HBU/210 MBU)—60 minutes boiling
½ oz.	(14 g) Cascade hops—5 minutes boiling
¼ tsp.	(1 g) powdered Irish moss
German or Bavarian-type lager yeast	
¾ cup	(175 ml measure) corn sugar (priming bottles) or 0.33 cups (80 ml) corn sugar for kegging

Spread 8 oz. of whole pale malt on a cookie sheet and toast in a moderate oven until you hear popping noises and smell the aroma of toasted malt. Do not toast to a dark brown. Cool this malt before crushing.

Heat 3 quarts (3 l) water to 172 degrees F (77.5 C) and then add crushed grains to the water. Stir well to distribute heat. Temperature should stabilize at about 155 degrees F (68 C). Wrap a towel around the pot and set aside for about 45 minutes. Have a homebrew.

After 30 minutes, add heat to the mini-mash and raise the temperature to 167 degrees F (75 C). Then pass the liquid and grains into a strainer and rinse with 170-degree F (77 C) water. Discard the grains.

To the sweet extract you have just produced, add more water, bringing the volume up to about 2.5 gallons (9.5 l). Add malt extract and 60-minute hops and bring to a boil.

The total boil time will be 60 minutes. When 10 minutes remain, add the Irish moss. When 5 minutes remain, add the 5-minute hops. After a total wort boil of 60 minutes, turn off the heat and place the pot (with cover on) in a running cold-water bath for 30 minutes. Continue to chill in the immersion or use other methods to chill your wort. Then strain and sparge the wort into a sanitized fermenter. Bring the total volume to 5 gallons (19 l) with additional cold water if necessary. Aerate the wort very well.

Pitch the yeast when temperature of wort is about 70 degrees F (21 C). Once visible signs of fermentation are evident, ferment at about 55 degrees F (12.5 C) for about 1 week, or until fermentation shows signs of calm and stopping. Rack from your primary to a secondary fermenter and if you have the capability, "lager" the beer at temperatures between 35 and 45 degrees F (1.5–7 C) for 3 to 6 weeks.

Prime with sugar and bottle or keg when complete.

KLIBBETY JIBBIT

- TARGET ORIGINAL GRAVITY: 1.046 (11.5 B)
- APPROXIMATE FINAL GRAVITY: 1.010 (2.5 B)
- IBU: ABOUT 29
- APPROXIMATE COLOR: 4 SRM (8 EBC)
- ALCOHOL: 4.8% BY VOLUME

6 lbs.	(2.7 kg) 6-row pale malt
1.5 lbs.	(680 g) flaked corn
¾ oz.	(21 g) German Northern Brewers hops 8% alpha (6 HBU/168 MBU)—60 minutes boiling

1 oz.	(28 g) Czech Saaz hops 3% alpha (3 HBU/84 MBU)—20 minutes boiling
½ oz.	(14 g) German Hersbrucker-Hallertauer hops—2 minutes boiling
¼ oz.	(7 g) crystal hop pellets—dry hopping
¼ tsp.	(1 g) powdered Irish moss
	Pilsener-type lager yeast
¾ cup	(175 ml measure) corn sugar (priming bottles) or 0.33 cups (80 ml) corn sugar for kegging

A step infusion mash is employed to mash the grains. Add 7.5 quarts (7.1 l) of 140-degree F (60 C) water to the crushed grain, stir, stabilize and hold the temperature at 132 degrees F (53 C) for 30 minutes. Add 3.75 quarts (3.6 l) of boiling water, add heat to bring temperature up to 155 degrees F (68 C) and hold for about 30 minutes. Then raise temperature to 167 degrees F (75 C), lauter and sparge with 3.5 gallons (13.5 l) of 170-degree F (77 C) water. Collect about 5.5 gallons (21 l) of runoff. Add 60-minute hops and bring to a full and vigorous boil.

The total boil time will be 60 minutes. When 20 minutes remain, add the 20-minute hops. When 10 minutes remain, add the Irish moss. When 2 minutes remain, add the 2-minute hops. After a total wort boil of 60 minutes, turn off the heat and place the pot (with cover on) in a running cold-water bath for 30 minutes. Continue to chill in the immersion or use other methods to chill your wort. Then strain and sparge the wort into a sanitized fermenter. Bring the total volume to 5 gallons (19 l) with additional cold water if necessary. Aerate the wort very well.

Pitch the yeast when temperature of wort is about 70 degrees F (21 C). Once visible signs of fermentation are evident, ferment at about 55 degrees F (12.5 C) for about 1 week, or until fermentation shows signs of calm and stopping. Rack from your primary to a secondary fermenter and add the hop pellets for dry hopping. If you have the capability, "lager" the beer at temperatures between 35 and 45 degrees F (1.5–7 C) for 4 to 8 weeks.

Prime with sugar and bottle or keg when complete.

Mash/Extract Recipe *for 5 gallons (19 l)*

2.5 lbs.	(1.15 kg) light malt extract syrup or 2 lbs. (0.9 kg) light dried malt extract
3 lbs.	(1.36 kg) 6-row pale malt
1.5 lbs.	(680 g) flaked corn
1 oz.	(28 g) German Northern Brewers hops 8% alpha (8 HBU/224 MBU)—60 minutes boiling
1 oz.	(28 g) Czech Saaz hops 3% alpha (3 HBU/84 MBU)—20 minutes boiling
½ oz.	(14 g) German Hersbrucker-Hallertauer hops—2 minutes boiling
¼ oz.	(7 g) crystal hop pellets—dry hopping
¼ tsp.	(1 g) powdered Irish moss
Pilsener-type lager yeast	
¾ cup	(175 ml measure) corn sugar (priming bottles) or 0.33 cups (80 ml) corn sugar for kegging

Heat 1.5 gallons (5.7 l) water to 172 degrees F (77.5 C) and then add crushed grains to the water. Stir well to distribute heat. Temperature should stabilize at about 155 degrees F (68 C). Wrap a towel around the pot and set aside for about 45 minutes. Have a homebrew.

After 45 minutes, add heat to the mini-mash and raise the temperature to 167 degrees F (75 C). Then pass the liquid and grains into a strainer and rinse with 170-degree F (77 C) water. Discard the grains.

To the sweet extract you have just produced, add more water, bringing the volume up to about 2.5 gallons (9.5 l). Add malt extract and 60-minute hops and bring to a boil.

The total boil time will be 60 minutes. When 20 minutes remain, add the 20-minute hops. When 10 minutes remain, add the Irish moss. When 2 minutes remain, add the 2-minute hops. After a total wort boil of 60 minutes, turn off the heat.

Immerse the covered pot of wort in a cold-water bath and let sit for 30 minutes, or the time it takes to have a couple of homebrews.

Then strain out and sparge hops and direct the hot wort into a sanitized fermenter to which 2.5 gallons (9.5 l) of cold water has been added. Bring the total volume to 5 gallons (19 l) with additional cold water if necessary. Aerate the wort very well.

Pitch the yeast when temperature of wort is about 70 degrees F (21 C).

Once visible signs of fermentation are evident, ferment at about 55 degrees F (12.5 C) for about 1 week, or until fermentation shows signs of calm and stopping. Rack from your primary to a secondary fermenter and add the hop pellets for dry hopping. If you have the capability, "lager" the beer at temperatures between 35 and 45 degrees F (1.5–7 C) for 4 to 8 weeks.

Prime with sugar and bottle or keg when complete.

MILE-HIGH GREEN CHILE ALE

- TARGET ORIGINAL GRAVITY: 1.051 (12.6 B)
- APPROXIMATE FINAL GRAVITY: 1.012 (3 B)
- IBU: ABOUT 35
- APPROXIMATE COLOR: 9 SRM (18 EBC)
- ALCOHOL: 5.1% BY VOLUME

All-Grain Recipe *for 5 gallons (19 l)*

7.5 lbs.	(3.4 kg) pale malt
1 lb.	(454 g) crystal malt (20-L)
½ oz.	(14 g) UK Kent Goldings hops 7% alpha (3.5 HBU/98 MBU)—60 minutes boiling
½ oz.	(14 g) UK Fuggles hops 5% alpha (2.5 HBU/70 MBU)—60 minutes boiling
¾ oz.	(21 g) UK Kent Goldings hops 7% alpha (5.3 HBU/147 MBU)—20 minutes boiling
½ oz.	(14 g) UK Fuggles hops 5% alpha (2.5 HBU/70 MBU)—20 minutes boiling
1 lb.	(454 g) fire-roasted green Anaheim or Santa Fe green chilies with skins
¼ tsp.	(1 g) powdered Irish moss
American-type ale yeast	
¾ cup	(175 ml measure) corn sugar (priming bottles) or 0.33 cups (80 ml) corn sugar for kegging

A step infusion mash is employed to mash the grains. Add 8.5 quarts (8.1 l) of 140-degree F (60 C) water to the crushed grain, stir, stabilize and hold the temperature at 132 degrees F (53 C) for 30 minutes. Add 4 quarts (3.8 l) of boiling water, add heat to bring temperature up to 155 degrees F (68 C) and hold for about 30 minutes. Then raise temperature to 167 degrees F (75 C), lauter and sparge with 3.5 gallons (13.5 l) of 170-degree F (77 C) water. Collect about 5.5 gallons (21 l) of runoff. Add 60-minute hops and bring to a full and vigorous boil.

The total boil time will be 60 minutes. When 20 minutes remain, add the 20-minute hops. When 10 minutes remain, add the Irish moss. After a total wort boil of 60 minutes, turn off the heat and place the pot (with cover on) in a running cold-water bath for 30 minutes. Continue to chill in the immersion or use other methods to chill your wort. Then strain and sparge the wort into a sanitized fermenter. Bring the total volume to 5 gallons (19 l) with additional cold water if necessary. Aerate the wort very well.

Pitch the yeast when temperature of wort is about 70 degrees F (21 C). Ferment at about 70 degrees F (21 C) for about 1 week, or until fermentation shows signs of calm and stopping. Rack from your primary to a secondary fermenter and add chopped roasted chilies. If you have the capability, "cellar" the beer at about 55 degrees F (12.5 C) for about 1 week.

Prime with sugar and bottle or keg when complete.

Malt Extract Recipe *for 5 gallons (19 l)*

6.25 lbs.	(2.8 kg) light malt extract syrup or 5 lbs. (2.3 kg) light dried malt extract
1 lb.	(454 g) crystal malt (20-L)
½ oz.	(14 g) UK Kent Goldings hops 7% alpha (3.5 HBU/98 MBU)—60 minutes boiling
1 oz.	(28 g) UK Fuggles hops 5% alpha (5 HBU/140 MBU)—60 minutes boiling
¾ oz.	(21 g) UK Kent Goldings hops 7% alpha (5.3 HBU/147 MBU)—20 minutes boiling
½ oz.	(14 g) UK Fuggles hops 5% alpha (2.5 HBU/70 MBU)—20 minutes boiling
1 lb.	(454 g) fire-roasted green Anaheim or Santa Fe chilies with skins
¼ tsp.	(1 g) powdered Irish moss
American-type ale yeast	
¾ cup	(175 ml measure) corn sugar (priming bottles) or 0.33 cups (80 ml) corn sugar for kegging

Place crushed grains in 2 gallons (7.6 l) of 150-degree F (68 C) water and let steep for 30 minutes. Then strain out (and rinse with 3 quarts [3 l] hot water) and discard the crushed grains, reserving the approximately 2.5 gallons (9.5 l) of liquid to which you will now add malt extract and 60-minute hops. Bring to a boil.

The total boil time will be 60 minutes. When 20 minutes remain, add the 20-minute hops. When 10 minutes remain, add the Irish moss. After a total wort boil of 60 minutes, turn off the heat.

Immerse the covered pot of wort in a cold-water bath and let sit for 30 minutes, or the time it takes to have a couple of homebrews.

Then strain out and sparge hops and direct the hot wort into a sanitized fermenter to which 2.5 gallons (9.5 l) of cold water has been added. Bring the total volume to 5 gallons (19 l) with additional cold water if necessary. Aerate the wort very well.

Pitch the yeast when temperature of wort is about 70 degrees F (21 C). Ferment at about 70 degrees F (21 C) for about 1 week, or until fermentation shows signs of calm and stopping. Rack from your primary to a secondary fermenter and add chopped roasted chilies. If you have the capability, "cellar" the beer at about 55 degrees F (12.5 C) for about 1 week.

Prime with sugar and bottle or keg when complete.

PURITANICAL NUT BROWN ALE

- TARGET ORIGINAL GRAVITY: 1.049 (12 B)
- APPROXIMATE FINAL GRAVITY: 1.010 (2.5 B)
- IBU: ABOUT 31
- APPROXIMATE COLOR: 17 SRM (34 EBC)
- ALCOHOL: 5.2% BY VOLUME

All-Grain Recipe *for 5 gallons (19 l)*

6.5 lbs.	(3 kg) English mild malt
1 lb.	(454 g) Belgian aromatic malt
8 oz.	(225 g) English crystal malt (75-L)
4 oz.	(113 g) chocolate malt

1 oz.	(28 g) German black Caraffe malt
1 oz.	(28 g) Glacier hops 6% alpha (6 HBU/168 MBU)— 120 minutes boiling
¾ oz.	(21 g) Willamette hops 5% alpha (3.8 HBU/105 MBU)—30 minutes boiling
¼ oz.	(7 g) crystal hop pellets—dry hopping
¼ tsp.	(1 g) powdered Irish moss
English or American-type ale yeast	
¾ cup	(175 ml measure) corn sugar (priming bottles) or 0.33 cups (80 ml) corn sugar for kegging

A step infusion mash is employed to mash the grains. Add 8 quarts (7.6 l) of 140-degree F (60 C) water to the crushed grain, stir, stabilize and hold the temperature at 132 degrees F (53 C) for 30 minutes. Add 4 quarts (3.8 l) of boiling water, add heat to bring temperature up to 155 degrees F (68 C) and hold for about 30 minutes. Then raise temperature to 167 degrees F (75 C), lauter and sparge with 3.5 gallons (13.5 l) of 170-degree F (77 C) water. Collect about 5.5 gallons (21 l) of runoff. Add 120-minute hops and bring to a full and vigorous boil.

The total boil time will be 120 minutes. When 30 minutes remain, add the 30-minute hops. When 10 minutes remain, add the Irish moss. After a total wort boil of 120 minutes, turn off the heat and place the pot (with cover on) in a running cold-water bath for 30 minutes. Continue to chill in the immersion or use other methods to chill your wort. Then strain and sparge the wort into a sanitized fermenter. Bring the total volume to 5 gallons (19 l) with additional cold water if necessary. Aerate the wort very well.

Pitch the yeast when temperature of wort is about 70 degrees F (21 C). Ferment at about 70 degrees F (21 C) for about 1 week, or until fermentation shows signs of calm and stopping. Rack from your primary to a secondary fermenter and add the hop pellets for dry hopping. If you have the capability, "cellar" the beer at about 55 degrees F (12.5 C) for about 1 week.

Prime with sugar and bottle or keg when complete.

Malt Extract Recipe *for 5 gallons (19 l)*

6 lbs.	(2.7 kg) amber malt extract syrup or 4.8 lbs. (2.2 kg) amber dried malt extract
1 lb.	(454 g) English crystal malt (75-L)
2 oz.	(56 g) chocolate malt
1 oz.	(28 g) German black Caraffe malt
1.25 oz.	(35 g) Glacier hops 6% alpha (7.5 HBU/210 MBU)—120 minutes boiling
¾ oz.	(21 g) Willamette hops 5% alpha (3.8 HBU/105 MBU)—30 minutes boiling
¼ oz.	(7 g) crystal hop pellets—dry hopping
¼ tsp.	(1 g) powdered Irish moss
English or American-type ale yeast	
¾ cup	(175 ml measure) corn sugar (priming bottles) or 0.33 cups (80 ml) corn sugar for kegging

Place crushed grains in 2 gallons (7.6 l) of 150-degree F (68 C) water and let steep for 30 minutes. Then strain out (and rinse with 3 quarts [3 l] hot water) and discard the crushed grains, reserving the approximately 2.5 gallons (9.5 l) of liquid to which you will now add malt extract and 120-minute hops. Bring to a boil.

The total boil time will be 60 minutes. When 30 minutes remain, add the 30-minute hops. When 10 minutes remain, add the Irish moss. After a total wort boil of 120 minutes, turn off the heat.

Immerse the covered pot of wort in a cold-water bath and let sit for 30 minutes, or the time it takes to have a couple of homebrews.

Then strain out and sparge hops and direct the hot wort into a sanitized fermenter to which 2.5 gallons (9.5 l) of cold water has been added. Bring the total volume to 5 gallons (19 l) with additional cold water if necessary. Aerate the wort very well.

Pitch the yeast when temperature of wort is about 70 degrees F (21 C). Ferment at about 70 degrees F (21 C) for about 1 week, or until fermentation shows signs of calm and stopping. Rack from your primary to a secondary fermenter and add the hop pellets for dry hopping. If you have the capability, "cellar" the beer at about 55 degrees F (12.5 C) for about 1 week.

Prime with sugar and bottle or keg when complete.

TELLURIDE INDIA PALE ALE

- TARGET ORIGINAL GRAVITY: 1.058 (14.5 B)
- APPROXIMATE FINAL GRAVITY: 1.014 (3.5 B)
- IBU: ABOUT 50
- APPROXIMATE COLOR: 15 SRM (30 EBC)
- ALCOHOL: 6% BY VOLUME

All-Grain Recipe *for 5 gallons (19 l)*

7.75 lbs.	(3.5 kg) pale malt
1 lb.	(454 g) crystal malt (20-L)
8 oz.	(225 g) biscuit malt
4 oz.	(113 g) Belgian Special-B malt
½ oz.	(14 g) Centennial hops 10% alpha (5 HBU/140 MBU)—60 minutes boiling
¾ oz.	(21 g) Willamette hops 5% alpha (3.8 HBU/105 MBU)—60 minutes boiling
½ oz.	(14 g) Galena hops 12% alpha (6 HBU/168 MBU)—30 minutes boiling
1 oz.	(28 g) Cascade hops—1 minute boiling
½ oz.	(14 g) Cascade hop pellets—dry hopping
¼ tsp.	(1 g) powdered Irish moss
English or American-type ale yeast	
¾ cup	(175 ml measure) corn sugar (priming bottles) or 0.33 cups (80 ml) corn sugar for kegging

A step infusion mash is employed to mash the grains. Add 9 quarts (8.6 l) of 140-degree F (60 C) water to the crushed grain, stir, stabilize and hold the temperature at 132 degrees F (53 C) for 30 minutes. Add 4.5 quarts (4.3 l) of boiling water, add heat to bring temperature up to 155 degrees F (68 C) and hold for about 30 minutes. Then raise temperature to 167 degrees F (75 C), lauter and sparge with 3.5 gallons (13.5 l) of 170-degree F (77 C) water. Collect about 5.5 gallons (21 l) of runoff. Add 60-minute hops and bring to a full and vigorous boil.

The total boil time will be 60 minutes. When 30 minutes remain, add the 30-minute hops. When 10 minutes remain, add the Irish moss. When 1 minute remains, add the 1-minute hops. After a total wort boil of 60 minutes, turn off the heat and place the pot (with cover on) in a running cold-water bath for 30 minutes. Continue to chill in the immersion or use other methods to chill your wort. Then strain and sparge the wort into a sanitized fermenter. Bring the total volume to 5 gallons (19 l) with additional cold water if necessary. Aerate the wort very well.

Pitch the yeast when temperature of wort is about 70 degrees F (21 C). Ferment at about 70 degrees F (21 C) for about 1 week, or until fermentation shows signs of calm and stopping. Rack from your primary to a secondary fermenter and add the hop pellets for dry hopping. If you have the capability, "cellar" the beer at about 55 degrees F (12.5 C) for about 1 week.

Prime with sugar and bottle or keg when your priorities are clear.

Malt Extract Recipe *for 5 gallons (19 l)*

6.5 lbs.	(3 kg) light malt extract syrup or 5.2 lbs. (2.36 kg) light dried malt extract
1 lb.	(454 g) crystal malt (20-L)
8 oz.	(225 g) home-toasted pale malt
4 oz.	(113 g) Belgian Special-B malt
¾ oz.	(21 g) Centennial hops 10% alpha (7.5 HBU/210 MBU)—60 minutes boiling
1 oz.	(28 g) Willamette hops 5% alpha (5 HBU/140 MBU)—60 minutes boiling
½ oz.	(14 g) Galena hops 12% alpha (6 HBU/168 MBU)—30 minutes boiling
1 oz.	(28 g) Cascade hops—1 minute boiling
½ oz.	(14 g) Cascade hop pellets—dry hopping
¼ tsp.	(1 g) powdered Irish moss
English or American-type ale yeast	
¾ cup	(175 ml measure) corn sugar (priming bottles) or 0.33 cups (80 ml) corn sugar for kegging

Spread 8 oz. of whole pale malt on a cookie sheet and toast in a moderate oven until you hear popping noises and smell the aroma of toasted malt. Do not toast to a dark brown. Cool this malt before crushing.

Place crushed grains in 2 gallons (7.6 l) of 150-degree F (68 C) water and let steep for 30 minutes. Then strain out (and rinse with 3 quarts [3 l] hot water) and discard the crushed grains, reserving the approximately 2.5 gallons (9.5 l) of liquid to which you will now add malt extract and 60-minute hops. Bring to a boil.

The total boil time will be 60 minutes. When 30 minutes remain, add the 30-minute hops. When 10 minutes remain, add the Irish moss. When 1 minute remains, add the 1-minute hops. After a total wort boil of 60 minutes, turn off the heat.

Immerse the covered pot of wort in a cold-water bath and let sit for 30 minutes, or the time it takes to have a couple of homebrews.

Then strain out and sparge hops and direct the hot wort into a sanitized fermenter to which 2.5 gallons (9.5 l) of cold water has been added. Bring the total volume to 5 gallons (19 l) with additional cold water if necessary. Aerate the wort very well.

Pitch the yeast when temperature of wort is about 70 degrees F (21 C). Ferment at about 70 degrees F (21 C) for about 1 week, or until fermentation shows signs of calm and stopping. Rack from your primary to a secondary fermenter and add the hop pellets for dry hopping. If you have the capability, "cellar" the beer at about 55 degrees F (12.5 C) for about 1 week.

Prime with sugar and bottle or keg when your priorities are clear.

JOHN 1981—A HOMEBREWED VERSION OF CHARLIE 1981

- TARGET ORIGINAL GRAVITY: 1.075 (18.2 B)
- APPROXIMATE FINAL GRAVITY: 1.014 (3.5 B)
- IBU: ABOUT 75
- APPROXIMATE COLOR: 14 SRM (28 EBC)
- ALCOHOL: 8.2% BY VOLUME

All-Grain Recipe *for 5 gallons (19 l)*

5.5 lbs.	(2.5 kg) 2-row pale malt
5.5 lbs.	(2.5 kg) Munich malt
1.5 lbs.	(680 g) crystal malt (40-L)

1 oz.	(28 g) Horizon hops 10% alpha (10 HBU/280 MBU)—60 minutes boiling
1 oz.	(28 g) Sterling hops 6% alpha (6 HBU/128 MBU)—60 minutes boiling
1 oz.	(28 g) Amarillo hops 8% alpha (8 HBU/224 MBU)—30 minutes boiling
2.5 oz.	(70 g) Amarillo hop pellets—dry hopping
¼ tsp.	(1 g) powdered Irish moss

Culture "pac-man" yeast from a bottle-conditioned Rogue Ale, Wyeast Irish Ale yeast #1084, White Labs Dry English Ale yeast WLP007 or California Ale yeast WLP001

¾ cup	(175 ml measure) corn sugar (priming bottles) or 0.33 cups (80 ml) corn sugar for kegging

A step infusion mash is employed to mash the grains. Add 12.5 quarts (12 l) of 140-degree F (60 C) water to the crushed grain, stir, stabilize and hold the temperature at 132 degrees F (53 C) for 30 minutes. Add 6 quarts (5.7 l) of boiling water, add heat to bring temperature up to 155 degrees F (68 C) and hold for about 30 minutes. Then raise temperature to 167 degrees F (75 C), lauter and sparge with 3.5 gallons (13.5 l) of 170-degree F (77 C) water. Collect about 5.5 gallons (21 l) of runoff. Add 60-minute hops and bring to a full and vigorous boil.

The total boil time will be 60 minutes. When 30 minutes remain, add the 30-minute hops. When 10 minutes remain, add the Irish moss. After a total wort boil of 60 minutes, turn off the heat and place the pot (with cover on) in a running cold-water bath for 30 minutes. Continue to chill in the immersion or use other methods to chill your wort. Then strain and sparge the wort into a sanitized fermenter. Bring the total volume to 5 gallons (19 l) with additional cold water if necessary. Aerate the wort very well.

Pitch the yeast when temperature of wort is about 70 degrees F (21 C). Ferment at about 70 degrees F (21 C) for about 1 week, or until fermentation shows signs of calm and stopping. Rack from your primary to a secondary fermenter and add the hop pellets for dry hopping. If you have the capability, "cellar" the beer at about 55 degrees F (12.5 C) for about 1 week.

Prime with sugar and bottle or keg when complete.

Malt Extract Recipe *for 5 gallons (19 l)*

9 lbs.	(4 kg) amber malt extract syrup or 7.25 lbs. (3.3 kg) amber dried malt extract
1.5 lbs.	(680 g) crystal malt (30-L)
1.5 oz.	(42 g) Horizon hops 10% alpha (15 HBU/420 MBU)—60 minutes boiling
1.5 oz.	(42 g) Sterling hops 6% alpha (9 HBU/252 MBU)—60 minutes boiling
1.5 oz.	(42 g) Amarillo hops 8% alpha (12 HBU/336 MBU)—30 minutes boiling
2.5 oz.	(70 g) Amarillo hop pellets—dry hopping
¼ tsp.	(1 g) powdered Irish moss

Culture "pac-man" yeast from a bottle-conditioned Rogue Ale, Wyeast Irish Ale yeast #1084, White Labs Dry English Ale yeast WLP007 or California Ale yeast WLP001

¾ cup	(175 ml measure) corn sugar (priming bottles) or 0.33 cups (80 ml) corn sugar for kegging

Place crushed grains in 2 gallons (7.6 l) of 150-degree F (68 C) water and let steep for 30 minutes. Then strain out (and rinse with 3 quarts [3 l] hot water) and discard the crushed grains, reserving the approximately 2.5 gallons (9.5 l) of liquid to which you will now add malt extract and 60-minute hops. Bring to a boil.

The total boil time will be 60 minutes. When 30 minutes remain, add the 30-minute hops. When 10 minutes remain, add the Irish moss. After a total wort boil of 60 minutes, turn off the heat.

Immerse the covered pot of wort in a cold-water bath and let sit for 30 minutes, or the time it takes to have a couple of homebrews.

Then strain out and sparge hops and direct the hot wort into a sanitized fermenter to which 2.5 gallons (9.5 l) of cold water has been added. Bring the total volume to 5 gallons (19 l) with additional cold water if necessary. Aerate the wort very well.

Pitch the yeast when temperature of wort is about 70 degrees F (21 C). Ferment at about 70 degrees F (21 C) for about 1 week, or until fermentation shows signs of calm and stopping. Rack from your primary to a secondary fermenter and add the hop pellets for dry hopping. If you have the capability, "cellar" the beer at about 55 degrees F (12.5 C) for about 1 week.

Prime with sugar and bottle or keg when complete.

1447 BELGIUM ZWARTE ROSE ALE

- TARGET ORIGINAL GRAVITY: 1.057 (14.5 B)
- APPROXIMATE FINAL GRAVITY: 1.016 (4 B)
- IBU: ABOUT 28
- APPROXIMATE COLOR: 26 SRM (52 EBC)
- ALCOHOL: 5.5% BY VOLUME

6 lbs.	(2.7 kg) Munich malt
1 lb.	(454 g) wheat malt
1 lb.	(454 g) oat malt
1 lb.	(454 g) crystal malt (120-L)
8 oz.	(225 g) Belgian Caramunich malt
1 oz.	(28 g) Styrian Goldings hops 5% alpha (5 HBU/140 MBU)—60 minutes boiling
1 oz.	(28 g) Mt. Hood hops 6% alpha (6 HBU/168 MBU)—20 minutes boiling
¼ oz.	(7 g) grains of paradise
2 oz.	(56 g) fresh unsprayed rose petals
¼ tsp.	(1 g) powdered Irish moss
American-type ale yeast	
¾ cup	(175 ml measure) corn sugar (priming bottles) or 0.33 cups (80 ml) corn sugar for kegging

A step infusion mash is employed to mash the grains. Add 9 quarts (8.6 l) of 140-degree F (60 C) water to the crushed grain, stir, stabilize and hold the temperature at 132 degrees F (53 C) for 30 minutes. Add 4.5 quarts (4.3 l) of boiling water, add heat to bring temperature up to 155 degrees F (68 C) and hold for about 30 minutes. Then raise temperature to 167 degrees F (75 C), lauter and sparge with 3.5 gallons (13.5 l) of 170-degree F (77 C) water. Collect about 5.5 gallons (21 l) of runoff. Add 60-minute hops and bring to a full and vigorous boil.

The total boil time will be 60 minutes. When 20 minutes remain, add the 20-minute hops and grains of paradise. When 10 minutes remain, add the Irish moss. After a total wort boil of 60 minutes, turn off the heat and place the pot (with cover on) in a running cold-water bath for 30 minutes. Continue to chill in the immersion or use other methods to chill your wort. Then strain and sparge the wort into a sanitized fermenter. Bring the total volume to 5 gallons (19 l) with additional cold water if necessary. Aerate the wort very well.

Pitch the yeast when temperature of wort is about 70 degrees F (21 C). Ferment at about 70 degrees F (21 C) for about 1 week, or until fermentation shows signs of calm and stopping. Rack from your primary to a secondary fermenter and add the rose petals. If you have the capability, "cellar" the beer at about 55 degrees F (12.5 C) for about 1 week.

Prime with sugar and bottle or keg when complete.

Malt Extract Recipe *for 5 gallons (19 l)*

4.5 lbs.	(2 kg) amber malt extract syrup or 3.6 lbs. (1.6 kg) amber dried malt extract
2 lbs.	(908 g) wheat malt extract syrup
1 lb.	(454 g) crystal malt (120-L)
10 oz.	(280 g) Belgian caramunich malt
1.5 oz.	(42 g) Styrian Goldings hops 5% alpha (7.5 HBU/210 MBU)—60 minutes boiling
1 oz.	(28 g) Mt. Hood hops 6% alpha (6 HBU/168 MBU)—20 minutes boiling
¼ oz.	(7 g) grains of paradise
2 oz.	(56 g) fresh unsprayed rose petals
¼ tsp.	(1 g) powdered Irish moss
	American-type ale yeast
¾ cup	(175 ml measure) corn sugar (priming bottles) or 0.33 cups (80 ml) corn sugar for kegging

Place crushed grains in 2 gallons (7.6 l) of 150-degree F (68 C) water and let steep for 30 minutes. Then strain out (and rinse with 3 quarts [3 l] hot water) and discard the crushed grains, reserving the approximately 2.5 gallons (9.5 l) of liquid to which you will now add malt extract and 60-minute hops. Bring to a boil.

The total boil time will be 60 minutes. When 20 minutes remain, add the 20-minute hops and grains of paradise. When 10 minutes remain, add the Irish moss. After a total wort boil of 60 minutes, turn off the heat.

Immerse the covered pot of wort in a cold-water bath and let sit for 30 minutes, or the time it takes to have a couple of homebrews.

Then strain out and sparge hops and direct the hot wort into a sanitized fermenter to which 2.5 gallons (9.5 l) of cold water has been added. Bring the total volume to 5 gallons with additional cold water if necessary. Aerate the wort very well.

Pitch the yeast when temperature of wort is about 70 degrees F (21 C). Ferment at about 70 degrees F (21 C) for about 1 week, or until fermentation shows signs of calm and stopping. Rack from your primary to a secondary fermenter and add the rose petals. If you have the capability, "cellar" the beer at about 55 degrees F (12.5 C) for about 1 week.

Prime with sugar and bottle or keg when complete.

JEFF BAGBY'S HOP WHOMPUS 2004

Adapted from a recipe and notes submitted by Jeff Bagby

- TARGET ORIGINAL GRAVITY: 1.088 (21 B)
- APPROXIMATE FINAL GRAVITY: 1.020 (5 B)
- IBU: MATHEMATICALLY OFF THE CHARTS, BUT PROBABLY 90+
- APPROXIMATE COLOR: 18 SRM (36 EBC)—RED
- ALCOHOL: 9% BY VOLUME

All-Grain Recipe *for 5 gallons (19 l)*

NOTE: You will need a 10-gallon kettle, 10-gallon-size mash tun with screen, an additional 10-gallon vessel and a counter-flow-type wort chiller for this recipe. If you are brewing on a simpler system, adapt the hop additions to suit your system.

12.5 lbs.	(5.7 kg) 2-row pale malt
1.5 lbs.	(680 g) crystal malt (75-L)
8 oz.	(225 g) crystal malt (120-L)
2 oz.	(56 g) Liberty whole hops 4.5% alpha—mash hops
¾ oz.	(21 g) Centennial whole hops 7.5% alpha—mash hops

Jeff Bagby

1.75 oz.	(49 g) Liberty hop pellets 5% alpha—first wort hopping
1 oz.	(28 g) Centennial hop pellets 9% alpha—120 minutes boiling
½ oz.	(14 g) Simcoe hop pellets 12% alpha—120 minutes boiling
1 oz.	(28 g) Amarillo hop pellets 8% alpha—60 minutes boiling

1 oz.	(28 g) Amarillo hop pellets 8% alpha—steeping hops
3.5 oz.	(98 g) Amarillo whole hops 8% alpha—post-boil hop-back
2.75 oz.	(77 g) Centennial whole hops 7.7% alpha—post-boil hop-back
1 oz.	(28 g) Liberty whole hops 4.5% alpha—post-boil hop-back
⅔ oz.	(18 g) Liberty hop pellets—secondary fermenter
⅔ oz.	(18 g) Centennial hop pellets—secondary fermenter
⅔ oz.	(18 g) Amarillo hop pellets—secondary fermenter
½ oz.	(14 g) Simcoe hop pellets—secondary fermenter
½ oz.	(14 g) Liberty whole hops—keg hops (optional)
⅔ oz.	(18 g) Centennial whole hops—keg hops (optional)
⅓ oz.	(9 g) Simcoe whole hops—keg hops (optional)
1.75 oz.	(49 g) Amarillo whole hops—keg hops (optional)
¼ tsp.	(1 g) powdered Irish moss
Wyeast Irish Ale yeast #1084, White Labs English Ale yeast WLP007 or California Ale yeast WLP001	
¾ cup	(175 ml measure) corn sugar (priming bottles) or 0.33 cups (80 ml) corn sugar for kegging

A step infusion mash is employed to mash the grains with the mash hops. Add 14.5 quarts (13.75 l) of 140-degree F (60 C) water to the mixed crushed grain and mash hops, stir, stabilize and hold the temperature at 132 degrees F (53 C) for 30 minutes. Add 7 quarts (6.2 l) of boiling water, add heat to bring temperature up to 155 degrees F (68 C) and hold for about 30 minutes. Add first wort hops to empty and clean brew kettle. Then raise temperature of mash to 167 degrees F (75 C), lauter (recirculate runoff until liquid is reasonably clear before adding to brew kettle) and sparge with 3.5 to 4 gallons (13.5–15 l) of 170-degree F (77 C) water. Collect about 7.5 gallons (28.5 l) of runoff. Add 120-minute hops and bring to a full and vigorous boil.

The total boil time will be 120 minutes. When 60 minutes remain, add the 60-minute hops. When 10 minutes remain, add the Irish moss. After a total wort boil of 120 minutes, turn off the heat and add steeping hops.

Now add post-boil hop-back hops on top of your clean and sanitized screen in your lauter tun. Pass the hot wort through this bed of hops and through your counter-flow wort chiller and on into your sanitized fermenter. Sparge hops if necessary to bring total volume to 5 gallons (19 l). Aerate the wort very well.

Pitch the yeast when temperature of wort is about 70 degrees F (21 C). Ferment at about 70 degrees F (21 C) for about 1 week, or until fermentation shows signs of calm and stopping. Rack from your primary to a secondary fermenter and add secondary fermenter hops. Continue secondary fermentation at 70 degrees F (21 C) for 4 to 5 days more. If you have the capability, begin cellaring the beer by dropping the temperature 10 degrees F (about 6 C) per day until temperature is down to 36 degrees F (2 C). Cellar at this temperature for 7 to 10 days.

Prime with sugar and bottle. If kegging, you may add optional keg hops to your keg by placing them in a sanitized hop bag (nylon stockings can work well) and then into your keg. Prime and let naturally carbonate at 70 degrees F (21 C) for 3 to 5 days or until carbonated.

What can one say but "hop whompus?" and thank you, Jeff Bagby.

Malt Extract Recipe *for 5 gallons (19 l)*

10.5 lbs.	(4.8 kg) light malt extract syrup or 8.4 lbs. (3.8 kg) light dried malt extract
1.5 lbs.	(680 g) crystal malt (75-L)
8 oz.	(225 g) crystal malt (120-L)
2 oz.	(56 g) Liberty whole hops 4.5% alpha—mash hops
¾ oz.	(21 g) Centennial whole hops 7.5% alpha—mash hops
1.75 oz.	(49 g) Liberty hop pellets 5% alpha—first wort hopping
1 oz.	(28 g) Centennial hop pellets 9% alpha—120 minutes boiling
½ oz.	(14 g) Simcoe hop pellets 12% alpha—120 minutes boiling
1 oz.	(28 g) Amarillo hop pellets 8% alpha—60 minutes boiling
3.5 oz.	(98 g) Amarillo whole hops 8% alpha—steeping hops
2.75 oz.	(77 g) Centennial whole hops 7.7% alpha—steeping hops
1 oz.	(28 g) Liberty whole hops 4.5% alpha—steeping hops
⅔ oz.	(18 g) Liberty hop pellets—secondary fermenter
⅔ oz.	(18 g) Centennial hop pellets—secondary fermenter

⅔ oz.   (18 g) Amarillo hop pellets—secondary fermenter

½ oz.   (14 g) Simcoe hop pellets—secondary fermenter

½ oz.   (14 g) Liberty whole hops—keg hops

⅔ oz.   (18 g) Centennial whole hops—keg hops

⅓ oz.   (9 g) Simcoe whole hops—keg hops

1.75 oz.   (49 g) Amarillo whole hops—keg hops

¼ tsp.   (1 g) powdered Irish moss

Wyeast Irish Ale yeast #1084, White Labs Dry English Ale yeast
WLP007 or California Ale yeast WLP001

¾ cup   (175 ml measure) corn sugar (priming bottles) or 0.33
               cups (80 ml) corn sugar for kegging

Place crushed grains and mash hops in 2.5 gallons (9.5 l) of 150-degree F (68 C) water and let steep for 30 minutes. Then strain out (and rinse with 3 quarts [3 l] hot water) and discard the crushed grains and hops, reserving the approximately 3 gallons (11.5 l) of liquid to which you will now add malt extract, first wort hops and 120-minute hops. Bring to a boil.

The total boil time will be 120 minutes. When 60 minutes remain, add the 60-minute hops. When 10 minutes remain, add the Irish moss. After a total wort boil of 120 minutes, turn off the heat and add steeping hops.

Immerse the covered pot of wort in a cold-water bath and let sit for 30 minutes, or the time it takes to have a couple of homebrews.

Then strain out and sparge hops and direct the hot wort into a sanitized fermenter to which 2 gallons (7.6 l) of cold water has been added. Bring the total volume to 5 gallons (19 l) with additional cold water if necessary. Aerate the wort very well.

Pitch the yeast when temperature of wort is about 70 degrees F (21 C). Ferment at about 70 degrees F (21 C) for about 1 week, or until fermentation shows signs of calm and stopping. Rack from your primary to a secondary fermenter and add secondary fermenter hops. Continue secondary fermentation at 70 degrees F (21 C) for 4 to 5 days more. If you have the capability, begin cellaring the beer by dropping the temperature 10 degrees F (about 6 C) per day until temperature is down to 36 degrees F (2 C). Cellar at this temperature for 7 to 10 days.

Prime with sugar and bottle. If kegging, you may add optional keg hops to your keg by placing them into a sanitized hop bag (nylon stockings can work well) and then into your keg. Prime and let naturally carbonate at 70 degrees F (21 C) for 3 to 5 days or until carbonated.

"Hop whompus?" and thank you, Jeff Bagby.

STONE 03.03.03 VERTICAL EPIC ALE

Lee Chase, Head Brewer

THERE ARE several guidelines, recipes and homebrew "challenges" on Stone's website (www.stonebrewing.com). Among them are recipes for their annual "Stone Vertical Epic" series of beers. Here is the 2003 Vertical Epic released on March 3, 2003, with commentary (in italics) from head brewer Lee Chase.

Recipe adapted from Stone Brewing Company's website

All right, now this is going to be a little different than last year's (OK, a LOT different!!). By now you might know that these "Vertical" beers are not just the same recipe as each other, they are designed to be quite different from each other. We are not trying to make the recipe as difficult to brew as possible (we're not doing triple decoctions, or aging them in oak barrels for three years . . . yet!). Instead we're just trying to make what we think is a great beer, and have a little fun in the process. So read on, and do the best you can. That's kind of what I did . . .

Adapted from a recipe at www.stonebrewing.com

- TARGET ORIGINAL GRAVITY: 1.078 (19 B)
- APPROXIMATE FINAL GRAVITY: 1.014 (3.5 B)
- IBU: ABOUT 48
- APPROXIMATE COLOR: 17 SRM (34 EBC)
- ALCOHOL: 8.2% BY VOLUME

All-Grain Recipe *for 5 gallons (19 l)*

12 lbs.	(5.4 kg) 2-row pale malt
12 oz.	(340 g) flaked wheat
6 oz.	(168 g) Belgian Special-B malt
4 oz.	(113 g) chocolate wheat malt
0.85 oz.	(24 g) Warrior hops 16% alpha (13.6 HBU/380 MBU)—75 minutes boiling
¼ oz.	(7 g) Centennial hop pellets—dry hopping
½ oz.	(14 g) freshly crushed whole coriander seed
½ oz.	(14 g) freshly crushed grains of paradise (alligator pepper)
0.2 oz.	(6 g) freshly crushed whole coriander seed—added with dry hops
0.2 oz.	(6 g) freshly crushed grains of paradise (alligator pepper)—added with dry hops
¼ tsp.	(1 g) powdered Irish moss

White Labs Abbey Ale 500 yeast
Stone "house yeast" cultured from one of their bottle-conditioned ales

¾ cup	(175 ml measure) corn sugar (priming bottles) or 0.33 cups (80 ml) corn sugar for kegging

If at all possible (and at Stone, it is), put on the Bob Wills and his Texas Playboys song "What's a Matter with the Mill?" (Lyrics: Took my wheat down to get it ground / the man who runs the mill said the mill's broke down / what's a matter with the mill? / it done broke down / what's a matter with the mill? / it done broke down / can't get no grind . . . tell me what's a matter with the mill.)

A one-step infusion mash is employed to mash the grains. Add 13 quarts (12.4 l) of 168-degree F (76 C) water to the crushed grain, stir, stabilize and hold the temperature at 152 degrees F (66.5 C) for 60 minutes. Then raise temperature to 167 degrees F (75 C), lauter and sparge with 3.5 gallons (13.5 l) of 170-degree F (77 C) water.

I have found that the use of some down-home sounds from the Hot Club of Cowtown can also help to influence a smooth runoff and a faster conversion.

Collect about 5.5 gallons (21 l) of runoff. Bring to a full and vigorous boil. After 15 minutes of boiling, add your 75-minute hops.

You want to achieve a full rolling (radical) boil, and what we have found to help is putting on the Gogol Bordello song "Radical." Believe it or not, it can get the temperature up to 214 degrees if it is loud enough! My theory is that the Russian sound makes the wort think it is colder than it really is, so it lets in a little more heat than normal . . .

The total boil time will be 90 minutes. When 10 minutes remain, add the Irish moss.

Go ahead and let the Gogol Bordello play out while you are getting the spices ready.

After a total wort boil of 90 minutes, turn off the heat and add the crushed coriander and grains of paradise. Let steep for 10 minutes. Keep the cover on the brewing pot. After 10 minutes, place the pot (with cover on) in a running cold-water bath for 30 minutes. Continue to chill in the immersion or use other methods to chill your wort. Then strain and sparge the wort into a sanitized fermenter. Bring the total volume to 5 gallons (19 l) with additional cold water if necessary. Aerate the wort very well.

The yeast: This part is a little strange (not unlike a lot of Belgian beers). I did a lot of research on what yeast worked well with the style/flavor profile I wanted to achieve. I pitched about six different styles of Belgian "abbey" yeasts into their own fermenters, all with the same wort, and tasted the results. The yeast I chose was the abbey strain 500 from White Labs. With this yeast, I still thought that the phenolic character was a little over-the-

top, and wanted to mellow it out. That may be achievable with a cooler fermentation, but I was delighted with the balance struck when the same wort fermented with our house yeast was blended 1:1 with the beer from the Belgian yeast strain. This gives an assertive yeast flavor, but doesn't keep the hops and spices from showing through. So, to pitch this batch for fermentation, split it up into two equal-size batches. A few selections from a Hank Williams Sr. album will surely touch on the hardships of a split-up. Pitch one with the abbey and the other with the yeast you cultured out of a bottle of any of the Stone bottle-conditioned beers. Or ask the guys at White Labs what would be a similar strain to our house yeast.

Split the 5-gallon (19 l) batch evenly between two fermenters.

Pitch one culture of yeast into each fermenter when temperature of wort is about 70 degrees F (21 C). Ferment at about 70 degrees F (21 C) for about 1 week, or until fermentation shows signs of calm and stopping. Rack from each primary to two different secondary fermenters, add dry hop pellets and additional spices and let finish for another week.

When complete, blend the two batches into one. Prime with sugar and bottle or keg when complete.

Now the hard part . . . wait for 10 years to see what happens. Or just enjoy it when you feel the time is right.

Malt Extract Recipe *for 5 gallons (19 l)*

9.5 lbs.	(4.3 kg) light malt extract syrup or 7.6 lbs. (3.5 kg) light dried malt extract
1 lb.	(454 g) wheat malt extract syrup
6 oz.	(168 g) Belgian Special-B malt
4 oz.	(113 g) chocolate wheat malt
1.1 oz.	(30 g) Warrior hops 16% alpha (17.6 HBU/493 MBU)—75 minutes boiling
¼ oz.	(7 g) Centennial hop pellets—dry hopping
½ oz.	(14 g) freshly crushed whole coriander seed
½ oz.	(14 g) freshly crushed grains of paradise (alligator pepper)
0.2 oz.	(6 g) freshly crushed whole coriander seed—added with dry hops

| 0.2 oz. | (6 g) freshly crushed grains of paradise (alligator pepper)—added with dry hops |
| ¼ tsp. | (1 g) powdered Irish moss |

White Labs Abbey Ale 500 yeast
Stone "house yeast" cultured from one of their bottle-conditioned ales

| ¾ cup | (175 ml measure) corn sugar (priming bottles) or 0.33 cups (80 ml) corn sugar for kegging |

Place crushed grains in 2 gallons (7.6 l) of 150-degree F (68 C) water and let steep for 30 minutes. Then strain out (and rinse with 3 quarts [3 l] hot water) and discard the crushed grains, reserving the approximately 2.5 gallons (9.5 l) of liquid to which you will now add malt extract. Bring to a boil. After 15 minutes of boiling, add your 75-minute hops.

The total boil time will be 90 minutes. When 10 minutes remain, add the Irish moss. After a total wort boil of 90 minutes, turn off the heat and add the crushed coriander and grains of paradise. Let steep for 10 minutes. Keep the cover on the brewing pot. After 10 minutes, place the pot (with cover on) in a running cold-water bath for 30 minutes, or the time it takes to have a couple of homebrews. Then strain out and sparge hops and direct the hot wort into a sanitized fermenter to which 2.5 gallons (9.5 l) of cold water has been added. Bring the total volume to 5 gallons (19 l) with additional cold water if necessary. Aerate the wort very well.

Split the 5-gallon (19 l) batch evenly between two fermenters.

Pitch one culture of yeast into each fermenter when temperature of wort is about 70 degrees F (21 C). Ferment at about 70 degrees F (21 C) for about 1 week, or until fermentation shows signs of calm and stopping. Rack from each primary to two different secondary fermenters, add dry hop pellets and additional spices and let finish for another week.

When complete, blend the two batches into one. Prime with sugar and bottle or keg when complete.

. . . .

NEW WISCONSIN
APPLE/RASPBERRY/CHERRY BEER

- TARGET ORIGINAL GRAVITY: 1.050 (12.5 B)
- APPROXIMATE FINAL GRAVITY: 1.014 (3.5 B)
- IBU: ABOUT 16
- APPROXIMATE COLOR: INDICATIVE OF FRUIT USED
- ALCOHOL: 4.8–5% BY VOLUME

All-Grain Recipe *for 5 gallons (19 l)—*
you will need 6.5 gallon (25 l)–size fermenters

7.5 lbs.	(3.4 kg) 2-row pale malt
1 lb.	(454 g) crystal malt (10-L)
8 oz.	(225 g) 2-row pale malt—for the sour mash
10 lbs.	(4.54 kg) fresh or frozen raspberries or full-flavored cherries or 1 gallon (4 l) of fresh apple juice
¾ oz.	(21 g) Mt. Hood hops 6% alpha (4.5 HBU/126 MBU)—60 minutes boiling
¼ tsp.	(1 g) powdered Irish moss
English or American-type ale yeast	
¾ cup	(175 ml measure) corn sugar (priming bottles) or 0.33 cups (80 ml) corn sugar for kegging

A step infusion mash is employed to mash the grains. Add 8.5 quarts (8.1 l) of 140-degree F (60 C) water to the crushed grains (except the sour-mash pale malt), stir, stabilize and hold the temperature at 132 degrees F (53 C) for 30 minutes. Add 4 quarts (3.8 l) of boiling water, add heat to bring temperature up to 155 degrees F (68 C) and hold for about 30 minutes.

To make the sour mash: Transfer the full mash into an odorless, sanitized, food-grade, 5-gallon (19 l) bucket. Let the mash cool to 130–135 degrees F (54–57 C) and add the ½ pound of crushed malted barley. Stir to mix. Place a sheet of aluminum foil in contact with the surface to form a complete barrier from the air. Fit lid snugly on the pail. Insulate the pail on all sides with a sleeping bag and/or blankets to help maintain warm temperatures and promote lactic bacterial activity and souring. The lactobacillus will sour the mash and will be noticeable after about 15 hours. Fifteen to 24 hours should be adequate for your first experiment with this process. More time will produce more sourness.

After the souring process, open the container (it will smell quite foul), remove the aluminum foil and skim any scum from the surface and discard. Heat the mash to 160 degrees F (71 C) and then transfer the sour mash to a lauter-tun, drain and sparge with 4 gallons (15.2 l) of 170-degree F (77 C) water.

Collect about 5.5 gallons (21 l) of runoff. Add 60-minute hops and bring to a full and vigorous boil.

The total boil time will be 60 minutes. When 10 minutes remain, add the Irish moss. After a total wort boil of 60 minutes, turn off the heat and place the pot (with cover on) in a running cold-water bath for 30 minutes. Continue to chill in the immersion or use other methods to chill your wort. Then strain and sparge the wort into a sanitized fermenter. Bring the total volume to 5 gallons (19 l) with additional cold water if necessary. Aerate the wort very well.

Pitch the yeast when temperature of wort is about 70 degrees F (21 C). Ferment at about 70 degrees F (21 C) for about 1 week, or until fermentation shows signs of calm and stopping. Rack from your primary to a 6.5-gallon (25 l) secondary fermenter and add crushed fresh fruit, thawed frozen fruit or 1 gallon of apple juice to the secondary fermenter. Continue fermenting for another 7 to 10 days at 70 degrees F (21 C). Rack a third time into a third fermenter, while separating and discarding the used fruit. When fermentation has stopped, rack a fourth time into a clean fermenter and if you have the capability, "cellar" the beer at about 55 degrees F (12.5 C) for 1 to 3 weeks.

Prime with sugar and bottle or keg when complete.

ALTERNATE METHOD: Instead of utilizing a sour mash, you may use the following grain formulation:

6.5 lbs.	(3.4 kg) 2-row pale malt
1 lb.	(454 g) crystal malt (10-L)
1 lb.	(454 g) German sauer malt

Do not carry out a sour mash procedure. A step-infusion mash is employed to mash the grains. Add 8.5 quarts (8.1 l) of 140-degree F (60 C) water to the crushed grain, stir, stabilize and hold the temperature at 132 degrees F (53 C) for 30 minutes. Add 4 quarts (3.8 l) of boiling water, add heat to bring temperature up to 155 degrees F (68 C) and hold for about 30 minutes. Then raise temperature to 167 degrees F (75 C), lauter and sparge with 3.5 gallons (13.5 l) of 170-degree F (77 C) water. Collect about 5.5 gallons (21 l) of runoff. Add 60-minute hops and bring to a full and vigorous boil.

Mash/Extract Recipe *for 5 gallons (19 l)*

5.5 lbs.	(2.5 kg) light malt extract syrup or 4.4 lbs. (2 kg) light dried malt extract
1 lb.	(454 g) crystal malt (10-L)
1 lb.	(454 g) German sauer malt
10 lbs.	(4.54 kg) fresh or frozen raspberries or full flavored cherries or 1 gallon (4 l) of fresh apple juice
1 oz.	(28 g) Mt. Hood hops 6% alpha (6 HBU/168 MBU)— 60 minutes boiling
¼ tsp.	(1 g) powdered Irish moss
German or Bavarian-type lager yeast	
¾ cup	(175 ml measure) corn sugar (priming bottles) or 0.33 cups (80 ml) corn sugar for kegging

Heat 2 quarts (2 l) water to 172 degrees F (77.5 C) and then add crushed grains to the water. Stir well to distribute heat. Temperature should stabilize at about 155 degrees F (68 C). Wrap a towel around the pot and set aside for about 45 minutes. Have a homebrew.

After 45 minutes, add heat to the mini-mash and raise the temperature to 167 degrees F (75 C). Then pass the liquid and grains into a strainer and rinse with 170-degree F (77 C) water. Discard the grains.

To the sweet extract you have just produced, add more water, bringing the volume up to about 2.5 gallons (9.5 l). Add malt extract and 60-minute hops and bring to a boil.

The total boil time will be 60 minutes. When 10 minutes remain, add the Irish moss. After a total wort boil of 60 minutes, turn off the heat.

Immerse the covered pot of wort in a cold-water bath and let sit for 30 minutes, or the time it takes to have a couple of homebrews.

Then strain out and sparge hops and direct the hot wort into a sanitized fermenter to which 2.5 gallons (9.5 l) of cold water has been added. Bring the total volume to 5 gallons (19 l) with additional cold water if necessary. Aerate the wort very well.

Pitch the yeast when temperature of wort is about 70 degrees F (21 C).

Ferment at about 70 degrees F (21 C) for about 1 week, or until fermentation shows signs of calm and stopping. Rack from your primary to a 6.5-gallon (25 l) secondary fermenter and add crushed fresh fruit, thawed frozen fruit or 1 gallon of apple juice to the secondary fermenter. Continue fermenting for another 7 to 10 days at 70 degrees F (21 C). Rack a third time into a third fermenter, while separating and discarding the used fruit. When fermentation has stopped, rack a fourth time into a clean fermenter and if you have the capability, "cellar" the beer at about 55 degrees F (12.5 C) for about 1 week.

Prime with sugar and bottle or keg when complete.

· ·

65-65-65-6.5 INDIA PALE ALE

- TARGET ORIGINAL GRAVITY: 1.065 (16 B)
- APPROXIMATE FINAL GRAVITY: 1.014 (3.6 B)
- IBU: ABOUT 65
- APPROXIMATE COLOR: 7 SRM (14 EBC)
- ALCOHOL: 6.5% BY VOLUME

All-Grain Recipe *for 5 gallons (19 l)*

9.75 lbs.	(4.4 kg) pale malt
1.25 lbs.	(568 g) crystal malt (15-L)
	All of the following hops are added as a blend in incrementally designated amounts over a period of 65 minutes at 5-minute intervals
½ oz.	(14 g) Warrior pellet hops 16% alpha—1-gram increments at 14 × 5-minute intervals
1 oz.	(28 g) Amarillo pellet hops 8% alpha—2-gram increments at 14 × 5-minute intervals
¾ oz.	(21 g) Simcoe pellet hops 12% alpha—1.5-gram increments at 14 × 5-minute intervals
5 g	each of Warrior, Amarillo and Simcoe hop pellets for dry hopping
¼ tsp.	(1 g) powdered Irish moss

Wyeast Irish Ale yeast #1084 or White Labs California Ale yeast
WLP001

| ¾ cup | (175 ml measure) corn sugar (priming bottles) or |
| | 0.33 cups (80 ml) corn sugar for kegging |

A step infusion mash is employed to mash the grains. Add 11 quarts (10.5 l) of 140-degree F (60 C) water to the crushed grain, stir, stabilize and hold the temperature at 132 degrees F (53 C) for 30 minutes. Add 5.5 quarts (5.2 l) of boiling water, add heat to bring temperature up to 155 degrees F (68 C) and hold for about 30 minutes. Then raise temperature to 167 degrees F (75 C), lauter and sparge with 3.5 gallons (13.5 l) of 170-degree F (77 C) water. Collect about 5.5 gallons (21 l) of runoff. Bring to a boil, add the first increment of hop pellets and begin timing. Every 5 minutes, add another increment of hops until you have boiled a full 65 minutes, adding the final dose of hops at 0 minutes.

When 10 minutes remain, add the Irish moss. After a total wort boil of 65 minutes, turn off the heat and place the pot (with cover on) in a running cold-water bath for 30 minutes. Continue to chill in the immersion or use other methods to chill your wort. Then strain and sparge the wort into a sanitized fermenter. Bring the total volume to 5 gallons (19 l) with additional cold water if necessary. Aerate the wort very well.

Pitch the yeast when temperature of wort is about 70 degrees F (21 C). Ferment at about 70 degrees F (21 C) for about 1 week, or until fermentation shows signs of calm and stopping. Rack from your primary to a secondary fermenter and add the hop pellets for dry hopping. If you have the capability, "cellar" the beer at about 55 degrees F (12.5 C) for about 1 week.

Prime with sugar and bottle or keg when complete.

Malt Extract Recipe *for 5 gallons (19 l)*

8.25 lbs.	(3.7 kg) light malt extract syrup or 6.6 lbs. (3 kg)
	light dried malt extract
1.25 lbs.	(568 g) crystal malt (15-L)
	All of the following hops are added as a blend in
	incrementally designated amounts over a period of 65
	minutes at 5-minute intervals
1 oz.	(28 g) Warrior pellet hops 16% alpha—2-gram
	increments at 14 × 5-minute intervals

1 oz.	(28 g) Amarillo pellet hops 8% alpha—2-gram increments at 14 × 5-minute intervals
¾ oz.	(21 g) Simcoe pellet hops 12% alpha—1.5-gram increments at 14 × 5-minute intervals
5 g	each of Warrior, Amarillo and Simcoe hop pellets for dry hopping
¼ tsp.	(1 g) powdered Irish moss

Wyeast Irish Ale yeast #1084 or White California Ale yeast WLP001

| ¾ cup | (175 ml measure) corn sugar (priming bottles) or 0.33 cups (80 ml) corn sugar for kegging |

Place crushed grains in 2 gallons (7.6 l) of 150-degree F (68 C) water and let steep for 30 minutes. Then strain out (and rinse with 3 quarts [3 l] hot water) and discard the crushed grains, reserving the approximately 2.5 gallons (9.5 l) of liquid to which you will now add malt extract and bring to a boil. When boiling commences, add the first increment of hop pellets and begin timing. Every 5 minutes add another increment of hops until you have boiled a full 65 minutes, adding the final dose of hops at 0 minutes.

When 10 minutes remain, add the Irish moss. After a total wort boil of 65 minutes, turn off the heat. Immerse the covered pot of wort in a cold-water bath and let sit for 30 minutes, or the time it takes to have a couple of home-brews.

Then strain out and sparge hops and direct the hot wort into a sanitized fermenter to which 2.5 gallons (9.5 l) of cold water has been added. Bring the total volume to 5 gallons (19 l) with additional cold water if necessary. Aerate the wort very well.

Pitch the yeast when temperature of wort is about 70 degrees F (21 C). Ferment at about 70 degrees F (21 C) for about 1 week, or until fermentation shows signs of calm and stopping. Rack from your primary to a secondary fermenter and add the hop pellets for dry hopping. If you have the capability, "cellar" the beer at about 55 degrees F (12.5 C) for about 1 week.

Prime with sugar and bottle or keg when complete.

FLYING FISH BABY SAISON FARMHOUSE ALE

Adapted from a recipe submitted by Gene Muller

- TARGET ORIGINAL GRAVITY: 1.046 (11.5 B)
- APPROXIMATE FINAL GRAVITY: 1.010 (2.5 B)
- IBU: ABOUT 14
- APPROXIMATE COLOR: 4 SRM (8 EBC)
- ALCOHOL: 4.8% BY VOLUME

All-Grain Recipe *for 5 gallons (19 l)*

6 lbs.	(2.7 kg) 2-row pale malt
12 oz.	(340 g) white wheat (not malted)
8 oz.	(225 g) Briess Carapils malt
6 oz.	(168 g) German sauer malt
0.1 oz.	(3 g) Styrian Goldings hops 4% alpha (0.4 HBU/11.2 MBU)—75 minutes boiling
0.1 oz.	(3 g) Magnum hops 14% alpha (1.4 HBU/31 MBU)—75 minutes boiling
½ oz.	(14 g) Styrian Goldings hops 4% alpha (2 HBU/56 MBU)—30 minutes boiling
½ oz.	(14 g) Styrian Goldings—5 minutes boiling
¼ tsp.	(1 g) powdered Irish moss
White Labs British Ale yeast WLP005	
¾ cup	(175 ml measure) corn sugar (priming bottles) or 0.33 cups (80 ml) corn sugar for kegging

A step infusion mash is employed to mash the grains. Add 7.5 quarts (7.1 l) of 140-degree F (60 C) water to the crushed grain, stir, stabilize and hold the temperature at 132 degrees F (53 C) for 30 minutes. Add 3.75 quarts (3.6 l) of boiling water, add heat to bring temperature up to 155 degrees F (68 C) and hold for about 30 minutes. Then raise temperature to 167 degrees F (75 C), lauter and sparge with 3.5 gallons (13.5 l) of 170-degree F (77 C) water. Collect about 5.5 gallons (21 l) of runoff. Add 75-minute hops and bring to a full and vigorous boil.

The total boil time will be 75 minutes. When 30 minutes remain, add the 30-minute hops. When 10 minutes remain, add the Irish moss. When 5 minutes remain, add the 5-minute hops. After a total wort boil of 75 minutes, turn off the heat and place the pot (with cover on) in a running cold-water bath for 30 minutes. Continue to chill in the immersion or use other methods to chill your wort. Then strain and sparge the wort into a sanitized fermenter. Bring the total volume to 5 gallons (19 l) with additional cold water if necessary. Aerate the wort very well.

Pitch the yeast when temperature of wort is about 70 degrees F (21 C). Ferment at about 70 degrees F (21 C) for about 1 week, or until fermentation shows signs of calm and stopping. Rack from your primary to a secondary fermenter and if you have the capability, "cellar" the beer at about 55 degrees F (12.5 C) for about 1 week.

Prime with sugar and bottle or keg when complete.

Mash/Extract Recipe *for 5 gallons (19 l)*

3 lbs.	(1.36 kg) very light malt extract syrup or 2.4 lbs. (1.1 kg) very light dried malt extract
1.5 lbs.	(680 g) wheat malt extract syrup
1.5 lbs.	(680 g) 2-row pale malt
8 oz.	(225 g) Briess Carapils malt
6 oz.	(168 g) German sauer malt
0.25 oz.	(7 g) Styrian Goldings hops 4% alpha (1 HBU/28 MBU)—75 minutes boiling
0.14 oz.	(4 g) Magnum hops 14% alpha (2 HBU/56 MBU)—75 minutes boiling
½ oz.	(14 g) Styrian Goldings hops 4% alpha (2 HBU/56 MBU)—30 minutes boiling
½ oz.	(14 g) Styrian Goldings—5 minutes boiling
¼ tsp.	(1 g) powdered Irish moss
White Labs British Ale yeast WLP005	
¾ cup	(175 ml measure) corn sugar (priming bottles) or 0.33 cups (80 ml) corn sugar for kegging

Heat 2.5 quarts (2.4 l) water to 172 degrees F (77.5 C) and then add crushed grains to the water. Stir well to distribute heat. Temperature should stabilize

at about 155 degrees F (68 C). Wrap a towel around the pot and set aside for about 45 minutes. Have a homebrew.

After 45 minutes, add heat to the mini-mash and raise the temperature to 167 degrees F (75 C). Then pass the liquid and grains into a strainer and rinse with 170-degree F (77 C) water. Discard the grains.

To the sweet extract you have just produced, add more water, bringing the volume up to about 2.5 gallons (9.5 l). Add malt extract and 75-minute hops and bring to a boil.

The total boil time will be 75 minutes. When 30 minutes remain, add the 30-minute hops. When 10 minutes remain, add the Irish moss. When 5 minutes remain, add the 5-minute hops. After a total wort boil of 75 minutes, turn off the heat.

Immerse the covered pot of wort in a cold-water bath and let sit for 30 minutes, or the time it takes to have a couple of homebrews.

Then strain out and sparge hops and direct the hot wort into a sanitized fermenter to which 2.5 gallons (9.5 l) of cold water has been added. Bring the total volume to 5 gallons (19 l) with additional cold water if necessary. Aerate the wort very well.

Pitch the yeast when temperature of wort is about 70 degrees F (21 C). Ferment at about 70 degrees F (21 C) for about 1 week, or until fermentation shows signs of calm and stopping. Rack from your primary to a secondary fermenter and if you have the capability, "cellar" the beer at about 55 degrees F (12.5 C) for about 1 week.

Prime with sugar and bottle or keg when complete.

BROOKLYN'S ORIGINAL
CHOCOLATE STOUT

Based on Steve Hindy's original recipe

- TARGET ORIGINAL GRAVITY: 1.052 (13 B)
- APPROXIMATE FINAL GRAVITY: 1.014 (3.5 B)
- IBU: ABOUT 28
- APPROXIMATE COLOR: 52 SRM (104 EBC)
- ALCOHOL: 5.2% BY VOLUME

All-Grain Recipe *for 5 gallons (19 l)*

7.75 lbs.	(3.5 kg) pale malt
1 lb.	(454 g) chocolate malt
4 oz.	(113 g) roasted barley
6 oz.	(168 g) black patent malt
1 oz.	(28 g) UK Fuggles hops 5% alpha (5 HBU/140 MBU)—60 minutes boiling
1.5 oz.	(42 g) Willamette hops 5% alpha (7.5 HBU/210 MBU)—10 minutes boiling
8 tsp.	(32 g) gypsum
¼ tsp.	(1 g) powdered Irish moss
Irish ale yeast	
¾ cup	(175 ml measure) corn sugar (priming bottles) or 0.33 cups (80 ml) corn sugar for kegging

A step infusion mash is employed to mash the grains. Add 9 quarts (8.6 l) of 140-degree F (60 C) water to the crushed grain, stir, stabilize and hold the temperature at 132 degrees F (53 C) for 30 minutes. Add 4.5 quarts (4.3 l) of boiling water, add heat to bring temperature up to 155 degrees F (68 C) and hold for about 30 minutes. Then raise temperature to 167 degrees F (75 C), lauter and sparge with 3.5 gallons (13.5 l) of 170-degree F (77 C) water. Collect about 5.5 gallons (21 l) of runoff. Add 60-minute hops and the gypsum and bring to a full and vigorous boil.

The total boil time will be 60 minutes. When 10 minutes remain, add the Irish moss and the 10-minute hops. After a total wort boil of 60 minutes, turn off the heat and place the pot (with cover on) in a running cold-water bath for 30 minutes. Continue to chill in the immersion or use other methods to chill your wort. Then strain and sparge the wort into a sanitized fermenter. Bring the total volume to 5 gallons (19 l) with additional cold water if necessary. Aerate the wort very well.

Pitch the yeast when temperature of wort is about 70 degrees F (21 C). Ferment at about 70 degrees F (21 C) for about 1 week, or until fermentation shows signs of calm and stopping. Rack from your primary to a secondary fermenter and if you have the capability, "cellar" the beer at about 55 degrees F (12.5 C) for about 1 week.

Prime with sugar and bottle or keg when complete.

Malt Extract Recipe *for 5 gallons (19 l)*

6.5 lbs.	(3 kg) dark malt extract syrup or 5.2 lbs. (2.4 kg) dark dried malt extract
1 lb.	(454 g) chocolate malt
4 oz.	(113 g) roasted barley
4 oz.	(113 g) black patent malt
1.5 oz.	(42 g) UK Fuggles hops 5% alpha (7.5 HBU/210 MBU)—60 minutes boiling
1.5 oz.	(42 g) Willamette hops 5% alpha (7.5 HBU/210 MBU)—10 minutes boiling
8 tsp.	(32 g) gypsum
¼ tsp.	(1 g) powdered Irish moss
Irish ale yeast	
¾ cup	(175 ml measure) corn sugar (priming bottles) or 0.33 cups (80 ml) corn sugar for kegging

Place crushed grains in 2 gallons (7.6 l) of 150-degree F (68 C) water and let steep for 30 minutes. Then strain out (and rinse with 3 quarts [3 l] hot water) and discard the crushed grains, reserving the approximately 2.5 gallons (9.5 l) of liquid to which you will now add malt extract, gypsum and 60-minute hops. Bring to a boil.

The total boil time will be 60 minutes. When 10 minutes remain, add the Irish moss and 10-minute hops. After a total wort boil of 60 minutes, turn off the heat.

Immerse the covered pot of wort in a cold-water bath and let sit for 30 minutes, or the time it takes to have a couple of homebrews.

Then strain out and sparge hops and direct the hot wort into a sanitized fermenter to which 2.5 gallons (9.5 l) of cold water has been added. Bring the total volume to 5 gallons (19 l) with additional cold water if necessary. Aerate the wort very well.

Pitch the yeast when temperature of wort is about 70 degrees F (21 C). Ferment at about 70 degrees F (21 C) for about 1 week, or until fermentation shows signs of calm and stopping. Rack from your primary to a secondary fermenter and if you have the capability, "cellar" the beer at about 55 degrees F (12.5 C) for about 1 week.

Prime with sugar and bottle or keg when complete.

···

MAGIC BOLO #9.1

- TARGET ORIGINAL GRAVITY: 1.047 (12 B)
- APPROXIMATE FINAL GRAVITY: 1.012 (3 B)
- IBU: ABOUT 18
- APPROXIMATE COLOR: 9 SRM (18 EBC)
- ALCOHOL: 4.6% BY VOLUME

All-Grain Recipe *for 5 gallons (19 l)*

7 lbs.	(3.2 kg) pale malt
1 lb.	(454 g) crystal malt (15-L)
¼ oz.	(7 g) Warrior hops 16% alpha (4 HBU/112 MBU)— 60 minutes boiling
¼ oz.	(7 g) Cascade hops 5% alpha (1.3 HBU/35 MBU)— 5 minutes boiling
½ oz.	(14 g) American Tettnanger hops—1 minute boiling
1.25 fl. oz.	(37 ml) apricot essence
¼ tsp.	(1 g) powdered Irish moss

Wyeast Ringwood Ale yeast #1187 or other British/English ale yeast

¾ cup	(175 ml measure) corn sugar (priming bottles) or 0.33 cups (80 ml) corn sugar for kegging

A step infusion mash is employed to mash the grains. Add 8 quarts (7.6 l) of 140-degree F (60 C) water to the crushed grain, stir, stabilize and hold the temperature at 132 degrees F (53 C) for 30 minutes. Add 4 quarts (3.8 l) of boiling water, add heat to bring temperature up to 155 degrees F (68 C) and hold for about 30 minutes. Then raise temperature to 167 degrees F (75 C), lauter and sparge with 3.5 gallons (13.5 l) of 170-degree F (77 C) water. Collect about 5.5 gallons (21 l) of runoff. Add 60-minute hops and bring to a full and vigorous boil.

The total boil time will be 60 minutes. When 10 minutes remain, add the Irish moss. When 5 minutes remain, add the 5-minute hops. When 1 minute remains, add the 1-minute hops. After a total wort boil of 60 minutes, turn off the heat and place the pot (with cover on) in a running cold-water bath for 30 minutes. Continue to chill in the immersion or use other methods to chill your wort. Then strain and sparge the wort into a sanitized fermenter. Bring the total volume to 5 gallons (19 l) with additional cold water if necessary. Aerate the wort very well.

Pitch the yeast when temperature of wort is about 70 degrees F (21 C). Ferment at about 70 degrees F (21 C) for about 1 week, or until fermentation shows signs of calm and stopping. Rack from your primary to a secondary fermenter and add the apricot essence. If you have the capability, "cellar" the beer at about 55 degrees F (12.5 C) for about 1 week.

Prime with sugar and bottle or keg when complete.

Malt Extract Recipe *for 5 gallons (19 l)*

6 lbs.	(2.7 kg) very light malt extract syrup or 4.8 lbs. (2.2 kg) light dried malt extract
1 lb.	(454 g) crystal malt (15-L)
⅓ oz.	(9 g) Warrior hops 16% alpha (5.3 HBU/148 MBU)—60 minutes boiling
¼ oz.	(7 g) Cascade hops 5% alpha (1.3 HBU/35 MBU)— 5 minutes boiling
½ oz.	(14 g) American Tettnanger hops—1 minute boiling
1.25 fl. oz.	(37 ml) apricot essence
¼ tsp.	(1 g) powdered Irish moss
Wyeast Ringwood Ale yeast #1187 or other British/English ale yeast	
¾ cup	(175 ml measure) corn sugar (priming bottles) or 0.33 cups (80 ml) corn sugar for kegging

Place crushed grains in 2 gallons (7.6 l) of 150-degree F (68 C) water and let steep for 30 minutes. Then strain out (and rinse with 3 quarts [3 l] hot water) and discard the crushed grains, reserving the approximately 2.5 gallons (9.5 l) of liquid to which you will now add malt extract and 60-minute hops. Bring to a boil.

The total boil time will be 60 minutes. When 10 minutes remain, add the Irish moss. When 5 minutes remain, add the 5-minute hops. When 1 minute remains, add the 1-minute hops. After a total wort boil of 60 minutes, turn off the heat.

Immerse the covered pot of wort in a cold-water bath and let sit for 30 minutes, or the time it takes to have a couple of homebrews.

Then strain out and sparge hops and direct the hot wort into a sanitized fermenter to which 2.5 gallons (9.5 l) of cold water has been added. Bring the total volume to 5 gallons (19 l) with additional cold water if necessary. Aerate the wort very well.

Pitch the yeast when temperature of wort is about 70 degrees F (21 C). Ferment at about 70 degrees F (21 C) for about 1 week, or until fermentation shows signs of calm and stopping. Rack from your primary to a secondary fermenter and add the apricot essence. If you have the capability, "cellar" the beer at about 55 degrees F (12.5 C) for about 1 week.

Prime with sugar and bottle or keg when complete.

WOLAVER'S ORGANIC OATMEAL STOUT

Adapted from a recipe submitted by Steve Parkes

- TARGET ORIGINAL GRAVITY: 1.061 (15 B)
- APPROXIMATE FINAL GRAVITY: 1.016 (4 B)
- IBU: ABOUT 44
- APPROXIMATE COLOR: 56 SRM (112 EBC)
- ALCOHOL: 5.7% BY VOLUME

All-Grain Recipe *for 5 gallons (19 l)*

7 lbs.	(3.2 kg) organic Briess 2-row pale malt
1.5 lbs.	(680 g) organic roasted barley
12 oz.	(340 g) organic oats
12 oz.	(340 g) organic Munich malt
10 oz.	(280 g) organic crystal malt (120-L)
6 oz.	(168 g) organic wheat
¾ oz.	(21 g) Magnum hops 13% alpha (9.75 HBU/273 MBU)—90 minutes boiling
0.2 oz.	(3 g) Organic New Zealand Hallertau hop pellets 7% alpha (1.25 HBU/35 MBU)—30 minutes boiling
1 oz.	(28 g) Cascade hops—1-minute steep at end of boil
¼ tsp.	(1 g) powdered Irish moss
Irish ale yeast	
¾ cup	(175 ml measure) organic sugar (priming bottles) or 0.33 cups (80 ml) organic sugar for kegging

A step infusion mash is employed to mash the grains. Add 11 quarts (10.5 l) of 140-degree F (60 C) water to the crushed grain, stir, stabilize and hold the temperature at 132 degrees F (53 C) for 30 minutes. Add 5.5 quarts (5.2 l) of boiling water, add heat to bring temperature up to 155 degrees F (68 C) and hold for about 30 minutes. Then raise temperature to 167 degrees F (75 C), lauter and sparge with 3.5 gallons (13.5 l) of 170-degree F (77 C) water. Collect about 5.5 gallons (21 l) of runoff.

Add 90-minute hops and bring to a full and vigorous boil.

The total boil time will be 90 minutes. When 30 minutes remain, add the 30-minute hops. When 10 minutes remain, add the Irish moss. When 1 minute remains, add the 1-minute hops. After a total wort boil of 90 minutes, turn off the heat and place the pot (with cover on) in a running cold-water bath for 30 minutes. Continue to chill in the immersion or use other methods to chill your wort. Then strain and sparge the wort into a sanitized fermenter. Bring the total volume to 5 gallons (19 l) with additional cold water if necessary. Aerate the wort very well.

Pitch the yeast when temperature of wort is about 70 degrees F (21 C). Ferment at about 70 degrees F (21 C) for about 1 week, or until fermentation shows signs of calm and stopping. Rack from your primary to a secondary fermenter and if you have the capability, "cellar" the beer at about 55 degrees F (12.5 C) for about 1 week.

Prime with sugar and bottle or keg when complete.

Mash/Extract Recipe *for 5 gallons (19 l)*

4.5 lbs.	(2 kg) amber (organic if available) malt extract syrup
8 oz.	(225 g) wheat malt extract syrup (organic if available)
2 lbs.	(908 g) organic Briess 2-row pale malt
1.5 lbs.	(680 g) organic roasted barley
12 oz.	(340 g) organic oats
10 oz.	(280 g) organic crystal malt (120-L)

1 oz.	(28 g) Magnum hops 13% alpha (13 HBU/364 MBU)—90 minutes boiling
0.2 oz.	(3 g) Organic New Zealand Hallertau hop pellets 7% alpha (1.25 HBU/35 MBU)—30 minutes boiling
1 oz.	(28 g) Cascade hops—1-minute steep at end of boil
¼ tsp.	(1 g) powdered Irish moss
Irish ale yeast	
¾ cup	(175 ml measure) organic sugar (priming bottles) or 0.33 cups (80 ml) organic sugar for kegging

Heat 5 quarts (4.75 l) water to 172 degrees F (77.5 C) and then add crushed grains to the water. Stir well to distribute heat. Temperature should stabilize at about 155 degrees F (68 C). Wrap a towel around the pot and set aside for about 45 minutes. Have a homebrew.

After 45 minutes, add heat to the mini-mash and raise the temperature to 167 degrees F (75 C). Then pass the liquid and grains into a strainer and rinse with 170-degree F (77 C) water. Discard the grains.

To the sweet extract you have just produced, add more water, bringing the volume up to about 2.5 gallons (9.5 l). Add malt extract and 90-minute hops and bring to a boil.

The total boil time will be 90 minutes. When 30 minutes remain, add the 30-minute hops. When 10 minutes remain, add the Irish moss. When 1 minute remains, add the 1-minute hops. After a total wort boil of 90 minutes, turn off the heat.

Immerse the covered pot of wort in a cold-water bath and let sit for 30 minutes, or the time it takes to have a couple of homebrews.

Then strain out and sparge hops and direct the hot wort into a sanitized fermenter to which 2.5 gallons (9.5 l) of cold water has been added. Bring the total volume to 5 gallons (19 l) with additional cold water if necessary. Aerate the wort very well.

Pitch the yeast when temperature of wort is about 70 degrees F (21 C). Ferment at about 70 degrees F (21 C) for about 1 week, or until fermentation shows signs of calm and stopping. Rack from your primary to a secondary fermenter and if you have the capability, "cellar" the beer at about 55 degrees F (12.5 C) for about 1 week.

Prime with sugar and bottle or keg when complete.

ALASKAN WINTER SPRUCE OLD ALE

- TARGET ORIGINAL GRAVITY: 1.066 (16 B)
- APPROXIMATE FINAL GRAVITY: 1.016 (4 B)
- IBU: ABOUT 27
- APPROXIMATE COLOR: 17 SRM (34 EBC)
- ALCOHOL: 6.5% BY VOLUME

All-Grain Recipe *for 5 gallons (19 l)*

4.5 lbs.	(2 kg) pale malt
2.5 lbs.	(1.15 kg) Munich malt
2 lbs.	(908 g) wheat malt
1 lb.	(454 g) crystal malt (40-L)
8 oz.	(225 g) Caramunich malt
8 oz.	(225 g) crystal malt (80-L)
8 oz.	(225 g) fresh Sitka or other spring spruce tips
2 oz.	(56 g) Czech Saaz hops 3% alpha (6 HBU/168 MBU)—90 minutes boiling
½ oz.	(14 g) Czech Saaz hops 3% alpha (1.5 HBU/42 MBU)—15 minutes boiling
¼ oz.	(7 g) German Hallertauer hop pellets—dry hopping
¼ tsp.	(1 g) powdered Irish moss
English or American-type ale yeast	
¾ cup	(175 ml measure) corn sugar (priming bottles) or 0.33 cups (80 ml) corn sugar for kegging

A step infusion mash is employed to mash the grains. Add 11 quarts (10.5 l) of 140-degree F (60 C) water to the crushed grain, stir, stabilize and hold the temperature at 132 degrees F (53 C) for 30 minutes. Add 5.5 quarts (5.2 l) of boiling water, add heat to bring temperature up to 155 degrees F (68 C) and hold for about 30 minutes. Then raise temperature to 167 degrees F (75 C), lauter and sparge with 3.5 gallons (13.5 l) of 170-degree F (77 C) water. Collect about 5.5 gallons (21 l) of runoff. Add 90-minute hops and 6 oz. (168 g) spruce tips and bring to a full and vigorous boil.

The total boil time will be 90 minutes. When 15 minutes remain, add the 15-minute hops and 2 oz. (56 g) spruce tips. When 10 minutes remain, add the Irish moss. After a total wort boil of 90 minutes, turn off the heat and place the pot (with cover on) in a running cold-water bath for 30 minutes. Continue to chill in the immersion or use other methods to chill your wort. Then strain and sparge the wort into a sanitized fermenter. Bring the total volume to 5 gallons (19 l) with additional cold water if necessary. Aerate the wort very well.

Pitch the yeast when temperature of wort is about 70 degrees F (21 C). Ferment at about 70 degrees F (21 C) for about 1 week, or until fermentation shows signs of calm and stopping. Rack from your primary to a secondary fermenter and add the hop pellets for dry hopping. If you have the capability, "cellar" the beer at about 55 degrees F (12.5 C) for about 1 week.

Prime with sugar and bottle or keg when complete.

Malt Extract Recipe *for 5 gallons (19 l)*

5 lbs.	(2.3 kg) wheat malt extract syrup
3 lbs.	(1.36 kg) light malt extract syrup or 2.4 lbs. (1.1 kg) light dried malt extract
12 oz.	(340 g) crystal malt (40-L)
8 oz.	(225 g) Caramunich malt
4 oz.	(113 g) crystal malt (80-L)
8 oz.	(225 g) fresh Sitka or other spring spruce tips
3 oz.	(84 g) Czech Saaz hops 3% alpha (9 HBU/252 MBU)— 90 minutes boiling
½ oz.	(14 g) Czech Saaz hops 3% alpha (1.5 HBU/42 MBU)—15 minutes boiling
¼ oz.	(7 g) German Hallertauer hop pellets—dry hopping
¼ tsp.	(1 g) powdered Irish moss
English or American-type ale yeast	
¾ cup	(175 ml measure) corn sugar (priming bottles) or 0.33 cups (80 ml) corn sugar for kegging

Place crushed grains in 2 gallons (7.6 l) of 150-degree F (68 C) water and let steep for 30 minutes. Then strain out (and rinse with 3 quarts [3 l] hot water) and discard the crushed grains, reserving the approximately 2.5 gallons (9.5 l) of liquid to which you will now add malt extract, 6 oz. (168 g) spruce tips and 90-minute hops. Bring to a boil.

The total boil time will be 90 minutes. When 15 minutes remain, add the

15-minute hops and 2 oz. (56 g) spruce tips. When 10 minutes remain, add the Irish moss. After a total wort boil of 90 minutes, turn off the heat.

Immerse the covered pot of wort in a cold-water bath and let sit for 30 minutes, or the time it takes to have a couple of homebrews.

Then strain out and sparge hops and direct the hot wort into a sanitized fermenter to which 2.5 gallons (9.5 l) of cold water has been added. Bring the total volume to 5 gallons (19 l) with additional cold water if necessary. Aerate the wort very well.

Pitch the yeast when temperature of wort is about 70 degrees F (21 C). Ferment at about 70 degrees F (21 C) for about 1 week, or until fermentation shows signs of calm and stopping. Rack from your primary to a secondary fermenter and add the hop pellets for dry hopping. If you have the capability, "cellar" the beer at about 55 degrees F (12.5 C) for about 1 week.

Prime with sugar and bottle or keg when complete.

SAM ADAMS TRIPLE BOCK HOMEBREW

- EQUIVALENT TARGET ORIGINAL GRAVITY: 1.171 (40 B)
- APPROXIMATE FINAL GRAVITY: 1.035 (9 B)
- IBU: 39
- COLOR: 36 SRM (72 EBC)
- ALCOHOL: 18% BY VOLUME

Malt Extract Recipe *for 5 gallons (19 l)*

20 lbs.	(9 kg) very light malt extract syrup or 16 lbs. (7.3 kg) light dried malt extract
3 lbs.	(1.36 kg) maple syrup
2 lbs.	(908 g) crystal malt (60-L)
3 oz.	(84 g) Hallertauer hops—120 minutes boiling
¼ tsp.	(1 g) powdered Irish moss
6.5 ml	enzymes: amyloglucosidase, such as AMG3001; an alpha amylase enzyme such as termamyl can also be helpful

23 g	Safale brand dried ale yeast
23 g	Saflager brand dried lager yeast
	White Labs Super High Gravity ale yeast WLP099
23 g	Pries de Mousse champagne yeast
5 g	distillers' yeast
¼ g	zinc-fortified yeast such as Servomyces or 1½ Servomyces tablets
1½ cups	(360 ml) toasted (American) oak chips
2 cups	(500 ml) bourbon whiskey, port and sherry blend
½ cup	(115 ml measure) corn sugar (priming bottles)

Place crushed grains in 2 gallons (7.6 l) of 150-degree F (68 C) water and let steep for 30 minutes. Then strain out (and rinse with 3 quarts [3 l] hot water) and discard the crushed grains, reserving the approximately 2.5 gallons (9.5 l) of liquid to which you will now add 4.5 lbs (2 kg) malt extract and all of the maple syrup, all hops, and water necessary for a total volume of 4 gallons (15 l). Bring to a boil. Take care to avoid boil-over.

The total boil time will be 120 minutes. When 10 minutes remain, add the Irish moss and Servomyces (zinc-fortified yeast). After a total wort boil of 120 minutes, turn off the heat.

Immerse the covered pot of wort in a cold-water bath and let sit for 30 to 60 minutes, or however long it takes to reduce the temperature to about 70 degrees F (21 C). This could be the time it takes to have a few homebrews.

Then strain out and sparge hops and direct the hot wort into a sanitized fermenter. Make the extra effort to aerate the cooled wort as much as possible. Bring the total volume to 3.5 gallons (13.3 l) with additional cold water if necessary. Aerate the wort very well.

Rehydrate one-third each of the Safale, Saflager and champagne dried yeast in one pint (16 oz., or 475 ml) of boiled and cooled water at about 85 degrees F (30 C). This will take about 20 minutes.

Pitch the rehydrated yeast and the liquid high-alcohol yeast cultures when temperature of wort is about 70 degrees F (21 C). Also add 3.5 ml of enzymes. Ferment at about 70 degrees F (21 C) for about 1 to 3 weeks, or until fermentation shows signs of calm and stopping. Rack from your primary to a secondary fermenter.

Then add 5.5 lbs. (2.5 kg) malt extract to 3 quarts (3 l) water and boil for 30 minutes. Take care not to boil-over. Then cool, aerate and add the cooled wort and 1 ml of enzymes to fermenter. Rehydrate another one-third each of the Safale, Saflager and champagne dried yeast in one pint (16 oz., or 475 ml) of boiled and cooled water at about 85 degrees F (30 C). This will take about 20 minutes. Continue to ferment at 70 degrees F (21 C). When activity has slowed, rack once more to another fermenter.

Then add 5 lbs. (2.3 kg) malt extract to 2 quarts (2 l) water and boil for 30 minutes. During the final 10 minutes, add one half tablet of Servomyces. Then cool, aerate and add the cooled wort and 1 ml of enzymes to fermenter along with another rehydration of one-third each of the Safale, Saflager and champagne dried yeast in 1 pint (16 oz., or 475 ml) of boiled and cooled water at about 85 degrees F (30 C). This will take about 20 minutes. Continue to ferment at 70 degrees F (21 C). When activity has slowed, rack once more to another fermenter.

Then add the final 5 lbs. (2.3 kg) malt extract to 2 quarts (2 l) water and boil for 30 minutes. Cool, aerate and add the cooled wort and 1 ml of enzymes to fermenter and continue to ferment at 70 degrees F (21 C) until there is no active sign of fermentation at 70 degrees F (21 C).

Toast oak chips in a moderate-low oven until the chips begin to turn only slightly darker. Do not turn them dark brown. You can make your own toasted oak chips by simply putting them in a toaster oven at about 250 degrees F (121 C) for about 5 to 10 minutes. Add them to the aging beer. Lager the beer at 55 degrees F (12.5 C) for 6 months to a year. During the final months, add 2 cups (500 ml) of a bourbon whiskey, port and sherry blend.

This beer will be very difficult to carbonate. Yeast may not be able to withstand the strength of alcohol. Your attempt at bottle conditioning should include a fresh rehydration of alcohol-tolerant dried yeast. Rehydrate 5 grams of distillers' and champagne yeast in water for 10 minutes and add this along with priming corn sugar.

If kegging, use forced carbonation methods to carbonate. Consult other homebrewing sources for instructions.

Because of the high alcohol content, do not expect good head retention.

Adapt the recipe and procedures to fit your brewing systems. Good luck!

MICKVIRAY PAPAZIAN PILSENER

Based on a recipe by Mick, Vi and Ray Taylor, Fargo, North Dakota

- TARGET ORIGINAL GRAVITY: 1.049 (12 B)
- APPROXIMATE FINAL GRAVITY: 1.012 (3 B)
- IBU: ABOUT 36
- APPROXIMATE COLOR: 4 SRM (8 EBC)
- ALCOHOL: 4.9% BY VOLUME

All-Grain Recipe *for 5 gallons (19 l)*

7.25 lbs.	(3.6 kg) Pilsener malt
¼ lb.	(112 g) German sour malt
½ oz.	(14 g) Czech Saaz hops 4% alpha (2 HBU/56 MBU)—75 minutes boiling
1 oz.	(28 g) Czech Saaz hops 4% alpha (4 HBU/112 MBU)—60 minutes boiling
1.25 oz.	(35 g) Czech Saaz hops 4% alpha (5 HBU/140 MBU)—20 minutes boiling
1 oz.	(28 g) Czech Saaz hops 4%—2 minutes boiling
¼ tsp.	(1 g) powdered Irish moss

Wyeast Czech Pils yeast #2278 or White Labs Pilsner Lager yeast WLP800

¾ cup	(175 ml measure) corn sugar (priming bottles) or 0.33 cups (80 ml) corn sugar for kegging

The original recipe used a triple decoction method of mashing. Here, a step infusion mash is employed to mash the grains. Use soft water very low in minerals. Add 8 quarts (7.6 l) of 140-degree F (60 C) water to the crushed grain, stir, stabilize and hold the temperature at 132 degrees F (53 C) for 30 minutes. Add 4 quarts (3.8 l) of boiling water, add heat to bring temperature up to 155 degrees F (68 C) and hold for about 30 minutes. Then raise temperature to 167 degrees F (75 C), lauter and sparge with 3.5 gallons (13.5 l) of 170-degree F (77 C) water. Collect about 6 gallons (23 l) of runoff. Add 75-minute hops and bring to a full and vigorous boil.

The total boil time will be 75 minutes. When 60 minutes remain, add the 60-minute hops. When 20 minutes remain, add the 20-minute hops. When 10 minutes remain, add the Irish moss. When 2 minutes remain, add the 2-minute hops. After a total wort boil of 75 minutes, turn off the heat and place the pot (with cover on) in a running cold-water bath for 30 minutes. Continue to chill in the immersion or use other methods to chill your wort. Then strain and sparge the wort into a sanitized fermenter. Bring the total volume to 5 gallons (19 l) with additional cold water if necessary. Aerate the wort very well.

Pitch the yeast when temperature of wort is about 70 degrees F (21 C). Once visible signs of fermentation are evident, ferment at temperatures of about 55 degrees F (12.5 C) for about 1 week, or until fermentation shows signs of calm and stopping. Rack from your primary to a secondary fermenter. Lager the beer at temperatures between 35 and 45 degrees F (1.5–7 C) for 3 to 6 weeks.

Prime with sugar and bottle or keg when complete.

Malt Extract Recipe *for 5 gallons (19 l)*

6.75 lbs.	(3.06 kg) light malt extract syrup or 5.4 lbs. (2.45 kg) extra-light dried malt extract
¾ oz.	(21 g) Czech Saaz hops 4% alpha (3 HBU/84 MBU)—75 minutes boiling
1 oz.	(28 g) Czech Saaz hops 4% alpha (4 HBU/112 MBU)—60 minutes boiling
1.5 oz.	(42 g) Czech Saaz hops 4% alpha (6 HBU/168 MBU)—20 minutes boiling
1 oz.	(28 g) Czech Saaz hops 4%—2 minutes boiling
¼ tsp.	(1 g) powdered Irish moss

Wyeast Czech Pils yeast #2278 or White Labs Pilsner Lager yeast WLP800

¾ cup	(175 ml measure) corn sugar (priming bottles) or 0.33 cups (80 ml) corn sugar for kegging

Add malt extract and 75-minute hops to 2.5 gallons (9.5 l) of hot water. Use soft water very low in minerals. Stir well while bringing to a boil.

The total boil time will be 75 minutes. When 60 minutes remain, add the

60-minute hops. When 20 minutes remain, add the 20-minute hops. When 10 minutes remain, add the Irish moss. When 2 minutes remain, add the 2-minute hops. After a total wort boil of 75 minutes, turn off the heat.

Immerse the covered pot of wort in a cold-water bath and let sit for 30 minutes, or the time it takes to have a couple of homebrews.

Then strain out and sparge hops and direct the hot wort into a sanitized fermenter to which 2.5 gallons (9.5 l) of cold water has been added. Bring the total volume to 5 gallons (19 l) with additional cold water if necessary. Aerate the wort very well.

Pitch the yeast when temperature of wort is about 70 degrees F (21 C). Once visible signs of fermentation are evident, ferment at temperatures of about 55 degrees F (12.5 C) for about 1 week, or until fermentation shows signs of calm and stopping. Rack from your primary to a secondary fermenter. Lager the beer at temperatures between 35 and 45 degrees F (1.5–7 C) for 3 to 6 weeks.

Prime with sugar and bottle or keg when complete.

IRISH COCOA WOOD PORTER

- TARGET ORIGINAL GRAVITY: 1.050 (12.5 B)
- APPROXIMATE FINAL GRAVITY: 1.016 (4 B)
- IBU: ABOUT 32
- APPROXIMATE COLOR: 48 SRM (96 EBC)
- ALCOHOL: 4.6% BY VOLUME

All-Grain Recipe *for 5 gallons (19 l)*

6 lbs.	(2.7 kg) English 2-row malt (Maris Otter if available)
1 lb.	(454 g) English crystal (15—lovibond)
8 oz.	(225 g) Belgian aromatic malt
8 oz.	(225 g) German black Caraffe malt
8 oz.	(225 g) English black malt
12 oz.	(340 g) English chocolate malt
½ oz.	(14 g) UK Fuggle hops 5% alpha (2.5 HBU/70 MBU)— 60 minutes boiling

¼ oz.	(7 g) UK Wye Northdown hops 8.5% alpha (2.1 HBU/60 MBU)—60 minutes boiling
½ oz.	(14 g) UK Wye Northdown hops 8.5% alpha (4.2 HBU/118 MBU)—20 minutes boiling
1 oz.	(28 g) U.S. Santiam hops—5 minutes boiling
1½ tsp.	(6 g) gypsum (calcium sulfate) if your water has a low mineral content
2 oz.	(56 g) toasted oak chips
¼ tsp.	(1 g) powdered Irish moss
Irish-type ale yeast	
¾ cup	(175 ml measure) corn sugar (priming bottles) or 0.33 cups (80 ml) corn sugar for kegging

A step infusion mash is employed to mash the grains. Add 8.5 quarts (8.1 l) of 140-degree F (60 C) water to the crushed grain, stir, stabilize and hold the temperature at 132 degrees F (53 C) for 30 minutes. Add 4 quarts (3.8 l) of boiling water, add heat to bring temperature up to 155 degrees F (68 C) and hold for about 30 minutes. Then raise temperature to 167 degrees F (75 C), lauter and sparge with 3.5 gallons (13.5 l) of 170-degree F (77 C) water. Collect about 5.5 gallons (21 l) of runoff. Add 60-minute hops and optional gypsum and bring to a full and vigorous boil.

The total boil time will be 60 minutes. When 20 minutes remain, add the 20-minute hops. When 10 minutes remain, add the Irish moss. When 5 minutes remain, add the 5-minute hops. After a total wort boil of 60 minutes, turn off the heat and place the pot (with cover on) in a running cold-water bath for 30 minutes. Continue to chill in the immersion or use other methods to chill your wort. Then strain and sparge the wort into a sanitized fermenter. Bring the total volume to 5 gallons (19 l) with additional cold water if necessary. Aerate the wort very well.

Pitch the yeast when temperature of wort is about 70 degrees F (21 C). Ferment at about 70 degrees F (21 C) for about 1 week, or until fermentation shows signs of calm and stopping. Rack from your primary to a secondary fermenter and add 2 oz. of toasted oak chips. Toast oak chips in a moderate-low oven until the chips begin to turn only slightly darker. Do not turn them dark brown. You can make your own toasted oak chips by simply putting them in a toaster oven at about 250 degrees F (121 C) for about 5 to 10 minutes. If you have the capability, "cellar" the beer at about 55 degrees F (12.5 C) for about 1 week.

Prime with sugar and bottle or keg when complete.

Malt Extract Recipe *for 5 gallons (19 l)*

5 lbs.	(2.3 kg) light malt extract syrup or 4 lbs. (1.8 kg) light dried malt extract
1 lb.	(454 g) English crystal (15—lovibond)
8 oz.	(225 g) Belgian aromatic malt
8 oz.	(225 g) German black Caraffe malt
8 oz.	(225 g) English black malt
8 oz.	(225 g) English chocolate malt
1 oz.	(28 g) UK Fuggle hops 5% alpha (5 HBU/140 MBU)—60 minutes boiling
¼ oz.	(7 g) UK Wye Northdown hops 8.5% alpha (2.1 HBU/60 MBU)—60 minutes boiling
½ oz.	(14 g) UK Wye Northdown hops 8.5% alpha (4.2 HBU/118 MBU)—20 minutes boiling
1 oz.	(28 g) U.S. Santiam hops—5 minutes boiling
1½ tsp.	(6 g) gypsum (calcium sulfate) if your water has a low mineral content
2 oz.	(56 g) toasted oak chips
¼ tsp.	(1 g) powdered Irish moss
Irish-type ale yeast	
¾ cup	(175 ml measure) corn sugar (priming bottles) or 0.33 cups (80 ml) corn sugar for kegging

Place crushed grains in 2 gallons (7.6 l) of 150-degree F (68 C) water and let steep for 30 minutes. Then strain out (and rinse with 3 quarts [3 l] hot water) and discard the crushed grains, reserving the approximately 2.5 gallons (9.5 l) of liquid to which you will now add malt extract, optional gypsum and 60-minute hops. Bring to a boil.

The total boil time will be 60 minutes. When 20 minutes remain, add the 20-minute hops. When 10 minutes remain, add the Irish moss. When 5 minutes remain, add the 5-minute hops. After a total wort boil of 60 minutes, turn off the heat.

Immerse the covered pot of wort in a cold-water bath and let sit for 30 minutes, or the time it takes to have a couple of homebrews.

Then strain out and sparge hops and direct the hot wort into a sanitized fermenter to which 2.5 gallons (9.5 l) of cold water has been added. Bring the total volume to 5 gallons (19 l) with additional cold water if necessary. Aerate the wort very well.

Pitch the yeast when temperature of wort is about 70 degrees F (21 C). Ferment at about 70 degrees F (21 C) for about 1 week, or until fermentation shows signs of calm and stopping. Rack from your primary to a secondary fermenter and add 2 oz. of toasted oak chips. Toast oak chips in a moderate-low oven until the chips begin to turn only slightly darker. Do not turn them dark brown. You can make your own toasted oak chips by simply putting them in a toaster oven at about 250 degrees F (121 C) for about 5 to 10 minutes. If you have the capability, "cellar" the beer at about 55 degrees F (12.5 C) for about 1 week.

Prime with sugar and bottle or keg when complete.

OLD LIGHTHOUSE IN THE FOG
BARLEYWINE ALE

- TARGET ORIGINAL GRAVITY: 1.099 (23.5 B)
- APPROXIMATE FINAL GRAVITY: 1.032 (8 B)
- IBU: ABOUT 56
- APPROXIMATE COLOR: 9 SRM (9 EBC)
- ALCOHOL: 8.7% BY VOLUME

All-Grain Recipe *for 4 (four) gallons (15.2 l)*

13 lbs.	(5.9 kg) pale malt
1.25 oz.	(35 g) Northern Brewers hops 9% alpha (11.3 HBU/315 MBU)—120 minutes boiling
1 oz.	(28 g) UK Wye Northdown hops 7% alpha (7 HBU/196 MBU)—20 minutes boiling
¼ tsp.	(1 g) powdered Irish moss
English-type ale yeast—double dose	
¾ cup	(175 ml measure) corn sugar (priming bottles) or 0.33 cups (80 ml) corn sugar for kegging

A one-step infusion mash is employed to mash the grains. Add 13 quarts (12.4 liters) of 140-degree F (60 C) water to the crushed grain, stir, stabilize and hold the temperature at 132 degrees F (53 C) for 30 minutes. Add 6.5

quarts (6.2 l) of boiling water and add heat to bring temperature up to 155 degrees F (68 C) and hold for about 30 minutes. Then raise temperature to 167 degrees F (75 C), lauter and sparge with 3.5 gallons (13.5 l) of 170-degree F (77 C) water. Collect and save *only* the first 4.5 gallons (17 l) of runoff. Discard the remaining runoff or brew a separate small beer with it. Add 120-minute hops and bring to a full and vigorous boil.

The total boil time will be 120 minutes. When 20 minutes remain add the 20-minute hops. When 10 minutes remain, add the add Irish moss. After a total wort boil of 120 minutes, turn off the heat and place the pot (with cover on) in a running cold-water bath for 30 minutes. Continue to chill in the immersion or use other methods to chill your wort. Then strain and sparge the wort into a sanitized fermenter. Bring the total volume to 4 gallons (15.2 l) with additional cold water if necessary. Aerate the wort very well.

Pitch a double dose of yeast when temperature of wort is about 70 degrees F (21 C). Ferment at about 70 degrees F (21 C) for about 1 to 2 weeks or when fermentation shows signs of calm and stopping. Rack from your primary to a secondary fermenter. Continue to age at temperatures between 60 and 70 degrees F (15.5–21 C) for at least 2 months.

Prime with sugar and bottle or keg when complete.

Malt Extract Recipe *for 4 (four) gallons (15.2 l)*

11 lbs.	(5 kg) light malt extract syrup or 8.8 lbs. (4 kg) light dried malt extract
1.5 oz.	(42 g) Northern Brewer hops 9% alpha (13.5 HBU/378 MBU)—120 minutes boiling
1 oz.	(28 g) UK Wye Northdown hops 7% alpha (7 HBU/196 MBU)—20 minutes boiling
¼ tsp.	(1 g) powdered Irish moss
English-type ale yeast—double dose	
¾ cup	(175 ml measure) corn sugar (priming bottles) or 0.33 cups (80 ml) corn sugar for kegging

Add malt extract and 120-minute hops to 2.25 gallons (8.6 l) water and bring to a boil. The total boil time will be 120 minutes. When 20 minutes remain, add the 20-minute hops. When 10 minutes remain, add the add Irish moss. After a total wort boil of 120 minutes turn off the heat.

Immerse the covered pot of wort in a cold water bath and let sit for 30–45 minutes or the time it takes to have 2 or even 3 homebrews.

Then strain out and sparge hops and direct the hot wort into a sanitized fermenter to which 1 gallon (3.8 l) of cold water has been added. If necessary, add additional cold water to achieve a 4-gallon (15.2 l) batch size

Pitch a double dose of yeast when temperature of wort is about 70 degrees F (21 C). Ferment at about 70 degrees F (21 C) for about 1 to 2 weeks or when fermentation shows signs of calm and stopping. Rack from your primary to a secondary fermenter. Continue to age at temperatures between 60 and 70 degrees F (15.5–21 C) for at least 2 months.

Prime with sugar and bottle or keg when complete.

ORIGINAL DOGBOLTER ALE—GOOSE & FIRKIN

Based on Colin Summers's original recipe, submitted by David Bruce

- TARGET ORIGINAL GRAVITY: 1.060 (14.7 B)
- APPROXIMATE FINAL GRAVITY: 1.015 (3.5 B)
- IBU: ABOUT 48
- APPROXIMATE COLOR: 14 SRM (28 EBC)
- ALCOHOL: 6% BY VOLUME

All-Grain Recipe *for 5 gallons (19 l)*

10 lbs.	(4.5 kg) 2-row English pale ale malt
1.25 lbs.	(568 g) crystal malt (40-L)
⅓ oz.	(9 g) black malt
2 oz.	(56 g) UK Goldings hops 6% alpha (12 HBU/336 MBU)—60 minutes boiling
0.5 oz.	(14 g) UK Goldings hops 6% alpha (3 HBU/84 MBU)—15 minutes boiling
¼ tsp.	(1 g) powdered Irish moss
English-type ale yeast	
¾ cup	(175 ml measure) corn sugar (priming bottles) or 0.33 cups (80 ml) corn sugar for kegging

A one-step infusion mash is employed to mash the grains. Add 11 quarts (10.5 l) of 172-degree F (78 C) water to the crushed grain, stir, stabilize and hold the temperature at 155 degrees F (68 C) for 60 minutes. Then raise temperature to 167 degrees F (75 C), lauter and sparge with 4 gallons (15.2 l) of 170-degree F (77 C) water. Collect about 5.5 gallons (21 l) of runoff. Add 60-minute hops and bring to a full and vigorous boil.

The total boil time will be 60 minutes. When 15 minutes remain, add the 15-minute hops. When 10 minutes remain, add the Irish moss. After a total wort boil of 60 minutes, turn off the heat and place the pot (with cover on) in a running cold-water bath for 30 minutes. Continue to chill in the immersion or use other methods to chill your wort. Then strain and sparge the wort into a sanitized fermenter. Bring the total volume to 5 gallons (19 l) with additional cold water if necessary. Aerate the wort very well.

Pitch the yeast when temperature of wort is about 70 degrees F (21 C). Ferment at about 70 degrees F (21 C) for about 1 week, or until fermentation shows signs of calm and stopping. Rack from your primary to a secondary fermenter and if you have the capability, "cellar" the beer at about 55 degrees F (12.5 C) for about 1 week.

Prime with sugar and bottle or keg when complete.

Malt Extract Recipe *for 5 gallons (19 l)*

7.5 lbs.	(3.4 kg) light malt extract syrup or 6 lbs. (2.7 kg) light dried malt extract
1.25 lbs.	(568 g) crystal malt (40-L)
1/3 oz.	(9 g) black malt
2.5 oz.	(70 g) UK Goldings hops 6% alpha (15 HBU/420 MBU)—60 minutes boiling
0.75 oz.	(21 g) UK Goldings hops 6% alpha (4.5 HBU/126 MBU)—15 minutes boiling
1/4 tsp.	(1 g) powdered Irish moss
English-type ale yeast	
3/4 cup	(175 ml measure) corn sugar (priming bottles) or 0.33 cups (80 ml) corn sugar for kegging

Place crushed grains in 2 gallons (7.6 l) of 150-degree F (68 C) water and let steep for 30 minutes. Then strain out (and rinse with 3 quarts [3 l] hot water) and discard the crushed grains, reserving the approximately 2.5 gallons (9.5 l) of liquid to which you will now add malt extract and 60-minute hops. Bring to a boil.

The total boil time will be 60 minutes. When 15 minutes remain, add the 15-minute hops. When 10 minutes remain, add the Irish moss. After a total wort boil of 60 minutes, turn off the heat.

Immerse the covered pot of wort in a cold-water bath and let sit for 30 minutes, or the time it takes to have a couple of homebrews.

Then strain out and sparge hops and direct the hot wort into a sanitized fermenter to which 2.5 gallons (9.5 l) of cold water has been added. Bring the total volume to 5 gallons (19 l) with additional cold water if necessary. Aerate the wort very well.

Pitch the yeast when temperature of wort is about 70 degrees F (21 C). Ferment at about 70 degrees F (21 C) for about 1 week, or until fermentation shows signs of calm and stopping. Rack from your primary to a secondary fermenter and if you have the capability, "cellar" the beer at about 55 degrees F (12.5 C) for about 1 week.

Prime with sugar and bottle or keg when complete.

BEYOND-THE-ORDINARY ORDINARY BITTER

- TARGET ORIGINAL GRAVITY: 1.038 (9.5 B)
- APPROXIMATE FINAL GRAVITY: 1.007 (1.5 B)
- IBU: ABOUT 30
- APPROXIMATE COLOR: 6 SRM (12 EBC)
- ALCOHOL: 4% BY VOLUME

All-Grain Recipe *for 5 gallons (19 l)*

5 lbs.	(2.3 kg) English 2-row Maris Otter malt
8 oz.	(225 g) English crystal malt (15-L)
4 oz.	(113 g) Belgian aromatic malt
8 oz.	(225 g) #2 invert sugar or Brazilian dark rapadura sugar*

*Note: Invert sugar #2 is not easy to find in America, but what seems to be an excellent substitute is very dark rapadura. This is dried and granulated pure cane sugar juice from Brazil. Sucanat is another type of cane juice sugar, but it is not as full flavored as rapadura. It's available at health-food stores or in the "natural sugar" section of your more natural-conscious grocery store.

¾ oz.	(21 g) UK Northdown hops 7% alpha (5.3 HBU/147 MBU)—60 minutes boiling
¾ oz.	(21 g) UK Kent Goldings hops—5 minutes boiling
½ oz.	(14 g) UK Fuggles hops—5 minutes boiling
¼ oz.	(7 g) crystal hop pellets—dry hopping
¼ tsp.	(1 g) powdered Irish moss

Wyeast Thames Valley yeast or English-type ale yeast

¾ cup	(175 ml measure) corn sugar (priming bottles) or 0.33 cups (80 ml) corn sugar for kegging

A step infusion mash is employed to mash the grains. Add 6 quarts (5.7 l) of 140-degree F (60 C) water to the crushed grain, stir, stabilize and hold the temperature at 132 degrees F (53 C) for 30 minutes. Add 3 quarts (3 l) of boiling water, add heat to bring temperature up to 155 degrees F (68 C) and hold for about 30 minutes. Then raise temperature to 167 degrees F (75 C), lauter and sparge with 3.5 gallons (13.5 l) of 170-degree F (77 C) water. Collect about 5.5 gallons (21 l) of runoff. Add 60-minute hops and rapadura sugar and bring to a full and vigorous boil.

The total boil time will be 60 minutes. When 10 minutes remain, add the Irish moss. When 5 minutes remain, add the 5-minute hops. After a total wort boil of 60 minutes, turn off the heat and place the pot (with cover on) in a running cold-water bath for 30 minutes. Continue to chill in the immersion or use other methods to chill your wort. Then strain and sparge the wort into a sanitized fermenter. Bring the total volume to 5 gallons (19 l) with additional cold water if necessary. Aerate the wort very well.

Pitch the yeast when temperature of wort is about 70 degrees F (21 C). Ferment at about 70 degrees F (21 C) for 24 hours. Then rack/transfer the fermenting beer to another fermenter, aerating by splashing the first 1 gallon. Continue to ferment about 1 week, or until fermentation shows signs of calm and stopping. Rack from your primary to a secondary fermenter and add the hop pellets for dry hopping. If you have the capability, "cellar" the beer at about 55 degrees F (12.5 C) for about 1 week.

Prime with sugar and bottle or keg when complete.

Malt Extract Recipe *for 5 gallons (19 l)*

4 lbs.	(1.82 kg) light malt extract syrup or 3.2 lbs. (1.45 kg) light dried malt extract
1 lb.	(454 g) English crystal malt (15-L)
8 oz.	(225 g) invert sugar #2 or Brazilian dark rapadura sugar*
0.88 oz.	(25 g) UK Northdown hops 7% alpha (6.2 HBU/172 MBU)—60 minutes boiling
¾ oz.	(21 g) UK Kent Goldings hops—5 minutes boiling
½ oz.	(14 g) UK Fuggles hops—5 minutes boiling
¼ oz.	(7 g) crystal hop pellets—dry hopping
¼ tsp.	(1 g) powdered Irish moss
Wyeast Thames Valley yeast or English-type ale yeast	
¾ cup	(175 ml measure) corn sugar (priming bottles) or 0.33 cups (80 ml) corn sugar for kegging

Place crushed grains in 2 gallons (7.6 l) of 150-degrees F (68 C) water and let steep for 30 minutes. Then strain out (and rinse with 3 quarts [3 l] hot water) and discard the crushed grains, reserving the approximately 2.5 gallons (9.5 l) of liquid to which you will now add malt extract, rapadura sugar and 60-minute hops. Bring to a boil.

The total boil time will be 60 minutes. When 10 minutes remain, add the Irish moss. When 5 minutes remain, add the 5-minute hops. After a total wort boil of 60 minutes, turn off the heat.

Immerse the covered pot of wort in a cold-water bath and let sit for 30 minutes, or the time it takes to have a couple of homebrews.

Then strain out and sparge hops and direct the hot wort into a sanitized fermenter to which 2.5 gallons (9.5 l) of cold water has been added. Bring the total volume to 5 gallons (19 l) with additional cold water if necessary. Aerate the wort very well.

Pitch the yeast when temperature of wort is about 70 degrees F (21 C). Ferment at about 70 degrees F (21 C) for 24 hours. Then rack/transfer the fermenting beer to another fermenter, aerating by splashing the first 1 gallon

---

*Note: Invert sugar #2 is not easy to find in America, but what seems to be an excellent substitute is very dark rapadura. This is dried and granulated pure cane sugar juice from Brazil. Sucanat is another type of cane juice sugar, but not as full flavored as rapadura. It's available at health-food stores or in the "natural sugar" section of your more natural-conscious grocery store.

of fermenting beer. Continue to ferment about 1 week, or until fermentation shows signs of calm and stopping. Rack from your primary to a secondary fermenter and add the hop pellets for dry hopping. If you have the capability, "cellar" the beer at about 55 degrees F (12.5 C) for about 1 week.

Prime with sugar and bottle or keg when complete.

∙∙∙

ST. BARTHOLOMEW'S MEAD

- TARGET ORIGINAL GRAVITY: 1.138 (31.5 B)
- APPROXIMATE FINAL GRAVITY: 1.030 (7.5 B)
- ALCOHOL: 14.5% BY VOLUME

All-Grain Recipe *for 4 gallons (15.2 l)*

15 lbs.	(6.8 kg) light honey (such as clover, alfalfa or orange blossom)
¼ tsp.	(0.5 g) yeast extract or appropriate amount of other yeast nutrient as recommended by your local homebrew supply stop
0.1 g	zinc-fortified yeast as nutrient
3 tbsp.	(40 g) dried champagne or mead yeast (Prise de Mousse champagne yeast is an excellent choice)

Add honey, yeast extract and zinc-fortified yeast to 1 gallon of water, stir, dissolve and bring to a boil for 5 minutes. Skim off coagulated meringuelike protein and discard during the boil.

Then add the boiled water and honey to 2 gallons of cold water in a sanitized fermenter for a total yield of 4 gallons. Mix extremely well, introducing as much air and oxygen into the mixture as possible. Original gravity may vary depending on the quality of the honey you used.

Rehydrate yeast by adding the dry yeast to about 2 cups of preboiled and cooled (to 100 degrees F [37 C]) water in a covered sanitized glass container. Let stand for 10 minutes before adding to the honey-and-water mixture.

When temperature of the honey-and-water mixture is between 72 and 80 degrees F (22 to 26.5 C), add rehydrated yeast and ferment at temperatures above 70 degrees F (21 C).

Ferment in a closed primary fermenter until fermentation appears to have stopped and the mead begins to clear. Introducing as little oxygen as possible, carefully transfer by siphoning to a closed second fermenter and let sit for up to a year or until the mead has become crystal clear and there are no signs of fermentation. The mead is now ready to drink or bottle.

With careful bottling techniques and minimizing the introduction of air and oxygen, this mead will age well for several decades, especially if properly corked.

St. Bartholomew is the patron saint of mead. His day is August 24, but celebrate every day.

CASTLE METHEGLIN

- TARGET ORIGINAL GRAVITY: 1.130–1.138 (30.2–31.8 B)
- APPROXIMATE FINAL GRAVITY: 1.028–1.038 (7–9.5 B)
- ALCOHOL: 14 TO 15% BY VOLUME

Recipe *for 5 gallons (19 l)*

18.5 lbs.	(8.2 kg) light honey
2 oz.	(56 g) gruit

Formulate the gruit using the following proportions of whole dried herbs (use fresh herbs when available). After the herbs are combined, crush them all to the same consistency. Store in airtight container in your freezer. (Note: 28 grams equals approximately 1 ounce.)

5 g	fresh ground nutmeg
5 g	cloves
10 g	dried ground ginger
10 g	thyme
10 g	peppermint

10 g	cinnamon (powder)
20 g	lemon balm
20 g	rosemary
20 g	bog myrtle (sweet gale)
30 g	yarrow
50 g	dried elderberry flower
50 g	fennel seed (freshly crushed)
240 g	*Total (about 8.5 ounces)*
4 g	yeast extract or appropriate amount of other yeast nutrient as recommended by your local homebrew supply shop
0.1 g	zinc-fortified yeast as nutrient
3 tbsp.	(40 g) dried champagne or mead yeast (Prise de Mousse or champagne yeast is an excellent choice)

Combine honey and zinc-fortified yeast with 1 gallon (3.8 l) of water and heat to 150 degrees F (65.5 C). Hold at this temperature for 20 minutes. Add this hot honey-and-water mixture to 2 gallons of cold water in your primary fermenter. Add more cold water as needed to achieve 5 gallons total volume. Aerate extremely well and add dissolved yeast nutrient (yeast extract).

When temperature is below 80 degrees F (26.5 C), add rehydrated yeast. Mead is best initially fermented between 70 and 75 degrees F (21–24 C). Ferment until fermentation activity is very low; this may take from 3 weeks to 3 months.

Rack and transfer to a secondary fermenter. Secondary can be stored at cooler temperatures. Add 2 oz. (56 g) gruit. Rack off sediment of herbs after 6 months to a year. Bottle when clear. Cork in wine bottles for long-term aging. Store corked bottles on their side. If using beer or cappable champagne bottles, dip capped bottle top in melted paraffin to prevent air from entering bottle.

This will be sweet, still metheglin mead, whose flavors will blend and balance themselves over the years. It's best after 50 years, but worth indulging in after 1 year.

ANDECH'S WEEKDAY BOCK

- TARGET ORIGINAL GRAVITY: 1.066 (16.5 B)
- APPROXIMATE FINAL GRAVITY: 1.016 (4 B)
- IBU: ABOUT 34
- APPROXIMATE COLOR: 19 SRM (38 EBC)
- ALCOHOL: 6.8% BY VOLUME

All-Grain Recipe *for 5 gallons (19 l)*

9 lbs.	(4 kg) German pilsener malt
1 lb.	(454 g) Belgian aromatic malt
12 oz.	(340 g) German Caramunich malt
4 oz.	(113 g) German sauer malt
2 oz.	(56 g) German black Caraffe malt
1.5 oz.	(42 g) German Hallertauer hops 4.5% alpha (6.8 HBU/190 MBU)—60 minutes boiling
1.5 oz.	(42 g) German Hersbrucker Hallertauer hops 3.3% alpha (5 HBU/140 MBU)—15 minutes boiling
½ oz.	(14 g) crystal hops—1 minute boiling
⅓ oz.	(10 g) crystal hop pellets—dry hopping
¼ tsp.	(1 g) powdered Irish moss
0.1 g	zinc-fortified yeast as nutrient
German or Bavarian-type lager yeast	
¾ cup	(175 ml measure) corn sugar (priming bottles) or 0.33 cups (80 ml) corn sugar for kegging

A step infusion mash is employed to mash the grains. Add 11 quarts (10.5 l) of 140-degree F (60 C) water to the crushed grain, stir, stabilize and hold the temperature at 132 degrees F (53 C) for 30 minutes. Add 5.5 quarts (5.2 l) of boiling water, add heat to bring temperature up to 155 degrees F (68 C) and hold for about 30 minutes. Then raise temperature to 167 degrees F (75 C), lauter and sparge with 3.5 gallons (13.5 l) of 170-degree F (77 C) water. Collect about 5.5 gallons (21 l) of runoff. Add 60-minute hops and bring to a full and vigorous boil.

The total boil time will be 60 minutes. When 15 minutes remain, add the 15-minute hops. When 10 minutes remain, add the Irish moss and zinc-fortified yeast. When 1 minute remains, add the 1-minute hops. After a total wort boil of 60 minutes, turn off the heat and place the pot (with cover on) in a running cold-water bath for 30 minutes. Continue to chill in the immersion or use other methods to chill your wort. Then strain and sparge the wort into a sanitized fermenter. Bring the total volume to 5 gallons (19 l) with additional cold water if necessary. Aerate the wort very well.

Pitch the yeast when temperature of wort is about 70 degrees F (21 C). Once visible signs of fermentation are evident, ferment at temperatures of about 55 degrees F (12.5 C) for about 1 week, or until fermentation shows signs of calm and stopping. Rack from your primary to a secondary fermenter and add the hop pellets for dry hopping. Lager the beer at temperatures between 35 and 45 degrees F (1.5–7 C) for 4 to 8 weeks.

Prime with sugar and bottle or keg when complete.

Malt Extract Recipe *for 5 gallons (19 l)*

8.25 lbs.	(3.7 kg) light malt extract syrup or 6.6 lbs. (3.0 kg) light dried malt extract
1 lb.	(454 g) German Caramunich malt
3 oz.	(84 g) German sauer malt
2 oz.	(56 g) German Hallertauer hops 4.4% alpha (8.8 HBU/106 MBU)—75 minutes boiling
1.5 oz.	(42 g) German Hersbrucker Hallertauer hops 3.3% alpha (5 HBU/140 MBU)—15 minutes boiling
½ oz.	(14 g) crystal hops—1 minute boiling
⅓ oz.	(10 g) crystal hop pellets—dry hopping
¼ tsp.	(1 g) powdered Irish moss
0.1 g	zinc-fortified yeast as nutrient
German or Bavarian-type lager yeast	
¾ cup	(175 ml measure) corn sugar (priming bottles) or 0.33 cups (80 ml) corn sugar for kegging

Place crushed grains in 2 gallons (7.6 l) of 150-degree F (68 C) water and let steep for 30 minutes. Then strain out (and rinse with 3 quarts [3 l] hot water) and discard the crushed grains, reserving the approximately 2.5 gallons (9.5 l) of liquid to which you will now add malt extract and 75-minute hops. Bring to a boil.

The total boil time will be 75 minutes. When 15 minutes remain, add the

15-minute hops. When 10 minutes remain, add the Irish moss and zinc-fortified yeast. When 1 minute remains, add the 1-minute hops. After a total wort boil of 75 minutes, turn off the heat.

Immerse the covered pot of wort in a cold-water bath and let sit for 30 minutes, or the time it takes to have a couple of homebrews.

Then strain out and sparge hops and direct the hot wort into a sanitized fermenter to which 2.5 gallons (9.5 l) of cold water has been added. Bring the total volume to 5 gallons (19 l) with additional cold water if necessary. Aerate the wort very well.

Pitch the yeast when temperature of wort is about 70 degrees F (21 C). Once visible signs of fermentation are evident, ferment at about 55 degrees F (12.5 C) for about 1 week, or until fermentation shows signs of calm and stopping. Rack from your primary to a secondary fermenter and add the hop pellets for dry hopping. Lager the beer at temperatures between 35 and 45 degrees F (1.5–7 C) for 4 to 8 weeks.

Prime with sugar and bottle or keg when complete.

PUMPERNICKEL RYE STOUT

- TARGET ORIGINAL GRAVITY: 1.050 (12 B)
- APPROXIMATE FINAL GRAVITY: 1.014 (3.5 B)
- IBU: ABOUT 25
- APPROXIMATE COLOR: 39 SRM (78 EBC)
- ALCOHOL: 4.8% BY VOLUME

All-Grain Recipe *for 5 gallons (19 l)*

4.5 lbs.	(2 kg) 6-row pale malt
1 lb.	(454 g) rye malt
12 oz.	(340 g) wheat malt
12 oz.	(340 g) German Caramunich malt
12 oz.	(340 g) flaked corn
8 oz.	(225 g) rice hulls
8 oz.	(225 g) roasted barley
4 oz.	(113 g) German sauer malt

4 oz.	(113 g) chocolate malt
2 oz.	(56 g) German black Caraffe malt
½ oz.	(14 g) Liberty hops 5% alpha (2.5 HBU/70 MBU)—60 minutes boiling
1 oz.	(28 g) Mt. Hood hops 6% alpha (6 HBU/168 MBU)—30 minutes boiling
½ oz.	(14 g) crystal hops—1 minute boiling
¼ oz.	(7 g) German Hallertauer hop pellets—dry hopping
¼ tsp.	(1 g) powdered Irish moss
Irish or English/British-type ale yeast*	
¾ cup	(175 ml measure) corn sugar (priming bottles) or 0.33 cups (80 ml) corn sugar for kegging

A step infusion mash is employed to mash the grains. Add 9 quarts (8.6 l) of 140-degree F (60 C) water to the crushed grain and rice hulls, stir, stabilize and hold the temperature at 132 degrees F (53 C) for 30 minutes. Add 4.5 quarts (4.3 l) of boiling water, add heat to bring temperature up to 155 degrees F (68 C) and hold for about 30 minutes. Then raise temperature to 167 degrees F (75 C), lauter and sparge with 3.5 gallons (13.5 l) of 170-degree F (77 C) water. Collect about 5.5 gallons (21 l) of runoff. Add 60-minute hops and bring to a full and vigorous boil.

The total boil time will be 60 minutes. When 30 minutes remain, add the 30-minute hops. When 10 minutes remain, add the Irish moss. When 1 minute remains, add the 1-minute hops. After a total wort boil of 60 minutes, turn off the heat and place the pot (with cover on) in a running cold-water bath for 30 minutes. Continue to chill in the immersion or use other methods to chill your wort. Then strain and sparge the wort into a sanitized fermenter. Bring the total volume to 5 gallons (19 l) with additional cold water if necessary. Aerate the wort very well.

Pitch the yeast when temperature of wort is about 70 degrees F (21 C). Ferment at about 70 degrees F (21 C) for about 1 week, or until fermentation shows signs of calm and stopping. Rack from your primary to a secondary fermenter and add the hop pellets for dry hopping. If you have the capability, "cellar" the beer at about 55 degrees F (12.5 C) for about 1 week. If you use German-style wheat beer yeast, do not lower temperatures during cellaring.

Prime with sugar and bottle or keg when complete.

*If you enjoy the character of German-style wheat beer, use German wheat beer yeast.

Mash/Extract Recipe *for 5 gallons (19 l)*

4.5 lbs.	(2 kg) wheat malt extract syrup
1 lb.	(454 g) rye malt
12 oz.	(340 g) Caramunich malt
8 oz.	(225 g) roasted barley
6 oz.	(168 g) 6-row pale malt
6 oz.	(168 g) flaked corn
4 oz.	(113 g) rice hulls
4 oz.	(113 g) chocolate malt
2 oz.	(56 g) German black Caraffe malt
¾ oz.	(21 g) Liberty hops 5% alpha (3.8 HBU/105 MBU)— 60 minutes boiling
1 oz.	(28 g) Mt. Hood hops 6% alpha (6 HBU/168 MBU)— 30 minutes boiling
½ oz.	(14 g) crystal hops—1 minute boiling
¼ oz.	(7 g) German Hallertauer hop pellets—dry hopping
¼ tsp.	(1 g) powdered Irish moss
Irish or English/British-type ale yeast*	
¾ cup	(175 ml measure) corn sugar (priming bottles) or 0.33 cups (80 ml) corn sugar for kegging

Heat 1 gallon (3.8 l) water to 172 degrees F (77.5 C) and then add crushed grains and rice hulls. Stir well to distribute heat. Temperature should stabilize at about 155 degrees F (68 C). Wrap a towel around the pot and set aside for about 45 minutes. Have a homebrew.

After 45 minutes, add heat to the mini-mash and raise the temperature to 167 degrees F (75 C). Then pass the liquid and grains into a strainer and rinse with 170-degree F (77 C) water. Discard the grains.

To the sweet extract you have just produced, add more water, bringing the volume up to about 2.5 gallons (9.5 l). Add malt extract and 60-minute hops and bring to a boil.

The total boil time will be 60 minutes. When 30 minutes remain, add the 30-minute hops. When 10 minutes remain, add the Irish moss. When 1 minute remains, add the 1-minute hops. After a total wort boil of 60 minutes, turn off the heat.

*If you enjoy the character of German-style wheat beer, use German wheat beer yeast.

Immerse the covered pot of wort in a cold-water bath and let sit for 30 minutes, or the time it takes to have a couple of homebrews.

Then strain out and sparge hops and direct the hot wort into a sanitized fermenter to which 2.5 gallons (9.5 l) of cold water has been added. Bring the total volume to 5 gallons (19 l) with additional cold water if necessary. Aerate the wort very well.

Pitch the yeast when temperature of wort is about 70 degrees F (21 C). Ferment at about 70 degrees F (21 C) for about 1 week, or until fermentation shows signs of calm and stopping. Rack from your primary to a secondary fermenter and add the hop pellets for dry hopping. If you have the capability, "cellar" the beer at about 55 degrees F (12.5 C) for about 1 week. If you use German-style wheat beer yeast, do not lower temperatures during cellaring.

Prime with sugar and bottle or keg when complete.

CRAZY OLD MAN ALTBIER

- TARGET ORIGINAL GRAVITY: 1.049 (12 B)
- APPROXIMATE FINAL GRAVITY: 1.012 (3 B)
- IBU: ABOUT 48
- APPROXIMATE COLOR: 16 SRM (32 EBC)
- ALCOHOL: 4.8% BY VOLUME

All-Grain Recipe *for 5 gallons (19 l)*

6.75 lbs.	(3.06 kg) German pale malt
4 oz.	(113 g) German sauer malt
8 oz.	(225 g) Belgian aromatic malt
8 oz.	(225 g) German Caramunich malt
2 oz.	(56 g) German black Caraffe malt
1 oz.	(28 g) German Hallertauer hops 4.5% alpha (4.5 HBU/126 MBU)—120 minutes boiling
1.25 oz.	(35 g) German Spalt hops 5% alpha (6.25 HBU/175 MBU)—120 minutes boiling
¾ oz.	(21 g) German Hallertauer hops 4.5% alpha (3.4 HBU/95 MBU)—20 minutes boiling

¼ tsp.   (1 g) powdered Irish moss

German ale yeast

¾ cup   (175 ml measure) corn sugar (priming bottles) or
                 0.33 cups (80 ml) corn sugar for kegging

A step infusion mash is employed to mash the grains. Add 8 quarts (7.6 l) of 140-degree F (60 C) water to the crushed grain, stir, stabilize and hold the temperature at 132 degrees F (53 C) for 30 minutes. Add 4 quarts (3.8 l) of boiling water, add heat to bring temperature up to 155 degrees F (68 C) and hold for about 30 minutes. Then raise temperature to 167 degrees F (75 C), lauter and sparge with 3.5 gallons (13.5 l) of 170-degree F (77 C) water. Collect about 6 gallons (23 l) of runoff. Add 120-minute hops and bring to a full and vigorous boil.

The total boil time will be 120 minutes. When 20 minutes remain, add the 20-minute hops. When 10 minutes remain, add the Irish moss. After a total wort boil of 120 minutes, turn off the heat and place the pot (with cover on) in a running cold-water bath for 30 minutes. Continue to chill in the immersion or use other methods to chill your wort. Then strain and sparge the wort into a sanitized fermenter. Bring the total volume to 5 gallons (19 l) with additional cold water if necessary. Aerate the wort very well.

Pitch the yeast when temperature of wort is about 70 degrees F (21 C). Ferment at about 70 degrees F (21 C) for about 1 week, or until fermentation shows signs of calm and stopping. Rack from your primary to a secondary fermenter and "lager" the beer at temperatures between 35 and 45 degrees F (1.5–7 C) for 4 to 6 weeks.

Prime with sugar and bottle or keg when complete.

Malt Extract Recipe *for 5 gallons (19 l)*

6.5 lbs.   (3 kg) light malt extract syrup or 5.2 lbs. (2.36 kg)
                 light dried malt extract

8 oz.   (225 g) German Caramunich malt

2 oz.   (56 g) German black Caraffe malt

1.5 oz.   (42 g) German Hallertauer hops 4.5% alpha (4.5
                 HBU/126 MBU)—120 minutes boiling

1.25 oz.   (35 g) German Spalt hops 5% alpha (6.25 HBU/175
                 MBU)—120 minutes boiling

¾ oz.	(21 g) German Hallertauer hops 4.5% alpha (3.4 HBU/95 MBU)—20 minutes boiling
¼ tsp.	(1 g) powdered Irish moss
German ale yeast	
¾ cup	(175 ml measure) corn sugar (priming bottles) or 0.33 cups (80 ml) corn sugar for kegging

Place crushed grains in 2 gallons (7.6 l) of 150-degree F (68 C) water and let steep for 30 minutes. Then strain out (and rinse with 3 quarts [3 l] hot water) and discard the crushed grains, reserving the approximately 2.5 gallons (9.5 l) of liquid to which you will now add malt extract and 120-minute hops. Bring to a boil.

The total boil time will be 120 minutes. When 20 minutes remain, add the 20-minute hops. When 10 minutes remain, add the Irish moss. After a total wort boil of 120 minutes, turn off the heat.

Immerse the covered pot of wort in a cold-water bath and let sit for 30 minutes, or the time it takes to have a couple of homebrews.

Then strain out and sparge hops and direct the hot wort into a sanitized fermenter to which 2.5 gallons (9.5 l) of cold water has been added. Bring the total volume to 5 gallons (19 l) with additional cold water if necessary. Aerate the wort very well.

Pitch the yeast when temperature of wort is about 70 degrees F (21 C). Ferment at about 70 degrees F (21 C) for about 1 week, or until fermentation shows signs of calm and stopping. Rack from your primary to a secondary fermenter and "lager" the beer at temperatures between 35 and 45 degrees F (1.5–7 C) for 4 to 6 weeks.

Prime with sugar and bottle or keg when complete.

HANS WEISSBIER

- TARGET ORIGINAL GRAVITY: 1.048 (12 B)
- APPROXIMATE FINAL GRAVITY: 1.014 (3.5 B)
- IBU: ABOUT 17
- APPROXIMATE COLOR: 6 SRM (14 EBC)
- ALCOHOL: 4.6% BY VOLUME

All-Grain Recipe *for 5 gallons (19 l)*

4.5 lbs.	(2 kg) German pilsener malt
3 lbs.	(1.36 kg) German wheat malt
8 oz.	(225 g) German sauer malt
¾ oz.	(21 g) German Hallertauer hops 4.4% alpha (3.3 HBU/92 MBU)—60 minutes boiling
¾ oz.	(21 g) German Hallertauer hops 4.4% alpha (3.3 HBU/92 MBU)—20 minutes boiling
¼ tsp.	(1 g) powdered Irish moss
German wheat beer yeast	
¾ cup	(175 ml measure) corn sugar (priming bottles) or 0.33 cups (80 ml) corn sugar for kegging

A step infusion mash is employed to mash the grains. Add 8 quarts (7.6 l) of 140-degree F (60 C) water to the crushed grain, stir, stabilize and hold the temperature at 132 degrees F (53 C) for 30 minutes. Add 4 quarts (3.8 l) of boiling water, add heat to bring temperature up to 155 degrees F (68 C) and hold for about 30 minutes. Then raise temperature to 167 degrees F (75 C), lauter and sparge with 3.5 gallons (13.5 l) of 170-degree F (77 C) water. Collect about 5.5 gallons (21 l) of runoff. Add 60-minute hops and bring to a full and vigorous boil.

The total boil time will be 60 minutes. When 20 minutes remain, add the 20-minute hops. When 10 minutes remain, add the Irish moss. After a total wort boil of 60 minutes, turn off the heat and place the pot (with cover on) in a running cold-water bath for 30 minutes. Continue to chill in the immersion or use other methods to chill your wort. Then strain and sparge the wort into a sanitized fermenter. Bring the total volume to 5 gallons (19 l) with additional cold water if necessary. Aerate the wort very well.

Pitch the yeast when temperature of wort is about 70 degrees F (21 C). Ferment at about 70 degrees F (21 C) for about 1 week, or until fermentation shows signs of calm and stopping. Rack from your primary to a secondary fermenter and maintain temperature at 70 degrees F (21 C) until fermentation is complete.

Prime with sugar and bottle or keg when complete.

Malt Extract Recipe *for 5 gallons (19 l)*

6.75 lbs.	(3.06 kg) wheat malt extract syrup or 5.4 lbs. (2.5 kg) dried wheat malt extract
1 oz.	(28 g) German Hallertauer hops 4.4% alpha (4.4 HBU/123 MBU)—60 minutes boiling
¾ oz.	(21 g) German Hallertauer hops 4.4% alpha (3.3 HBU/92 MBU)—20 minutes boiling
¼ tsp.	(1 g) powdered Irish moss
German wheat beer yeast	
¾ cup	(175 ml measure) corn sugar (priming bottles) or 0.33 cups (80 ml) corn sugar for kegging

To 2.5 gallons (9.5 l) of hot water, add malt extract and 60-minute hops. Bring to a boil.

The total boil time will be 60 minutes. When 20 minutes remain, add the 20-minute hops. When 10 minutes remain, add the Irish moss. After a total wort boil of 60 minutes, turn off the heat.

Immerse the covered pot of wort in a cold-water bath and let sit for 30 minutes, or the time it takes to have a couple of homebrews.

Then strain out and sparge hops and direct the hot wort into a sanitized fermenter to which 2.5 gallons (9.5 l) of cold water has been added. Bring the total volume to 5 gallons (19 l) with additional cold water if necessary. Aerate the wort very well.

Pitch the yeast when temperature of wort is about 70 degrees F (21 C). Ferment at about 70 degrees F (21 C) for about 1 week, or until fermentation shows signs of calm and stopping. Rack from your primary to a secondary fermenter and maintain temperature at 70 degrees F (21 C) until fermentation is complete.

Prime with sugar and bottle or keg when complete.

PRINTZ HELLES GERMAN LAGER

- TARGET ORIGINAL GRAVITY: 1.054 (13 B)
- APPROXIMATE FINAL GRAVITY: 1.013 (3.5 B)
- IBU: ABOUT 27
- APPROXIMATE COLOR: 10 SRM (20 EBC)
- ALCOHOL: 5.5% BY VOLUME

All-Grain Recipe *for 5 gallons (19 l)*

7.5 lbs.	(3.4 kg) German pilsener malt
1 lb.	(454 g) Belgian aromatic malt
4 oz.	(113 g) German Caramunich malt
4 oz.	(113 g) German sauer malt
½ oz.	(14 g) Mt. Hood hops 6% alpha (3 HBU/84 MBU)— 60 minutes boiling
½ oz.	(14 g) German Tradition hops 6.5% alpha (3.3 HBU/91 MBU)—60 minutes boiling
½ oz.	(14 g) crystal hop pellets—1 minute boiling
⅓ oz.	(10 g) crystal hop pellets—dry hopping
¼ tsp.	(1 g) powdered Irish moss
German or Bavarian-type lager yeast	
¾ cup	(175 ml measure) corn sugar (priming bottles) or 0.33 cups (80 ml) corn sugar for kegging

A step infusion mash is employed to mash the grains. Add 9 quarts (8.6 l) of 140-degree F (60 C) water to the crushed grain, stir, stabilize and hold the temperature at 132 degrees F (53 C) for 30 minutes. Add 4.5 quarts (4.3 l) of boiling water, add heat to bring temperature up to 155 degrees F (68 C) and hold for about 30 minutes. Then raise temperature to 167 degrees F (75 C), lauter and sparge with 3.5 gallons (13.5 l) of 170-degree F (77 C) water. Collect about 5.5 gallons (21 l) of runoff. Add 60-minute hops and bring to a full and vigorous boil.

The total boil time will be 60 minutes. When 10 minutes remain, add the Irish moss. When 1 minute remains, add the 1-minute hops. After a total wort boil of 60 minutes, turn off the heat and place the pot (with cover on) in a running cold-water bath for 30 minutes. Continue to chill in the immersion or use other methods to chill your wort. Then strain and sparge the wort into a sanitized fermenter. Bring the total volume to 5 gallons (19 l) with additional cold water if necessary. Aerate the wort very well.

Pitch the yeast when temperature of wort is about 70 degrees F (21 C). Once visible signs of fermentation are evident, ferment at temperatures of about 55 degrees F (12.5 C) for about 1 week, or until fermentation shows signs of calm and stopping. Rack from your primary to a secondary fermenter and add the hop pellets for dry hopping. If you have the capability, "lager" the beer at temperatures between 35 and 45 degrees F (1.5–7 C) for 3 to 6 weeks.

Prime with sugar and bottle or keg when complete.

Mash/Extract Recipe *for 5 gallons (19 l)*

5.5 lbs.	(2.5 kg) light malt extract syrup or 4.4 lbs. (2 kg) light dried malt extract
1 lb.	(454 g) aromatic malt
1 lb.	(454 g) German pilsener malt
4 oz.	(113 g) German Caramunich malt
¾ oz.	(21 g) Mt. Hood hops 6% alpha (4.5 HBU/126 MBU)—60 minutes boiling
½ oz.	(14 g) German Tradition hops 6.5% alpha (3.3 HBU/91 MBU)—60 minutes boiling
½ oz.	(14 g) crystal hop pellets—1 minute boiling
⅓ oz.	(10 g) crystal hop pellets—dry hopping
¼ tsp.	(1 g) powdered Irish moss
German or Bavarian-type lager yeast	
¾ cup	(175 ml measure) corn sugar (priming bottles) or 0.33 cups (80 ml) corn sugar for kegging

Heat 2 quarts (2 l) water to 172 degrees F (77.5 C) and then add crushed grains to the water. Stir well to distribute heat. Temperature should stabilize at about 155 degrees F (68 C). Wrap a towel around the pot and set aside for about 45 minutes. Have a homebrew.

After 45 minutes, add heat to the mini-mash and raise the temperature to 167 degrees F (75 C). Then pass the liquid and grains into a strainer and rinse with 170-degree F (77 C) water. Discard the grains.

To the sweet extract you have just produced, add more water, bringing the volume up to about 2.5 gallons (9.5 l). Add malt extract and 60-minute hops and bring to a boil.

The total boil time will be 60 minutes. When 10 minutes remain, add the Irish moss. When 1 minute remains, add the 1-minute hops. After a total wort boil of 60 minutes, turn off the heat.

Immerse the covered pot of wort in a cold-water bath and let sit for 30 minutes, or the time it takes to have a couple of homebrews.

Then strain out and sparge hops and direct the hot wort into a sanitized fermenter to which 2.5 gallons (9.5 l) of cold water has been added. Bring the total volume to 5 gallons (19 l) with additional cold water if necessary. Aerate the wort very well.

Pitch the yeast when temperature of wort is about 70 degrees F (21 C). Once visible signs of fermentation are evident, ferment at temperatures of about 55 degrees F (12.5 C) for about 1 week, or until fermentation shows signs of calm and stopping. Rack from your primary to a secondary fermenter and add the hop pellets for dry hopping. If you have the capability, "lager" the beer at temperatures between 35 and 45 degrees F (1.5–7 C) for 3 to 6 weeks.

Prime with sugar and bottle or keg when complete.

FROG & ROSBIF'S BROWN WHEAT CORIANDER ALE

- TARGET ORIGINAL GRAVITY: 1.049 (12.5 B)
- APPROXIMATE FINAL GRAVITY: 1.014 (3.5 B)
- IBU: ABOUT 24
- APPROXIMATE COLOR: 15 SRM (30 EBC)
- ALCOHOL: 5% BY VOLUME

All-Grain Recipe *for 5 gallons (19 l)*

6.5 lbs.	(3 kg) pale malt
12 oz.	(340 g) wheat malt
12 oz.	(340 g) crystal malt (40-L)
4 oz.	(113 g) chocolate malt

¾ oz.   (21 g) Czech Saaz hops 4% alpha (3 HBU/84 MBU)—
                  60 minutes boiling
½ oz.   (14 g) German Hersbrucker-Hallertauer hops 3.3%
                  alpha (1.7 HBU/46 MBU)—60 minutes boiling
½ oz.   (14 g) German Hersbrucker-Hallertauer hops 3.3%
                  alpha (1.7 HBU/46 MBU)—30 minutes boiling
½ oz.   (14 g) German Hersbrucker-Hallertauer hops 3.3%
                  alpha (1.7 HBU/46 MBU)—15 minutes boiling
1.25 oz.   (35 g) freshly crushed coriander seeds
¼ tsp.   (1 g) powdered Irish moss
English/British-type ale yeast
¾ cup   (175 ml measure) corn sugar (priming bottles) or 0.33
                  cups (80 ml) corn sugar for kegging

A step infusion mash is employed to mash the grains. Add 8 quarts (7.6 l) of 140-degree F (60 C) water to the crushed grain, stir, stabilize and hold the temperature at 132 degrees F (53 C) for 30 minutes. Add 4 quarts (3.8 l) of boiling water, add heat to bring temperature up to 155 degrees F (68 C) and hold for about 30 minutes. Then raise temperature to 167 degrees F (75 C), lauter and sparge with 3.5 gallons (13.5 l) of 170-degree F (77 C) water. Collect about 5.5 gallons (21 l) of runoff. Add 60-minute hops and bring to a full and vigorous boil.

The total boil time will be 60 minutes. When 30 minutes remain, add the 30-minute hops. When 15 minutes remain, add the 15-minute hops. When 10 minutes remain, add the Irish moss and ¾ oz. (21 g) crushed coriander seeds. After a total wort boil of 60 minutes, turn off the heat and place the pot (with cover on) in a running cold-water bath for 30 minutes. Continue to chill in the immersion or use other methods to chill your wort. Then strain and sparge the wort into a sanitized fermenter. Bring the total volume to 5 gallons (19 l) with additional cold water if necessary. Aerate the wort very well.

Pitch the yeast when temperature of wort is about 70 degrees F (21 C). Ferment at about 70 degrees F (21 C) for about 1 week, or until fermentation shows signs of calm and stopping. Rack from your primary to a secondary fermenter, add ½ oz. (14 g) of crushed coriander seeds and if you have the capability, "cellar" the beer at about 55 degrees F (12.5 C) for about 1 week.

Prime with sugar and bottle or keg when complete.

Malt Extract Recipe *for 5 gallons (19 l)*

4 lbs.	(1.82 kg) light malt extract syrup or 3.2 lbs. (1.45 kg) light dried malt extract
2 lbs.	(908 g) wheat malt extract syrup
12 oz.	(340 g) crystal malt (40-L)
4 oz.	(113 g) chocolate malt
1.25 oz.	(35 g) Czech Saaz hops 4% alpha (5 HBU/140 MBU)—60 minutes boiling
½ oz.	(14 g) German Hersbrucker-Hallertauer hops 3.3% alpha (1.7 HBU/46 MBU)—60 minutes boiling
½ oz.	(14 g) German Hersbrucker-Hallertauer hops 3.3% alpha (1.7 HBU/46 MBU)—30 minutes boiling
½ oz.	(14 g) German Hersbrucker-Hallertauer hops 3.3% alpha (1.7 HBU/46 MBU)—15 minutes boiling
1.25 oz.	(35 g) freshly crushed coriander seeds
¼ tsp.	(1 g) powdered Irish moss
English/British-type ale yeast	
¾ cup	(175 ml measure) corn sugar (priming bottles) or 0.33 cups (80 ml) corn sugar for kegging

Place crushed grains in 2 gallons (7.6 l) of 150-degree F (68 C) water and let steep for 30 minutes. Then strain out (and rinse with 3 quarts [3 l] hot water) and discard the crushed grains, reserving the approximately 2.5 gallons (9.5 l) of liquid to which you will now add malt extract and 60-minute hops. Bring to a boil.

The total boil time will be 60 minutes. When 30 minutes remain, add the 30-minute hops. When 15 minutes remain, add the 15-minute hops. When 10 minutes remain, add the Irish moss and ¾ oz. (21 g) crushed coriander seeds. After a total wort boil of 60 minutes, turn off the heat.

Immerse the covered pot of wort in a cold-water bath and let sit for 30 minutes, or the time it takes to have a couple of homebrews.

Then strain out and sparge hops and direct the hot wort into a sanitized fermenter to which 2.5 gallons (9.5 l) of cold water has been added. Bring the total volume to 5 gallons (19 l) with additional cold water if necessary. Aerate the wort very well.

Pitch the yeast when temperature of wort is about 70 degrees F (21 C). Ferment at about 70 degrees F (21 C) for about 1 week, or until fermentation

shows signs of calm and stopping. Rack from your primary to a secondary fermenter, add ½ oz. (14 g) of crushed coriander seeds and if you have the capability, "cellar" the beer at about 55 degrees F (12.5 C) for about 1 week.

Prime with sugar and bottle or keg when complete.

POETIC BRIGHELLA ITALIAN-BELGIAN-GERMAN-ENGLISH-AMERICAN ALE

- TARGET ORIGINAL GRAVITY: 1.074 (18 B)
- APPROXIMATE FINAL GRAVITY: 1.016 (4 B)
- IBU: ABOUT 27
- APPROXIMATE COLOR: 16 SRM (32 EBC)
- ALCOHOL: 7.9% BY VOLUME

All-Grain Recipe *for 5 gallons (19 l)*

7.25 lbs.	(3.3 kg) pale malt
3.5 lbs.	(1.6 kg) Munich malt
1.5 lbs.	(680 g) German sauer malt
4 oz.	(113 g) German black Caraffe malt
¾ oz.	(21 g) German Hallertauer hops 4.5% alpha (3.4 HBU/94 MBU)—60 minutes boiling
½ oz.	(14 g) Perle hops 8% alpha (4 HBU/112 MBU)—60 minutes boiling
¼ tsp.	(1 g) powdered Irish moss
SafAle dried ale yeast*	
¾ cup	(175 ml measure) corn sugar (priming bottles) or 0.33 cups (80 ml) corn sugar for kegging

A step infusion mash is employed to mash the grains. Add 12 quarts (11.5 l) of 140-degree F (60 C) water to the crushed grain, stir, stabilize and hold the temperature at 132 degrees F (53 C) for 30 minutes. Add 6 quarts (6 l) of boiling

---

*This is the ale yeast used by Birrificio Lambrate. A well-attenuating English-type yeast can also be used.

water, add heat to bring temperature up to 155 degrees F (68 C) and hold for about 30 minutes. Then raise temperature to 167 degrees F (75 C), lauter and sparge with 3.5 gallons (13.5 l) of 170-degree F (77 C) water. Collect about 5.5 gallons (21 l) of runoff. Add 60-minute hops and bring to a full and vigorous boil.

The total boil time will be 60 minutes. When 10 minutes remain, add the Irish moss. After a total wort boil of 60 minutes, turn off the heat and place the pot (with cover on) in a running cold-water bath for 30 minutes. Continue to chill in the immersion or use other methods to chill your wort. Then strain and sparge the wort into a sanitized fermenter. Bring the total volume to 5 gallons (19 l) with additional cold water if necessary. Aerate the wort very well.

Pitch the yeast when temperature of wort is about 70 degrees F (21 C). Ferment at about 70 degrees F (21 C) for about 1 week, or until fermentation shows signs of calm and stopping. Rack from your primary to a secondary fermenter and if you have the capability, "cellar" the beer at about 55 degrees F (12.5 C) for about 1 week.

Prime with sugar and bottle or keg when complete.

Mash/Extract Recipe *for 5 gallons (19 l)*

7 lbs.	(3.2 kg) amber malt extract or 5.6 lbs. (2.5 kg) amber dried malt extract
2.5 lbs.	(1.15 kg) pale malt
1.25 lbs.	(568 g) German sauer malt
4 oz.	(113 g) German black Caraffe malt
1 oz.	(28 g) German Hallertauer hops 4.5% alpha (4.5 HBU/126 MBU)—60 minutes boiling
¾ oz.	(21 g) Perle hops 8% alpha (6 HBU/168 MBU)—60 minutes boiling
¼ tsp.	(1 g) powdered Irish moss
SafAle dried ale yeast*	
¾ cup	(175 ml measure) corn sugar (priming bottles) or 0.33 cups (80 ml) corn sugar for kegging

Heat 1 gallon (3.8 l) water to 172 degrees F (77.5 C) and then add crushed grains to the water. Stir well to distribute heat. Temperature should stabilize

---

*This is the ale yeast used by Birrificio Lambrate. A well-attenuating English-type yeast can also be used.

at about 155 degrees F (68 C). Wrap a towel around the pot and set aside for about 45 minutes. Have a homebrew.

After 45 minutes, add heat to the mini-mash and raise the temperature to 167 degrees F (75 C). Then pass the liquid and grains into a strainer and rinse with 170-degree F (77 C) water. Discard the grains.

To the sweet extract you have just produced, add more water, bringing the volume up to about 2.5 gallons (9.5 l). Add malt extract and 60-minute hops and bring to a boil.

The total boil time will be 60 minutes. When 10 minutes remain, add the Irish moss. After a total wort boil of 60 minutes, turn off the heat.

Immerse the covered pot of wort in a cold-water bath and let sit for 30 minutes, or the time it takes to have a couple of homebrews.

Then strain out and sparge hops and direct the hot wort into a sanitized fermenter to which 2.5 gallons (9.5 l) of cold water has been added. Bring the total volume to 5 gallons (19 l) with additional cold water if necessary. Aerate the wort very well.

Pitch the yeast when temperature of wort is about 70 degrees F (21 C). Ferment at about 70 degrees F (21 C) for about 1 week, or until fermentation shows signs of calm and stopping. Rack from your primary to a secondary fermenter and if you have the capability, "cellar" the beer at about 55 degrees F (12.5 C) for about 1 week.

Prime with sugar and bottle or keg when complete.

PIOZZO ITALIAN PALE ALE

- TARGET ORIGINAL GRAVITY: 1.052 (13 B)
- APPROXIMATE FINAL GRAVITY: 1.014 (3.5 B)
- IBU: ABOUT 47
- APPROXIMATE COLOR: 15 SRM (30 EBC)
- ALCOHOL: 5% BY VOLUME

All-Grain Recipe *for 5 gallons (19 l)*

8 lbs.	(3.6 kg) pale malt
12 oz.	(340 g) crystal malt (80-L)
1.5 oz.	(42 g) Styrian Goldings hops 5% alpha (7.5 HBU/210 MBU)—60 minutes boiling

1 oz.	(28 g) Santiam whole hops 5% alpha (5 HBU/140 MBU)—30 minutes boiling
1 oz.	(28 g) Cascade hops 5% alpha (5 HBU/140 MBU)—5 minutes boiling
½ oz.	(14 g) Santiam hop pellets—dry hopping
¼ tsp.	(1 g) powdered Irish moss
American-type ale yeast	
¾ cup	(175 ml measure) corn sugar (priming bottles) or 0.33 cups (80 ml) corn sugar for kegging

A step infusion mash is employed to mash the grains. Add 9 quarts (8.6 l) of 140-degree F (60 C) water to the crushed grain, stir, stabilize and hold the temperature at 132 degrees F (53 C) for 30 minutes. Add 4.5 quarts (4.3 l) of boiling water, add heat to bring temperature up to 155 degrees F (68 C) and hold for about 30 minutes. Then raise temperature to 167 degrees F (75 C), lauter and sparge with 3.5 gallons (13.5 l) of 170-degree F (77 C) water. Collect about 5.5 gallons (21 l) of runoff. Add 60-minute hops and bring to a full and vigorous boil.

The total boil time will be 60 minutes. When 30 minutes remain, add the 30-minute hops. When 10 minutes remain, add the Irish moss. When 5 minutes remain, add the 5-minute hops. After a total wort boil of 60 minutes, turn off the heat and place the pot (with cover on) in a running cold-water bath for 30 minutes. Continue to chill in the immersion or use other methods to chill your wort. Then strain and sparge the wort into a sanitized fermenter. Bring the total volume to 5 gallons (19 l) with additional cold water if necessary. Aerate the wort very well.

Pitch the yeast when temperature of wort is about 70 degrees F (21 C). Ferment at about 70 degrees F (21 C) for about 1 week, or until fermentation shows signs of calm and stopping. Rack from your primary to a secondary fermenter and add the hop pellets for dry hopping. If you have the capability, "cellar" the beer at about 55 degrees F (12.5 C) for about 1 week.

Prime with sugar and bottle or keg when complete.

Might I suggest exposing this beer to Indian sitar music during primary fermentation and Italian opera during cellaring?

Malt Extract Recipe *for 5 gallons (19 l)*

6.75 lbs.	(3.06 kg) light malt extract syrup or 5.4 lbs. (2.6 kg) light dried malt extract
12 oz.	(340 g) crystal malt (80-L)
2 oz.	(56 g) German Hallertauer hops 4.4% alpha (8.8 HBU/246 MBU)—60 minutes boiling
1.25 oz.	(35 g) Santiam whole hops 5% alpha (6.3 HBU/175 MBU)—30 minutes boiling
1 oz.	(28 g) Cascade hops 5% alpha (5 HBU/140 MBU)—5 minutes boiling
½ oz.	(14 g) Santiam hop pellets—dry hopping
¼ tsp.	(1 g) powdered Irish moss
American-type ale yeast	
¾ cup	(175 ml measure) corn sugar (priming bottles) or 0.33 cups (80 ml) corn sugar for kegging

Place crushed grains in 2 gallons (7.6 l) of 150-degree F (68 C) water and let steep for 30 minutes. Then strain out (and rinse with 3 quarts [3 l] hot water) and discard the crushed grains, reserving the approximately 2.5 gallons (9.5 l) of liquid to which you will now add malt extract and 60-minute hops. Bring to a boil.

The total boil time will be 60 minutes. When 30 minutes remain, add the 30-minute hops. When 10 minutes remain, add the Irish moss. When 5 minutes remain, add the 5-minute hops. After a total wort boil of 60 minutes, turn off the heat.

Immerse the covered pot of wort in a cold-water bath and let sit for 30 minutes, or the time it takes to have a couple of homebrews.

Then strain out and sparge hops and direct the hot wort into a sanitized fermenter to which 2.5 gallons (9.5 l) of cold water has been added. Bring the total volume to 5 gallons (19 l) with additional cold water if necessary. Aerate the wort very well.

Pitch the yeast when temperature of wort is about 70 degrees F (21 C). Ferment at about 70 degrees F (21 C) for about 1 week, or until fermentation shows signs of calm and stopping. Rack from your primary to a secondary fermenter and add the hop pellets for dry hopping. If you have the capability, "cellar" the beer at about 55 degrees F (12.5 C) for about 1 week.

Prime with sugar and bottle or keg when complete.

Might I suggest exposing this beer to Indian sitar music during primary fermentation and Italian opera during cellaring?

VELLO'S GOTLANDSDRICKE

- TARGET ORIGINAL GRAVITY: 1.046 (11.5 B)
- APPROXIMATE FINAL GRAVITY: 1.012 (3 B)
- IBU: ABOUT 30
- APPROXIMATE COLOR: 7 SRM (14 EBC)
- ALCOHOL: 6.5% BY VOLUME

All-Grain Recipe *for 5 gallons (19 l)*

5 lbs.	(2.3 kg) birch-smoked pale malt
1.5 lbs.	(680 g) Munich malt
1.5 lbs.	(680 g) pale malt
¾ oz.	(21 g) Northern Brewer hops 8% alpha (6 HBU/168 MBU)—60 minutes boiling
1 oz.	(28 g) German Hersbrucker-Mittelfrueh hops 4% alpha (4 HBU/112 MBU)—15 minutes boiling
6	10-to-12-inch boughs/branches of juniper for brewing water*
4	10-to-12-inch boughs/branches of juniper for base water and lautering
¼ tsp.	(1 g) powdered Irish moss
1	square centimeter of fresh compressed "caked" bread yeast.**
¾ cup	(175 ml measure) corn sugar (priming bottles) or 0.33 cups (80 ml) corn sugar for kegging

Boil 4 boughs of juniper branches in 6½ gallons (25 l) of water for 1 hour. After removing the "spent" branches, use the water for mashing and sparging.

A step infusion mash is employed to mash the grains. Add 8 quarts (7.6 l) of 140-degree F (60 C) juniper water to the crushed grain, stir, stabilize and hold the temperature at 132 degrees F (53 C) for 30 minutes. Add 4 quarts (3.8 l) of boiling juniper water, add heat to bring temperature up to 155 degrees F (68 C) and hold for about 30 minutes. Then raise temperature to 167

*The juniper I used were laden with green berries. Juniper is not cedar. The needles on these branches were very thornlike and difficult to handle without gloves.

**Of course you may use lager or ale yeast, but keep in mind this recipe attempts to be true to style.

degrees F (75 C). Place 2 branches of juniper on the bottom of the lauter vessel and lauter and sparge with 3.5 gallons (13.5 l) of 170-degree F (77 C) juniper water. Collect about 5.5 gallons (21 l) of runoff. Add 60-minute hops
and bring to a full and vigorous boil.

The total boil time will be 60 minutes. When 15 minutes remain, add the
15-minute hops. When 10 minutes remain, add the Irish moss. After a total
wort boil of 60 minutes, turn off the heat and place the pot (with cover on) in
a running cold-water bath for 30 minutes. Continue to chill in the immersion
or use other methods to chill your wort. Then strain and sparge the wort into
a sanitized fermenter. Bring the total volume to 5 gallons (19 l) with additional cold juniper water if necessary. Aerate the wort very well.

Dissolve the compressed yeast in a small amount of boiled and cooled water. Use a jar and a teaspoon previously sterilized in boiling water to contain
and mix the yeast and water. Pitch the yeast when temperature of wort is
about 65 degrees F (18 C). Ferment at about 65 degrees F (18 C) for about 1
week, or until fermentation shows signs of calm and stopping. Rack from
your primary to a secondary fermenter and if you have the capability, "cellar"
the beer at about 55 degrees F (12.5 C) for about 1 week.

Prime with sugar and bottle or keg when complete.

Relax. Don't worry. Have a homebrew and hope that you never find yourself smelling the dandelions on Folknykterhetens Dag.

Mash/Extract Recipe *for 5 gallons (19 l)*

4 lbs.	(1.82 kg) birch-smoked pale malt
3 lbs.	(1.36 kg) amber malt extract syrup or 2.4 lbs. (1.1 kg) amber dried malt extract
1 oz.	(28 g) Northern Brewer hops 8% alpha (8 HBU/224 MBU)—60 minutes boiling
¾ oz.	(21 g) German Hersbrucker-Mittelfrueh hops 4% alpha (3 HBU/84 MBU)—15 minutes boiling
4	10-to-12-inch boughs/branches of juniper for brewing water*
4	10-to-12-inch boughs/branches of juniper for base water preparation

*The juniper I used were laden with green berries. Juniper is not cedar. The needles on these
branches were very thornlike and difficult to handle without gloves.

¼ tsp.	(1 g) powdered Irish moss
1	square centimeter of fresh compressed "caked" bread yeast*
¾ cup	(175 ml measure) corn sugar (priming bottles) or 0.33 cups (80 ml) corn sugar for kegging

Boil 4 boughs of juniper branches in 6½ gallons (25 l) of water for 1 hour. After removing the "spent" branches, use the water for mashing and sparging.

Heat 1 gallon (3.8 l) juniper water to 172 degrees F (77.5 C) and then add crushed grains to the juniper water. Stir well to distribute heat. Temperature should stabilize at about 155 degrees F (68 C). Wrap a towel around the pot and set aside for about 45 minutes. Have a homebrew.

After 45 minutes, add heat to the mini-mash and raise the temperature to 167 degrees F (75 C). Then pass the liquid and grains into a strainer and rinse with 170-degree F (77 C) juniper water. Discard the grains.

To the sweet extract you have just produced, add more juniper water, bringing the volume up to about 2.5 gallons (9.5 l). Add malt extract and 60-minute hops and bring to a boil.

The total boil time will be 60 minutes. When 15 minutes remain, add the 15-minute hops. When 10 minutes remain, add the Irish moss. After a total wort boil of 60 minutes, turn off the heat.

Immerse the covered pot of wort in a cold-water bath and let sit for 30 minutes, or the time it takes to have a couple of homebrews.

Then strain out and sparge hops and direct the hot wort into a sanitized fermenter to which 2.5 gallons (9.5 l) of cold juniper water has been added. Bring the total volume to 5 gallons (19 l) with additional cold water if necessary. Aerate the wort very well.

Dissolve the compressed yeast in a small amount of boiled and cooled water. Use a jar and a teaspoon previously sterilized in boiling water to contain and mix the yeast and water. Pitch the yeast when temperature of wort is about 65 degrees F (18 C). Ferment at about 65 degrees F (18 C) for about 1 week, or until fermentation shows signs of calm and stopping. Rack from your primary to a secondary fermenter, and if you have the capability, "cellar" the beer at about 55 degrees F (12.5 C) for about 1 week.

Prime with sugar and bottle or keg when complete.

Relax. Don't worry. Have a homebrew and hope that you never find yourself smelling the dandelions on Folknykterhetens Dag.

---

*Of course you may use lager or ale yeast, but keep in mind this recipe attempts to be true to style.

··

ZEEZUIPER SPICED NEDERLANDER STRONG ALE

- TARGET ORIGINAL GRAVITY: 1.072 (17.5 B)
- APPROXIMATE FINAL GRAVITY: 1.016 (4 B)
- IBU: ABOUT 20
- APPROXIMATE COLOR: 6 SRM (12 EBC)
- ALCOHOL: 7.5% BY VOLUME

All-Grain Recipe *for 5 gallons (19 l)*

11 lbs.	(5 kg) pale malt
1 lb.	(454 g) flaked corn
1 oz.	(28 g) Styrian Goldings hops 5% alpha (5 HBU/140 MBU)—60 minutes boiling
½ oz.	(14 g) Brewers Gold hops—5 minutes boiling
1 oz.	(28 g) freshly crushed coriander seed
¾ oz.	(21 g) dried Curaçao orange peel
½ oz.	(14 g) woodruff
¼ tsp.	(1 g) powdered Irish moss

Belgian ale yeasts, such as Wyeast 1762 Belgian Abbey yeast II or White Labs Bastogne Belgian Ale yeast WLP510

¾ cup	(175 ml measure) corn sugar (priming bottles) or 0.33 cups (80 ml) corn sugar for kegging

A step infusion mash is employed to mash the grains. Add 12 quarts (11.5 l) of 140-degree F (60 C) water to the crushed grain, stir, stabilize and hold the temperature at 132 degrees F (53 C) for 30 minutes. Add 6 quarts (6 l) of boiling water, add heat to bring temperature up to 155 degrees F (68 C) and hold for about 30 minutes. Then raise temperature to 167 degrees F (75 C), lauter and sparge with 3.5 gallons (13.5 l) of 170-degree F (77 C) water. Collect about 5.5 gallons (21 l) of runoff. Add 60-minute hops and bring to a full and vigorous boil.

The total boil time will be 60 minutes. When 10 minutes remain, add the Irish moss, coriander, orange peel and woodruff. When 5 minutes remain, add the 5-minute hops. After a total wort boil of 60 minutes, turn off the heat and place the pot (with cover on) in a running cold-water bath for 30 minutes. Continue to chill in the immersion or use other methods to chill your wort. Then strain and sparge the wort into a sanitized fermenter. Bring the total volume to 5 gallons (19 l) with additional cold water if necessary. Aerate the wort very well.

Pitch the yeast when temperature of wort is about 70 degrees F (21 C). Ferment at about 70 degrees F (21 C) for about 10 days, or until fermentation shows signs of calm and stopping. Rack from your primary to a secondary fermenter and continue to lager at 40 degrees F (4 C) for 3 additional weeks.

Prime with sugar and bottle or keg when complete. Condition the beer at warm temperatures of about 70 to 75 degrees F (21–24 C) for 10 days and then enjoy this wonderfully creamy exotic brew.

Mash/Extract Recipe *for 5 gallons (19 l)*

7.25 lbs.	(3.3 kg) light malt extract or 5.8 lbs. (2.6 kg) light dried malt extract
2 lbs.	(908 g) 6-row pale malt
1 lb.	(454 g) flaked corn
1.25 oz.	(35 g) Styrian Goldings hops 5% alpha (6.3 HBU/175 MBU)—60 minutes boiling
½ oz.	(14 g) Brewers Gold hops—5 minutes boiling
1 oz.	(28 g) freshly crushed coriander seed
¾ oz.	(21 g) dried Curaçao orange peel
½ oz.	(14 g) woodruff
¼ tsp.	(1 g) powdered Irish moss

Belgian ale yeasts, such as Wyeast 1762 Belgian Abbey yeast II or White Labs Bastogne Belgian Ale yeast WLP510

¾ cup	(175 ml measure) corn sugar (priming bottles) or 0.33 cups (80 ml) corn sugar for kegging

Heat 3 quarts (3 l) water to 172 degrees F (77.5 C) and then add crushed grains to the water. Stir well to distribute heat. Temperature should stabilize at about 155 degrees F (68 C). Wrap a towel around the pot and set aside for about 60 minutes. Have a homebrew.

After 60 minutes, add heat to the mini-mash and raise the temperature to 167 degrees F (75 C). Then pass the liquid and grains into a strainer and rinse with 170-degrees F (77 C) water. Discard the grains.

To the sweet extract you have just produced, add more water, bringing the volume up to about 2.5 gallons (9.5 l). Add malt extract and 60-minute hops and bring to a boil.

The total boil time will be 60 minutes. When 10 minutes remain, add the Irish moss, coriander, orange peel and woodruff. When 5 minutes remain, add the 5-minute hops. After a total wort boil of 60 minutes, turn off the heat.

Immerse the covered pot of wort in a cold-water bath and let sit for 30 minutes, or the time it takes to have a couple of homebrews.

Then strain out and sparge hops and direct the hot wort into a sanitized fermenter to which 2.5 gallons (9.5 l) of cold water has been added. Bring the total volume to 5 gallons (19 l) with additional cold water if necessary. Aerate the wort very well.

Pitch the yeast when temperature of wort is about 70 degrees F (21 C). Ferment at about 70 degrees F (21 C) for about 10 days, or until fermentation shows signs of calm and stopping. Rack from your primary to a secondary fermenter and continue to lager at 40 degrees F (4 C) for 3 additional weeks.

Prime with sugar and bottle or keg when complete. Condition the beer at warm temperatures of about 70 to 75 degrees F (21–24 C) for 10 days and then enjoy this wonderfully creamy exotic brew.

SWITCH AND TOGGLES PREPOSTEROUS POORTER

- TARGET ORIGINAL GRAVITY: 1.060 (14.5 B)
- APPROXIMATE FINAL GRAVITY: 1.016 (4 B)
- IBU: ABOUT 25
- APPROXIMATE COLOR: 32 SRM (64 EBC)
- ALCOHOL: 5.8% BY VOLUME

All-Grain Recipe *for 5 gallons (19 l)*

8.75 lbs.	(4 kg) Belgian amber malt
8 oz.	(225 g) Belgian aromatic malt
8 oz.	(225 g) Belgian biscuit malt
4 oz.	(113 g) Belgian Special-B malt

4 oz.	(113 g) Belgian chocolate malt
4 oz.	(113 g) German black Caraffe malt
1 oz.	(28 g) German Spalt hops 5% alpha (5 HBU/140 MBU)—120 minutes boiling
1 oz.	(28 g) Styrian Goldings hops—5 minutes boiling
½ oz.	(14 g) German or American Tettnanger or Santiam hops—5 minutes boiling
¼ tsp.	(1 g) powdered Irish moss

White Labs California Ale yeast WLP001 or Wyeast 1762 Belgian Abbey yeast II

¾ cup	(175 ml measure) corn sugar (priming bottles) or 0.33 cups (80 ml) corn sugar for kegging

A step infusion mash is employed to mash the grains. Add 10.5 quarts (10.4 l) of 140-degree F (60 C) water to the crushed grain, stir, stabilize and hold the temperature at 132 degrees F (53 C) for 30 minutes. Add 5 quarts (4.8 l) of boiling water, add heat to bring temperature up to 155 degrees F (68 C) and hold for about 30 minutes. Then raise temperature to 167 degrees F (75 C), lauter and sparge with 3.5 gallons (13.5 l) of 170-degree F (77 C) water. Collect about 6 gallons (23 l) of runoff. Add 120-minute hops and bring to a full and vigorous boil.

The total boil time will be 120 minutes. When 10 minutes remain, add the Irish moss. When 5 minutes remain, add the 5-minute hops. After a total wort boil of 120 minutes, turn off the heat and place the pot (with cover on) in a running cold-water bath for 30 minutes. Continue to chill in the immersion or use other methods to chill your wort. Then strain and sparge the wort into a sanitized fermenter. Bring the total volume to 5 gallons (19 l) with additional cold water if necessary. Aerate the wort very well.

Pitch the yeast when temperature of wort is about 70 degrees F (21 C). Ferment at about 70 degrees F (21 C) for about 7 to 10 days, or until fermentation shows signs of calm and stopping. Rack from your primary to a secondary fermenter and continue in the fermenter at the same temperature for another 1 to 2 weeks, or until fermentation is complete. If you have the capability, "cellar" the beer at about 40 to 45 degrees F (4.5–7.5 C) and lager for 2 to 3 weeks.

Prime with sugar and bottle or keg when complete.

Mash/Extract Recipe *for 5 gallons (19 l)*

7.5 lbs.	(3.4 kg) amber malt extract syrup or 6 lbs. (2.7 kg) amber dried malt extract
8 oz.	(225 g) Belgian aromatic malt
8 oz.	(225 g) Belgian biscuit malt
4 oz.	(113 g) Belgian Special-B malt
4 oz.	(113 g) Belgian chocolate malt
4 oz.	(113 g) German black Caraffe malt
1.25 oz.	(35 g) German Spalt hops 5% alpha (6.25 HBU/175 MBU)—90 minutes boiling
1 oz.	(28 g) Styrian Goldings hops—5 minutes boiling
½ oz.	(14 g) German or American Tettnanger or Santiam hops—5 minutes boiling
¼ tsp.	(1 g) powdered Irish moss

White Labs California Ale yeast WLP001 or Wyeast 1762 Belgian Abbey yeast II

¾ cup	(175 ml measure) corn sugar (priming bottles) or 0.33 cups (80 ml) corn sugar for kegging

Heat 2 quarts (2 l) water to 172 degrees F (77.5 C) and then add crushed grains to the water. Stir well to distribute heat. Temperature should stabilize at about 155 degrees F (68 C). Wrap a towel around the pot and set aside for about 45 minutes. Have a homebrew.

After 45 minutes, add heat to the mini-mash and raise the temperature to 167 degrees F (75 C). Then pass the liquid and grains into a strainer and rinse with 170-degree F (77 C) water. Discard the grains.

To the sweet extract you have just produced, add more water, bringing the volume up to about 3 gallons (10.5 l). Add malt extract and 90-minute hops and bring to a boil.

The total boil time will be 90 minutes. When 10 minutes remain, add the Irish moss. When 5 minute remain, add the 5-minute hops. After a total wort boil of 90 minutes, turn off the heat.

Immerse the covered pot of wort in a cold-water bath and let sit for 30 minutes, or the time it takes to have a couple of homebrews.

Then strain out and sparge hops and direct the hot wort into a sanitized fermenter to which 2.5 gallons (9.5 l) of cold water has been added. Bring the total volume to 5 gallons (19 l) with additional cold water if necessary. Aerate the wort very well.

Pitch the yeast when temperature of wort is about 70 degrees F (21 C). Ferment at about 70 degrees F (21 C) for about 7 to 10 days, or until fermentation shows signs of calm and stopping. Rack from your primary to a secondary fermenter and continue in the fermenter at the same temperature for another 1 to 2 weeks, or until fermentation is complete. If you have the capability, "cellar" the beer at about 40 to 45 degrees F (4.5–7.5 C) and lager for 2 to 3 weeks.

Prime with sugar and bottle or keg when complete.

BELGIAN-STYLE CHERRY–BLACK CURRANT (KRIEK-CASSIS) LAMBIC

- TARGET ORIGINAL GRAVITY: 1.048 (12 B)
- APPROXIMATE FINAL GRAVITY: 1.006 (1.5 B)
- IBU: ABOUT 6
- APPROXIMATE COLOR: RED-PURPLE
- ALCOHOL: 6.5% BY VOLUME

All-Grain Recipe *for 5 gallons (19 l)*

NOTE: this beer takes two years to prepare for bottling.

6 lbs.	(2.7 kg) pilsener malt
2 lbs.	(908 g) flaked wheat
3 oz.	(84 g) old stale (low alpha) aroma hops, aged for at least one year at room temperature
10 lbs.	(4.5 kg) red sour cherries
6 lbs.	(2.7 kg) chokecherries or black currants, or a blend of both
1 oz.	(28 g) cedar chips
¼ tsp.	(1 g) powdered Irish moss

Wyeast Lambic Blend (yeast and bacteria)
Yeast from quality bottle-conditioned sour or lambic beers
Saflager dried yeast at bottling

¾ cup	(175 ml measure) corn sugar (priming bottles)

Boil the wheat flakes and a half-pound (225 g) crushed pilsener malt in 5 quarts (4.7 l) of water for 10 minutes. Then add enough cold water to bring the volume to 8 quarts (7.6 l) and the temperature to about 147 degrees F (65.5 C). Immediately add what remains of the 6 pounds (2.7 kg) crushed pilsener malt, stabilizing the temperature at 133 degrees F (56 C). Hold for 30 minutes. Then add 4 quarts (3.8 l) of 200-degree F (93 C) water. Stir and stabilize at about 158 degrees F (70 C). Hold for 60 minutes. Then raise temperature to 167 degrees F (75 C), lauter and sparge with 3.5 gallons (13.5 l) of 170-degree F (77 C) water. Collect about 5.5 gallons (21 l) of runoff. Add hops and bring to a full and vigorous boil.

When 10 minutes remain, add the Irish moss. After a total wort boil of 60 minutes, turn off the heat and place the pot (with cover on) in a running cold-water bath for 30 minutes. Continue to chill in the immersion or use other methods to chill your wort. Then strain and sparge the wort into a sanitized 6.5-gallon (23 l) closed fermenter. Bring the total volume to 5 gallons (19 l) with additional cold water if necessary. Aerate the wort very well.

Add the lambic blend of yeast and bacteria and ferment at 70 to 72 degrees F (21–22 C). After 1 month, add any other sour/lambic beer cultures you may have acquired. After 1 to 3 months of primary fermentation, rack the beer into a secondary fermenter and add sour cherries (pits are okay). If the cherries are fresh, you will need to crush them without cracking the pits. If they have been previously frozen, crushing is not necessary. Secondary ferment with cherries at temperatures between 65 and 70 degrees F (18–21 C). After an additional month, rack off the beer from the cherries to another fermenter. Discard cherries. Continue to ferment beer for an additional 1 year. During this time, a substantially evident white film will form on the surface of the beer. Don't be alarmed. It should be there and should not be disturbed.

After 1 year, add crushed chokecherries and/or black currants. Three months later, rack the beer off of the fruit into another fermenter. Add cedar chips. Discard fruit.

Six to 9 months later, prepare to bottle your lambic. Dissolve in water, boil priming sugar and add to the bottling vessel. Siphon/rack the beer into the bottling vessel and avoid siphoning the sediment and white film on the surface. Rehydrate one package of Saflager dried lager yeast in one cup of 90-degree F (32 C) sterile water for 15 minutes. Then add the rehydrated yeast to the beer and stir gently to evenly disburse yeast. Prime with sugar, bottle and cap.

To preserve your lambic for decades, melt paraffin and dip tops of crown-capped bottles in the melted wax. Age at room temperature for 1 to 2 months and then store at cellar temperatures. It begins to mature well after 6 months in the bottle.

Malt Extract Recipe *for 5 gallons (19 l)*

3.5 lbs. (1.6 kg) wheat malt extract *plus* 3.25 lbs. (1.5 kg) of light malt extract syrup may be substituted for all of the above grains. Skip the mashing process and simply boil the extract in 3 gallons (11.5 l) of water with hops, later adding cold water to bring the volume to 5 gallons (21 l).

CZECH-MEX TIJUANA URQUELL

- TARGET ORIGINAL GRAVITY: 1.047 (12 B)
- APPROXIMATE FINAL GRAVITY: 1.012 (3 B)
- IBU: ABOUT 34
- APPROXIMATE COLOR: 7 SRM (14 EBC)
- ALCOHOL: 4.6% BY VOLUME

All-Grain Recipe *for 5 gallons (19 l)*

5.5 lbs.	(2.5 kg) German or Czech pilsener malt
1.5 lbs.	(680 g) honey malt
12 oz.	(340 g) aromatic malt
1.5 oz.	(42 g) Czech Saaz hops 4% alpha (6 HBU/168 MBU)—90 minutes boiling
½ oz.	(14 g) Czech Saaz hops 4% alpha (2 HBU/56 MBU)—30 minutes boiling
1.25 oz.	(35 g) Czech Saaz hops 4% alpha (5 HBU/140 MBU)—15 minutes boiling
¼ tsp.	(1 g) powdered Irish moss
Czech-style pilsener yeast	
¾ cup	(175 ml measure) corn sugar (priming bottles) or 0.33 cups (80 ml) corn sugar for kegging

A step infusion mash is employed to mash the grains. Add 7.5 quarts (7.1 l) of 140-degree F (60 C) water to the crushed grain, stir, stabilize and hold the temperature at 132 degrees F (53 C) for 30 minutes. Add 3.75 quarts (3.6 l) of boiling water, add heat to bring temperature up to 155 degrees F (68 C) and hold for about 30 minutes. Then raise temperature to 167 degrees F (75 C), lauter and sparge with 3.5 gallons (13.5 l) of 170-degree F (77 C) water. Collect about 6 gallons (23 l) of runoff. Add 90-minute hops and bring to a full and vigorous boil.

The total boil time will be 90 minutes. When 30 minutes remain, add the 30-minute hops. When 15 minutes remain, add the 15-minute hops. When 10 minutes remain, add the Irish moss. After a total wort boil of 90 minutes, turn off the heat and place the pot (with cover on) in a running cold-water bath for 30 minutes. Continue to chill in the immersion or use other methods to chill your wort. Then strain and sparge the wort into a sanitized fermenter. Bring the total volume to 5 gallons (19 l) with additional cold water if necessary. Aerate the wort very well.

Pitch the yeast when temperature of wort is about 70 degrees F (21 C). Once visible signs of fermentation are evident, ferment at temperatures of about 55 degrees F (12.5 C) for about 1 week, or until fermentation shows signs of calm and stopping. Rack from your primary to a secondary fermenter and if you have the capability, "lager" the beer at temperatures between 35 and 45 degrees F (1.5–7 C) for 3 to 6 weeks.

Prime with sugar and bottle or keg when complete.

Mash/Extract Recipe *for 5 gallons (19 l)*

5 lbs.	(2.3 kg) light malt extract syrup or 4 lbs. (1.8 kg) light dried malt extract
1.25 lbs.	(568 g) honey malt
8 oz.	(225 g) aromatic malt
1.5 oz.	(42 g) Czech Saaz hops 4% alpha (6 HBU/168 MBU)—60 minutes boiling
1 oz.	(28 g) Czech Saaz hops 4% alpha (4 HBU/112 MBU)—30 minutes boiling
1.5 oz.	(42 g) Czech Saaz hops 4% alpha (6 HBU/168 MBU)—15 minutes boiling

¼ tsp.   (1 g) powdered Irish moss

Czech-style pilsener yeast

¾ cup   (175 ml measure) corn sugar (priming bottles) or
                 0.33 cups (80 ml) corn sugar for kegging

Heat 2 quarts (2 l) water to 172 degrees F (77.5 C) and then add crushed grains to the water. Stir well to distribute heat. Temperature should stabilize at about 155 degrees F (68 C). Wrap a towel around the pot and set aside for about 45 minutes. Have a homebrew.

After 45 minutes, add heat to the mini-mash and raise the temperature to 167 degrees F (75 C). Then pass the liquid and grains into a strainer and rinse with 170-degree F (77 C) water. Discard the grains.

To the sweet extract you have just produced, add more water, bringing the volume up to about 2.5 gallons (9.5 l). Add malt extract and 60-minute hops and bring to a boil.

The total boil time will be 60 minutes. When 30 minutes remain, add the 30-minute hops. When 15 minutes remain, add the 15-minute hops. When 10 minutes remain, add the Irish moss. After a total wort boil of 60 minutes, turn off the heat.

Immerse the covered pot of wort in a cold-water bath and let sit for 30 minutes, or the time it takes to have a couple of homebrews.

Then strain out and sparge hops and direct the hot wort into a sanitized fermenter to which 2.5 gallons (9.5 l) of cold water has been added. Bring the total volume to 5 gallons (19 l) with additional cold water if necessary. Aerate the wort very well.

Pitch the yeast when temperature of wort is about 70 degrees F (21 C). Once visible signs of fermentation are evident, ferment at temperatures of about 55 degrees F (12.5 C) for about 1 week, or until fermentation shows signs of calm and stopping. Rack from your primary to a secondary fermenter and if you have the capability, "lager" the beer at temperatures between 35 and 45 degrees F (1.5–7 C) for 3 to 6 weeks.

Prime with sugar and bottle or keg when complete.

QUITO ABBEY ALE—1534

Based on the 1966 recipe

- TARGET ORIGINAL GRAVITY: 1.042 (10.5 B)
- APPROXIMATE FINAL GRAVITY: 1.010 (2.5 B)
- IBU: ABOUT 20
- APPROXIMATE COLOR: 27 SRM (54 EBC)
- ALCOHOL: 4.2% BY VOLUME

Mash/Extract Recipe *for 5 gallons (19 l)*

1 lb.	(454 g) pilsener malt
1.5 lbs.	(680 g) crystal malt (20-L)
10 oz.	(280 g) black malt
3 lbs.	(1.36 kg) brown sugar
1 oz.	(28 g) Styrian Goldings hops 5% alpha (5 HBU/140 MBU)—60 minutes boiling
¼ tsp.	(1 g) powdered Irish moss

Belgian Abbey–style yeast of your choice

¾ cup   (175 ml measure) corn sugar (priming bottles) or 0.33 cups (80 ml) corn sugar for kegging

Heat 3 quarts (3 l) water to 172 degrees F (77.5 C) and then add crushed grains to the water. Stir well to distribute heat. Temperature should stabilize at about 155 degrees F (68 C). Wrap a towel around the pot and set aside for about 45 minutes. Have a homebrew.

After 45 minutes, add heat to the mini-mash and raise the temperature to 167 degrees F (75 C). Then pass the liquid and grains into a strainer and rinse with 170-degree F (77 C) water. Discard the grains.

To the sweet extract you have just produced, add more water, bringing the volume up to about 2.5 gallons (9.5 l). Add brown sugar and hops and bring to a boil.

The total boil time will be 60 minutes. When 10 minutes remain, add the Irish moss. After a total wort boil of 60 minutes, turn off the heat.

Immerse the covered pot of wort in a cold-water bath and let sit for 30 minutes, or the time it takes to have a couple of homebrews.

Then strain out and sparge hops and direct the hot wort into a sanitized fermenter to which 2.5 gallons (9.5 l) of cold water has been added. Bring the total volume to 5 gallons (19 l) with additional cold water if necessary. Aerate the wort very well.

Pitch the yeast when temperature of wort is about 70 degrees F (21 C). Ferment at about 70 degrees F (21 C) for about 1 week, or until fermentation shows signs of calm and stopping. Rack from your primary to a secondary fermenter and continue to age about 1 more week, until clear.

Prime with sugar and bottle or keg when complete.

VIENNA-STYLE OURO DE HABANERA (HAVANA GOLD)

- TARGET ORIGINAL GRAVITY: 1.048 (12 B)
- APPROXIMATE FINAL GRAVITY: 1.012 (3 B)
- IBU: ABOUT 32
- APPROXIMATE COLOR: 10 SRM (20 EBC)
- ALCOHOL: 4.8% BY VOLUME

All-Grain Recipe *for 5 gallons (19 l)*

3.5 lbs.	(1.6 kg) pilsener malt
2 lbs.	(908 g) Vienna malt
1.5 lbs.	(680 g) flaked corn
8 oz.	(225 g) crystal malt (40-L)
8 oz.	(225 g) aromatic malt
⅔ oz.	(18 g) Perle hops 8% alpha (5.3 HBU/148 MBU)—60 minutes boiling
¾ oz.	(21 g) Mt. Hood hops 6% alpha (4.5 HBU/126 MBU)—30 minutes boiling
½ oz.	(14 g) Santiam hop pellets—1-minute steep
¼ tsp.	(1 g) powdered Irish moss
German or Bavarian-type lager yeast	
¾ cup	(175 ml measure) corn sugar (priming bottles) or 0.33 cups (80 ml) corn sugar for kegging

A step infusion mash is employed to mash the grains. Add 8 quarts (7.6 l) of 140-degree F (60 C) water to the crushed grain, stir, stabilize and hold the temperature at 132 degrees F (53 C) for 30 minutes. Add 4 quarts (3.8 l) of boiling water, add heat to bring temperature up to 155 degrees F (68 C) and hold for about 30 minutes. Then raise temperature to 167 degrees F (75 C), lauter and sparge with 3.5 gallons (13.5 l) of 170-degree F (77 C) water. Collect about 5.5 gallons (21 l) of runoff. Add 60-minute hops and bring to a full and vigorous boil.

The total boil time will be 60 minutes. When 30 minutes remain, add the 30-minute hops. When 10 minutes remain, add the Irish moss. When 1 minute remains, add the 1-minute hops. After a total wort boil of 60 minutes, turn off the heat and place the pot (with cover on) in a running cold-water bath for 30 minutes. Continue to chill in the immersion or use other methods to chill your wort. Then strain and sparge the wort into a sanitized fermenter. Bring the total volume to 5 gallons (19 l) with additional cold water if necessary. Aerate the wort very well.

Pitch the yeast when temperature of wort is about 70 degrees F (21 C). Once visible signs of fermentation are evident, ferment at temperatures of about 55 degrees F (12.5 C) for about 1 week, or until fermentation shows signs of calm and stopping. Rack from your primary to a secondary fermenter. If you have the capability, "lager" the beer at temperatures between 35 and 45 degrees F (1.5–7 C) for 3 to 6 weeks.

Prime with sugar and bottle or keg when complete.

Mash/Extract Recipe *for 5 gallons (19 l)*

2 lbs.	(908 g) amber malt extract syrup or 1.6 lbs. (726 g) amber dried malt extract
2 lbs.	(908 g) pilsener malt
2 lbs.	(908 g) Vienna malt
1 lb.	(454 g) flaked corn
8 oz.	(225 g) aromatic malt
¾ oz.	(21 g) Perle hops 8% alpha (6 HBU/168 MBU)—60 minutes boiling
¾ oz.	(21 g) Mt. Hood hops 6% alpha (4.5 HBU/126 MBU)—30 minutes boiling
½ oz.	(14 g) Santiam hop pellets—1-minute steep

¼ tsp.	(1 g) powdered Irish moss
	German or Bavarian-type lager yeast
¾ cup	(175 ml measure) corn sugar (priming bottles) or 0.33
	cups (80 ml) corn sugar for kegging

Heat 1.5 gallons (5.7 l) water to 172 degrees F (77.5 C) and then add crushed grains to the water. Stir well to distribute heat. Temperature should stabilize at about 155 degrees F (68 C). Wrap a towel around the pot and set aside for about 45 minutes. Have a homebrew.

After 45 minutes, add heat to the mini-mash and raise the temperature to 167 degrees F (75 C). Then pass the liquid and grains into a strainer and rinse with 170-degree F (77 C) water. Discard the grains.

To the sweet extract you have just produced, add more water, bringing the volume up to about 3 gallons (9.5 l). Add malt extract and 60-minute hops and bring to a boil.

The total boil time will be 60 minutes. When 30 minutes remain, add the 30-minute hops. When 10 minutes remain, add the Irish moss. When 1 minute remains, add the 1-minute hops. After a total wort boil of 60 minutes, turn off the heat.

Immerse the covered pot of wort in a cold-water bath and let sit for 45 minutes, or the time it takes to have a few homebrews.

Then strain out and sparge hops and direct the hot wort into a sanitized fermenter to which 2 gallons (7.6 l) of cold water has been added. Bring the total volume to 5 gallons (19 l) with additional cold water if necessary. Aerate the wort very well.

Pitch the yeast when temperature of wort is about 70 degrees F (21 C). Once visible signs of fermentation are evident, ferment at temperatures of about 55 degrees F (12.5 C) for about 1 week, or until fermentation shows signs of calm and stopping. Rack from your primary to a secondary fermenter. If you have the capability, "lager" the beer at temperatures between 35 and 45 degrees F (1.5–7 C) for 3 to 6 weeks.

Prime with sugar and bottle or keg when complete.

ZIMBABWE ZEPHYR SORGHUM BEER

- TARGET ORIGINAL GRAVITY: VARIABLE
- APPROXIMATE FINAL GRAVITY: VARIABLE
- IBU: NONE
- APPROXIMATE COLOR: PALE PINK-BROWN7 SRM (14 EBC)
- ALCOHOL: 1–5% BY VOLUME

All-Grain Recipe *for 1 gallon (4 l)*

1.5 lbs.	(680 g) medium-finely crushed sorghum malt*
¼ cup	(50 g) medium-finely crushed sorghum malt for fermentation
Ale yeast	

Add the malt flour to 3 quarts of 156-degree F (69 C) water. Hold this temperature for 60 minutes. Complete conversion is not critically important. Quickly pour the mash through a kitchen strainer. Rinse with 165-degree F (74 C) water until a volume of 1 gallon is reached. Cool to about 75 degrees F. Add yeast and about ¼ cup of freshly milled sorghum malt flour. Keep temperature above 75 degrees F.

Begin to experience after 12 to 24 hours. And please don't forget to keep your thumbs out of the bucket.

SWAKAPMUND COWBOY LAGER

- TARGET ORIGINAL GRAVITY: 1.050 (12.5 B)
- APPROXIMATE FINAL GRAVITY: 1.016 (4 B)
- IBU: ABOUT 33
- APPROXIMATE COLOR: 7 SRM (14 EBC)
- ALCOHOL: 4.6% BY VOLUME

*You might also experiment by trying this with barley malt processed in this same manner.

All-Grain Recipe *for 5 gallons (19 l)*

8.5 lbs.	(3.9 kg) pilsener malt
1 oz.	(28 g) German Hersbrucker Hallertauer hops 3.3% alpha (3.3 HBU/92 MBU)—60 minutes boiling
1 oz.	(28 g) Czech Saaz hops 3% alpha (3 HBU/84 MBU)—60 minutes boiling
½ oz.	(21 g) German Hersbrucker Hallertauer hops 3.3% alpha (3.3 HBU/92 MBU)—20 minutes boiling
¾ oz.	(21 g) Santiam hops—3 minutes boiling
¼ oz.	(7 g) German Hersbrucker Hallertauer hops—3 minutes boiling
¼ tsp.	(1 g) powdered Irish moss
German or Bavarian-type lager yeast	
¾ cup	(175 ml measure) corn sugar (priming bottles) or 0.33 cups (80 ml) corn sugar for kegging

A step infusion mash is employed to mash the grains. Add 8.5 quarts (8.1 l) of 140-degree F (60 C) water to the crushed grain, stir, stabilize and hold the temperature at 132 degrees F (53 C) for 30 minutes. Add 4 quarts (3.8 l) of boiling water, add heat to bring temperature up to 155 degrees F (68 C) and hold for about 30 minutes. Then raise temperature to 167 degrees F (75 C), lauter and sparge with 3.5 gallons (13.5 l) of 170-degree F (77 C) water. Collect about 5.5 gallons (21 l) of runoff. Add 60-minute hops and bring to a full and vigorous boil.

The total boil time will be 60 minutes. When 20 minutes remain, add the 20-minute hops. When 10 minutes remain, add the Irish moss. When 3 minutes remain, add the 3-minute hops. After a total wort boil of 60 minutes, turn off the heat and place the pot (with cover on) in a running cold-water bath for 30 minutes. Continue to chill in the immersion or use other methods to chill your wort. Then strain and sparge the wort into a sanitized fermenter. Bring the total volume to 5 gallons (19 l) with additional cold water if necessary. Aerate the wort very well.

Pitch the yeast when temperature of wort is about 70 degrees F (21 C). Once visible signs of fermentation are evident, ferment at temperatures of about 55 degrees F (12.5 C) for about 1 week, or until fermentation shows signs of calm and stopping. Rack from your primary to a secondary fermenter and if you have the capability, "lager" the beer at temperatures between 35 and 45 degrees F (1.5–7 C) for 3 to 6 weeks.

Prime with sugar and bottle or keg when complete.

Malt Extract Recipe *for 5 gallons (19 l)*

7 lbs.	(3.2 kg) light malt extract syrup or 5.6 lbs. (2.5 kg) light dried malt extract
1.5 oz.	(42 g) German Hersbrucker Hallertauer hops 3.3% alpha (3.3 HBU/92 MBU)—60 minutes boiling
1.25 oz.	(35 g) Czech Saaz hops 3% alpha (3 HBU/84 MBU)—60 minutes boiling
½ oz.	(21 g) German Hersbrucker Hallertauer hops 3.3% alpha (3.3 HBU/92 MBU)—20 minutes boiling
¾ oz.	(21 g) Santiam hops—3 minutes boiling
¼ oz.	(7 g) German Hersbrucker Hallertauer hops—3 minutes boiling
¼ tsp.	(1 g) powdered Irish moss
German or Bavarian-type lager yeast	
¾ cup	(175 ml measure) corn sugar (priming bottles) or 0.33 cups (80 ml) corn sugar for kegging

Add malt extract and 60-minute hops to 2 gallons (7.6 l) of water. Bring to a boil. The total boil time will be 60 minutes. When 20 minutes remain, add the 20-minute hops. When 10 minutes remain, add the Irish moss. When 3 minutes remain, add the 3-minute hops. After a total wort boil of 60 minutes, turn off the heat.

Immerse the covered pot of wort in a cold-water bath and let sit for 30 minutes, or the time it takes to have a couple of homebrews.

Then strain out and sparge hops and direct the hot wort into a sanitized fermenter to which 2.5 gallons (9.5 l) of cold water has been added. Bring the total volume to 5 gallons (19 l) with additional cold water if necessary. Aerate the wort very well.

Pitch the yeast when temperature of wort is about 70 degrees F (21 C). Once visible signs of fermentation are evident, ferment at temperatures of about 55 degrees F (12.5 C) for about 1 week, or until fermentation shows signs of calm and stopping. Rack from your primary to a secondary fermenter and if you have the capability, "lager" the beer at temperatures between 35 and 45 degrees F (1.5–7 C) for 3 to 6 weeks.

Prime with sugar and bottle or keg when complete.

···

ZALTITIS BALTIC PORTER

- TARGET ORIGINAL GRAVITY: 1.080 (19.3 B)
- APPROXIMATE FINAL GRAVITY: 1.018 (4.5 B)
- IBU: ABOUT 28
- APPROXIMATE COLOR: 7 SRM (14 EBC)
- ALCOHOL: 8.3% BY VOLUME

All-Grain Recipe *for 5 gallons (19 l)*

7 lbs.	(3.2 kg) pilsener malt
4 lbs.	(1.82 kg) Munich malt
1 lb.	(454 g) Caramunich malt
12 oz.	(340 g) German black Caraffe malt
12 oz.	(340 g) aromatic malt
8 oz.	(225 g) chocolate malt
¾ oz.	(21 g) Northern Brewer hops 8% alpha (6 HBU/168 MBU)—90 minutes boiling
¾ oz.	(21 g) Liberty hops 5% alpha (3.8 HBU/106 MBU)—20 minutes boiling
1 oz.	(28 g) Santiam hop pellets—1 minute boiling
¼ tsp.	(1 g) powdered Irish moss
Wyeast 2042 Danish Lager yeast or White Labs German Lager yeast WLP830	
¾ cup	(175 ml measure) corn sugar (priming bottles) or 0.33 cups (80 ml) corn sugar for kegging

A step infusion mash is employed to mash the grains. Add 14 quarts (13.3 l) of 140-degree F (60 C) water to the crushed grain, stir, stabilize and hold the temperature at 132 degrees F (53 C) for 30 minutes. Add 7 quarts (6.7 l) of boiling water, add heat to bring temperature up to 155 degrees F (68 C) and hold for about 30 minutes. Then raise temperature to 167 degrees F (75 C), lauter and sparge with 3.5 gallons (13.5 l) of 170-degree F (77 C) water. Collect about 5.5 gallons (21 l) of runoff. Add 90-minute hops and bring to a full and vigorous boil.

The total boil time will be 90 minutes. When 20 minutes remain, add the 20-minute hops. When 10 minutes remain, add the Irish moss. When 1 minute remains, add the 1-minute hops. After a total wort boil of 90 minutes, turn off the heat and place the pot (with cover on) in a running cold-water bath for 30 minutes. Continue to chill in the immersion or use other methods to chill your wort. Then strain and sparge the wort into a sanitized fermenter. Bring the total volume to 5 gallons (19 l) with additional cold water if necessary. Aerate the wort very well.

Pitch the yeast when temperature of wort is about 70 degrees F (21 C). Once visible signs of fermentation are evident, ferment at temperatures of about 55 degrees F (12.5 C) for about 7 to 10 days, or until fermentation shows signs of calm and stopping. Rack from your primary to a secondary fermenter and "lager" the beer at temperatures between 35 and 45 degrees F (1.5–7 C) for 3 to 6 weeks.

Prime with sugar and bottle or keg when complete.

Mash/Extract Recipe *for 5 gallons (19 l)*

9 lbs.	(4 kg) amber malt extract syrup or 7.25 lbs. (3.3 kg) amber dried malt extract
1 lb.	(454 g) Caramunich malt
1 lb.	(454 g) aromatic malt
12 oz.	(340 g) German black Caraffe malt
8 oz.	(225 g) chocolate malt
1 oz.	(28 g) Northern Brewer hops 8% alpha (8 HBU/224 MBU)—60 minutes boiling
¾ oz.	(21 g) Liberty hops 5% alpha (3.8 HBU/106 MBU)— 20 minutes boiling
1 oz.	(28 g) Santiam hop pellets—1 minute boiling
¼ tsp.	(1 g) powdered Irish moss

Wyeast 2042 Danish Lager yeast or White Labs German Lager yeast WLP830

¾ cup	(175 ml measure) corn sugar (priming bottles) or 0.33 cups (80 ml) corn sugar for kegging

Heat 3 quarts (3 l) water to 172 degrees F (77.5 C) and then add crushed grains to the water. Stir well to distribute heat. Temperature should stabilize at about 155 degrees F (68 C). Wrap a towel around the pot and set aside for about 45 minutes. Have a homebrew.

After 45 minutes, add heat to the mini-mash and raise the temperature to 167 degrees F (75 C). Then pass the liquid and grains into a strainer and rinse with 170-degree F (77 C) water. Discard the grains.

To the sweet extract you have just produced, add more water, bringing the volume up to about 3 gallons (11.4 l). Add malt extract and 60-minute hops and bring to a boil.

The total boil time will be 60 minutes. When 20 minutes remain, add the 20-minute hops. When 10 minutes remain, add the Irish moss. When 1 minute remains, add the 1-minute hops. After a total wort boil of 60 minutes, turn off the heat.

Immerse the covered pot of wort in a cold-water bath and let sit for 30 minutes, or the time it takes to have a couple of homebrews.

Then strain out and sparge hops and direct the hot wort into a sanitized fermenter to which 2.5 gallons (9.5 l) of cold water has been added. Bring the total volume to 5 gallons (19 l) with additional cold water if necessary. Aerate the wort very well.

Pitch the yeast when temperature of wort is about 70 degrees F (21 C). Once visible signs of fermentation are evident, ferment at temperatures of about 55 degrees F (12.5 C) for about 7 to 10 days, or until fermentation shows signs of calm and stopping. Rack from your primary to a secondary fermenter and "lager" the beer at temperatures between 35 and 45 degrees F (1.5–7 C) for 3 to 6 weeks.

Prime with sugar and bottle or keg when complete.

QINGDAO DARK LAGER

- TARGET ORIGINAL GRAVITY: 1.056 (14 B)
- APPROXIMATE FINAL GRAVITY: 1.014 (3.5 B)
- IBU: ABOUT 27
- APPROXIMATE COLOR: 21 SRM (42 EBC)
- ALCOHOL: 5.5% BY VOLUME

All-Grain Recipe *for 5 gallons (19 l)*

7 lbs.	(3.2 kg) pilsener malt
1.5 lbs.	(680 g) flaked corn
12 oz.	(340 g) crystal malt (80-L)
4 oz.	(113 g) German black Caraffe malt

1 oz.	(28 g) Mt. Hood hops 6% alpha (6 HBU/168 MBU)— 60 minutes boiling
½ oz.	(14 g) Mt. Hood hops 6% alpha (3 HBU/84 MBU)—20 minutes boiling
¼ tsp.	(1 g) powdered Irish moss
	German or Bavarian-type lager yeast
¾ cup	(175 ml measure) corn sugar (priming bottles) or 0.33 cups (80 ml) corn sugar for kegging

A step infusion mash is employed to mash the grains. Add 9.5 quarts (9 l) of 140-degree F (60 C) water to the crushed grain, stir, stabilize and hold the temperature at 132 degrees F (53 C) for 30 minutes. Add 4.75 quarts (4.5 l) of boiling water, add heat to bring temperature up to 155 degrees F (68 C) and hold for about 30 minutes. Then raise temperature to 167 degrees F (75 C), lauter and sparge with 3.5 gallons (13.5 l) of 170 degree F (77 C) water. Collect about 5.5 gallons (21 l) of runoff. Add 60-minute hops and bring to a full and vigorous boil.

The total boil time will be 60 minutes. When 20 minutes remain, add the 20-minute hops. When 10 minutes remain, add the Irish moss. After a total wort boil of 60 minutes, turn off the heat and place the pot (with cover on) in a running cold-water bath for 30 minutes. Continue to chill in the immersion or use other methods to chill your wort. Then strain and sparge the wort into a sanitized fermenter. Bring the total volume to 5 gallons (19 l) with additional cold water if necessary. Aerate the wort very well.

Pitch the yeast when temperature of wort is about 70 degrees F (21 C). Once visible signs of fermentation are evident, ferment at temperatures of about 55 degrees F (12.5 C) for about 1 week, or until fermentation shows signs of calm and stopping. Rack from your primary to a secondary fermenter. If you have the capability, "lager" the beer at temperatures between 35 and 45 degrees F (1.5–7 C) for 3 to 6 weeks.

Prime with sugar and bottle or keg when complete.

Mash/Extract Recipe *for 5 gallons (19 l)*

4 lbs.	(1.82 kg) light malt extract syrup or 3.2 lbs. (1.45 kg) light dried malt extract
2.5 lbs.	(1.15 kg) pilsener malt
1 lb.	(454 g) flaked corn

12 oz.	(340 g) crystal malt (80-L)
5 oz.	(140 g) German black Caraffe malt
1.25 oz.	(35 g) Mt. Hood hops 6% alpha (7.5 HBU/210 MBU)—60 minutes boiling
½ oz.	(14 g) Mt. Hood hops 6% alpha (3 HBU/84 MBU)—20 minutes boiling
¼ tsp.	(1 g) powdered Irish moss
German or Bavarian-type lager yeast	
¾ cup	(175 ml measure) corn sugar (priming bottles) or 0.33 cups (80 ml) corn sugar for kegging

Heat 5 quarts (4.75 l) water to 172 degrees F (77.5 C) and then add crushed grains to the water. Stir well to distribute heat. Temperature should stabilize at about 155 degrees F (68 C). Wrap a towel around the pot and set aside for about 45 minutes. Have a homebrew.

After 45 minutes, add heat to the mini-mash and raise the temperature to 167 degrees F (75 C). Then pass the liquid and grains into a strainer and rinse with 170-degree F (77 C) water. Discard the grains.

To the sweet extract you have just produced, add more water, bringing the volume up to about 2.5 gallons (9.5 l). Add malt extract and 60-minute hops and bring to a boil.

The total boil time will be 60 minutes. When 20 minutes remain, add the 20-minute hops. When 10 minutes remain, add the Irish moss. After a total wort boil of 60 minutes, turn off the heat.

Immerse the covered pot of wort in a cold-water bath and let sit for 30 minutes, or the time it takes to have a couple of homebrews.

Then strain out and sparge hops and direct the hot wort into a sanitized fermenter to which 2.5 gallons (9.5 l) of cold water has been added. Bring the total volume to 5 gallons (19 l) with additional cold water if necessary. Aerate the wort very well.

Pitch the yeast when temperature of wort is about 70 degrees F (21 C). Once visible signs of fermentation are evident, ferment at temperatures of about 55 degrees F (12.5 C) for about 1 week, or until fermentation shows signs of calm and stopping. Rack from your primary to a secondary fermenter. If you have the capability, "lager" the beer at temperatures between 35 and 45 degrees F (1.5–7 C) for 3 to 6 weeks.

Prime with sugar and bottle or keg when complete.

FIJI HOMEBREW—VALE VAKAVITI

Recipe *for 2 gallons (7.6 l)*

3 lbs.	(1.36 kg) cassava (tapioca) root
2.25 lbs.	(1 kg) corn sugar
1–3	packs bread yeast

Peel the cassava root. Cut into small pieces. Boil for one hour in 1 gallon (4 l) water. Mash the cooked cassava root in the water in which it was cooked. When it becomes a purée, add water and sugar to make 2 gallons. Stir to dissolve the sugar. Pour into a fermenter. If you desire homebrew in 24 hours, use 3 packs of yeast. If you can be a bit more patient, use only 1 package of yeast. Add yeast when temperatures are below 75 degrees F (24 C). For a smoother and more refined taste, ferment at temperatures between 65 and 70 degrees F (18.5–21 C). Serve warm and while still fermenting, anytime after 24 hours. And "drink cowboy-style."

SPARKLING MEAD—TROPICAL CHAMPAGNE

- TARGET ORIGINAL GRAVITY: 1.060 (15 B)
- APPROXIMATE FINAL GRAVITY: 0.995 (–1 B)
- APPROXIMATE COLOR: SUNLIGHT
- ALCOHOL: 8.4% BY VOLUME

Recipe *for 5 gallons (19 l)*

8 lbs.	(3.6 kg) light honey, such as orange blossom or clover
4 oz.	(113 g) extra-light dried malt extract
2 oz.	(56 g) freshly grated ginger root
1 tsp.	(4 g) gypsum
1 tsp.	(5 g) citric acid

¼ oz.	(7 g) yeast extract (as nutrient)
0.1 g	zinc-fortified yeast
¼ tsp.	(1 g) powdered Irish moss
23 g	Pries de Mousse champagne yeast
¾ cup	(175 ml measure) corn sugar (priming bottles) or 0.33 cups (80 ml) corn sugar for kegging

Place all ingredients except for yeast and corn sugar in 2 gallons (7.6 l) of water and bring to a boil. The total wort boil time will be 10 minutes. After boiling, turn off the heat.

Immerse the covered pot of wort in a cold-water bath and let sit for 30 minutes, or the time it takes to have a couple of homebrews.

Then strain out and sparge ginger root and direct the hot wort into a sanitized fermenter to which 3 gallons (11.4 l) of cold water has been added. Bring the total volume to 5 gallons (19 l) with additional cold water if necessary. Aerate the must very well.

Rehydrate the dry yeast in 1 cup (250 ml) of sterile water at about 90 degrees F (32 C) for about 10 to 15 minutes. Pitch the yeast when temperature of must is about 70 degrees F (21 C). Ferment at about 70 degrees F (21 C) until fermentation seems to have stopped. Rack from your primary to a secondary fermenter and continue to ferment at room temperature until the mead becomes reasonably clear.

Prime with sugar and bottle or keg when complete.

MONASTIC BLEUE STRONG BELGIAN-STYLE ALE

- TARGET ORIGINAL GRAVITY: 1.081 (19.5 B)
- APPROXIMATE FINAL GRAVITY: 1.014 (3.5 B)
- IBU: ABOUT 40
- APPROXIMATE COLOR: 8 SRM (16 EBC)
- ALCOHOL: 9% BY VOLUME

All-Grain Recipe *for 5 gallons (19 l)*

13 lbs.	(5.9 kg) pale malt
2.25 lbs.	(1 kg) corn sugar
1.25 oz.	(35 g) Styrian Goldings hops 5% alpha (6.25 HBU/175 MBU)—60 minutes boiling
½ oz.	(14 g) Northern Brewer hops 8% alpha (4 HBU/112 MBU)—60 minutes boiling
½ oz.	(14 g) Styrian Goldings hops 5% alpha (2.5 HBU/70 MBU)—15 minutes boiling
1 oz.	(28 g) Styrian Goldings hops—1 minute boiling
¼ tsp.	(1 g) powdered Irish moss
0.1 g	zinc-fortified yeast (as nutrient)

White Labs Bastogne Belgian Ale yeast WLP510 or Wyeast 1762 Belgian Abbey yeast II

¾ cup	(175 ml measure) corn sugar (priming bottles) or 0.33 cups (80 ml) corn sugar for kegging

A step infusion mash is employed to mash the grains. Add 10 quarts (9.5 l) of 140-degree F (60 C) water to the crushed grain, stir, stabilize and hold the temperature at 132 degrees F (53 C) for 30 minutes. Add 5 quarts (4.8 l) of boiling water, add heat to bring temperature up to 155 degrees F (68 C) and hold for about 30 minutes. Then raise temperature to 167 degrees F (75 C), lauter and sparge with 3.5 gallons (13.5 l) of 170-degree F (77 C) water. Collect about 5.5 gallons (21 l) of runoff. Add 60-minute hops and corn sugar and bring to a full and vigorous boil.

The total boil time will be 60 minutes. When 15 minutes remain, add the 15-minute hops. When 10 minutes remain, add the Irish moss and zinc-fortified yeast. When 1 minute remains, add the 1-minute hops. After a total wort boil of 60 minutes, turn off the heat and place the pot (with cover on) in a running cold-water bath for 30 minutes. Continue to chill in the immersion or use other methods to chill your wort. Then strain and sparge the wort into a sanitized fermenter. Bring the total volume to 5 gallons (19 l) with additional cold water if necessary. Aerate the wort very well.

Pitch the yeast when temperature of wort is about 70 degrees F (21 C). Ferment at about 70 degrees F (21 C) for about 1 week, or until fermentation shows signs of calm and stopping. Rack from your primary to a secondary fermenter and continue to secondary ferment at 70 degrees F (21 C) for about 1 to 3 weeks.

Prime with sugar and bottle or keg when complete. This beer ages well at temperatures between 65 and 70 degrees F (18–21 C).

Malt Extract Recipe *for 5 gallons (19 l)*

8.5 lbs.	(3.9 kg) light malt extract syrup or 6.8 lbs. (3.1 kg) light dried malt extract
2.25 lbs.	(1 kg) corn sugar
1.75 oz.	(49 g) Styrian Goldings hops 5% alpha (8.8 HBU/245 MBU)—60 minutes boiling
½ oz.	(14 g) Northern Brewer hops 8% alpha (4 HBU/112 MBU)—60 minutes boiling
½ oz.	(14 g) Styrian Goldings hops 5% alpha (2.5 HBU/70 MBU)—15 minutes boiling
1 oz.	(28 g) Styrian Goldings hops—1 minute boiling
¼ tsp.	(1 g) powdered Irish moss
0.1 g	zinc-fortified yeast (as nutrient)

White Labs Bastogne Belgian Ale yeast WLP510 or Wyeast 1762 Belgian Abbey yeast II

¾ cup	(175 ml measure) corn sugar (priming bottles) or 0.33 cups (80 ml) corn sugar for kegging

Add malt extract, corn sugar and 60-minute hops to 2.5 gallons (9.5 l) of hot water and bring to a boil. The total boil time will be 60 minutes. When 15 minutes remain, add the 15-minute hops. When 10 minutes remain, add the Irish moss and zinc-fortified yeast. When 1 minute remains, add the 1-minute hops. After a total wort boil of 60 minutes, turn off the heat.

Immerse the covered pot of wort in a cold-water bath and let sit for 30 minutes, or the time it takes to have a couple of homebrews.

Then strain out and sparge hops and direct the hot wort into a sanitized fermenter to which 2.5 gallons (9.5 l) of cold water has been added. Bring the total volume to 5 gallons (19 l) with additional cold water if necessary. Aerate the wort very well.

Pitch the yeast when temperature of wort is about 70 degrees F (21 C). Ferment at about 70 degrees F (21 C) for about 1 week, or until fermentation

shows signs of calm and stopping. Rack from your primary to a secondary fermenter and continue to secondary ferment at 70 degrees F (21 C) for about 1 to 3 weeks.

Prime with sugar and bottle or keg when complete. This beer ages well at temperatures between 65 and 70 degrees F (18–21 C).

19TH-CENTURY LEIPZIGER GOSE

- TARGET ORIGINAL GRAVITY: 1.042 (10.5 B)
- APPROXIMATE FINAL GRAVITY: 1.010 (2.5 B)
- IBU: ABOUT 12
- APPROXIMATE COLOR: 4 SRM (8 EBC)
- ALCOHOL: 4.5% BY VOLUME

While modern Leipzig versions of this beer do not contain any hint of brettanomyces yeast or other wild yeast character, there is little doubt that the original versions of this style of beer were spontaneously fermented. Spontaneous fermentation begins with the introduction of airborne microorganisms that would include a variety of wild yeast and bacteria. The beer was very likely fermented in the similar tradition of Belgian gueuze/lambic ales. Quite obviously even the names are similar in spelling and certainly very similarly pronounced. No current German breweries introduce any microorganism into the fermentation other than pure beer yeast strains. The acidity often is developed by adding pasteurized lactic acid. Modern versions lack the complexity of flavor and aroma the original Gose surely portrayed.

You may develop the character of 19th-century Gose by employing several options.

Option 1: Develop acidity through a sour mash. See the recipe in the chapter "Apples in a Big Beer—New Glarus Brewing Company, Wisconsin."

Option 2: Develop acidity by using German sauer malt. See the recipe in the chapter "Poetic Justice in Italy, Year 2000, The Microbrewers of Italy."

Option 3: Develop acidity and other traditional Gose character by introducing wild yeast and bacteria into the fermentation.

THE FIRST TWO options offer a degree of stability in the final beer. This recipe challenges your brewing skills by employing various microorganisms to develop the complexity that surely was a character typical of traditional Gose ale from the northern German town of Leipzig. The traditional beer was likely enjoyed fresh, cloudy and with some fermentation activity. Enjoy this beer when fully carbonated. It is not intended to age for long periods. CAUTION: The introduction of wild yeast and bacteria will continue to slowly ferment the beer over a long period of time. Excessive pressure may result, and there is also a risk of foaming, gushing or even exploding bottles. Do not age this beer once it has reached desired level of carbonation. You may chill the ale to very cold temperatures to inhibit fermentation, extending its "drinking life."

All-Grain Recipe *for 5 gallons (19 l)*

4 lbs.	(1.82 kg) pilsener malt
3 lbs.	(1.36 kg) wheat malt
½ tsp.	(3 g) pure salt (sodium chloride)
¼ oz.	(7 g) Northern Brewer hops 8% alpha (2 HBU/56 MBU)—60 minutes boiling
½ oz.	(14 g) Northern Brewer hops 8% alpha (4 HBU/112 MBU)—15 minutes boiling
¼ oz.	(7 g) coriander seed

German-type ale yeast
Brettanomyces yeast cultures and lactobacillus bacteria culture, both available as a Belgian lambic mix of microorganisms

¾ cup   (175 ml measure) corn sugar (priming bottles) or 0.33 cups (80 ml) corn sugar for kegging

A step infusion mash is employed to mash the grains. Add 7 quarts (6.7 l) of 140-degree F (60 C) water to the salt and crushed grain. Stir, stabilize and hold the temperature at 132 degrees F (53 C) for 30 minutes. Add 3.5 quarts (3.3 l) of boiling water, add heat to bring temperature up to 155 degrees F (68 C) and hold for about 30 minutes. Then raise temperature to 167 degrees F (75 C), lauter and sparge with 3.5 gallons (13.5 l) of 170-degree F (77 C) water. Collect about 5.5 gallons (21 l) of runoff. Add 60-minute hops, salt and bring to a full and vigorous boil.

The total boil time will be 60 minutes. When 15 minutes remain, add the 15-minute hops. When 1 minute remains, add the freshly crushed coriander seed. After a total wort boil of 60 minutes, turn off the heat and place the pot (with cover on) in a running cold-water bath for 30 minutes. Continue to chill in the immersion or use other methods to chill your wort. Then strain and sparge the wort into a sanitized fermenter. Bring the total volume to 5 gallons (19 l) with additional cold water if necessary. Aerate the wort very well.

Pitch the German ale yeast, brettanomyces yeast cultures and lactobacillus bacteria culture when temperature of wort is about 70 degrees F (21 C). Ferment at about 70 degrees F (21 C) for about 10 days, or until fermentation appears to show signs of stopping and begins to clear. Rack from your primary to a secondary fermenter and if you have the capability, "cellar" the beer at about 55 degrees F (12.5 C) for about 2 weeks.

Prime with sugar and bottle or keg when complete.

Malt Extract Recipe *for 5 gallons (19 l)*

6 lbs.	(2.7 kg) wheat malt extract syrup (50% barley malt/ 50% wheat malt)
0.36 oz.	(10 g) Northern Brewer hops 8% alpha (2.8 HBU/80 MBU)—60 minutes boiling
0.36 oz.	(10 g) Northern Brewer hops 8% alpha (2.8 HBU/80 MBU)—15 minutes boiling
¼ oz.	(7 g) coriander seed
½ tsp.	(3 g) pure salt (sodium chloride)
German-type ale yeast	
Brettanomyces yeast cultures and lactobacillus bacteria culture, both available as a Belgian lambic mix of microorganisms	
¾ cup	(175 ml measure) corn sugar (priming bottles) or 0.33 cups (80 ml) corn sugar for kegging

Add malt extract, salt and 60-minute hops to 2 gallons (7.6 l) of water. Bring to a boil. The total boil time will be 60 minutes. When 15 minutes remain, add the 15-minute hops. When 1 minute remains, add freshly crushed coriander seed. After a total wort boil of 60 minutes, turn off the heat.

Immerse the covered pot of wort in a cold-water bath and let sit for 30 minutes, or the time it takes to have a couple of homebrews.

Then strain out and sparge hops and direct the hot wort into a sanitized fermenter to which 2.5 gallons (9.5 l) of cold water has been added. Bring the total volume to 5 gallons (19 l) with additional cold water if necessary. Aerate the wort very well.

Pitch the German ale yeast, brettanomyces yeast cultures and lactobacillus bacteria culture when temperature of wort is about 70 degrees F (21 C). Ferment at about 70 degrees F (21 C) for about 10 days, or until fermentation appears to show signs of stopping and begins to clear. Rack from your primary to a secondary fermenter, and if you have the capability, "cellar" the beer at about 55 degrees F (12.5 C) for about 2 weeks.

Prime with sugar and bottle or keg when complete.

Glossary of Terms

a.b.v.: Alcohol by volume.

Ale: A style of beer, usually brewed at temperatures between 60 and 70 degrees F (16–21 C) using ale yeast. Often referred to as a "top-fermented" because of the tendency for some strains of ale yeast to rise to the surface for a period during fermentation.

Balling: A scale of measurement used by professional brewers worldwide to measure the density of a liquid as compared to water. See also Specific gravity.

Barrel: One U.S. barrel equals 31 gallons equals about 13½ cases of 12-oz. bottles. One typical American keg equals 15.5 gallons, or a half-barrel.

Bottle conditioned: Term describing lager or ale that is carbonated naturally by the action of yeast on fermentable sugars while in the bottle. Sometimes referred to as bottle fermentation.

Bottom-fermenting: See Lager yeast.

F and C: Abbreviations for degrees Fahrenheit and degrees Celsius (Centigrade).

Gravity dispensed: Term describing beer that is dispensed from a keg by the force of gravity, rather than by "pushing" the beer out with added pressure. A spigot is employed while air is permitted to enter from an opening at the top of the keg.

Hops: Flowers from the hop vine that impart different types of bitterness, flavor and aroma to beer.

Lager: From the German word, to store. Also a style of beer. Traditionally, a "bottom-fermented" beer brewed at temperatures of 40 to 50 degrees F (4–10 C) and stored for a period of time at temperatures as low as 32 degrees F (0 C).

Lagering: The period during which lager beer is aged.

Lager yeast: *Saccharomyces uvarum* (formerly known as *S. carlsbergensis*) type of yeast. Generally speaking, true lager yeast does best at fermentation temperatures of 33 to 50 degrees F. It is also known as "bottom-fermenting yeast" because of its tendency to form sediment while fermenting.

Lauter or **lautering:** The process of removing spent grains or hops from wort. This is simply done by the utilization of a strainer and a subsequent quick, hot water rinse (sparging) of the caught spent grains or hops.

Lauter vessel or **lauter tun:** The brewing vessel that is used to separate grains from sweet wort by a straining process.

Lovibond and malt color (-L): A measure of malt color. Ten is low; 40 is amber; above 80 is dark.

Lupulin: Tiny bright yellow-golden capsules of oil and resin located at the base of the hop flower petal, responsible for the flavor and aroma of hops.

Mash or **mashing:** The process of converting grain starches to fermentable sugars by carefully sustaining a water and grain "soup" at temperatures ranging from 140 to 160 degrees F for a period of time.

Naturally carbonated: Term describing beer that has developed carbonation from the natural carbon dioxide byproduct of fermentation. Forced carbonation adds carbonation to beer by forcing high-pressure carbon dioxide into otherwise flat beer.

Pitch the yeast: To "throw in" or add yeast to the wort.

Rack (Racking): Process of transferring unfinished homebrew from a primary fermenter to a secondary fermenter. A siphon is often used by homebrewers so yeast sediments remain undisturbed in the primary.

Refermentation: A second fermentation that may develop in the bottle because of added sugars at bottling time.

Secondary fermenter (the secondary): Any vessel in which secondary fermentation occurs.

Sparge or sparging: The act of sprinkling hot water on grains or hops to wash off desired sugars. See Lautering.

Specific gravity: A measure of the density of a liquid as compared to water. Readings above 1.000 indicate a density higher than that of plain water. Adding fermentable sugar to water will increase density. Fermentation will decrease density. Degrees balling and degrees plato are other scales for measuring the density of wort.

Top fermenting: See Ale.

Wort: Unfermented beer.

Photo Credits

All photos taken by the author except:

Page 5. Gordon Bowker, co-founder of Red Hook Ale. By David Bjorkman.

Page 12. Founding brewer Ken Grossman. Courtesy Sierra Nevada Brewing Co.

Page 29. Louis Koch's Brewery. Courtesy Jim Koch.

Page 59. Book with the Little Rose. Courtesy of Peter Bouckaert, New Belgium Brewing Co.

Page 70. Sam Calagione, photo by Bruce Weber.

Page 73. Gene Muller. Courtesy Flying Fish Brewing Co.

Page 76. Steve Hindy. Courtesy of Brooklyn Brewing Co.

Page 81 and 82. Morgan Wolaver and Steve Parkes. Courtesy Otter Creek/Wolavers Organic Beer.

Page 98. Limos with the Prairie Homebrewing Companions. Courtesy Prairie Homebrewing Companions.

Page 104. Tapping into a keg of real ale at Boscos. Courtesy Boscos.

Page 114. David Bruce and the beginning of the Firkin Empire. Courtesy David Bruce.

Page 280. Jeff Bagby. Courtesy Brewers Association.

Page 284. Lee Chase. Courtesy Stone Brewing Co.

Acknowledgments

Many thanks to Guillermo Moscoso, who worked for Anheuser-Busch Inc., St. Louis, for first introducing to me the tale of the Brewery of the Monastery of San Francisco (Quito, Ecuador); Dori Whitney, editor of *The Brewer's Digest*, who uncovered the January 1966 issue that featured the brewery; and Lilian Bejarano, working on the restoration of the monastery, who graciously arranged for a tour of the brewery.

Index

Charlie Papazian is one of the most prominent and recognized names in the world of beer and brewing. Since founding the Association of Brewers in 1978, which in 2005 merged with the Brewers Association of America to become the Brewers Association, he has guided the development of the American Homebrewers Association (AHA), the Great American Beer Festival and the World Beer Cup. He is the author of the bible of brewing, *The Complete Joy of Homebrewing*, and is the founding publisher of *Zymurrgy* (the magazine for homebrewers) and *The New Brewer* (the magazine for small, professional craftbrewers). He lives in Boulder, Colorado, with his wife, Sandra.

RELAX, HAVE A HOME BREW!

THE COMPLETE JOY OF HOMEBREWING

ISBN 0-06-053105-3

Papazian presents a fully revised edition of his essential guide to homebrewing, including a complete update of all instructions, recipes, charts, and guidelines. Everything you need to get started is here, including classic and new recipes for brewing stouts, ales, lagers, pilseners, porters, specialty beers, and honey meads.

THE HOMEBREWER'S COMPANION

ISBN 0-06-058473-4

What's different about *The Homebrewer's Companion*? There are 60 additional recipes and more detailed charts, tables, techniques, and equipment information for the advanced brewer.

Available wherever books are sold, or call 1-800-331-3761 to order.

Learn More • Do More • Live More

 **Collins**   *An Imprint of HarperCollinsPublishers*   www.harpercollins.com